THE MODERN INVENTION
OF MEDIEVAL MUSIC

Medieval music has been made and remade over the past two hundred years. For the nineteenth century it was vocal, without instrumental accompaniment, but with barbarous harmony that no one could have wished to hear. For most of the twentieth century it was instrumentally accompanied, increasingly colourful and increasingly enjoyed. At the height of its popularity it sustained an industry of players and instrument-makers, all engaged in re-creating an apparently medieval performance practice. During the 1980s it became vocal once more, exchanging colour and contrast for cleanliness and beauty. But what happens to produce such radical changes of perspective? And what can we learn from them about the way we interact with the past? How much is really known about how medieval music sounded? Or have modern beliefs been formed and sustained less by evidence than by the personalities of scholars and performers, their ideologies and their musical tastes?

DANIEL LEECH-WILKINSON is a writer and broadcaster on medieval music. He is Reader in Historical Musicology at King's College, London. His previous books include studies and editions of the fourteenth-century poet and composer Guillaume de Machaut.

CAMBRIDGE MUSICAL TEXTS AND MONOGRAPHS
General editors: John Butt and Laurence Dreyfus

This series has as its centres of interest the history of performance and the history of instruments. It includes annotated translations of authentic historical texts on music and monographs on various aspects of historical performance and instrument history

Recent titles

John Butt
Bach Interpretation: Articulation Marks in the Sources of J. S. Bach

Nicholas Thistlethwaite
The Making of the Victorian Organ

Christopher Page (trans. and ed.)
Summa musice: A Thirteenth-Century Manual for Singers

Ardal Powell (trans. and ed.)
The Virtuoso Flute Player by Johann George Tromlitz

Beth Bullard (trans. and ed.)
Musica getutscht: A Treatise on Musical Instruments by Sebastian Virdung

David Rowland
A History of Pianoforte Pedalling

John Butt
Music Education and the Art of Performance in the German Baroque

Rebecca Harris Warrick and Carol Marsh
Musical Theatre at the Court of Louis XIV
Le Mariage de la Grosse Cathos

Julianne C. Baird (trans. and ed.)
Introduction to the Art of Singing by Johann Friedrich Agricola

Valerie Walden
One Hundred Years of Violoncello
A History of Technique and Performance Practice, 1740–1840

Bernard Brauchli
The Clavichord

Suzanne J. Beicken (trans. and ed.)
Vocal Performance and Ornamentation by Johann Adam Hiller

Hugh Macdonald (trans. and ed.)
Berlioz's Orchestration Treatise

MUSICAL PERFORMANCE AND RECEPTION
General editors: John Butt and Laurence Dreyfus

This series continues the aim of Cambridge Musical Texts and Monographs to
publish books centred on the history of musical instruments and the history of
performance, but broadens the focus to include musical reception in relation
· to performance and as a reflection of period expectations and practices.

Published titles

John Butt
**Playing with History: The Historical Approach to Musical
Performance**

James Garratt
**Palestrina and the German Romantic Imagination: Interpreting
Historicism in Nineteenth-Century Music**

Daniel Leech-Wilkinson
**The Modern Invention of Medieval Music: Scholarship, Ideology,
Performance**

Michael Musgrave and Bernard Sherman
Performing Brahms: Early Evidence of Performance Style

THE MODERN INVENTION
OF MEDIEVAL MUSIC

Scholarship, Ideology, Performance

DANIEL LEECH-WILKINSON

CAMBRIDGE
UNIVERSITY PRESS

PUBLISHED BY THE PRESS SYNDICATE OF THE UNIVERSITY OF CAMBRIDGE
The Pitt Building, Trumpington Street, Cambridge, United Kingdom

CAMBRIDGE UNIVERSITY PRESS
The Edinburgh Building, Cambridge CB2 2RU, UK
40 West 20th Street, New York NY 10011–4211, USA
10 Stamford Road, Oakleigh, VIC 3166, Australia
Ruiz de Alarcón 13, 28014 Madrid, Spain
Dock House, The Waterfront, Cape Town 8001, South Africa

http://www.cambridge.org

First published 2002

Printed in the United Kingdom at the University Press, Cambridge

Typeface Baskerville Monotype 11 / 12.5 pt.   *System* LaTeX 2$_\varepsilon$ [TB]

A catalogue record for this book is available from the British Library

ISBN 0 521 81870 2

Whereof we cannot speak,
thereof we will go on guessing,
I suppose
(Philip Hensher)

Contents

Acknowledgements		*page* x
Introduction		1
1	The invention of the voices-and-instruments hypothesis	13
2	The re-invention of the *a cappella* hypothesis	88
3	Hearing medieval harmonies	157
4	Evidence, interpretation, power and persuasion	215
Conclusion		257
Notes		262
Bibliography		301
Index		323

Acknowledgements

I suspect that if I had known where this project would lead, or how long it would take, I should never have started it. The enthusiasm of many friends and colleagues has encouraged me, and I owe them collectively, and often individually, a debt too great to repay.

Irene Auerbach offered colloquial English equivalents of many invented compounds unknown to the dictionary (or even to her). Jon Banks discussed with me evidence for instrumental participation in polyphony. Alexander Bird commented expertly on my discussion of Thomas Kuhn. Rachel Beckles Willson saw everything we discussed from quite a different angle, and so, among other things, was an invaluable critic. Anna Maria Busse Berger helped in so many different ways that I hardly know where to begin to thank her, passing on rare materials, arranging lectures that gave me precious feedback at a crucial stage, and providing, together with Karol Berger, the most generous hospitality.

I was fortunate to be granted interviews with a number of scholars and performers who remember predecessors now long dead, or who grew up in traditions now forgotten. For sharing their recollections I am deeply grateful to Reinhold Brinkman, Martin Chusid, René Clemencic, Ursula Günther, Michel Huglo, Theodore Karp, Rena Mueller, Martin Picker, Andrea von Ramm, Joshua Rifkin, Edward Roesner and Denis Stevens. Key players in the *a cappella* movement were similarly helpful, including David Fallows, Christopher Page, Andrew Parrott and Ted Perry.

John Butt and Laurence Dreyfus both read the complete typescript and commented incisively, much to its advantage. Others who read extracts and offered comments include Susanne Dunlap, John Fallas, Mary Gifford, Don Greig, Andrew Kirkman, Richard Parncutt, Yolanda Plumley, Anne Stone, Richard Taruskin, Rob Wegman and Kirsten Yri. Colleagues who have kept me generously supplied with typescripts of their own, for which I owe them many thanks, include Lawrence

Earp, James Garratt, John Haines, Andrew Kirkman, Elizabeth Leach, Hartmut Möller, Stefan Morent, Alexander Rehding and Stephen Rice.

Timothy Day is the kindest curator one could ever hope to meet, just as Jerome Weber is the most phenomenally knowledgeable discographer: both have helped me greatly in tracing and dating early recordings. Gwendolyn Tietze has taught me much about German musicology of the 1920s and 1930s, and added regularly to my collection of musicological portraits. Noel O'Regan kindly sent me an article I could find nowhere else. For answering various and often mysterious questions I'm happy to be able to thank, in addition to many of those named already, Neil Gregor, Michael Heath, David Hiley, Tess Knighton, Patricia van Ness, Antony Pitts, Pamela Potter and Richard Wood. I am deeply grateful to all of them and to the many others who have helped, often without knowing how.

I should also like to pay tribute to the staff of the British Library, especially the staff of the library's National Sound Archive; in the USA the library staff of Columbia, Harvard, Stanford and New York universities and the University of California, Berkeley; in Germany the universities of Hamburg, Heidelberg and Göttingen, and the State Library of Berlin. I have received generous financial support from The British Council and Deutscher Akademischer Austauschdienst enabling me to work jointly on materials in German libraries with Annette Kreutziger-Herr, to whom, and to whose family, I owe my warmest thanks for innumerable kindnesses.

Introduction

A sketch from the classic television comedy series *Not only . . . but also* set in a London nightclub, La Maison Sophistiquée, showed Peter Cook, playing a humourless BBC arts presenter, interviewing Dudley Moore, playing jazz singer/pianist Bo Dudley.[1] Moore begins with a song from his new show, a boogie-woogie with the following lyrics:

> Momma's gotta bran' new bag, yeah.
> We're gonna groove it the whole night long, Baby.
> We're gonna work it out, Baby, hnnh.
> We're gonna shake it tonight.
> Stretch out, stretch out Baby.
> I hear you talkin', I hear you talkin' now.
> You turn me on, Baby.
> You're burning up now, Baby.

Following Moore's spirited performance, Cook, who shows no sign of ever having heard such a song before, takes him through the text line by line, explaining the slang for the benefit of English viewers. After extensive exegesis, in which every reading is suggested by Cook in his most earnest academic mode and enthusiastically endorsed by Moore, a résumé is offered to round off the sketch:

Well, to summarise, basically this is a simple story. The momma has gone out into the gay, bustling streets of Harlem. She's seen a brand new bag, she's bought it, this gaily coloured plastic bag. She brings it home, spends the whole night grooving it for her child. Then she discovers she's grooved it badly, she hasn't worked it out, and so in her rage she shakes all night, attempts to go to sleep, but the neighbours start talking. She asks her child to turn on the light, but she fuses it, and the whole [house] goes up in flames.

Anyone who has read an interpretation of a medieval text will recognise what's happened here, and why. Like many an academic hypothesis that pieces together fragments of evidence to form a story, this reading of the text seems coherent and tenable – or at least it would if we didn't have other ways of checking it. Cook, of course, hasn't the faintest idea of what he is talking about, but he knows that the BBC's mission is to educate and explain, and so he applies what seems to him to be reasonable common sense to this fragmentary text and arrives at what is apparently a perfectly plausible explanation, albeit one that reflects rather badly on the characters in the story (as he goes on to point out, in a passage which would nowadays cause too much offence for me to repeat). Note that Cook offers the reading and Moore simply agrees, knowing (as a passing remark makes clear) that the true meaning of the text is not sufficiently decent to be divulged on television (the show went out in February 1966, just months after Kenneth Tynan, to almost universal outrage, broke the four-letter-word barrier on the BBC).[2]

For the purposes of this book the Bo Dudley sketch, naturally, is a parable, but one that is in several respects all too close to reality. Perhaps the main difference is that medieval musicians are absent; they cannot validate, let alone contradict, our blithely unintentional misinterpretations of their work. Strangely, that seems to make us no less confident than Peter Cook's interviewer that our readings make correct sense of the evidence. On the contrary, musicologists offer explanations of their own for the patterns they see in the surviving fragments of evidence and hope to convince their readers that 'they' – medieval composers, performers, experts – would agree. But why does anyone do it, when the chances of being wrong, crazily wrong, are so high? Perhaps the most important reason is that it is enormously enjoyable. Trying to find ways of answering questions not answered by the hard evidence is endlessly fascinating, a battle of wits between the lack of evidence and one's own ingenuity. There is a great deal of pleasure to be had from piecing together fragments of evidence into a story that seems plausible. If others find it so, they will build on it, creating further plausible hypotheses that, gratifyingly, take one's own as a starting-point. The grooved bag and the fused lights can thus become the basis for further work, leading step by step to a more detailed understanding of grooving and shaking in mid-twentieth-century Harlem. And so scholars have the satisfaction of gradually building up – recovering, it seems – a history, and of feeling that each is playing an essential part in the process, which indeed they are.

That the whole argument is based on a misinterpretation is obvious enough in this example, because we have so much evidence about the context: Cook's interviewer may have been an idiot, but at least the information he needed in order to arrive at a historically appropriate reading of Moore's song was easily available elsewhere. But that is not true for medieval music. We don't have nearly enough context to answer even simple questions definitively. Who performed ars antiqua motets? What kinds of voices and/or instruments did they use? We have to use what little information there is if we want to arrive at an answer, but we cannot possibly know that it is correct; we can only believe it, or not. But while the absence of medieval musicians able to give us their view prevents us from achieving certainty, it also puts us in a very powerful position to propose answers of our own. We can present medieval musicians in any way we like, and contradiction can come only from colleagues who believe they have better reason to argue for something else. Inevitably the freedom we have to represent medieval people makes it easy for us to create views of them that are useful to us. We have to create something, because if we confined ourselves strictly to the hard evidence we should never be able to present a coherent picture, nor one that would be of any interest in the wider world, and medieval music would never be heard. But along the way we inevitably start to invent, and what we invent reflects our own personal beliefs about the Middle Ages, our preferences for particular kinds of stories, our background and our tastes. Often it's not easy to see exactly where this invention happens, because each step that a scholar takes in forming and setting out their view is a small one, and necessarily fits well with views that colleagues already hold. Otherwise it could never be accepted, and scholars never propose views that have no chance of being taken up: there are market forces that limit what they may safely propose if they want any kind of career. But when you add all those small steps together, over a long enough time, a view of the subject gets built up that is far more specific and detailed than can possibly be confirmed by the small amount of hard evidence that survives. Each new step uses some medieval evidence as its basis, but the way that evidence is read is very largely determined by the nature of views already accepted. At any one moment, then, musicology is highly conservative, both in discouraging radically new views of the subject and in discouraging radical questioning of existing ones. But over a long time-span it is extremely creative, building up pictures that look plausible but that could be wildly wrong. All we can know for sure is that these pictures have become complex and interesting in themselves and have led to a wonderfully rich tradition of music-making.

Considering the achievements of musicology in recovering something of medieval music, my comparison with Cook and Moore is an unkind one, no doubt, yet not as irrelevant as one might wish. And looking over the field as a whole it is hard to think of any area in which it is more likely to offer a fair analogy than that examined in this book: the understanding of medieval music as sound. Almost everything we might wish to know about the sound of medieval music is lost to us. Without living in the Middle Ages and experiencing that culture we are never going to be able to make the sense of those fragments of evidence that was made of them when they were set down. Even the things we recognise – that people set texts, sang and played instruments – can have no reality in sound except in so far as we can imagine them in relation to the way people sing and play around the world today. Ways of singing and ways of playing change too fast for us to be able to guess backwards.

To get some perspective on the size of the problem, imagine for a moment what scholars 600 years from now would make of a twentieth-century orchestral score with no instrument names, no evidence for the make-up of an orchestra, no indication, even, that it was an *orchestral* score. Or to make it easier, imagine that they had everything from the twentieth century that was written down, but nothing else: no instruments, no recordings, just words and pictures. How would they re-create a violin, how would they learn to play it, how would they sound, once they had taught themselves? There would be no oral tradition, only an evolving musical practice over the intervening 600 years, taking them . . . wherever it took them. In those circumstances, how would *La Mer* sound? They are us, except that we don't even know whether we are supposed to play it or sing it.

What, then, has musicology been doing over the first century or two of its existence?[3] How did we get to a point where medieval music is an established part of our cultural life? And if so little evidence for the sound of medieval music survives, where has all this knowledge of performance practice come from? The only way to understand where we are is to see how we got here, and in this book that is what I want to try to do. My plan is to follow the research done on performance practice between the eighteenth century and the present day, to see how views emerged and how and why they changed. I shall be asking when evidence was found, what was made of it, by whom, how their interpretations related to contemporary views of music and culture, and also how interpretations reflect the individuals who created them. I shall be looking at how these ideas were turned into performances and, over time, into an evolving performance practice.

Understanding medieval music in sound is not just about performance practice; it is also about how we make sense of the musical language, the way the notes fit together into compositions: and so I also want to look at the emergence and development of ideas about how the music works, especially about its melodic and harmonic structures. I shall try to persuade you that these two kinds of research – performance practice and musical analysis – are closely related and feed off each other, so that we need to see them working together if we are to understand the making of our current beliefs. Arising out of this, inevitably, will be some more general conclusions about how musicology works, more precisely about how musicologists work. I shall suggest that findings and procedures in this kind of research are not always what they seem, but that what they are is actually more interesting than what they are supposed to be. In particular, I shall be suggesting that historical work on medieval music is not as historical as it pretends, but that it is actually more interesting than it could be if it were constrained by the evidence that survives. That is not to say that I shall be trying to invalidate a historical approach to studying music of the past. Historical musicology may not always be quite what it seems but it is immensely productive, not as productive as it could be with a little opening up of its borders, but creative and inspiring nevertheless. And we have the performances to prove it. Without a sense that things could be known if only we looked and thought hard enough it seems unlikely that performers, just like performers of later repertories inspired by authenticist ideology, would have put so much effort into remaking the music. But I shall be suggesting that trying to find out how it was 'then' is just one approach and that others too could produce valuable results.

In a book with these rather specific intentions it would have been foolish to try to cover every repertory of medieval music that survives. There is far too much of it, and many of the points made for one body of music would have been repeated in looking at the others. Besides which, it makes sense to write about what one knows best. For me that is late medieval polyphony, especially the music of thirteenth-, fourteenth- and early fifteenth-century France and Italy. Specialists in other fields will be able to decide how much of what I say is relevant to them. Even with that restriction there is an enormous amount of scholarship to consider, and I have tried not to skate over the twists and turns in the story in order to keep it artificially straightforward. Because every step in scholarship is taken in relation to many previous (especially recent) steps, details are essential if we are to be able to understand what was believed at any one time and place. It is important, though, not to mistake detail for comprehensiveness. It will never be feasible to tell this story with historical verisimilitude, even though events happened so recently and are so well recorded. Naturally others will see the subject quite differently and would have written a different book, even with the same materials. Some may wish that it were a straight history of musicology, or a historical study of the modern performance practice of medieval music; others might have preferred a social, psychological or cultural-theoretical study. Although it is perhaps each of these things on occasion, I am not trying to achieve anything so categorised: the interaction of views in this specific area of musicology (the understanding of medieval music as music) is what I want to look at, and it's the complexity of those interactions that I think is interesting and typical. Neither have I covered aspects of medieval music in modern culture beyond the classical music world, in pop music, new-age, advertising, film and others. Some of those are considered, together with a more explicit use of cultural theory, in the book written in parallel to this one by my friend and colleague Annette Kreutziger-Herr.[4] We worked on many of the essential materials together in the early stages, but we have written radically different books. I'm delighted that that's so, in fact it provides the most encouraging indication that our field is opening up, just as at the end of this book I shall argue it should.

Even so, there is a theoretical side to *The Modern Invention of Medieval Music*, one that emerges as the book proceeds and that crystallised gradually during the writing of chapters 1 to 3. As I reconstructed in my own mind the evolution of a modern tradition of performing and analysing medieval polyphony, I found myself led inexorably towards a more sceptical view than I'd had when I began, more sceptical not just of arguments about medieval performance but of historical musicology as a method capable of arriving at historical truth. Seeing how one idea led to another, seeing how they interacted with other period concerns, and keeping always in mind what evidence was available at the time, it was impossible to avoid seeing also how much invention was going on and how firmly it was shaped by the preferences and beliefs of scholars. Here, then, was a beautiful illustration of the argument set out by Hans-Georg Gadamer in *Truth and Method*, and developed so much further by others during the past few decades. At the same time, I found this interaction of past materials with present imaginations more and more acceptable, more and more a legitimate way of using historical materials. All that was wrong, it seemed to me, was the continuing pretence (which, I shall suggest, lies beneath the surface rhetoric of scholarly caution) that all this invention corresponds to medieval fact. Whether this makes me an extreme positivist or an out-and-out relativist depends on your point of view, but there comes a point where the two attitudes meet, and that may be where this book has led me. At any rate, I shall be suggesting that we need to take away from this story a collection of related ideas, including:

(1) That historical musicology has tended to claim too much for its findings.

I have perhaps said enough already to explain why I think that. My response to it will be to call for more emphasis on the hypothetical and personal nature of research findings whenever they are offered. Silently assuming that readers understand that findings are ultimately unverifiable leads very easily to no longer recognising it oneself, and from there to claiming that one has *adequately* proved the historical correctness of an interpretation whose historical correctness cannot in fact be proved.

(2) That there is no special ethical virtue, as far as medieval music history goes, in the faithful recovery of the past.

This is not to say that there is anything less valuable about it than about any other approach, simply that the search for accurate knowledge of the far-distant past has no special value greater than the value of other uses that can be made of the surviving materials. Just to be clear, I do not extend this to recent history: the importance of knowing exactly what happened and why declines as events get further and further away. The lessons of the Nazi genocide or of ethnic cleansing in the Balkans or in Rwanda matter desperately. Similar lessons are there to be learned from the distant past; origins are there to be understood if only we can find out enough about them. But the context of those more distant events, especially the mental world in which they took place, was so different from our own that they can have only limited application to our own situation. In so far as there are fundamental lessons of human behaviour, there are plenty more recent examples from which to learn, and their contexts will be more relevant to our world. Therefore an accurate recovery of the distant past is a matter of interest rather than a matter of duty. Similarly, it would be fascinating to know how medieval musicians thought about their music, and that in itself is a good enough reason to try to find out, but there is no ethical imperative we must obey that requires us to share their view. Thus the aim of historical musicology as current understood – to recover and experience the past as it was – is not more worthy than the aim of any other kind of musical study, for example the interpretation or adaptation of medieval music to suit the present. There will be more to say about this later on, especially in relation to the rights of individuals present and past.

(3) Work on medieval music therefore can be done from an infinite range of viewpoints and with a great many worthwhile aims.

'Worthwhile' can only be defined in relation to current interests. Assessments of the value or importance of musicological work cannot be made in relation to its historical correctness, both because correctness cannot be determined clearly enough, and because historically correct work is not absolutely preferable. How then is work to be assessed? Until now, because work on medieval music has had just one aim, to show 'how it was', assessing the value of studies has been easy. You ask, 'could it have happened like this?', and the excellence of the work is proportional to the conviction with which you can say 'yes'. It seems perfectly reasonable to continue to apply that test to work that aims to be historical. But what of work that does not? This is not a noticeable problem with non-historical work on later music, so it's hard to see why it should be a problem here. Work will more often than not set its own criteria by defining its aims; in such cases it may reasonably be judged by how well it achieves them in the view of the reader making the judgement. It seems perfectly reasonable for the writer to set those aims rather than to be required to work to criteria set institutionally. Whether they are worthwhile aims will be largely a matter of opinion, and it is the writer's job to persuade her readers that they are. It seems reasonable to judge work by how far it persuades its readers that it matters. This leads to a second and more general criterion, which is that work should be interesting and useful; by 'interesting' I mean that it should engage the mind of the reader pleasurably and rewardingly, leaving him with ideas he had not had before, ideas that he is glad to have considered; by 'useful' I mean that it should engage with wider current concerns in such a way as to be transferable to other situations. For example, a piece of work might arrive at conclusions that can lead further, or that allow other questions to be seen in a new and potentially fruitful light. I am not arguing that every piece of work should be revolutionary, therefore, or return to first principles, only that it should be found to stimulate interest or further ideas in those who read it.

(4) Of all Western musics, therefore, medieval music more than any should be open to the practice of many different kinds of musicology, and there is no good reason why they should not co-exist or even – whenever a scholar can make them – intermingle.

For students of other musical repertories this may not sound an especially radical agenda. For specialists in cultural studies, much of what I say in chapter 4 – where I look at these questions in most detail – will be over-familiar, indeed old-hat, especially to those working in later fields for whom covert and casual values began to be exposed almost a quarter of a century ago. It may be helpful, then, to say a few words about the relationship between my arguments here and work done on later music from a postmodernist perspective. I have tried to avoid using references to the classics of postmodernist thought as a membership badge, partly because to do so is to play exactly the game I discuss in chapter 4, dropping names to show one's ideological currency (remarkably hard to resist, I must say), and partly because my position is a slightly different one to any of those set out by the major figures of musicological postmodernism.

That there can be no objective knowledge of music, either through a historical or an analytical approach, seems clear. Interpretation conscious of its cultural position seems at the moment (though this may change) to be the best that can be hoped for when we try to understand music, whether in the present or the past. But while I wish to see removed the special privileges accorded by musicology to historicist approaches, so that they become no more legitimate than others, I do not wish to see those approaches underprivileged or abandoned. It may deserve no special status, but an attempt to find out what happened and how it seemed at the time is, in my view, perfectly legitimate and a thoroughly worthwhile aim. Certainly it's impossible to recover the past, let alone the way it was experienced, just as it's impossible to get to the bottom of what music might mean, to oneself or anyone else. But one doesn't do musicology because it's possible: one does it because it is fascinating. Thus, unlike Lawrence Kramer, I do think that there is a place in musicology for a narrow, though perhaps not a 'phobically narrow . . . notion of contestable knowledge';[5] and I want to see evidence from the past subjected to a hard epistemology; for while I recognise that that is an ideal that can never be realised I still think it is a reasonable way of making sense of material remains of the past. But I do not think it is the only way, or better on principle than any other possible way. And this is one respect in which I part company from many of my medievalist colleagues. Another may be in believing that a product of hard epistemology, for example a hypothesis about past events, because it is inevitably not what it purports to be – that is, it cannot be an accurate description of what happened as it seemed at the time – needs to be recognised more vocally by historians, drawing on the insights of postmodernist scholarship, as nothing more than a modern hypothesis created in accordance with its author's ideology. Historical studies claim, and have always claimed, to take this as read. But it very soon gets forgotten in the excitement of piecing together a story about the past that seems newly and provocatively coherent. We need the constant admonition of postmodern thought to remind us of the thoroughly unhistorical nature of anything we may say today that interprets the material evidence that survives.

A consequence of this argument, though, is that the material evidence needs to be more clearly separated from the interpretations that gather around it. We need to be clear about what we *really* know, and to separate that rigorously from what we think it means. And in this sense my view is, if anything, more strictly positivist than is quite respectable today. We need to know what the surviving materials are and, since most are documents, what texts they preserve. Finding and making available those materials is, in my view, historicism in its most valuable form. If we do want to try to know something, however mistaken, about what happened in the past, we need all the hard evidence we can get. When we use it, of course, we are not impartial observers; indeed, we may not wish to be observers at all, but rather to use medieval materials quite openly to construct something new. I have no problem with that. I would oppose any permanent or irreversible changes being made to the surviving remains, because to alter them for ever would be to deny future historians the little but invaluable contact with the Middle Ages that they offer; but as far as interpretation goes I don't see that there can be any boundaries that must never be crossed, save only those imposed by generally agreed beliefs about human rights. It is perhaps this negotiation between positivism and freedom of interpretation that defines my project, if anything does, as postmodernist.

However one labels them, though, such views are currently, for many in my field, well beyond the pale. Medievalism is perhaps the last stronghold of old musicology, and still repels invaders with remarkable success. At the same time, because there is so little evidence, it presents exactly the same problems as face scholars of later music, but in a much more extreme form. This makes it an ideal case to take on if one wishes to learn something about musicology's needs and beliefs. Perhaps if critical musicology had not been so seduced by the overt emotional and personal subtexts of nineteenth-century music, with which it has been overwhelmingly occupied so far, it might have got to the Middle Ages rather sooner. They offer an irresistible wealth of examples of personal and emotional overlay imposed upon fragmentary and largely formless material. Similarly, medievalists who interpret evidence, and especially musical evidence, have close to hand in other kinds of musicology new ways of thinking about what they do. There ought to be exciting possibilities for meetings of minds. And yet, the gulf that separates traditional medievalists from colleagues in later fields is still huge, at its most extreme wider than ever, and it is almost impossible for a scholar on one side to see how things look from the other. Talking to both sides at once can be a thankless task, for one inevitably seems unsatisfactory to both. But the alternative is to see the two communities moving further and further apart, and given the extremely weak position of musical studies in our society a radical split is not going to work in anyone's interests. Medievalists need to understand and be understood by students of later music, and a view of what medieval studies has and has not achieved may be a small step towards that.

Non-specialists may be forgiven for thinking that musicology is tearing itself apart. There is plenty of evidence that could be offered in support.[6] But in fact the situation is not nearly that bad. We're living through a period in which fundamental questions are being asked about what musicology is for and what it should be. Asking them has to be healthy. While we're asking them it's not really possible, or at least not for me, to write a 'straight' history of the subject, because it's not possible to know what a 'straight' history would be.[7] Instead we need to go back a bit and look at how the last straight histories – the ones that set out the story more or less as it's currently believed – were reached. How did we get here, and did we do it right? Could the story be told differently? This is not just an academic question: it affects profoundly everything that is believed about the subject. Everyone who is interested in medieval music needs to know whether they are being told what it was really like, or something else. That something else may not be bad; far from it. But it would be nice to know what it really is.

It will be obvious from everything I've said that this is a personal view. I shall try to keep that clear throughout. One of my points is that all musicology is personal to a larger degree than is sometimes admitted: who writes it determines what it says. And that is certainly true here. I am very much part of the world I am describing and sometimes criticising. If I appear to be standing outside and taking an overview, that is an illusion: it may be in some respects a broad view, but it's seen from inside, not above or beyond. Quite a bit of it, especially in chapter 2, is written from personal experience, drawing on my memories of what happened and why. My ideas about this music took their first shape during the years when all-vocal performance, related to a view of the harmony as purposefully directed, was becoming the ideal. The importance of what was achieved in those years seemed especially great because my own view and the new approach grew up in tandem, and it's hard to escape that entirely later on. That experience is certainly responsible for one of the main biases in this book. Vocal performance seemed right, or more right anyway, and it sounded wonderful. But that is not to say that it was right or that it will always sound so good. Tastes and beliefs change all the time, and I can now see that far less is certain than seemed certain at the time. So in what follows there are the remains of deep-rooted preferences, albeit ones I no longer try so hard to justify by calling on history. But perhaps readers will be able to allow for that. Without biases, after all, one would have nothing particular to say.

CHAPTER I

The invention of the voices-and-instruments hypothesis

INTRODUCTION

Anyone interested in early music, unless they are British and under about twenty-five, will have grown up with the idea that medieval polyphony uses instruments, and lots of them: in songs they play the tenor and contratenor, and often join the singer of the cantus in unison or at the octave; in sacred music they play the cantus firmus and accompany the voices singing the other parts. Equally, anyone who has kept abreast of the early music scene during the last twenty years or so will know that there has been a phenomenal growth in performances by voices alone, especially from groups based in the UK. The earlier 'instrumental' view, however, has continued to be practised everywhere else (and even to some extent by British groups), so that a newcomer taking an overview of concerts and recordings would certainly conclude that instruments had an important part to play in medieval music as a whole. But if such a newcomer were to go backstage after some concerts and ask the groups' directors why they used voices alone or voices with instruments it is a fair bet that the answers would be not just different but of different kinds. The all-vocal director might refer them to some recent articles citing documentary evidence for the vocal performance of specific pieces that survive,[1] or descriptions in medieval literature that leave no doubt that composed polyphony is being sung,[2] in other words they would cite scholarship; but the instrumentalist might (experience suggests) be more likely to cite a long tradition of modern performance, or the lack of text in manuscripts, contacts between medieval Europe, North Africa and the Middle East, or simply the group's training and preferences, answers whose reasoning is harder to pin down.

These different kinds of answers, the certainty of a little evidence against the conviction of a rich tradition of belief, point not so much to the rightness of one and the delusion of the other (a conclusion that has yet to be substantiated) as to their very different histories. The vocal movement sprang quite recently from fresh evidence and a new look at existing information, and because it began within recent memory its origins in that evidence are still clear in people's minds: the evidence and its application are still closely associated, with little in the way of a tradition of performance separating the two. But for the voices-and-instruments movement that is no longer true: the origins of that approach are lost in the past; even experienced performers have only a vague idea of what the original evidence was and none at all of when it was gathered. There is a long and rich tradition of performances with instruments, and on the whole it is from this that performers take their cue, not from 'basic musicology'. But what was that tradition based on, where did it start, and when, and why? The answers to these questions were still remembered as late as the 1950s, and were partially recovered at least once since then,[3] but seemed to have been almost entirely forgotten by the end of the century; yet without them in front of us we can hardly begin to treat these two theories of performance on an equal footing and to the scrutiny they deserve. An essential step towards understanding where we are with the performance of medieval music can only be taken, then, by looking back to the beginnings of modern writing on medieval performance practice in search of the origins of the voices-and-instruments hypothesis.

One might ask why this was not done when the all-vocal revolution began. Even if the fathers of the new hypothesis were more concerned to promote their new view than to question the past, one might expect the defenders of the old to look back in search of a secure basis for instrumental practices. Perhaps they did. But if so, what they found will have seemed more alarming than reassuring. For as this chapter will explain, the voices-and-instruments hypothesis was invented on the basis of a single observation about the texting of one manuscript, mixed, soon after, with a large dose of nationalistic, modernist assumption about the nature of art song. It may seem strange that these suspect origins have been so long forgotten; but then, while the all-vocal people have already begun to scrutinise their own work, questioning its origins in a peculiarly English view of singing,[4] they belong to a self-reflective generation for whom the questioning of assumptions is a sub-discipline in itself, whereas the scholars who wrote in support of the instrumental hypothesis were not of a generation that questioned themselves, however enthusiastically they may have questioned one another. Our generation has replaced the certainty that we must be right with the certainty that we cannot be, so that it comes as no surprise to see scholars who advocate voices guarding their backs by refusing to rule out instruments, while arguing against them. And it is interesting to see them and others making tentative moves now to rehabilitate them. What *do* you do when a position, vigorously sought and finally achieved, after a while becomes stale? The crucial difference is that this time the case is being argued on documentary evidence and not simply on the basis of taste and cultural assumption. It may not be the least of the vocal movement's achievements that this time the case for instruments will be argued properly.

This chapter, however, is not primarily intended to contribute to that argument. Its purpose is to recover the origins of the instrumental hypothesis and to examine its development and its influence on performers up to the 1950s, the coming-of-age of professional medieval music groups. It looks at the foundations of the state that the vocal revolutionaries sought to overturn. It is therefore not so much concerned with what is right, with what actually happened, as with what scholars wanted to have happened, and why. It is about the origin, in fact, as I shall argue, the *invention* of the idea that medieval music generally, and late medieval song in particular, was composed for voice accompanied by instruments. This is not just an issue for historiography. It matters now because that is how medieval music was heard and described and thought about for three-quarters of a century, indeed for the first three-quarters of a century in which it was widely perceived at all. To all intents and purposes, this was how medieval music became established in our culture; the impression it made in this form is still strongly evident in current views of the music and may never be wholly erased. If the whole picture was based on wishful thinking, as I shall argue, we need to know. Of course, further research may show the wishful thinking to have hit the historical mark. But it has not been possible to know that up till now, and thus for most of the time our discipline has promoted this music it has been making claims it could not possibly substantiate, claims that tell us only about us and our tastes and needs. It is arguable, especially in the present climate of musicology, that our tastes and needs are the proper focus of our work, and that what happened in the Middle Ages concerns 'them', not us. But in any case, whatever our position on that we (both sides) need to know what we are doing; we all need to know what we are making up and what we are not. Then we can use it plausibly within our own work.

An apology may be necessary for my going in detail through a lot of early musicology and reporting what it said. Presenting this chapter in lectures in various parts of the world has shown that the story it tells has been almost wholly lost sight of. We need to reclaim an appreciation of what musicology's early medievalists found, and of what they claimed, if we are to understand how we were trained and why we think about the subject as we do. Put bluntly, Ludwig and Riemann – and their students and followers – formed the subject for us. We need to understand why they made it that way.

THE NINETEENTH-CENTURY BACKGROUND

What scholars thought about performance practice depended on the pieces they knew as well as on the documentary evidence available to them. Both were very limited until the early twentieth century when, as we shall see, the question quite suddenly came to life. Consequently the nineteenth-century histories of medieval music have very little to offer; they print few pieces and can suggest very little context for them.[5] At the same time they did provide the starting-point for the scholars with whose work we will mainly be concerned. Riemann, Ludwig and Johannes Wolf, like Kretzschmar and Adler, the giants of early musicology, necessarily used Kiesewetter, Fétis, Coussemaker and Ambros as sources for their general view of medieval music. It is therefore worth looking briefly at what the eighteenth- and nineteenth-century historians knew before we try to understand what changed around 1900.

Among the earliest music historians, Charles Burney (1789) depends heavily on Martin Gerbert's collection of treatises published only a few years earlier (Gerbert 1784). Without Gerbert, Burney – like Sir John Hawkins the previous decade (Hawkins 1776) – would have been even more dependent on the atypical English sources that they knew best. But for both writers, the history of medieval music was largely a history of theorists. Burney used literary sources to provide information about the troubadours and trouvères, from which he deduced that jongleurs were 'employed to sing the works of those Troubadours who, for want of voice or knowledge in Music, were unable to do it for themselves' and that 'At that time melody seems to have been little more than plainsong, or *chanting*. The notes were square, and written on four lines only, like those of the Romish church, in the clef of C, without any marks for time. The movement [i.e., the rhythm] and embellishments of the air depend on the abilities of the singer ... The singer always accompanied himself on an instrument *in unison*.'[6] He also provides editions of two songs by the Chatelain de Coucy, with others from the *Roman d'Alexandre* and by Thibaut de Navarre, to which he adds editorial accompaniment. But on the whole he can say little about performance practice: he had too few pieces and too little documentary evidence to begin to discuss it.

Johann Nicolaus Forkel (1801), though heavily dependent on Gerbert, Hawkins and Burney, attempts to divide his survey of medieval music ('Von Guido bis auf den Franchinus Gafor') into two parts, the first ('Von dem Mensural-gesang') dealing with mensural theory, the second ('Von der Harmonie') with counterpoint theory. The titles are revealing: measured song was a matter only of notation, as a reading of the theorists would lead one to believe; while the few surviving examples, for a reader of Forkel's generation, were remarkable only for their extraordinary harmony, the subject of so many sarcastic comments from Burney to at least the 1930s.[7] But for the modern reader perhaps the most striking aspect of Forkel's second part is the enormous hole between organum and the fifteenth century, a hole that is filled only in part during the nineteenth century, mainly by Coussemaker's publication of thirteenth-century motets. The fourteenth century remains almost entirely blank until the discoveries of Ludwig and Wolf a century later. The only significant exception, one that subsequent authors reproduce again and again in the absence of any alternative, is François-Joseph Fétis' brief description in the first issue of his *Revue musicale* (1827) of the music of Adam de la Halle. Although Fétis found the parallel fourths and fifths of early polyphony horrible,[8] Adam's rondels at least intermingled thirds, sixths and contrary motion, and he was willing to admit that while 'this is still very ill-mannered music', nevertheless 'it is a first step towards better, a necessary intermediary between diaphony proper and more improved pieces'.[9] He was well aware of the importance of his discovery for music history: since nothing was known of music between Franco (whom Fétis believed to be active towards the end of the eleventh century) and the late fifteenth century, the rondeaux of Adam could provide an identifiable stage in the development of harmony after Guido.[10] As well as printing a specimen rondeau *Tant con je vivrai*, wrongly transcribed in duple time,[11] Fétis offers the first description of a medieval motet (commenting that 'These motets were sung in processions'[12]) and introduces *Le Jeu de Robin et Marion* as the oldest existing opéra-comique.

By far the most assiduous collector of specimens, however, was Raphael Georg Kiesewetter.[13] Kiesewetter's aim, in a series of books and articles through the 1830s and 1840s, was to show a development in music leading from the earliest times towards the pinnacle of modern music, and in that sense the music of his own time is the real subject of his work and informs all his (numerous) judgements. To illustrate his argument he had necessarily to provide examples of the stages through which he saw music developing, and he seems to have trawled earlier publications with unusual thoroughness, often providing his own transcriptions in place of those he found; consequently he was used repeatedly by later writers as a ready source of material, and his examples continue to turn up in histories of music throughout the rest of the century. Kiesewetter's interest was mainly in the harmonic language of music, so that questions of its performance are hardly raised, though it is clear from his discussion of instrumental music, in his history of Western European music (1834), that he saw instruments participating with voices from at least the fifteenth century. (The quotations come from the 1848 translation that made Kiesewetter's work familiar to English audiences.)

During the periods of which we have previously treated [i.e., before the 'Epoch of Josquin'], there never existed the smallest idea of a proper, artistical, and substantial instrumental music: for strengthening or supporting the chorus, i.e., the singers, cornetti, trombones, and perhaps trumpets, were mostly employed, all of which moved in unison with the voices.[14]

It has, moreover, been noticed by many writers, – and their observations are evidently confirmed by a perusal of the compositions of that early period [late fifteenth-century contemporaries of Paumann], which contain a great extension of the parts, and frequent change of key, – that counterpoint, particularly such as was set to familiar songs, was performed by instruments of one kind or another, whatever may have been their nature or construction.[15]

But he had already seen enough archival evidence to know that 'still the instrumentalists, with the exception of the organists, were totally separated from the real or proper (scientifically educated) musicians, i.e., from the singers (for the music masters were singers); they formed a peculiar sect, under the name of town-fifers, music-fifers, or warders', a point that has been picked up only in recent times to argue for the separation of instrumentalists and singers in performance.

Kiesewetter's history of the origins of opera, *Schicksale und Beschaffenheit des weltlichen Gesanges vom frühen Mittelalter bis zu der Erfindung des dramatischen Styles und den Anfängen der Oper* (1841), which is essentially a history of secular song, provides by far the richest and most varied collection of medieval music yet published, including monophonic songs taken from treatises, songs extracted from mass tenors (drawing on Kiesewetter's seminal study of the Netherlands school), troubadour songs copied from La Borde and Burney, monophonic songs by Adam taken from Bottée de Toulmon, along with a lay stanza and a virelai by Machaut; also polyphonic works by Adam and Landini taken from Fétis; Machaut's *Dous viaire* transcribed by Kiesewetter (with his famous Ciceronian annotation 'O tempora! o mores!'[16]), likewise Dufay's *Je prens congié* and *Ce moys de may* (the latter attributed to Binchois), an anonymous song from Gerbert, Busnoys' *Dieu quel mariage* from Petrucci, as well as pieces by Regis, Josquin, Cara, and so on. Whether or not his readers regarded these works as leading inexorably towards opera, as an introduction to medieval music they must have come as a revelation.

To this stock of published music relatively little is added before the last few years of the nineteenth century. The most substantial, and certainly the most influential publications of music were Coussemaker's 1865 collection of thirteenth-century motets and his wider-ranging history of harmony from 1852, containing polyphonic pieces from the twelfth to the fourteenth centuries, which together added around seventy works to those already available; both publications included facsimiles as well as transcriptions, offering the first opportunity to study medieval music in its original form. Of the histories of music published later in the century, Ambros (Kiesewetter's nephew and clearly much in his debt) provided the fullest treatment of medieval music but, even so, provided only a handful of examples taken from primary sources, the rest coming mainly from Coussemaker and Kiesewetter.

Although, as we have seen, a good deal of medieval music was available before the path-breaking publications of the 1890s, the focus of interest for writers on the subject changed very little after Kiesewetter. Schluter (1863), Ambros (1864), Fétis (1876), Schletterer (1884), Rockstro (1886) and Riemann (1882, 2/1884, 3/1887 and Riemann 1888) were above all concerned with the development of forms and styles, showing far less interest in how the music might have sounded. Nevertheless, their curiosity is from time to time aroused by the question, and the scattered remarks they make do allow us to begin to reconstruct the assumptions that were general before – at the end of the century – Stainer's seminal studies, and the ideas developed from them by Riemann, changed the whole picture. For Coussemaker (1865) the notation of conductus in score, with the text underneath the system, indicates that it applied only to the lowest voice; and while he thinks it possible that the upper two parts were vocalised, he finds it probable that they were instrumental. When he considers whether motet tenors were sung or played he notes that no theorist is explicit, but thinks instrumental performance more likely on account of the provision of a text incipit only (i.e., not an underlaid chant text) and also because of the repetition of the tenor melody, but he readily admits that this is just conjecture in the absence of further evidence.[17]

At any rate, Coussemaker shows us that instrumental participation was conceivable in his time.[18]

One might not think so from reading other writers. Ambros discusses the possibility that untexted parts in organum might have been vocalised,[19] a suggestion that surfaces again as late as 1905 in Wooldridge's survey of late medieval music for the original Oxford History of Music:

With respect to the number of voices employed in Machaut's form of rondeau, these might either be two, three, or four; the text, which is only to be found in one of the parts, was always given to the upper voice, the remaining voices probably singing upon some vowel, in the old manner.[20]

It is also perfectly clear from numerous entries in his Musik-Lexikon that Hugo Riemann believed, at least until after the fifth edition of 1900, that medieval polyphony was purely vocal:

Accompanying Parts: The older contrapuntists of the 14th to the 16th century were unacquainted with *A. p.* in the real sense of the term. In purely vocal compositions, with strict or free imitations, which they exclusively cultivated, each part contained melody (was a *concerted* part). . . . The songs of the troubadours were accompanied by the minstrels on the viol or *vielle*. . . . It appears, however, that the instrumental accompaniment only doubled the vocal part in unison, or in octave, and possibly only those notes which fell upon strong beats. Accompaniment, in the modern sense of the term, appears first about 1600, and its cradle was Italy.[21]

Music, History of: *Middle Ages IV: (14th–16th cents.)*: the possibility of various kinds of mensural determination soon led to the artifice of coupling various kinds of time in simultaneous vocal parts. . . . During the whole of this period music became more [*recte* is always] polyphonic and, as a rule, in four parts, seldom more than five, and [always] *a cappella*.[22]

on Modern Times: . . . Next came [*recte* First we find] monody with instrumental accompaniment in chords . . . from this sprang the opera and the oratorio, also singing in parts with instrumental accompaniment . . . , and finally, pure instrumental music.[23]

Cappella: As in old times sacred compositions were written for voices only without any kind of instrumental accompaniment (up to 1600), the term *a cappella* . . . received the meaning of polyphonic vocal music without accompaniment.[24]

Their appearance here in what was already the standard reference work on music suggests fairly strongly that these were generally held views at the end of the nineteenth century (and if they were not before, their circulation through the Musik-Lexikon certainly made them so).

Consequently we should see Riemann's 1892 and 1893 editions of late medieval songs texted in all voices as reflecting prevailing opinion rather than (with the benefit of hindsight) as a wilful modernisation uncharacteristic of its time. In *Sechs bisher nicht gedruckte dreistimmige Chansons* (1892) Riemann transcribed six songs from a fragmentary source in Munich that had been catalogued by J. J. Maier in 1879, substituting for the original French text of the cantus a German translation applied to all voices, and transposing pieces as necessary to suit modern women's (or boys') and men's voices.[25] Some of these pieces he reused in the following year in his *Illustrationen zur Musikgeschichte. I: Weltlicher mehrstimmiger Gesang im 13.–16. Jahrhundert*, which includes songs by Binchois and Dunstable (attributed to Binchois), again fully texted in German (Illustration 1.1).

What is particularly interesting about these editions is that they were transcribed from original sources, not taken over from existing publications. This is significant not only because the transcriptions so clearly indicate current assumptions about medieval performance but also because Riemann had not previously worked from original notation. Indeed his 1878 textbook on the history of notation shows no signs of familiarity with any manuscript, but relies entirely on rules for notation provided by treatises in Gerbert and Coussemaker.[26] It seems unlikely that Riemann had never seen a manuscript of medieval polyphony before he began to transcribe the Munich fragments for Riemann 1892, and anyway facsimiles of both song and motet notation, including untexted voices, were easily available to him in Coussemaker 1852 and 1865, but what is interesting for the present argument is that while he was transcribing these songs, and was faced with three separate voices, two of which were untexted, he nevertheless found it reasonable to apply the cantus text to all three in order to make a performable edition. The same view was taken by Guido Adler and Oswald Koller in the first volume of pieces from the Trent Codices published in the series Denkmäler der Tonkunst in Österreich in 1900 (as in all three volumes Adler edited, 1900, 1904 and 1912). For reasons touched on in the introduction to *Sechs Trienter Codices I* and set out in detail in an article published (provocatively, one might think) in the Riemann Festschrift of 1909, the cantus text was applied to the lower voices, breaking ligatures where necessary. For Adler, as for Riemann in his early publications, medieval polyphony was vocal and therefore the text must apply to all voices. No one who knew only his later writings on medieval music (from 1905 on) would suppose that Riemann could ever have believed this, for it is the exact

1.1 John Dunstable, *O Rosa Bella*, ed. Hugo Riemann (1893: 4)

opposite of the view that he and his disciples so vigorously promoted later on. The evidence of these early editions shows beyond a doubt that before about 1900 late medieval song was generally believed to be vocal in all parts.[27] Some time around then Riemann was converted and the voices-and-instruments hypothesis took wing. But what changed his mind, and why does it matter?

INVENTION

The answer to the second question will become clearer during this chapter, but for now an indication of Riemann's importance in the process may be seen by attempting to trace backwards, from publications later in the twentieth century, footnotes pointing to the evidence for using instruments in late medieval songs. Inexorably they converge, not on any primary sources or any documentary evidence, but on studies by Riemann, above all his *Handbuch der Musikgeschichte* of 1905. Riemann, as we shall see, was the first and most influential publicist for the voices-and-instruments hypothesis. How he was converted is also clear, for he makes no secret of his reasoning (although his motivation will need some elucidation). The evidence is largely incorporated into the story he sets out in the *Handbuch*, but it finds its clearest presentation in an article that appeared the following year under the revealing title 'Das Kunstlied im 14.–15. Jahrhundert' (*Artsong* in the 14th and 15th centuries) and whose first half sets out Riemann's new view of late medieval performance practice.[28] Riemann makes a potent argument, powerfully presented, out of a variety of ingredients including observations from two previous studies, Stainer (1898) and (rather grudgingly) Ludwig (1902–3), together with the materials assembled by Wolf for his path-breaking *Geschichte der Mensuralnotation* (1904), transmuted through Riemann's preconceptions about the nature of art music. To understand more precisely how his argument formed it will help to look briefly at each of these ingredients.

As Riemann implicitly acknowledges in both studies, the voices-and-instruments hypothesis has its ultimate origin in the Stainer family's work on the Oxford manuscript Canonici misc. 213. Although Riemann seems only to have known the final product of their research, *Dufay and his Contemporaries* of 1898, Sir John Stainer had already published the essentials two years earlier, in a paper read to the Musical Association on 12 November 1895 and published in the Proceedings for 1895–6. In studying the Canonici songs the Stainers were inevitably struck by the number of pieces that began with an untexted phrase in the cantus, as well as by the frequency of untexted phrases within and at the ends of pieces; given the untexted lower voices, and the nature of contemporary (late nineteenth-century) song, it would have been surprising if they had not considered the possibility that instruments were involved. In fact to Sir John Stainer it was obvious:

From the fact that it is rather the exception than the rule that the words should begin with the music, and also from the fact that a long series of notes often occurs in the middle or at the end of a song, without any words being written under them, I think it may safely be inferred that instruments of the viol family were employed throughout; they would be in unison with the voices when the words were being sung, and, when the voices were silent, they would supply short symphonies. The existence of these preliminary and final instrumental symphonies in Dufay's compositions is of considerable interest.[29]

He goes on to suggest that it may represent a further stage of the developmental progression proposed by Gevaert from Greek song accompanied by a lyre, via the Romans, into the plainchant antiphon (in which, Gevaert suggested, voices took the place of the instrumental introduction),[30] leading in turn (Stainer proposes) to the instrumental introductions in songs of Handel and Bach and 'the modern drawing-room or St James's Hall ballad'. While this may seem too ridiculous to mention now, it provides a useful reminder of just how little was known about medieval and early Renaissance music at the end of the nineteenth century, and of how important the evidence of the Canonici manuscript must therefore have seemed. Between the Montpellier motets published by Coussemaker (1865) and the later Netherlands composers,[31] *Dufay and his Contemporaries* offered the largest body of music yet published. Inevitably it was read as a crucial intervening stage in the development of music.

At the end of his paper Stainer introduced a performance – probably the first modern performance – of some Dufay songs, the introduction to which offers another small clue as to why the voices-and-instruments hypothesis seemed to make so much sense:

I had great difficulty in finding out how to let you *hear* some of Dufay's compositions. It would have been a hopeless task to try to find three or four good singers who were sufficiently advanced philologists to sing the old French words; it would require a vocal quartet of Max Müllers![32] But as they were without doubt accompanied by an early form of viol (a fact which may have had an important influence on the compass of the parts), I at last determined to place the music in your hands and have it performed on three or four violas; these instruments will probably give you the nearest approach to the old viol tone which can be found in our modern instruments.[33]

It is a recurring theme of pre-war performances of, and writings on, medieval music that the music is too difficult to sing without instrumental accompaniment,[34] so that it is possible that in referring to difficulties with old French (in which a modern French accent would surely have been serviceable) Stainer was drawing a veil over a more serious obstacle to vocal performance. If so, one can hardly expect a writer in late Victorian England (least of all a composer of choral music) to suppose that medieval singers might have been very much more skilled than their own.

In the introduction to *Dufay and his Contemporaries* the Stainers offer more detailed arguments in favour of performance with instruments on all parts:

It is abundantly clear from our MS that some form of instrumental accompaniment was employed; to take one instance only – Dufay's song 'Ce jour de l'an' – it will be seen from the facsimile that there are three groups of notes, one at the beginning, one in the middle, and one at the end of each of the three vocal parts, under which no words are written. It is possible of course that in the case of the two latter groups the last preceding syllable of the words was intended to be carried on in spite of the intervening rests: numerous instances of this may be found in the music of the period, and Thomas Morley quotes a passage from a motet of Dunstable's to illustrate the absurdity of the practice;[35] but with regard to the first group of notes, it is clear that they can only have been written as an introductory symphony for instruments, such as viols, preceding and leading up to the entry of the voices, and we shall probably not err in supposing that these instruments were employed not only for symphonies, but to accompany the voices throughout. In the case of 'Ce jour de l'an' the words are written out in full under each part, but in many, indeed in the majority of the songs in this MS, the words are placed under the upper part only, while the tenor and the contra-tenor parts have only the first two or three words written at their beginning, generally in such a way as not to correspond with the notes above them. Perhaps one is not justified in inferring from this that in every case where it occurs the lower parts were not intended to be sung at all, but to be played only, but in some cases this must clearly be so; if you will look, for instance, at the first song in this collection, 'Je demande ma bienvenue', you will see that the two lower parts cannot possibly be sung to the words of the song, even if the phrasing indicated by the ligatures is entirely disregarded. Another good illustration of the employment of instruments is afforded by Dufay's song 'Estrines moy, je vous estrineray' on folio 20 verso of the MS. This song is in three parts, but the words are in the form of a dialogue between *two* persons only, and are distributed accordingly between the two upper parts, while the third or contra-tenor part has merely the words 'Est[r]ines moy' written at its commencement. Here, therefore, it is clear that the contra-tenor part must have been played and not sung, and that of the two upper parts which sustain the dialogue, those portions only can have been sung to which the words of the dialogue are allotted, the remaining portions which occur while the singer is not speaking, but being spoken to, being rendered by instruments alone.[36]

The editors go on to quote Olivier de la Marche's description of motets being played.[37] On the face of it this was powerful evidence, and until Wolf published his much wider-ranging collection in 1904 no one, apart from Ludwig (who by the end of 1904 had already transcribed the bulk of fourteenth-century polyphony, as is clear from his dated transcriptions in the Ludwig Nachlass)[38] was in a position to see that these songs were not entirely representative of medieval song as a whole. Ludwig, however, had come to somewhat similar conclusions. He seems not to have believed that instruments took part in the cantus line – at any rate, when Riemann built on the Stainers' hypothesis, describing in the *Handbuch der Musikgeschichte* 'instrumental introductory-, between- and after-phrases', Ludwig annotated the margin of his copy 'unbelievable'.[39] But he certainly shared the Stainers' assumption that the untexted lower voices were instrumental. In his ground-breaking 1903 study of fourteenth-century polyphony Ludwig was at first rather coy about his view of performance practice:

in the manner of performance, by comparison with the other voices it [the Tenor] must have contrasted very much; unfortunately, for lack of sufficient clues, we still do not know how this happened in the performance of the whole composition, whether by being purely instrumental or in another way.[40]

But right at the end of the article, after warning that speculation about questions of vocal and instrumental music has frequently led scholars into madness, he becomes much more specific, to the extent that his repeated disclaimer at the end has a hollow ring to it. His views have become quite clear:

That instrumental accompaniment also plays a large role in the expert performance of the French and Italian vocal works of our epoch is without a doubt. For example we see the composers often shown playing a portative organ; I can well imagine that the tenor was played on this instrument, one that is capable of holding on the longest notes of the tenor and, like bowed and plucked instruments, allows self-accompaniment. It should not, however, be my task here to add to the many hypotheses about the instrumental practice of the Middle Ages a new one, like them based for the most part only on supposition.[41]

By 1903, then, Riemann would have been aware that instrumental accompaniment for these new repertories was beginning to look like a real possibility. Although it was an English publication with a restricted circulation, he must have known of the Stainer volume by 1900, when Adler cited it in his introduction to *Sechs Trienter Codices I* and Wolf reviewed it in the *Sammelbände der internationalen Musikgesellschaft*.[42] We do not know when he first saw a copy, but even if, as early as 1898, he had seen Stainer's support for instrumental participation in all voices, it is possible that that observation's potential for a redrawn history of late medieval music was not apparent to him until he came to work on the second half-volume of his *Handbuch der Musikgeschichte*, probably around 1903–4 (the first half-volume was issued in 1904 and was presumably completed some time before since the second appeared already in 1905). This would provide a context for his short article on two canons in the Canonici manuscript published in the *Zeitschrift der internationalen Musikgesellschaft* for 1904–5. But, crucially, it was also during this same period that he could first have seen the full range of music that Wolf would be publishing in his *Geschichte der Mensuralnotation* in 1904. In 'Das Kunstlied im 14.–15. Jahrhundert' Riemann acknowledges this:

Since Wolf made the individual page-sheets available to me during the printing, I was in the happy position of being able to use the contents for the second half-volume of my Handbuch der Musikgeschichte.[43]

Again this points to *c.* 1903–4 for Riemann's detailed working-out of his new view of fourteenth-century song. During this period he must for the first time have come to appreciate the range of late medieval music that survives (entirely unknown to him before Wolf), the marked differences between French and Italian forms and styles, and the layout and notation of these pieces in the manuscripts. It is worth remembering that he had been writing music history of this period in one form or another for twenty-five years;[44] he must immediately have begun to think about how all this material might fit into or might alter the story he had been outlining during that time; as a musician and a thinker about music (which to Riemann was always more important than being a historian) he must have wanted above all else to understand the language of these pieces, where it might have come from and what it might lead to. He was thus bringing a knowledgeable and immensely fertile mind to bear on a mass of new and fascinating music.

What seems to have struck Riemann more powerfully than anything, even than questions of performance practice (though they proved to be crucial to his argument), was the repertory of trecento polyphony, which was entirely new to him and to all his contemporaries apart from Ludwig, who had transcribed it for himself but had published only an overview and without music examples.[45] Ludwig's article shows his own preference for trecento music over what we now call *ars subtilior*, saying of the latter, 'how disappointing is the kernel that hides behind the shell', and then 'What a different effect, on the other hand, the Italian trecento has on us!'[46] This passage may have been another factor in the growth of Riemann's view. But in any case, the music of fourteenth-century Italy came as a revelation to him, the excitement of it palpable in the language of the *Handbuch*. Two features of trecento song struck Riemann as crucial, first that it was more nearly tonal than French music, and might therefore point more directly towards the music of the future, and secondly (and more specifically) that it consisted of simple quasi-tonal accompanying parts supporting a graceful melodic line and in that sense showed values that for Riemann were essential to art song. In setting it into context, therefore, he looks not to thirteenth-century French music, which seems to have little in common with it, but rather to English music (which he knew from the English series *Early Bodleian Music*), where the thirds and sixths Riemann so appreciated in trecento pieces could be found at an even earlier date. Hence:

Johannes Wolf (Gesch. der Mensuralnotation etc) would like to ascribe . . . the greater advance to the French. [But] English parallel discant in 3rds or 6ths or in 3rds and 6ths beginning and ending in perfect consonances (unison, octave, fifth) is after all undoubtedly at least the starting-point of the style that, through the Ars nova, became Continental, perhaps as earlier stressed, even the starting-point for the whole of polyphony, including the old organum.[47]

It follows that French music needs to be sidelined, for, seen from this angle, there is a continuous development from early English music, through the ars nova of trecento Italy, to the music of modern times, a development to which fourteenth-century French music contributes very little and fifteenth-century English music much less than had been supposed. Thus:

Curiously enough, Johannes Wolf, in this the first collection of the musical art of the 14th century made available to us in a substantial quantity, has not observed that the *Italians* have not only prepared the revolution in notation that Philippe de Vitry imparted to France and the Netherlands, but moreover – something that is more important – also created the new style, which for the Ars nova is after all the most important thing, the style that breaks conspicuously with the tradition of organum and in composition is based on parallel motion in 3rds and 6ths instead of on contrary motion. This result of investigating [Wolf's] collection is highly surprising, and opens whole new perspectives which could strongly reduce the role that England played at the time of the origin of the type of fully developed compositions recognised even until today as contrapuntally correct, so that Power, Benet, Dunstable etc. do not appear to be phenomena emerging especially from English musical roots. Florence thus becomes the birthplace of a style-change scarcely less important than the return 300 years later to (accompanied) monody.[48]

Riemann then begins to examine trecento polyphony in detail, in a chapter boldly entitled 'Florence, the cradle of Ars nova'. Acknowledging the work of Wolf and Ludwig in making fourteenth-century music available, he sets out to show that in stressing the importance of the French ars nova they both failed to see what was revolutionary about the Italian. To lend weight to his argument he begins by making an analogy between 'the fresh pulsing life' of troubadour poetry and music, and the development of the Italian language in Dante, suggesting a line of development between two bodies of work already widely admired on to which he can peg a similar musical development; for it is easily understandable that 'the young bloom' of Italian poetry coincides with that of Italian music:[49]

Certainly the Florentine Ars nova of the trecento did not take up the laborious studies of the Parisian school, as emerges clearly enough from the fact that it does not build motets over a tenor that uses just a few pitches, nor rondeaux and conductus put together in a ponderous organal style,[50] but rather appears with a whole new fundamental form and further with such security and natural liveliness that any suspicion of a theoretical starting-point is out of the question. No, this Florentine New Art is very much an authentic indigenous offspring of Italian genius . . .[51]

The language is reminiscent of Jacob Burckhardt, whose *Die Kultur der Renaissance in Italien* (1860) had by 1905 already reached its ninth edition. As well as Burckhardt's repeated presentation of Florence as the birthplace of the Renaissance, Riemann here seems to be echoing especially the language of Part IV, 'The Discovery of the World and of Man', which from so many angles contrasts the Italians' new-found interest in the natural world with the medieval traditions of the Church. Riemann's use of this rhetoric may have been unconscious, for Burckhardt was by now an inextricable part of any intellectual's understanding of European culture. But by bringing music into this view, and seeing it too as progressive and anti-medieval, Riemann is able to draw on other prejudices widely shared by scholars from a similar background. Supported by the hint that French ars nova music had in Vitry a purely theoretical basis, Riemann's rhetoric is of course designed to denigrate any French contribution and, coupled with his preference for England as an ultimate source for trecento style, reflects a nationalistic element in Riemann's thought that surfaces elsewhere in his writings and that is entirely in keeping with his place and time. Anti-French sentiment was as strong in Riemann's Leipzig as anywhere in Germany. It found a particular focus in the Battle of Leipzig – one of the first mass battles of modern times – which saw the final defeat of Napoleon in 1813, and had been stoked within recent memory by the Franco-Prussian war of 1870. Germany had been in alliance with Italy since 1882. Riemann's historical argument could hardly have been better adapted to his surroundings. He had been building up to it for several years. Alexander Rehding cites a similar passage in the *Geschichte der Musiktheorie* of 1898:

As historical research keeps confirming, it is hardly a coincidence that *Germanic nations brought the raw beginnings [of simultaneous singing] to a certain artistic height, and that England of all places became the actual cradle of fully developed counterpoint.*

We have seen Riemann withdrawing the credit from England somewhat in 1905 and redirecting it towards Italy. But his determination to exclude French music from any kind of formative role is just as strong, for this 1898 extract continues:

The third as the foundation of harmony is something remote, something completely unthinkable for the peoples educated in the theories of the ancients [i.e., the French]. This healthy core of harmonic music could not be found through speculation; rather it was the vocation of the nations to whom this notion was self-evident, familiar for centuries, to bring order and meaning at once into the theory and practice of an art, which the heirs of the ancient culture had fundamentally ruined in their attempt to assimilate an element alien to them.[52]

A further argument he offers deals with compositional procedure. Just as the ballata derives not from the French virelai but from troubadours' dance songs, so the caccia, he insists, is a wholly original Tuscan product, not derived from the French chace; it is:

a canon for two voices with or without a fundamental bass voice. The musical construction of the Florentines at this time astounds first of all through the fact that the cantus prius factus, normal almost without exception for the Parisian school, is very obviously lacking; thus successive voice invention is abandoned. Even in the cases where a low voice proceeds in long notes it appears not so much as a cantus firmus as a *fundamental bass*. It goes without saying that the canonic voices cannot have been made one after another, but rather are worked out together.[53]

It must be evident by now that barely hidden behind these apparently music-historical facts lies a mass of cultural prejudice. Not only did Riemann wish to exclude the French from any significant role in the formation of modern music; as a Protestant intellectual he shared a widespread distaste for the enthusiasm for the Middle Ages shown by Catholic historians. For them, the central part played by (pre-Reformation) religious belief in medieval life, gave the Middle Ages an appeal that to Protestant historians was positively objectionable. If Riemann was to find a crucial role for medieval music in his history of music then it was going to have to be found outside the music of the Church. The long-standing German love affair with Italy, which went back through Burckhardt at least as far as Goethe and Heine, together with the anti-French and anti-clerical sentiments so characteristic of his class, almost inevitably converged in his preference for trecento song over French cantus-firmus based compositions, especially given their very different approaches to melody and accompaniment, the one so much easier to relate to modern music than the other. All this feeds into his preference for Italy as the birthplace of secular song and, with it, of all those fundamental ingredients in Western classical music (instrumental music, tonality, abstract music) for whose fullest development, through the eighteenth and nineteenth centuries, Germans of Riemann's generation felt they could reasonably take the credit.

Before going on to deal with the tonal construction of trecento compositions and its (for Riemann) clear anticipation of later developments, he introduces another and in this context a more surprising ingredient into his argument, but one that plays a major role in showing how trecento song marks the origin of modern music. It seems clear to Riemann, in the light of the Stainers' work, that these songs are accompanied melodies, and that the accompaniment is instrumental, and in that sense they mark the beginning of song as it became known in later centuries, particularly since, for Riemann, the texting is not melismatic as it appears in the manuscripts, but rather syllabic as in later song, the melismas belonging to the accompanying instruments. This is almost breathtaking in its boldness and its ruthlessness with the manuscript evidence, though in an environment where German Lieder marked the pinnacle of song, and where an understanding of the medieval context had so little evidence on which to rest, it makes much more sense than it might today (though, as we shall see, its influence is in some respects still with us).

Riemann begins his presentation of this extraordinary hypothesis by raising the difficulties that Ludwig had in approving of the extensive melismas he found in trecento vocal lines. Ludwig, Riemann tells us, wonders in his 1902 survey of fourteenth-century polyphony, about the Florentines' 'excessive extension of the individual parts through melismas delighting in notes [tonfreudige Melismen], such as never appear in French secular art'; and Riemann notes that in Wolf's published transcriptions from the manuscripts that is indeed what one sees. To Riemann, however, this is to read the manuscripts far too literally, without considering how they would have been performed. Far from being excessive vocal melismas, he believes, these are in fact '*instrumental introductory-, between- and end-phrases*' (Riemann's italics) that in performance 'wrap up the sung melody'.[54]

I have pointed out many times [earlier in Riemann 1905] that even monody notations of the 13th century not infrequently contain elements that can only be understood as instrumental preludes, interludes and postludes. . . . For polyphonic pieces Stainer's recent 'Dufay and his contemporaries' (1898) includes a large number of perfect proofs.[55]
. . .in any case, an unprejudiced look at the madrigals of the oldest Florentines teaches that we stand here before a richly developed form *combining instrumental music with vocal music* whose existence at so early a time one had not suspected. Whether the lower voice is at all intended to be sung seems to me questionable even if it is not impossible.[56]

Taking as an example Giovanni da Cascia's madrigal *Nel mezzo a sei*, Riemann then shows how his tonal reading, combined with his rearrangement of the text, produces something that he can relate directly to the later Florentine monodists, and thus to the birth of modern music. Although he makes no reference to Kiesewetter here, it is clear that his agenda is not unlike Kiesewetter's in the *Schicksale*, using late medieval song as a step along the road to opera. An extract from Riemann's example is reproduced here as Illustration 1.2.

A quick glance soon teaches that here we stand before a new art; in the whole of the older literature one seeks in vain for such a piece, one that so clearly *rests on a harmonic basis*, so systematically disposed over *harmonic progression*. Cadences and half-cadences are found on $d, g, a, g, d, a, d, \overset{b}{g}, \overset{(\sharp)}{a}, \overset{\sharp}{g}, d, d, \overset{b}{g}, d, \overset{\sharp}{a}, d, f, \overset{(\sharp)}{a}$, only twice (bar 15 and bar 4 of the $\frac{3}{2}$, section) comes the typical . . . old style divergence from 3rd to 5th $\overset{c\sharp}{a} \overset{d}{g}$, and even there with a tension-creating effect [mit einer

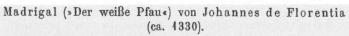

1.2 Giovanni da Cascia, *Nel mezzo a sei,* ed. Hugo Riemann (1905: 309)

Ausnutzung für eine Spannungswirkung] that is still possible even today. The few parallels still occurring are, as my revealing of the simple foundation shows, only the chance result of the noticeably skilful figuration . . .[57]

Through my clearly implemented extraction of the instrumental parts, the excessive melismas are removed and the declamation appears simple, almost syllabic. It is worthwhile to treat the piece, as it is here, like a figured bass notation and complete it in accordance with the practice of 300 years later – it can easily be left to stand beside the Nuove musiche of the 17th century![58]

What Riemann has done, then, is to move the first and last syllables of each line up against the rest of the text, so that each line is set syllabically and is surrounded by textless phrases. The piece thus has the untexted introduction, interludes and conclusion that the Stainers found in early fifteenth-century song, and like them Riemann has no difficulty with the notion that those untexted phrases were instrumental. Indeed, that is exactly what he would have expected to find in art song of any period, whether by Dufay, Handel or Brahms. Its very nature is that a sensitively set text is introduced and accompanied by instruments. Riemann's view of performance practice, then, grew out of his conviction – based on nationalistic and musical preferences – that trecento music provided the starting-point for European art music in its every aspect. And this is not out of keeping with Riemann's treatment of other topics. To take only two examples, Pierre Aubry in 1907 complained of Riemann's treatment of the rhythm of thirteenth-century song earlier in the *Handbuch* that his method for determining rhythm depended not on notation but on his modern understanding of musical metre in general; hence 'in truth, it results in an easy and permanent procedure for accommodating to a modern ear the melodies of the past'.[59] Much more recently, Dieter Christensen has shown how Riemann's view of music theory validated the ethnocentric and evolutionist beliefs of his time, noting how effective was his popularisation of them,[60] a point to which we shall come in a moment. But at any rate, it seems clear enough from Riemann's presentation of the argument that his aim here was to achieve a special historical status for trecento song, but in the process he has invoked, and to some extent (in editing the upper voice and assigning its melismas to instruments) has created a theory of performance practice that was to have more far-reaching consequences than anyone but Riemann might have imagined, for as we shall see, while his editorial practice and his historical outline were implicitly rejected by the musicologists who formed our view of fourteenth-century music history, those who wrote about performance found them far more attractive; indeed, they shaped the following seventy-five years of medieval music in sound.

DISSEMINATION

Riemann's hypothesis received some immediate support from quite different evidence the following year with the publication of Hugo Leichtentritt's investigation of medieval representations of music-making.[61] This potentially rich source of evidence had been opened up as recently as 1903 in a book on musical instruments in early medieval miniatures by Edward Buhle which, since it was published in the city where he was professor of music and by his regular publisher (Breitkopf & Härtel), Riemann must have known.[62] Leichtentritt confirms the ubiquity of *a cappella* assumptions before Riemann, but goes on to deduce from a literal reading of the pictorial evidence, which assumes that the miniatures show composed polyphony being performed, that *a cappella* ensembles were far less common than instrumental groupings:

According to present views concerning older music one should assume that *a cappella* singing was by far predominant. The pictorial representations, however, show something quite other. Singers alone, without instruments, are relatively rarely shown, now and then singing with accompaniment and conspicuously frequently instrumental playing without singing.[63]

Drawing heavily on representations of religious scenes including angel musicians, Leichtentritt observes that 'In all centuries from 1300 on the artists show groups of singers that are accompanied by a very rich orchestra'[64] and further that 'It is clearly apparent that the earliest representations, at least from the 13th century on until into the 16th, always show three singers, only rarely four or more. What we know of the music of this time agrees with that. Three voices are the norm.'[65] At the end of his discussion of medieval scenes Leichtentritt adds a short paragraph (perhaps introduced at proof stage?) linking his findings to the few suggestions of instrumental participation in polyphony made by earlier writings, namely Coussemaker's 1865 remarks quoted above and Riemann's newly published *Handbuch*.

Another early application of Riemann's ideas came from Pierre Aubry in France who, in the introduction to his facsimile and edition of the Bamberg motets of 1908, extended Riemann's ideas (of which he cautiously remarks, 'The idea is fruitful [féconde], it requires only to be applied prudently and with restraint'[66]) to the thirteenth-century motet, incidentally picking up Coussemaker's suggestion of forty years before, arguing that the tenors must be instrumental, both because of their notation in ligatures and their lack of text; and he then extends the idea, following Riemann, to the untexted introductions and postludes found in a few motets, as well as to untexted hockets. He is also quite specific about the kinds of instruments required, in a remark that needs to be read in the light of early twentieth-century vocal style: 'We can very well imagine that this role would have been entrusted to a string instrument, vielle or rebec: the bow has a keenness and a precision that the singer cannot attain'.[67]

But the major work of disseminating his views was done by Riemann himself in the years immediately following publication of the *Handbuch*. His first move, before the real work of popularisation began, was to write up his theory in more detail for a scholarly audience. This was the purpose of 'Das Kunstlied im 14.–15. Jahrhundert' published in the International Musicological Society papers for 1905–6. Riemann goes through many of the same points made in the *Handbuch*. Of various amplifications and additions to his argument, perhaps the most interesting is his reading of the sixteenth-century Spanish lute arrangements published in 1902 (again by Breitkopf & Härtel in Leipzig) under the editorship of Don G. Morphy. Here the original vocal line is distinguished from the instrumental elaboration by the use of red notes indicating that the plain vocal part was sung at the same time that the lute played the elaboration:

Because what should be sung and what not is always marked like this, or similarly, there is in these Spanish songs with obbligato lute no argument about what is vocal and what not. It is thus of very great consequence that *nowhere* are any of these 'song-fond melismas' found in the vocal line. Where something like passage-work occurs, it is without any doubt instrumental![68]

Combined with an entirely mistaken reading of *noté* and *nota* in descriptions of music, Riemann returns to a still more confident interpretation of a remark already quoted in 1905 from the fourteenth-century Florentine author Franco Sacchetti, 'he speaks with many notes as one would utter a madrigal'.[69] For Riemann this is simply 'a proof for the wrapping up of the plainly declaimed sung phrases in richly figured instrumental parts'.[70] This theory was to be taken very much further a few years later by Riemann's younger colleague Arnold Schering.

Another point made considerably clearer here is the impossibility for Riemann of accepting that trecento composers could have intentionally broken up text-lines by rests (and we shall see this in Schering too). Similarly,

the thought that a new flowering of art song, making a great stir, might have *begun* with such excesses of coloratura must appear outrageous, whereas one stands admiring before a purposefully set out manner of design as soon as one assumes that the text is without exception entirely plainly recited with the correct stresses ... and that everything remaining is instrumental.[71]

One may feel today that Riemann's argument is so shaped by his preconceptions about what is vocal and what instrumental, and what is suitable in the setting of a text, that it becomes irredeemably contaminated; but of course it is precisely to those preconceptions, generally shared by his musical contemporaries, that he is appealing in offering this as evidence, and it would be unreasonable, and certainly unhistorical, to expect his appeal to have been rejected. Riemann was a brilliant self-publicist and promoter of his own musical vision, as his continuing influence testifies: whatever other scholars may have thought (and most seem to have largely agreed with him) he was certainly not out of touch with the views of his public. It is entirely in keeping with his style that his argument ends with an advertisement:

It is not necessary to add to the examples of evidence. Anyone who has Wolf's Geschichte der Mensuralnotation, Stainer's Dufay, the selections from the Trent codices and Fr.As. Barbieri's Cancionero musical de los siglos XV e XVI (1890)[72] to hand can easily convince himself that it actually amounts to a universally dispersed, developed style. My collection 'Hausmusik aus alter Zeit. Intime Gesänge mit Instrumentalbegleitung aus dem 14.–15. Jahrhundert', appearing from Breitkopf und Härtel in Leipzig, will, however, give wider circles the opportunity to convince themselves that throughout the 200 years before the coming of the 16th-century madrigalists a most respectable flowering of art song had existed, one that is still well worth being studied today, which is why I publish the collection in a form intended directly for living practice, in score and parts.[73]

The *Hausmusik* was duly published by Breitkopf in 1906, a collection of fourteenth- and early fifteenth-century songs scored for voice and strings (the strings playing all the parts, with only the texted parts sung as well), including optional double bass on 'the bass voice' in which case multiple strings were recommended for the upper parts.[74] Text is underlaid in full for all stanzas (an improvement on most later editions) and is

provided in the original language and in an underlaid German translation (Illustration 1.3). Intended for amateur performance, the score is
heavily marked with indications of tempo and expression – Appassion-
ato, Sostenuto, Larghetto, Andantino con grazia, Lento – that bend over
backwards to make the music look familiar and that tell us much about
Riemann's conception of it, founded on an assumption that a love-sick
text must call forth sad music. This is an assumption widely shared; it
resurfaces vigorously around 1930 in Rudolf Ficker's work and, significantly, is invariably reflected in recordings from the 1930s and for several
decades thereafter.

Having dealt with scholars, and having provided some music for people to play, Riemann now turned to his wider readership. To understand
the breadth of his influence it helps to see the range of Riemann's publications and, especially, the regularity with which they were updated
and reissued in revised editions. In their range, Riemann aimed to cover
nothing less than the entire field of musical study; including tonal theory
(1873, 1877, 1882, 1905, 1913 – the dates are all of separate publications,
not reprints or new editions), notation (1878, 1881, 1896, 1907, 1909,
1910, 1915), expression (1883), dynamics and accentuation (1884), opera
(1887), aesthetics (1888, 1890, 1900), orchestration (1888), music history
(1888, 1900, 1901, 1904–13, 1908), organ playing (1888), general musical knowledge (1888), anthologies (1893, 1906, 1911–12), theorists (1898),
Beethoven (1903, 1918–19), rhythm and metre (1903), and musicology
(1908). The latter years of his life (and much time earlier as well) were
taken up with overseeing new editions. Thus his ever-expanding musical
dictionary, the Musik-Lexikon, went through eight editions by Riemann
between 1882 and 1916, before the editing was handed over to Alfred
Einstein following Riemann's death in 1919. His list of publications in
the 1909 Festschrift, some ten years before he died, runs to over 200
items. There were thus ample opportunities, both in updating earlier
books and in writing new ones, for Riemann to set out his vision of the
origins of instrumentally accompanied art song in fourteenth-century
Italy. Over the next few years, it appears in the 1908 *Kleines Handbuch
der Musikgeschichte*,[75] a very much abbreviated retelling of the *Handbuch*
(the later volumes of which were still in progress); in the seventh edition of the Musik-Lexikon in 1909; in the fourth edition of the *Katechismus der Musikgeschichte* of 1910;[76] and in the *Musikgeschichte in Beispielen* of
1911 and 1912.[77] Each of these was aimed at a different audience, the
examples at performers and music readers, the catechism at students, the
small handbook at trainee music teachers and for private instruction,[78]

1.3 Guillaume du Fay, *Ce jour de l'an*, ed. Hugo Riemann (1906: II, 12)

and the *Handbuch* itself, of course, at the widest possible audience for a
definitive history of Western music.

It is worth looking at some of these publications in a little more detail
in order to see the ease with which Riemann could exploit his influence
and rewrite music history. His first opportunity came with the third edition of the *Katechismus der Musikgeschichte* published in 1906. The previous
1901 edition included, in answer to its Question 154, 'What was secular
music like at the time of the development of counterpoint?', fifteen lines
on polyphony 1300–1500 dealing with the Lochamer Liederbuch and
early sixteenth-century German printed collections, mentioning similar
French and Italian publications almost as an afterthought.[79] In the 1906
edition he simply replaced this passage (leaving its context somewhat un-
satisfactorily intact) with a larger one outlining his new story. Riemann
generally made less use of academic ifs and buts than most scholars, but
even so, like all brief summaries from experts, this usefully shows exactly
how he understood late medieval music as a whole: Italian song develops out of the troubadours, French out of Italian, sacred music follows
secular, and vocal polyphony returns only around 1500:

> One is not mistaken when one supposes that the 'travelling musicians', the
> jongleurs and minstrels in their performances of secular songs gradually built
> up a practice of instrumental accompaniment, which from the beginning of the
> 14th century takes artistic shape, first of all in the madrigals, caccias and canzonas
> of the central and north Italian composers of the time of Petrarch and Boccaccio,
> [a practice which] soon wholly supersedes the stiff organal style in France, too,
> and already before 1400 leads to an admirable blooming of art song; ... Also
> sacred songs of all types (Marian songs, hymns, paraphrased antiphons) show
> the same mixture of vocal and instrumental music. Polyphonic song without
> instrumental accompaniment, already known in various forms in the 12th and
> 13th centuries (both in the form of rondeaux with the same text simultaneously
> in all voices, for example those of Adam de la Hale, as well as in motets with
> different unrelated texts coupled together [this phrase marked '!!' by Ludwig in
> both the 1906 and 1910 editions, probably because of the exorbitant German
> phrase construction]), was, it seems, wholly in the background in the 14th to 15th
> centuries, and returned to favour again only at the end of the 15th century in the
> Spanish Strambottas and Villancicos, the Italian frottolas and villanellas. . .[80]

Similarly in the *Kleines Handbuch der Musikgeschichte*, first published in
1908, the section on 'The Era of Instrumentally Accompanied Song:
(Early Renaissance in the 14th–15th Centuries)' works through the same
material in its opening (four-page) paragraph:

> *The Florentine Ars nova.* A wholly new composition style arises at the beginning of
> the 14th century in Florence [Ludwig's copy is marked '?' here], from where it

spreads at first through middle- and upper-Italy, then France, The Netherlands, Spain and England and rapidly eliminates the old style of the Paris school. Just as the Parisian ars antiqua grew out of holy ground, so on the contrary the Florentine new art is secular in origin and, probably under the ennobling and deepening influence of the Renaissance in the sphere of the other arts, grew directly out of the poetic-musical practice of the troubadours [and so on].[81]

But it was undoubtedly the Musik-Lexikon that spread Riemann's views farthest and widest (as a glance through the catalogue of any university library more than a hundred years old will confirm). In fact it took him rather longer to update than other publications; the text of those passages quoted above, showing his earlier view, changes only to a limited extent before the seventh edition of 1909; it seems probable that Riemann's workload was such (he produced at least eighteen other publications in 1904–5), and the size of the Lexikon – and thus the lead-time for a new edition – so great, that it was impractical even for him to rewrite all the entries that would be effected by his change of view in time for the 1905 sixth edition. In this respect the popularity of Riemann's publications, and the frequency of new editions, works very much to our benefit, for it is possible to trace more exactly than for any other early musicologist the development of his beliefs. We can see his ideas about instrumental participation gradually shifting through editions of the Lexikon in the light first of Stainer, and then his own work. Thus under 'Accompanying voices', a description of troubadour song's melodic accompaniment is shifted back towards antiquity, and a new clause introduced to allow for the development through the troubadours of the kind of chordal accompaniment required (as Riemann saw it) by Stainer's examples:

Third and fourth editions, 1887 & 1894:
The songs of the troubadours were accompanied by the minstrels on the viol or *vielle*, the Bards sang to the chrotta, the Greeks to the cithara, lyre or aulos, the Hebrews to the psaltery. It appears, however, that the instrumental accompaniment only doubled the vocal part in unison, or in octave, and possibly only those notes which fell upon strong beats. Accompaniment, in the modern sense, first appears only about 1600, and its cradle was Italy.[82]

Fifth and <sixth> editions, 1900 & <1905>:
The songs of the troubadours were accompanied by the minstrels on the viol or *vielle*, the Bards sang to the chrotta, the Greeks to the cithara, lyre or aulos, the Hebrews to the psaltery; it appears <6th ed.: it is certain>, however, that in antiquity the instrumental accompaniment only doubled the vocal part in unison, or in octave, and decorated at most here and there; while in the Middle Ages chordal accompaniment gradually developed. Artistically developed

accompaniment in the modern sense, however, appears first from 1600, and its cradle was Italy.[83]

By the time we reach the seventh edition, of 1909, the development of chordal accompaniment in the Middle Ages remains in place, but with 'chordal' emphasised, and a new – if now familiar – continuation:

while in the Middle Ages *chordal* accompaniment gradually developed. Already at the beginning of the 14th century instrumental accompaniment of secular and sacred song had developed into artful forms, and shows decorated preludes, interludes and postludes, compared to which even the treatment of the vocal part appears simpler, as in the Florentine madrigals, caccie, ballate and canzone and in French rondeaux after *c.* 1400.[84]

Similarly, under 'Kappelle', Riemann in the fourth edition of 1894 describes all sacred music before 1600 as *a cappella*;[85] in the fifth edition of 1900 he allows the possibility of instrumental accompaniment in unison with the voices.[86] By the seventh edition, appearing in 1909, there was obbligato instrumental participation in church music until the development of imitative polyphony at the time of Ockeghem finally introduced *a cappella* polyphony.[87]

Just as interesting is the new arrangement of the entry for 'History of Music', whose paragraph dealing with the fourteenth and fifteenth centuries, previously the last paragraph of the sub-section 'Middle Ages', is now entitled 'Era of Instrumentally Accompanied Art Song', and appears as the opening of 'Renaissance Period (1300–1600)'.[88] For Riemann, and his readers, it marked the beginning of the modern musical world. His new view crops up all over the seventh edition: in 'Dufay', where he manages to slip in another advertisement,

Some monophonic and polyphonic chansons by Dufay are in Riemann's *Alte Hausmusik* (with separation of the sung and instrumental parts)[89]

in 'Florenz in der Musikgeschichte',

Twice in music history Florence has opened important periods, the first time *c.* 1300 as the cradle of instrumentally accompanied art song . . . in which a completely new style (the *Ars nova*) replaces the organal style of the Parisian school [90]

in 'Instrumentalmusik' (this whole passage in Ludwig's copy (understandably) annotated with an exclamation mark),

In the textless compositions of the Parisian school of the 12th to 13th centuries called *organum purum* we apparently have the beginning of independent organ music before us. The *Ars nova* of the Florentines of the 14th century then brings an artistic instrumental accompaniment of monophonic, rarely polyphonic songs, probably grown out of the accompanimental practice of the troubadours and jongleurs[91]

in 'Machaut', who in the sixth edition was placed on a par with Landini ('Machaut is for France … as Landini is for Italy'[92]), now, along with Vitry, becomes a follower of the Italians,

Machaut is, so long as no compositions of the oft-praised Philippe de Vitry are found, for us the first French representative of the 14th-century *Ars nova* that comes out of Florence[93]

and so on, in many other entries.

It would be impossible, in effect, for anyone after 1905 who wanted to acquire some general knowledge of medieval music to avoid absorbing Riemann's view of it. It was written up in all the most convenient and up-to-date books. However sceptical Ludwig, the unparalleled expert, might be – as the ever-present marginal annotations in his books testify – Ludwig did not publish except very rarely and very densely in small-circulation specialist journals.

EXTENSION

Only one scholar in the early days challenged Riemann's view in print, and then only partially. Guido Adler, whom Riemann had criticised in his 1905–6 article 'Das Kunstlied' for adding text to the lower voices of songs from the Trent codices,[94] took the opportunity to respond in the most prominent possible place, Riemann's sixtieth birthday Festschrift published in 1909. Pointing out that his edition had made absolutely clear what was in the manuscript and what was editorial (something Riemann didn't trouble to do) and welcoming the opportunity offered by the volume to comment on 'the setting up of an instrumentally accompanied solo-song', he continued:

On the legitimacy of setting up an epoch of 'early Renaissance' in the music of the 14th century I want to refrain from making any comment and only give some clarifying remarks on the situation of the text underlay in the Trent codices[95]

which makes his view of Riemann's theory as a whole fairly clear. He then proceeds to work through a number of observations made after study of a large number of pieces, managing to imply that Riemann had not done the same, which was almost certainly true; and one can well understand

the irritation of a meticulous scholar like Adler (or Ludwig, or Wolf)
at the sight of such an influential figure repeatedly riding roughshod
over the evidence. He notes that in most pieces most voices are provided
with at least some text; that in liturgical pieces the well-known texts are
often entered only fragmentarily but the less well-known texts more fully,
likewise in widely distributed songs the text may be less complete; that
when text is present it is relatively precisely underlaid; that while text may
be absent in one source it is often present in another, so that one cannot
deduce instrumental performance from any one source; that there is
a continuum from wholly texted to wholly untexted; and that nothing
definite will be determined until a much fuller comparative study of the
sources has been carried out. In other words, it is far too early to be
coming to conclusions, let alone to Riemann's. Certainly in some pieces
one or other voice is instrumental (and he cites *In Hydraulis* and the *Et in
terra ad modum tubae*), but everywhere else the evidence is unclear, and in
view of the pattern of texting in the sources it is legitimate to attempt to
apply text to all voices, breaking ligatures and dividing notes if necessary,
since the ligature patterns and note values also vary. It is impossible to
infer that absence of text indicates none in performance. Adler was thus
presenting exactly the opposite of Riemann's theory, and, as he points
out over and over, with a much firmer grounding in the sources.

Perhaps Adler's vote for texted vocal performance would have had
more impact, and would have been followed up with more detailed
research, if only two years later the pendulum had not swung wildly
in the opposite direction, so that fire that might have been directed at
Riemann was instead drawn on to his more radical follower (and later
colleague), Arnold Schering. Schering's 'Das kolorierte Orgelmadrigal
des Trecento' (The decorated organ-madrigal of the trecento), published
in the *Sammelbände der Internationalen Musik-Gesellschaft* for 1911–12, was the
article that caused so much trouble, and it is not hard to see why. The
introduction speaks both to his boldness and to his reliance on instinct to
an even greater extent than Riemann; above all it shows the importance
for him of the experience of performance, something that was to be
characteristic of his later and most influential work as well:

One cannot deny that Riemann's hypothetical positions are very brilliant . . .
However, they were and remain hypothesis, and it is open to me to prove that this
hypothesis was false. From the start I harboured some doubt about the rightness
and naturalness of Riemann's attempted interpretations without being able to
put a better one in their place. Particularly when I heard his practical edition of
trecento compositions [the *Hausmusik alter Zeit* mentioned above] in performance

with viol accompaniment, my belief was strongly shaken. Should highly sensitive [feinbesaiteten] poets in the age of Petrarch really have tolerated these tearings-apart and choppings-up of their strophes, this arrogant incessant contribution [Hineinspielen] of the instruments, the contemporaries of a Landino this worse than meagre musical declamation without life and expression? Unthinkable. I go, rather, a step further than Riemann and assert: this literature is pure instrumental music, to be precise, originally organ music.[96]

The key word here, of course, is 'unthinkable'. Schering simply could not conceive of word-setting so far from following the principles of his own age. Great poetry (and here the influence of Burckhardt is again very apparent) could never have been treated like this when sung; therefore it must be instrumental music, and the manuscript texting must have some other purpose. In working out this idea in greater detail he proposes that these pieces, both Italian and French, are decorated versions for organ of simple 'folksongs', the elaborated tune accompanied by the simpler lower voices. Were a singer to take part, he would sing the original unelaborated melody with its text:

the text underlay of the original manuscript is set out for the most part completely independently from the sense of the music, even from time to time producing the wildest nonsenses through dismemberment by rests.... [Thus] here the words are neither intended for a singer, nor are they underlaid at all with the purpose of somehow reliably indicating the relevant associated notes. Rather, they were meant as a purely practical means of orientation for the eyes of the organ player.... One uses the words of the text as a signpost on the journey through the piece, precisely in the sense of the rehearsal letters or numbers in our orchestral parts and scores.... They indicate which line of words fits the music they delimit, without however marking the actual beginning and end of the sung phrases.[97]

Not surprisingly, the late medieval Robertsbridge codex (represented in Wolf's 1904 collection), which preserves what appears to be keyboard music with underlaid text, provides Schering with a perfect example of the same practice in a different notation. He goes on to propose that the same is true of fifteenth-century song and of sacred music, in the latter case the choir taking the cantus firmus while the organist – or an orchestra – plays the other, decorative parts. The article concludes with a series of examples (of some analytical interest) in which the melodic core is extracted from decorative cantus lines.

With the benefit of hindsight, and particularly after half a century of performances that have accustomed us to medieval polyphony more or less as notated, Schering's theory must seem quite mad. And while recognising that, by our standards at any rate, Adler was right to insist on further research before coming to any conclusions about performance practice, nevertheless there is something rather admirable about Schering's ability to imagine a completely different reading of the evidence, and something rather attractive about a period in which such wild theorising was still possible. Having said that, few of the major scholars seem to have been persuaded. One of the few to give him house room was Riemann who, perhaps rather generously in view of Schering's disagreement with him, allowed his younger colleague to suggest his view as an alternative to Riemann's in the notes to the latter's anthology of music, *Musikgeschichte im Beispielen*, first published in 1911 and reissued the following year with Schering's commentary.[98]

In the same year, Schering published the first of several books developing his theory in greater detail, *Die niederländische Orgelmesse im Zeitalter des Josquin: Eine stilkritische Untersuchung* (Leipzig, 1912), which he dedicated to Riemann. Working through an ordered series of criteria, Schering argued that, while the cantus firmus might be sung, the other musical lines were intrinsically instrumental in character. 'What from the mouth of singers seemed unnatural and grotesque, now assumes the most natural and self-recommending form.'[99] The key to Schering's view thus remained his inability to conceive that such lines could sensibly be sung.

Within weeks of the book's publication Schering was publicly challenged by Wolf.[100] At a local chapter meeting in Berlin of the International Musicological Society on 2 April, following presentations by Otto Kinkeldey (who argued that the trecento song manuscript we know as the Squarcialupi codex was an organ book) and by Schering, Wolf demolished their arguments point by point. If this repertory was all organ music, he said, it would be amazing that no collection of vocal music had come down to us, and if these were instrumentally decorated songs it was astonishing that not one of these pieces survived in its simple form; the text could not function as a means of aligning the voice parts; the large size and complex notation of the Squarcialupi codex would make playing from the manuscript extremely difficult; Wolf did not accept that Squarcialupi himself (1416–80, Florentine organist and a later owner) must have played the pieces in his manuscript, since that would have given them a life of over a hundred years. Wolf likewise disagreed with Schering about the mass music of the following century: while some sources had incomplete text, others were fully texted; the voice that Schering thought could be sung, the Tenor, was the one voice Wolf thought could be instrumental; the sophistication of the parts simply showed the high level

of vocal training; had Schering had a better knowledge of the sources
he would have known that in the Basle print of Obrecht's *Missa Sub tuum
praesidium* text had been added in manuscript, obviously for the use of the
singer; conversely one finds partial texting in material from the Cappella
Sistina, where only singers were used. And so on. The meeting and the
ensuing discussion is reported in enjoyable detail by Hermann Springer
in the *Zeitschrift der Internationalen Musik-Gesellschaft* for 1911–12. Ludwig's
annotated copy makes clear his agreement, writing beside each of Wolf's
numerous points 'gut'.[101]

Wolf was not the only scholar to dissect Schering's arguments. In
the following volume of the *Zeitschrift* Hugo Leichtentritt took the num-
bered criteria of *Die niederländische Orgelmesse* and knocked them down
one by one, commenting effectively on Schering's narrow view of what
was singable and what was instrumental by nature.[102] Schering replied
in the next volume, followed by further comments by Leichtentritt.[103]
Undaunted, apparently, Schering went on to publish a further book
in 1914, *Studien zur Musikgeschichte der Frührenaissance*, working out his
theory over a wide range of fourteenth- and fifteenth-century music,
supported by musical and pictorial illustrations. It may be tempting to
dismiss Schering at this stage, but we shall need to return to his ideas
below, since they resurface as late as 1931 in two books whose influence
on later performances of medieval and Renaissance music can clearly
be seen, Schering's own *Aufführungspraxis alter Musik* and Robert Haas'
Aufführungspraxis der Musik, the latter published as part of the influential
Handbuch der Musikwissenschaft edited by Heinrich Besseler. And his
influence is acknowledged as late as 1966 by Gilbert Reaney, reporting
his own, Schering-like performance in 1958 of Machaut's Mass with
his London Medieval Group.[104] Just as with Riemann, then, scholars
may have believed that they had seen off Schering, but the influence of
both writers on subsequent performers was extensive and long-lived and,
as we shall see, did much to shape the twentieth-century performance
practice of early music.

ORTHODOXY

While scholars might hold individual views about how instruments were
used in these repertories, it was generally accepted by the second decade
of the twentieth century that their role was an important one. Johannes
Wolf, in his 1913 *Handbuch der Notationskunde*, could safely write:

Instrumental impact is especially clear in polyphonic secular pieces of the 14th
and 15th centuries. In the trecento it is above all the art of the Florentines

that provides numerous problems to solve. Scarcely is Italian, the vulgar tongue, established in literature, when a polyphonic song technique blossoms, within which a special role is given to instruments. It is difficult to separate the closely mixed up vocal and instrumental parts. Since in these folklike songs their syllabic character is unquestionably emphasised, it would be wrong to take every melisma from the voice. The indications for instrumental performance are: use of small note values suited to coloratura, leaping voice-leading, short motives and emphasis on sequence. The question whether vielles, organ or other types of instruments provided the means of performance is fundamentally less important than the clear separation of vocal and instrumental sections. Textless and extensively ligated voices can automatically be assigned to instruments.[105]

The battle for instrumental participation was now won, and although a few writers spoke up for vocal performance as an option, above all Theodore Kroyer (see below) but also Besseler (see below), and later Reaney and Frank Harrison,[106] the battle was not to be fought again for almost seventy years. But as yet the case for instruments had been made only on paper. Performances that would turn this scholarly vision into sound, and introduce medieval music into mainstream musical life had not yet been attempted.

The first such attempt came in a single concert devoted to 'Les Primitifs de la Musique Française' at the Sainte-Chapelle on 8 June 1914, presented as part of the Paris congress of the International Musicological Society.[107] The concert was organised by Amédée Gastoué, who provided the transcriptions, most apparently newly made from the manuscripts, though he also acknowledges Coussemaker, Aubry and the research of Ludwig and Jean Beck. Arranged in three sections the programme began with an instrumental 'Ouverture' (in fact the motet *O Maria/O Maria/Misit Dominus*),[108] then covered liturgical monophony, ars antiqua and trouvères (Aquitanian and Notre Dame polyphony, including the *Alleluia Posui* attributed to Perotin, and monophonic songs on religious themes from troubadour and trouvère collections), and the ars nova (the four-voice motet *Impudenter/Virtutibus* and mass movements from the Apt manuscript which Gastoué was to publish in transcription in 1936 and first encountered soon before this concert).[109] Gastoué explains in the booklet that:

the difficulty of performance by voices, and also our current ignorance concerning the interpretation of organum in the style of Perotin, has led us to perform it on instruments. . . . On account of the length [longueur] and extreme monotony of the development we offer only the first and last sections of the verse with their delicate and charming outlines. . . . The role of instruments in the music of these periods is plainly indicated by the pieces and the notation. . . . We have chosen instruments whose timbre seems to us closest to those of the Middle Ages. . .[110]

We can get a rough idea of the sound of Gastoué's choir, though without any instruments, from his recording of plainchant made in 1930 with the Schola Cantorum of Paris:[111] fast vibrato, portamento leading up to the initial notes of each phrase and across any interval of more than a second, strong crescendi and diminuendi matched to the rising and falling melody. The instruments must have gone some way to stabilise and focus the pitches, but it is not hard to see why singing Notre Dame polyphony would have seemed impossibly hard: the sound was simply not stable enough to make sense of rapid step-wise oscillations in several voices at once. Gastoué remembered the concert fondly in his 1922 book adopting the same title, *Les Primitifs de la Musique Française*:

I need not remind those who were there of the beautiful and deserved success obtained in June 1914 – on the eve of the Great War – by the concert dedicated to the Primitives of French Music in the marvellous setting of the Sainte Chapelle in Paris, the first demonstration of a series of artistic enterprises at that time planned and which still remain unfulfilled.[112]

In fact the first successor of Gastoué's pioneering concert was already being planned as he wrote, and although it proved to be more significant and of greater influence its debt to his programme is obvious. This was the first of two concert-series put on in Germany in 1922 and 1924. Both were carefully researched and prepared, and lavishly presented; on both occasions the director was Wilibald Gurlitt, a former student of both Riemann and Schering. Both consisted of three concerts under the general title 'Musik des Mittelalters', the first of plainchant, the second of sacred polyphony, the third of secular, so that in structure they followed closely the model provided by Gastoué in 1914. The 1922 series was performed among the Old German Masters of the Badische Kunsthalle in Karlsruhe from Sunday 24 to Tuesday 26 September, the 1924 series in the small hall of the Hamburg Musikhalle on Thursday 3, Saturday 5 and Tuesday 8 April. Both were preceded by a lecture from Gurlitt. For both the programme booklet survives, and both were written up by major scholars in the *Zeitschrift für Musikwissenschaft*. Consequently we can recover quite a bit of detail about the programme and the forces used.

The first evening of the 1922 series, 'Musica ecclesiastica', consisted of chants from the Vatican gradual and antiphonary. The second concert, 'Musica composita', offered sacred polyphony, the organum *Alleluia pascha nostrum* here attributed to Leonin, together with two motets on related clausulae attributed to Perotin, all edited by Ludwig,[113] the atypical but German motet *Brumans est mors* edited by Aubry, Machaut's Kyrie published by Wolf but (as the programme notes) emended by Ludwig, and Dufay's *Alma redemptoris mater* and *Salve regina* from Adler's DTÖ volumes.[114] The third concert, 'Musica vulgaris', ranged from a Bamberg motet, *Au cuer/Ja ne/Jolietement*, and Walter von der Vogelweide's 'Palästinalied', through three of the thirteenth-century instrumental dances, to Landini's ballata *Gran piant'agl'occhi*, a three-part song from the Lochamer Liederbuch and, finally, a group of four early fifteenth-century songs attributed to Binchois and Dufay. Musical items on both the second and third evenings were separated by readings from medieval Latin and middle high German, a solution to the problem of too many short pieces that has been adopted innumerable times since.

The Karlsruhe performances were written up for the *Zeitschrift für Musikwissenschaft* by Ludwig (who, since he provided the editions for the Notre Dame music and included them as an appendix to his report, could hardly be a dispassionate critic).[115] The pieces were scored for varying combinations of singer, two recorders (usually supported by a flute), two violas and gamba, with a small choir for the motets and sacred music, as well as three 'Karlsruher Kunstfreunde' who took the upper lines in some songs and motets. Ludwig clearly supports the use of instruments on untexted lines, indeed he regards those parts as instrumental accompaniments: thus for him a double motet consists of an instrumentally accompanied duet, a three-part song of a melody with two-part instrumental accompaniment, and so on.[116] But given that he was so certain, and that the Karlsruhe performances shared his view, it is interesting that he nevertheless felt it necessary to offer a defence against Riemann's and 'other' (presumably Schering's) more extreme opinions; clearly this was still a hot issue and it offers some indication of how deep a shadow Riemann and Schering still cast:

Apart from this obbligato role that instruments play in that branch of the development of medieval secular polyphony that I have just sketched, they are also, in the Middle Ages, often used as support for the sung voices, without it being indicated in the sources to what extent that happened. Further they are also invoked, as is well known (again in obbligato use), for the vocal parts in the preludes, interludes and postludes, though again it remains very controversial as to how far such melismas in the vocal parts are to be regarded as only instrumental. It is well known that, ever since H. Riemann brought this question under the spotlight, the most extreme opinions are held on some sides – seeing 'instrumentalisms' already in even modest melismas, they therefore take them from the singing voice and give them a completely instrumental performance – opinions that for the Middle Ages are already disproved simply through the existence of Gregorian chant and the wholly vocal performance of its melodies. The Karlsruhe presentations of such works (of Landini's ballata and the chansons of Dufay and Binchois) followed no rigid principle, but rather sought to bring forth for each work, according to its particular characteristics, a solution to the question – which of course cannot have any solution that is absolutely binding. So in the chansons some melismas were performed vocally (the instruments, here the flutes, naturally in this case play together with the vocal part throughout); and in Landini's ballata all melismas of the Tenor and the Cantus were (correctly, I believe) reserved for the vocal performance (strings playing together with them).[117]

The Hamburg concerts followed very much the same pattern, even including some of the same pieces, though the programmes were much more ambitious, their greater length allowing the thirteenth century to be much better represented, and a wider range of fifteenth-century sacred music to be offered.[118] The instrumentation was essentially the same. The report in the *Zeitschrift* was written by Heinrich Besseler, who had studied with Ludwig and Adler but also with Gurlitt, so that, like Ludwig two years earlier, he was not an entirely disinterested observer. That makes the more intriguing his notable interest in those items performed by voices alone:

We find the same attitude [as in the Dufay mass movements] in Dunstable's wonderfully fresh-sounding *Quam pulcra es* (DTÖ 7, 190), performed vocally in all three voices [and a footnote cites the texted contratenor in the Bologna manuscript Q15].[119]
...*Der wallt hat sich entlaubet*, a two-section German strophic song, was given as a Tenorlied with two instruments. The purely vocal performance used in Karlsruhe seems just as sonorous and, with hindsight, as regards the polyphonic writing to comply better with the intention of the composer.[120]

We can also see in his report evidence of a fight-back against Riemann's much publicised preference for Italian music and his insistence that ars nova was first and foremost an Italian achievement:

Machaut's four-voice double-motet *Christe qui lux es – Veni creator* (No. 21, still unedited ...) represented French motet style of the 14th century with a work that, next to Perotin's organa and pieces like *O Maria maris stella* and *Je me cuidoie*, marks a high point. The performance of such a composition is alone enough to refute, at least, the *artistic* over-estimation of the Florentine so-called *Ars nova* at the cost of French music.[121]

While the French ars nova is now seen as, if anything, more influential than the Italian – in line with Ludwig's view and against Riemann's – at the time of Besseler's review Riemann's influence was still strong. Thus Wolf in 1925, in his popular *Geschichte der Musik in allgemeinverständlicher Form* (History of Music in a Readily Comprehensible Form), still opened his chapter on 'The Renaissance' with '*Ars nova* in Italy', followed only in section two with '*Ars nova* in France'.[122]

Besseler here goes on to comment in some detail on the harmony, especially chord colour and progression. His views on the Hamburg performances are thus valuable (if rather early) signals of a gradual shifting of emphasis among several aspects of late medieval music. Equally, the concerts themselves show a willingness to experiment with different kinds of scorings that is appropriate given the continuing absence of any reliable evidence as to medieval practices. Scholars now had a strong sense that instruments were involved, yet there was too little evidence for them to know how: experimentation was another way of gathering evidence, enabling them to gauge what seemed to work and what not.

This openness to many possibilities in performance was given theoretical justification in several articles by Jacques Handschin published between 1928 and 1931.[123] Handschin proposed that medieval music began as vocal music but gradually became more and more instrumental. For much of the later Middle Ages instrumental performance was a 'secondary' practice, texted pieces or voices or parts of voices (a gesture to the Riemann–Schering view of melismas) being performed instrumentally at will, drawing on a great variety of instruments, and sometimes omitting voices.[124] (Interestingly, in his own series of concerts given in Zurich, Bern and Basel in May 1928, Handschin took a more cautious line, explicitly distancing himself from Riemann's instrumental melismas.)[125] Other kinds of pieces, such as estampies, were primarily instrumental and only – since there is evidence that words were sometimes added to them – secondarily vocal.[126] In other words, almost anything was possible and from time to time probably happened. This all-inclusive view – one in which almost anyone who beats their head against the brick wall of medieval performance practice will find at least momentary relief – not only legitimised the varied scorings tried in concerts but also offered a justification for the orchestrations that began to appear at about the same time from Ficker and Schering. Certainly the 1920s concerts were influential; because of their scale, their scholarly grounding, their musical success and the publicity they attracted, they were playing a significant role in creating a defensible, but still an undeniably invented performance practice for medieval music. An interesting indication of their influence comes from the discussion of medieval performance practice in Robert Haas's 1931 *Aufführungspraxis der Musik.* This widely read book was essentially a work of synthesis, reporting previous theories, and used the Karlsruhe and Hamburg concerts to provide detailed examples of plausible scorings for the repertories covered by the concerts.[127] Haas also gave lengthy and sympathetic consideration to Schering's ideas in a discussion which, because of the book's prominent publication in a standard series coinciding with the publication of Schering's own *Aufführungspraxis alter Musik* (1931), can only have helped to prolong their life.[128] Haas' book thus offers another medium through which instrumental participation, in various forms, was fostered.

Throughout these years only one scholar stood out for greater use of voices. As Adler in 1909 had argued against Riemann without apparently finding support, so Theodore Kroyer argued against the tide in a 1925 article that, appearing in a Dutch Festschrift, was probably little read, and certainly went unheeded. His point was that there was ample manuscript evidence for the singing of lower voices, and that Riemann, in particular, had deliberately misrepresented the manuscript texting in order to make instrumental participation seem more likely.[129] In a particularly pointed example Kroyer took one of the very pieces Riemann had edited fully texted in 1893, and showed how Riemann's later edition falsifies the manuscript evidence he knew so well. Kroyer concluded that therefore *a cappella* scorings were more likely than was generally believed, and the instrumental hypothesis was correspondingly less secure.[130] But in his generation Kroyer was a lone voice. A few years later his disagreement with Schering on just this point was to lead to the sacking of Einstein as editor of the *Zeitschrift für Musikwissenschaft* (see below). And this may point to a political dimension to the failure of Kroyer's view to be noticed. Schering became one of the most powerful figures in German musicology during these years, and was not to be contradicted.

Another factor in the rapid growth of interest in medieval music in Germany in the 1920s was social. As inflation made public music less and less affordable and nationalist sentiment ever stronger, an increasing interest developed in amateur music-making, creating a market for music – and particularly German music – that could be performed at home and by amateur and youth ensembles. An enthusiastic contributor of such publications was Johannes Wolf whose 1925 *Geschichte der Musik in allgemeinverständlicher Form* (mentioned above) set out a brief narrative of early music history aimed at non-specialists, closely followed by a companion anthology *Sing- und Spielmusik aus älterer Zeit herausgegeben als Beispielband zur Allgemeinen Musikgeschichte* (Vocal and Instrumental

Music from Olden Times) in which Wolf edited relatively undemanding polyphony from the later Middle Ages onwards (including motets and songs by Machaut, Landini, Cesaris, Power, Grenon, Dufay, Binchois and many others) issued in the same small and inexpensive format. The introduction aims the volume at both music lovers and experts, though primarily at the former, and sets out for them the principles of performance practice that by now were taken for granted by specialists, mixing voices and instruments at will, using instruments for the untexted voices but also, if one wished, allowing instruments to play texted parts as well. Wolf hopes that the collection may win new and well-deserved friends for this old artistic practice.[131] Over the next two years Wolf went on to publish *Chor- und Hausmusik aus alter Zeit*, four volumes of mainly German compositions from the fifteenth to the seventeenth centuries consisting of two volumes of songs for mixed choir followed by two more containing just instrumental music, drawing on works by Senfl, Stoltzer, Haussmann, Josquin des Prés, Isaac and many other northern composers. A few years later, in 1930, Wolf wrote enthusiastically in support of Hausmusik for use at home, at school and in the youth movement, and volumes such as these were exactly what this wider market required.[132] This early popularisation of medieval music did much to strengthen its position in the increasingly difficult social conditions of the Weimar Republic, and set the pattern for musicology's self-protection through collaboration which characterised German musicologists' dealings with National Socialism.[133]

That this activity was gradually creating a view of medieval music as relevant to modern times is indicated by Bärenreiter's 1927 publication of an inexpensive collection of twelve songs from the Canonici and Trent manuscripts, arranged for voice accompanied by string instruments (which also doubled the voice), with editorial bowing marks, fingering, phrasing and dynamic markings all indicated. The editor, Oskar Dischner, testifies to a new aspect of the growing interest in medieval music when, in his introduction, he speaks of similarities between our modern musical tendencies and those of the fifteenth century, including 'linearity, asymmetrically caesuraed melody, harmony with loosened functionality':

We know that we late 'post-classical' men cannot return to the simple, pure sounds of Dufay's time, no more to its organically grown – not organised – lines, without confusing contemporary art and archaic arts-and-crafts: this world has for us the melancholy magic of the irretrievable. . . . For to various problems troubling modern art the Middle Ages . . . already have a solution to offer . . .[134]

There may be an element of wishful thinking at work here; Pamela Potter has shown how important it was for musicologists during the Weimar period to make their work relevant to the *Volk*, and this edition surely belongs to that movement.[135] But even so, and partly because it is a peripheral publication, it is likely to reflect ideas that are already in the air, even if they have not yet been discussed formally in print; and these ideas are some of the most persistent in modern images of medieval music: linearity, lack of organisation, craft rather than art. At the same time Dischner is happy to admit, as a scholar only could in moments of despair, that the Middle Ages are unrecoverable. And of course the modern performance of medieval music absolutely requires that one believe both incompatible things together: we try to do it the way it was, and we know we cannot, and we argue for both. The dichotomy with which postmodern musicology faces medievalists so mercilessly is first raised, one may argue, by the growth of this modern performance tradition in the 1920s.

The growing confidence of editors in offering concrete advice on performance is reflected in another selection published in 1927, this time in France, the *Trois Chansonniers Français du XVe Siècle* begun in 1922 by André Pirro, the music completed by Yvonne Rokseth and Geneviève Thibault and the commentary, with its advice on scoring, provided by Eugénie Droz and Thibault. Droz and Thibault recommend scorings for each piece based on the extent of its homophony or polyphony. For the former group, pieces like *J'ay prins amours*, they propose instruments from the same family for each of the lower voices, or in the case of extremely simple lower voices, as in Hayne's *De tous biens plaine*, a single polyphonic instrument such as clavichord, harp or lute; for the latter group, where the lower voices move more independently (e.g. Ockeghem's *Ma bouche rit*),[136] contrasting instrumental sounds for the non-cantus voices. Only reluctantly do they recommend more than one voice, as in Ockeghem's *L'autre d'antan*.[137] The recommended instruments include winds in general, trombone in particular, bowed strings in general, viols in particular, keyboard (including small organ), harp and lute. We see reflected here a gradual expansion in the kinds of instruments found suitable, as well as an increasing sense that texture had to be reflected in scoring, as would be the case in a Classical work.

Nothing better illustrates the acceptance into the canon of medieval music in performance than another major concert, on the model of the Karlsruhe and Hamburg series, put together by the Austrian (though Munich-born) musicologist Rudolf Ficker for the Beethoven centenary

festival and congress in 1927. Performed in the Burgkapelle in Vienna
on the penultimate day of the festival (30 March) under the title 'Gothic
Polyphony', the programme (for which the booklet also survives) included organa tripla by Perotin, early motets, motets by Vitry (an early,
tentative attribution of *Garrit/In nova*) and Machaut (the late four-voice
motet not included in the Karlsruhe or Hamburg programmes), songs
by Giovanni and Machaut, and motets by Dunstable and Gemblaco, a
suitable cross-section of evident masterworks by the earliest precursors
of Beethoven.[138] The instruments were again viola and gamba, but now
with boy soloists for the upper vocal lines, together with the State Opera
chorus, students from the Hochschule and the Academy for Music and
Dramatic Art, and the boys from the Burgkapelle choir, the editing and
conducting undertaken by Ficker. Those, at any rate, are the forces listed
in the programme; but in his report on the festival for the *Zeitschrift* Einstein notes that for the *Alleluya Posui adjutorium* Ficker also used oboes
and bassoons to accompany the men's and boys' voices and trombones
and trumpets on the cantus firmus, while other works included celesta,
glockenspiel, horn and cor anglais.[139] One may think that a rather large
ensemble for the works in the programme, but Ficker must already have
been working towards his well-known reading of Notre Dame polyphony
as among the grandest repertories of Western music. It was in fact in the
same venue, almost exactly two years later (11 April 1929), that Ficker directed the first performance of his monumental arrangement of Perotin's
Sederunt principes for a chorus of men and boys (singing in octaves, which
explains the use of oboes with bassoons, trumpets with trombones in
the 1927 Perotin performance), three-part violas, three oboes, three bassoons, two trumpets, two tenor trombones, glockenspiel (or celesta) and
three tubular bells. The following year (1930) a vocal score was published
by Universal-Edition using a title page based on that for the Beethoven
centenary concert. Marked 'Langsam, schwebend' (Slow, floating), the
music begins *p*, reducing during the first chord to *pp*, then from bar 38
(about half-way through the first sonority-section) 'Allmählich steigern'
(gradually increase) becomes faster and louder towards a climax at the
second chant note; and so on. Ficker's own description needs no further
comment:

Above a syllabic chant of mystical profundity flows a far-flung stream of inter-
woven tones, now like shadowy, fugitive apparitions, now swelling to an orgiastic
rout.... Above the seven tones of the initial word 'sederunt' soars a mighty
'Sinfonia' leading up through 142 measures to a tremendous climax.[140]

Aside from the later *Carmina Burana* of Orff (1937), which owed much to Ficker,[141] perhaps the closest musical analogy to this opening is the Rheingold prelude, with *Sederunt* as the beginning of the great drama of Western music. Ficker's student Josef Mertin reported some fifty years later: 'When we sang the great organum quadruplum "Sederunt principies" in 1926 [*sic*] under Ficker, . . . we were in a trance'.[142] The later recording, with the Bavarian Radio chorus and orchestra conducted by Eugen Jochum, begins at $\quarternote$. = 40, accelerating to 84 during the first chant-note section, following a similar pattern in later sections (occasionally, near the end, touching 120) with a long 'slow movement' in the middle (accompanied by celesta) centring on about 68. The slower end of this spectrum is astonishingly slow according to modern assumptions,[143] but, together with the orchestration, brings a vast grandeur to the work (making it very much a 'work') and speaking to a view of gothic polyphony matched to its buildings.[144] In a characteristically imaginative survey of medieval music in context, Ficker related the organa of St Martial in Limoges (now known as Aquitanian polyphony) to the 'mystical half-light' and massive walls of the romanesque cathedral (Dom), and those of Leonin and Perotin to the 'coloured shimmering glass' and slender columns of the gothic cathedral (Kathedrale) where 'the whole building breathes movement'.[145] The religious mystical ingredient in Ficker's view is also strong: he speaks of the way that the short chant phrase 'descendit de coelis' when set as organum 'leads one to imagine that one sees from the distant heights the light-form of the Saviour floating down to bring salvation to guilt-laden Mankind'.[146] Ficker's is a romantic and intensely religious view of medieval art, brilliantly expressed in the sound-world of his arrangements. But he offered a historical justification as well, one that was beginning to occur to others at about the same time.

The period around 1930 marked the end of the discreet instrumentation that had characterised the Karlsruhe and Hamburg performances and that is reflected in Dischner's anthology. Up to this point assumptions about plausible instrumentation were cautious; but Ficker saw support for more colourful orchestras:

In these compositions, besides men's and boys' voices, a large share of the musical effect results more especially from the numerous instruments employed. True, the manuscripts contain no information whatever on this point. . . . But on the other hand we know, from pictured presentations and from many written records, what a vast array of instrumental forces in divers varieties of bowed, plucked, wind and percussion instruments that period could muster. Hence one who only sees these staves with the note-heads, without sensing the mighty orchestral apparatus hidden behind those note-heads, will naturally fail to comprehend a certain ancient report concerning the effect of this music, which states that the performance of such music provoked indignation and public disturbances on the part of 'educated' hearers, whereas the common people listened in awe-stricken and trembling admiration to the strident creaking of the organ-bellows, the shrill clangor of the cymbals, the harmony of the flutes.[147]

The attraction was clearly irresistible. Just as medieval music was being offered up for membership of the canon of great Western art by votaries like Ficker, here was a further way to bring it to life, turning the plain notes on the page into a riot of colourful sounds. Just as for Riemann (who, incidentally, would have been horrified by Ficker's Catholic mysticism) medieval song took on the habits of the nineteenth-century Lied,[148] so for Ficker and his colleagues organum and by extension other medieval polyphony became orchestral, leaving the chamber and the closed world of scholarship, and entering mainstream musical life in the concert hall. It seems likely that an influence in this process was the 'bright colours, sharp contrasts' vision of the Middle Ages promoted in Johan Huizinga's immensely successful book, *The Autumn of the Middle Ages*, first published in Dutch in 1919, and in German and English translations in 1924 (a French translation was made in 1923 but not published until 1932).[149] Ficker referred to Huizinga almost as soon as the German translation was published;[150] later he borrows Huizinga's title to describe fourteenth-century France,[151] and images from *The Autumn of the Middle Ages* resonate in Ficker's description of one of Machaut's late isorhythmic motets:[152]

Now let your mind conceive how the metallic boy-voices were mingled with all the gentle tintinnabulation of the glockenspiel, cymbals, triangle, etc., then in use, together with the dulcet tones of the viols, while the long-sustained notes of the lower parts were sung by smooth tenor voices supported by manifold wind-instruments, and you will get a fair idea of the dazzling tone-magic of such motets. Fancy yourself attending one of those great assemblies of the estates honored by the Regent's presence and accompanied by the most lavish display, for which the courts of France and Burgundy were then conspicuous. All the bewildering splendor radiated by the cerebral action finds an echo in the scintillant rhythms and interlinked tones of this music.[153]

And this was clearly what Ficker had in mind when he orchestrated this motet, *Tu/Plange*, for the 1927 Beethoven festival concert, strengthening the triplum with horn and bassoon, marking the rhythmic accents in the motetus with glockenspiel and celesta, and having the tenor line sung by six tenors *pianissimo*.[154] 'The splendour of the royal court', as a popular LP of medieval music later had it, was what Ficker aimed to re-create.[155]

ORCHESTRATION

Certainly Netherlands art played a part in the process of translating an image of the colourful Middle Ages into colourful sound, as we can see from a fascinating example in Arnold Schering's 1931 guide, *Aufführungspraxis alter Musik*. Schering had been teaching performance practice to students at Leipzig and then Berlin universities since at least 1915 (and before that at the Leipzig Conservatorium), where his students had included Gurlitt, Friedrich Blume and Helmut Osthoff (his assistant at Berlin from 1928), Heinrich Husmann and Walter Wiora. His influence as a teacher was thus already far-reaching, but his book, a compendium of his beliefs and deductions over twenty-five years, reached a far wider audience (indeed it was reissued in Germany in 1969, and again in 1975 and 1983). The book is thus valuable for providing a detailed record of what was widely assumed, assumptions that inevitably fed back into editions and, later, performances. It may be worth remembering, while reading Schering's advice, that the hard evidence for medieval performance practice was exactly what it had been in Riemann's day, and before. And in many respects Schering's view of late medieval song has changed little since 1911, so that the early sections of his new book offer only a limited number of ideas not already set out in more detail in his 1914 *Studien*.[56] The text-underlay in the manuscripts is still 'senseless' and if one follows it 'one will have to accept that this word stammering separated by long instrumental phrases is nothing less than appropriate to the beautiful poetry'.[57] Just as in the 1914 book he begins with the trecento before going on to illustrate the same decorating of a simple (though otherwise unknown) melodic core in the songs of Machaut. A brief example from Machaut's *Se pour ce muir* stands in for the fuller demonstration using *S'amours ne fait* that he provided in 1914.[58] And, just as in the *Studien*, he rather inconsistently proposes that nevertheless Machaut's two-part virelais, whose texting is syllabic throughout, are correctly sung with instrumental accompaniment, since they continue the troubadours' practice of accompanying themselves with a vielle.[59] He also extends his approach backwards to earlier medieval music: phrases such as 'cum organicis modulis' indicate organ participation, for example in extemporised organa in which the still primitive organ would have been joined by strings and wind instruments.[160] Conductus is sung in the bottom, texted voice of the score (the 'cantus firmus', Schering thinks) and is instrumental in the voices above (as Coussemaker thought possible in 1865), with the sung voice also played; the caudae (which Schering calls Vor- and Nachspiele) are played.[161] Thirteenth-century motets are sung in the texted voices, with instruments on all voices, the tenor played on, for example, organ, trombone or viola. A footnote cautions that the glockenspiel should not be forgotten.[162]

But as well as applying his earlier work more widely, Schering also offers some new comments on the sound of medieval performances which usefully illustrate the gradual extension of the voices-and-instruments hypothesis beyond the stage documented by the Karlsruhe and Hamburg concerts. Drawing on pictorial evidence from published collections he lists some of the ensembles illustrated in medieval miniatures, going on to argue that their combination produced not a unity of sound but rather a contrast; each voice is heard distinctly, sharp and clear:

Light and dark, sharp and soft, flowing and broken up do not mix together, but rather remain side by side.[163]

Nowhere is this better illustrated than towards the end of the book where Schering offers a scoring up of the opening of Ockeghem's *L'Homme armé* mass for the ensemble shown in Memling's panels from Santa Maria de Real, Najera (repeatedly illustrated in books on early music, almost always without the central – vocal – panel: Illustration 1.4). Schering seems to have been clearly aware that paintings could not always be read literally, that musical instruments could be included for symbolic reasons rather than for realism, for he insists (defensively?) that this is no painter's fantasy. That he could be so sure – for there was still no documentary evidence for such an ensemble – can only have been due to his conviction, based on so many years' repetition, that colourful instrumental groupings were a characteristic feature of the medieval soundscape, even in the performance of a polyphonic mass. Schering's examination of the altarpiece leads on from a discussion of ensembles for festive music, both sacred and secular, in the fifteenth and sixteenth centuries:

Hans Memling's 10 musical angels in the Antwerp altar (*c.* 1480) show such an original festive ensemble, the arrangement of which by no means only springs from the painter's fantasy. The wind quartet stands in the middle, then follows on both sides a chordal instrument (lute, portative organ), then to the left and right a plucked and a bowed one: tromba marina and psalterium, harp and viola. Despite all individually decorating the notes we have a blended totality of sounds, where both lower and upper voices are brought together through the combination of different sound characters, and the linear sharpness of the voice-leading thereby becomes softened.

1.4 Hans Memling, 'Christ surrounded by musician angels', Koninklijk Museum, Antwerp (Copyright IRPA-KIK, Brussels)

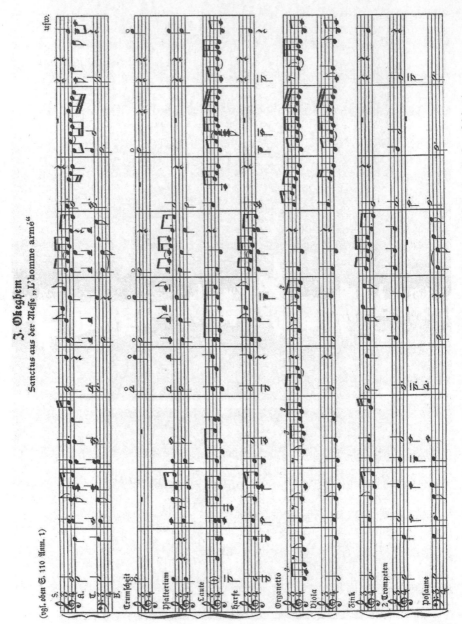

1.5 Jean de Ockeghem, 'Sanctus', *Missa L'Homme armé*, arr. Arnold Schering (1961 a: foldout)

And Schering then uses a footnote to explain the principles behind his arrangement. Before looking at what he says, it will be helpful to know something of the context in which his views of the capabilities of each instrument were formed. The growth of academic interest in medieval instruments was marked at this period, going hand-in-hand with the appreciation of collections, although it was not to have practical results in performance until after the Second World War. Notable contributions to research in these years included a pair of dissertations that sought out references to instruments in Old French literature, one on wind instruments from 1926, another on strings and percussion from 1932.[164] Two of the first guides for curators of instrument collections appeared in 1916 and 1920.[165] Early surveys of instruments include studies by Curt Sachs in 1920 and 1923 and, specifically dealing with medieval instruments, one by Théodore Gérold from 1928.[166] Also widely read was the anthology of pictures assembled by Georg Kinsky in 1929. Important primary sources reissued during the same years include Max Schneider's edition of Ganassi's *Regola Rubertina* (1924), Gurlitt's of Praetorius's *De organographia* (1929), and Leo Schrade's of Virdung's *Musica getuscht* (1931).[167] Not translated from Danish but very probably read in Germany was Hortense Panum's important book on medieval string instruments that first appeared in 1915. A fundamental study of sources of early keyboard music was Schrade's of 1931. Thus Schering was one of the first scholars of performance practice to have a substantial amount of information about medieval instruments on which to draw. All this helps to explain why it was now possible for him, in arranging this Ockeghem Sanctus for instruments, to be so specific about what each instrument could play. Hence:

Experiments in the reconstruction of the old sound-forms can naturally only produce positive results when the technique and playing-method of each individual instrument have been perfectly established. Here we stand only at the beginning. Taking as an example for the above-mentioned ensemble a four-part composition ... of Ockeghem, the instruments could be distributed as shown in the accompanying score [Illustration 1.5]. As the tromba marina uses only two open strings and harmonics, it can only ever sound occasionally. The psalterium players shown in illustrations always use both hands, at about the interval of an octave. The lute would still be strung with metal strings and could produce chords only through strokes with the plectrum. The harp in the old days as a rule plays in two-voices; for the sake of simplicity some possible contra notes are left out. On the coloratura voices of the organetto with their many rests see my 'Studien' p. 62. Cornetts and trombones play all pitches; not so the trumpets, which have semitones in series only in the high register.[168]

This orchestration is fascinating and ingenious; and yet it is reached only after travelling down a spiral of deductions whose starting-point remains the Stainers' reaction to the Canonici songs. To summarise the journey crudely: lack of text leads the Stainers to propose plain instrumental participation (viols); concerts extending the ensemble to include recorders and flutes are successful; pictures encourage a wider range of instruments to be tried; Schering believes that even sacred music is instrumental; Memling's painting – for a church – shows singers and a decidedly mixed group of instruments; Ockeghem was a Netherlands composer who wrote sacred music at the same time; *ergo* . . . Put like this the conclusion may seem weak, but spread over two generations, during which assumptions about instrumental participation became almost universal and went almost entirely unchallenged, it must have seemed entirely reasonable. As a result, orchestrations like this became widely heard in later years. An early example was the third concert of Paul Hindemith's Yale Collegium musicum, on 20 May 1946, which used instruments borrowed from the Metropolitan Museum of Art (loaned by their curator, Emmanuel Winternitz) and the Yale University collection, plus chorus and female soloist, to perform fifteenth-century songs using this same ensemble of Memling's.[169]

THE ORIENTAL HYPOTHESIS

Another major ingredient in the developing picture of medieval performance practice has its origins not long before Schering's book and is considered in it. This is the Oriental hypothesis. Schering argues that although singing in the Middle Ages has not yet been properly studied, nevertheless we can deduce that it would have contained Oriental elements,

> both in the treatment of the voice in itself (nasal and guttural sound-colour, falsetto, trembling of the voice, pulling intervals up and down, staccati, etc.) and in the performance (sprinklings of improvised melismas (*flores armonici*), hockets, trills (*reverberationes*), appoggiaturas, grace-notes etc.). We rightly accept today that the various ornamentations, loop- and slide-notes that neumatic notation knows, have been nothing other than attempts of the West to record improvised Oriental singing style in the form of writing. Their actual performance was assured through the living oral tradition.[170]

This is one of the earliest statements of this view applied to polyphony, although Schering's matter-of-fact presentation suggests that he had been teaching it for some time. And indeed it turned up a year earlier in the thesis of a student in his Department, Marius Schneider, which acknowledges Schering's influence in its foreword.[171] Schneider relates the vocal ornaments described by the fourteenth-century Walter Odington to Oriental influences surviving in Gregorian chant,[172] the use of percussion instruments to Oriental practice,[173] and even rhythm and text-setting.[174] He also explores potential ensembles, classifying medieval instruments by type; he lists some of the combinations shown in pictures,[175] and for each musical form lists a range of ensembles that he finds workable.[176] The issue was one that had surfaced only within the previous decade, mainly thanks to the work of Julián Ribera y Tarragó on Arabic influence on the *Cantigas*, and was just becoming a matter for lively debate,[177] filtering through to more general studies by the late 1920s, for example in Ficker (1929) who traces Gothic architecture and the (for him) related decoration of Leoninian organa to the influence of returning Crusaders,[178] and in Besseler (1931) who imagines the impersonal, anonymous character of medieval melody reflected in a stylised performance, perhaps even nasal in the Oriental manner.[179] Schneider thus stands near the beginning of the process, setting out views that were taken up in more popular writings over the next twenty-five years until, by the time early music groups routinely adopted them in the 1950s and 1960s, they had become ingrained.

Although in his conclusion Schneider leaves a door open for Schering's pure-instrumental hypothesis, allowing that an organist might play 'some madrigal or motet' on his instrument[180] – and as a student in Schering's department he may have had little choice – it is clear that he believes that fourteenth-century music is intended for voice and instruments together. But his emphasis on Oriental influence and in particular on improvisation points towards another aspect of later performances that was to be widely pursued:

Perhaps, on the basis of music still alive in the Orient today, with which the 14th century shows so many connections, we can imagine the performance of these works as a free, simultaneously vocal and instrumental performance that always bears the character of an improvisation. The Oriental sings melodies whose texts now are underlaid in quite syllabic style, now are spread out in wide stretched melismas. The word has for him only a little significance. He makes rests, breaks up his words, in order to take a breath, accompanies himself at the same time in unison, plays the instrument now here, now there, without singing, or he sings without accompanying himself on the instrument. He never performs the same composition twice in the same manner and always gives the whole an improvised character.[181]

This is exactly the sort of effect that we hear performers aiming at in recordings from the 1960s and after, starting with the Studio der frühen Musik under Thomas Binkley.[182] Again, there is a large time-lag before it becomes sound, but that has to do both with the war, which sent so many German and Austrian scholars to the USA where they handed on their beliefs to a younger generation of players, and also with the lack of editions. The lack of editions is the more benign factor: without editions there are no early music groups, and the large collected editions were mostly still some way in the future. Much more disturbing today is the fact that so much of this approach was developed through an extremely ethnocentric view of non-Western music, well represented in the quotation above and all too characteristic of its place and time.[183] It can only have been the perceived advantages for musical performance that allowed assumptions about 'Oriental' influence to be promoted in America with the help of scholars driven out of their homeland by precisely those sorts of prejudices. When, in a passage quoted below, Karl Geiringer (exiled from Vienna in 1938) writes of 'the highly civilised Orient', he is perhaps consciously taking a more positive view of the East while promoting the same theory of performance practice.[184] Although it is noticeable today that in all these discussions there is a marked similarity in attitudes to the otherness of the East and of the medieval West, a similarity that goes far beyond this hypothetical Oriental influence, it was not necessary in the 1930s to be racist for the comparison to seem quite natural. However positively one viewed non-Western or medieval Western music, both were imagined as primitive in a similar sense, the product of cultures that had yet to achieve modernity.

ENGLAND AND AMERICA

Schneider's view of instruments playing with voices of course chimes with the view that, as we have seen, had already become standard outside the immediate circle of Riemann and Schering and that was reflected in the Karlsruhe and Hamburg performances. One can see its increasingly widespread acceptance in two publications of the 1930s from England and America. One of the first books in English to devote itself entirely to medieval polyphony was H. E. Wooldridge's two-volume contribution to the original Oxford History of Music. (He was preceded, more briefly and eccentrically, by Robert Hope (1899), who shows no sign of having seen any medieval music other than plainsong, which he hates.) Wooldridge had the misfortune to complete his survey at just the moment – 1905 – that a wealth of new information was appearing. Had he been up-to-date with the *Sammelbände* it is possible, depending on the publication schedule for the Oxford History, that he might have taken some account of Ludwig's and Wolf's studies of the last few years, but for whatever reason he did not, and thanks to the huge amount of new research over the next twenty-five years his volumes of the OHM required early up-dating. At the end of the 1920s Oxford reorganised the early parts of the History: they added an Introductory volume before volume 1 covering in more detail music before and other than Western polyphony, and they commissioned Percy Buck to revise Wooldridge's volumes 1 and 2 (1929 and 1932). Buck's changes to Wooldridge's survey of late medieval song provide a ready measure of the extent to which the new German view of performance practice had been accepted elsewhere. Wooldridge's treat-ment of Machaut is cut down, excising his harsh judgement on the motets (that they hardly developed beyond their thirteenth-century models),[185] no doubt in the light of Ludwig's and Besseler's published descriptions and the examples in Wolf;[186] also omitted is the comparison of Machaut's songs with Adam's, and its remark cited above proposing vocalisation.[187] Wooldridge's extended description of Italian notation has gone, though his preference for Italian over French ars nova music remains;[188] indeed, Buck leaves in place most of Wooldridge's numerous complaints about medieval harmony. More were added, however, by Jack Westrup in his new chapter for the revised vol. II on 'Song'. Westrup's purpose in his discussion of France and Italy, he tells us, is to consider not style but 'the changes which came about in the conception of melody and the function of instrumental accompaniment';[189] he builds on Riemann in tracing the emergence of ars nova song from the jongleurs via l'Escurel and Machaut's monophonic pieces, continues with a judgement on Machaut's polyphony that accepts the Ludwig/Wolf view of the primacy of the French over Italian ars nova, and Riemann's view of instrumental accompaniment as integral to art song; but Westrup departs from his sources in offering an alternative to instrumental participation:

The importance for the history of song of Machault's works for two or more voices is that the secondary part or parts are in many cases undoubtedly written for instruments. . . . We have in these works the beginnings of instrumental ac-companiment as an integral part of an art form. The technique is hardly yet dis-tinguishable from that of vocal composition, and many of these accompanying parts could be, and doubtless were on occasion, sung. Where words are supplied, the instruments probably accompanied the voices in unison throughout.[190]

Westrup develops this idea in his discussion of Italian music in a passage in which his distaste for Italian coloratura leads him to disagree with the German assumption that melismas must be instrumental; on the contrary, Westrup implies, that sort of thing is all too typical of Italian vocal writing. He is commenting on an extract from Jacopo's *Un bel sparver*:

The extended runs and the decoration of phrases are not altogether unexpected in an Italian composition. Vocal expression always seems to have come naturally to the Italians, and this same tendency to extravagance is still noticeable at a much later date in the operas of the eighteenth and nineteenth centuries ... in the fourteenth century it was still more or less a purely national disease. Dissatisfaction with these vocal gambols has led some German historians [he footnotes Riemann 1905–6 and 1905: 316, and Schering 1914a] to suggest either that the florid passages were intended to be executed on instruments, the simple phrases only being assigned to the voice, or that these compositions are highly decorated organ arrangements of originally simple and unembroidered vocal melodies. Riemann, who is responsible for the first opinion, would rewrite Ex. 34 [Jacopo's *Un bel sparver gentil*] as bracketed [Westrup shows as an alternative the first and last syllables of the text line moved inwards, leaving the melismas untexted].[191]

And Westrup goes on to disagree, citing clear manuscript underlay and the suitability of the vowels so set for 'vocal display'. He is willing to accept that the first syllable only appears at the beginning of the music because it is copied as a decorated initial, and should be moved to the start of the rest of the text, but,

Apart from this it is extremely unwise to rearrange these compositions. The florid instrumental style probably developed from the vocal style. . . . These runs and triplets for the voice need not dismay us. Their origin may be sought in those 'endless Alleluias' which were the delight of the church. . . . Florid ornamentation for the voice, far from being something new or requiring explanation, was in fact almost as ancient as Western European music itself.[192]

Westrup's independence seems to come from two characteristically English sources, a dislike of Italian vocal 'excesses' coupled with a greater willingness than German scholars showed to believe that florid passages are singable, very probably a consequence of his experience of the English cathedral tradition (which proved to be an important element in the vocal revival of the 1980s, as Page has argued).[193]

Across the Atlantic, very similar attitudes may be found in Leonard Ellinwood's 1936 article on Landini's music. Ellinwood reports Riemann's and Schering's theories of (respectively) instrumental cantus melismas and organ decorations of a simple vocal core and, while agreeing that 'parts without text were intended for and performed on instruments' he argues carefully against them, using some of the same arguments as Westrup and Adler before him, 'only the ballate (dance pieces) have purely instrumental parts without texts'; the lower, certainly instrumental voices are simpler, so why simplify the texted voice in order to sing it; lower voices with text in one manuscript but not in another sometimes have longer notes split in the former; syllable are sometimes tied by dashes to their notes, indicating a direct connection with the music; repeated text sometimes shows a melisma to be sung; chant offers examples of sung melismas:[194]

For these reasons, we believe that, while the parts *without* text were undoubtedly played on the lute, organ, or possibly viol, the florid parts *with* text were primarily sung in the manner indicated in the manuscripts, either alone or with the support of instruments.[195]

INSTRUMENTAL COLOUR

By the mid-1930s, then, a fairly consistent view seems to have been held by musicologists everywhere: Riemann had exaggerated, but late medieval song was instrumentally accompanied, and probably in all parts. This view, of course, was irresistibly attractive to historians of musical instruments, for it gave the medieval instruments they described something to do. Karl Geiringer's classic *Musical Instruments* was begun in Vienna in 1936, continued in London in 1938–9 and completed in America in 1940, eventually being published in 1943 (in English) – a production history plainly reflecting the circumstances of its time. Geiringer sees the use of instruments in medieval music in far grander terms than we have yet encountered; and this is itself a symptom of the security with which instrumental participation was established: other views could be tied up to it:

The early Middle Ages were dominated by the idea of Universality. As there were still no national boundaries, so there was only *one* science, only *one* acknowledged language – Latin – only *one* religion – the Catholic – and, similarly, only *one* art of music. The division between vocal and instrumental music which seems so natural to us to-day had not yet been made.[196]

Like most organologists, Geiringer (a pupil of Sachs) has an interest in bringing together Oriental and Western medieval instruments:

Thus the early Middle Ages, which were peculiarly receptive to influences from the highly civilized Orient, gathered on Western soil a motley host of Oriental instruments ... there is good reason for assuming that so far as single-voiced music is concerned, as soon as instruments co-operated the performance took place in the Oriental manner. All the musicians played the same melody in unison, and the melody as a rule would be sung as well. Each player, however, would decorate and adorn the tune in his own particular manner, according to the qualities of his own instrument.[197]

And just as for Schering and Schneider, this leads on to a link between instrumental colour and the nature of medieval polyphony. It is easy to see how the gradual elaboration of this view by successive writers brought it towards a state of orthodoxy, especially when, as in this case, an author is able to tie it in to some wider assumptions about the medieval mind, here its predilection for independent thought:

Generally speaking, the main line of development [1300–1500] was in the direction of the free expression of the performer's personality. ... The late Middle Ages laid greater stress on individuality in music, as in all other activities. ... The instruments of the late Middle Ages were far too delicate and weak to stand alone. In the painting of the fourteenth and fifteenth centuries, which are our chief sources of information concerning the instruments of the period, they appear almost invariably in groups. Yet instruments of like tone were seldom combined; indeed, the groupings were plainly so arranged as to provide the greatest wealth of contrast and variety. This becomes intelligible if we turn from the painting to the actual scores that have come down to us. The essentially different, shrill, and apparently discordant instruments were able to differentiate the separate parts, to which the period of Landino, Dunstable and Dufay aimed to give individual characters. Effects of harmony were not sought after in that heyday of contrapuntal virtuosity, and the contrasting tones of the instruments gave full emphasis to the polyphonic life of the composition. The orchestra of the late Middle Ages was instinct with light, radiant, imponderable colours, like the paintings of the Primitives.[198]

The linear view of medieval music was now firmly tied in with the voices-and-instruments hypothesis, just as their opposites – the all-vocal hypothesis and a vertical view of late medieval harmony – have been tied together more recently.

SURVEYS AND SYNTHESES

The first and, arguably, even now the most influential history of medieval music was Heinrich Besseler's *Die Musik des Mittelalters und der Renaissance* of 1930–4 which set out the story in broadly the form it has taken ever since. Although Ludwig had published a long chapter surveying the period in Adler's 1924 *Handbuch der Musikgeschichte*, establishing an overview of the

development of medieval polyphony, it reflected the nature of its author in severely limiting its interpretation of the evidence. Besseler's was
thus the first survey to present the story of medieval music as a directed
imaginative conception. Being less austerely scholarly than Ludwig's, it
was far more influential in shaping perceptions of medieval music. Our
view of great schools of medieval composition, of changing medieval
attitudes to construction and affect, of the aesthetics of the music, of
the place of individual masters, of the slow progression from craft to
art are all set out, for the first time, in a coherent vision of the subject.
Besseler's unquestioning assumption of instrumental accompaniment in
motet and song is unsurprising in this context and becomes brilliantly integrated into the story so that, for example, the solo voice in Machaut's
polyphonic ballades, set against its 'restlessly crumbling background'
of 'instrumental accompanying voices', produces a 'new excitement of
sound ... intensified through occasional shifts of harmony to romantic luminosity. Such music ... has become an art of enchantment, that
abducts the listening hearer from reality and seeks to entice him across
into its dreamworld.'[199] So a theory of accompaniment helps to shape
an inspired, romantic view of musical development. Of all the general
histories Besseler's was the most creative and, as a result, the most coher-
ently formed. Like Ficker, Besseler continually emphasises concepts of
Nordic and Gothic, annexing French and English medieval music into
a greater Northern alliance with Germany, a view that in some ways is
not so far from Riemann's despite its different emphasis. For both writers Northern and Italian approaches combine to lead music towards its
tonal destiny, and although Riemann was more concerned to exclude
the French – a strategy that after Ludwig was no longer possible – all
three writers (Riemann, Besseler and Ficker) manage indirectly, by their
continual use of evocative Northern adjectives and frequent references
to Minnesang, to imply that German values remain central to music's
onward march through history.

For French speakers the equivalent task was performed, albeit less
imaginatively, by Théodore Gérold in two histories of early music published in the 1930s. They share a lot of text, though the later book incor-
porates a few recent ideas not sufficiently developed in 1932 to have been
mentioned. Foremost among these is the Oriental hypothesis, which as
we have seen, and as Gérold remarks, was just emerging.[200] Like Reese in
1940, Gérold includes no single treatment of the voices-and-instruments
question simply because he takes for granted that untexted parts must
be instrumental.[201] This, coupled with a natural preference for French

music, leads him, for example, to credit Philippe de Vitry with one of the earliest vocal compositions to have an instrumental introduction, the motet *Tuba/In arboris* which begins with upper-voice melismas, a judgement that extends Riemann's beliefs far beyond the trecento madrigal and shows just how deeply the idea was now ingrained in scholars' minds.[202] Italian music, for Gérold, is relegated to a chapter on 'Music of the 14th century outside France',[203] its performance seen in more or less Riemann's terms.[204] Both books are widely cited in subsequent publications (including Reese) for their treatment of medieval instruments, and indeed Gérold is particularly generous in citing lists of instruments from medieval French literature and in describing their characteristics.[205] His books were thus well-placed to serve as reference tools for subsequent performers. Much the same service was provided, but in more detail drawn directly from literary and archival sources, by André Pirro's 1940 history of late medieval and Renaissance music, which begins with a long Huizingan chapter evoking the late medieval soundscape in terms that can only have encouraged performers to seek colourful and varied scorings.[206]

Almost all the beliefs outlined in the preceding sections are collected together for the general reader in the first edition of Gustave Reese's enormously influential *Music in the Middle Ages* (1940). Reese was a student at New York University in the 1920s and in his early professional life was a lawyer; thus as a medievalist he was self-taught, so that his view would have been shaped mainly by the German musicology he read. The return of fellow Americans who had studied in Germany and the influx of German scholars to America in the 1930s provided further stimuli: Kinkeldy – whom we met earlier, arguing in Berlin in April 1912 that the Squarcialupi codex was a collection of organ music – was an American, who studied in Berlin with Kretzschmar and then taught at Breslau until 1914; Kinkeldy's student at Cornell, Oliver Strunk, had spent a year studying with Wolf and Schering in Berlin in 1927–8; in 1936, after completing his Ph.D. in Berlin, Willi Apel moved to Cambridge, Mass., joining the Harvard faculty in 1938; in 1937 Curt Sachs came as a visiting professor to New York University; in 1938 Leo Schrade joined the faculty at Yale; in 1939 came Alfred Einstein, Otto Gombosi, Dragan Plamenac and also Manfred Bukofzer, who had studied in Heidelberg with Besseler and then in Berlin with Wolf, Schering, Blume, Sachs and Hindemith, and who had taken his doctorate at Basel under Handschin.[207] The later names on this list surely came too late to have any personal influence on *Music in the Middle Ages*, though the list gives some sense of the meeting of minds that was to transform American musicology. In his turn, Reese became a close influence on Noah Greenberg and the New York Pro Musica and on the Waverly Consort (founded within his own Department at NYU).[208] In his contribution to the Reese Festschrift, Greenberg writes,

Reese's ... monumental work in the music of the Middle Ages and the Renaissance has served, and continues to serve, as our basic and trusted guide. ... In my own case, when I first came to his publications, I was a mere enthusiast; but it was the extraordinary impact of his work that persuaded me to devote my entire life to the study and performance of this music.[209]

Music in the Middle Ages is the book on which generations of English-speaking musicologists were raised and to which generations of performers have turned for a first overview of the subject and a guide to repertories and their performance. Reese passes on all the received traditions of his time, drawing them in from the far corners of musicology and distilling from them an agreed core, their simplest possible expression. The thirteenth-century motet with instrumental tenor gave 'rise to the vocal solo, duet, and trio with composed accompaniment',[210] and he naturally takes it for granted that any untexted part from the fourteenth century is instrumental.[211] Reese's teaching materials, preserved at New York University, flesh out the same story with examples: in course listening notes on Machaut he draws attention to 'the occasional highly dissonant leaps in the undoubtedly instrumental contratenor' of the Kyrie of the Mass;[212] similarly his notes on the various fifteenth-century pieces imitating trumpets make clear his view that they were intended to be performed on those instruments.[213] The extent to which Reese used recordings, reflected also in the discographies to his medieval and Renaissance textbooks, is evident from his teaching materials and only serves to emphasise his unquestioning support for current performance practices. *Music in the Middle Ages* also promotes the idea of contrasting sonorities encouraged by Schering:

some thought seems to have been given, where more than one instrument participated, to the obtaining of contrasting sonorities ... [214]
Pictorial evidence furnishes some clues to the type of instrumental ensemble preferred. This shows a strong liking for contrast. Where two stringed instruments chance to form a group one is almost certain to be bowed, the other plucked. If the group is larger, the additional instruments are likely to include aerophones, membranophones, or idiophones.[215]

His footnote here includes references to Schneider 1931, for a picture illustrating the principle of contrast, and to Leichtentritt 1905.[216] Like so many other writers, Reese still reports Riemann's view of trecento melismas and Schering's organ-music theory, despite the fact that, like most of the others who report them, he does not believe either.[217] It is interesting, too, to see echoes of Riemann in phrases such as '*trecento* music shakes off the shackles of a *cantus firmus*',[218] a form of words that in Riemann intended to downplay the importance of France, though Reese was no doubt using it unconsciously. Because it has been a standard work for so long, it is easy to forget that *Music in the Middle Ages*, though magisterially done, is simply a faithful synthesis of early musicology.

Similar to Reese in that it brought together received opinion in a useful package, and hardly less influential on performers, was the British scholar and performer Thurston Dart's *The Interpretation of Music* (1954), whose final chapter dealt with the Middle Ages.[219] Dart dispenses with references, so that it is not possible to trace his immediate sources for each piece of advice, but his text paints exactly the same picture that we have seen assembled over the preceding half-century. We learn that parts were composed successively, and therefore pieces were performable with fewer than all parts; musicians who could add parts to existing pieces were considered cleverer than composers of new pieces; the main melodic line must be the clearest, the rest are subordinate; instrumental accompaniment is to be taken for granted; music and instruments from the mountains of Sardinia and Sicily, and Catalan bands, 'are medieval in flavour'; Arabic lute, rebec and shawm are 'still much the same' as in medieval Europe; Spanish flamenco singers give some idea of medieval performance of roulades; traditional Irish harp accompaniments notated in the eighteenth century preserve the style found in fifteenth-century ducal courts; drones on the tonic need to be added; percussion must be added; ornamentation must be added; the lower voices in chansons were instrumental (because they have no words); the tenor in chansons is more important than the contratenor and therefore needs 'a cantabile melody instrument' and the contratenor 'a lighter tone-colour' [and we hear this again and again in recordings, for example a bowed tenor and a plucked contra]; mass tenors should be made prominent by organ or bells; other parts could be doubled by brass; and in trecento madrigals and ballate 'certain scholars have concluded that the melodic lines should be split up between voices and instrument'.

Dart, who was to play a key role in modernising historical musicology in Britain in the 1960s, studied immediately after the war with Charles van den Borren in Brussels. Van den Borren's view was that instruments were used in all secular and much sacred music, and in any combination that happened to be available.[220] Under van den Borren's influence, his son-in-law, Safford Cape, had already – from the mid-1930s to the mid-1950s – put into practice with his ensemble Pro Musica Antiqua of Brussels almost every one of the ideas summarised by Dart. Cape's tastes are well demonstrated in an article on the Machaut Mass published (in instalments) in 1959 and 1960, offering a detailed account of the decisions he took in preparing the work for performance. These include emphasising the isorhythmic and other formal elements by changes in scoring; using instruments for the Gloria and Credo link passages (which 'are impossible for the voices') as well to create contrast in middle sections; stressing repeating melodic figures; octave doubling at climaxes.[221] The result can be heard on one of the early Deutsche Grammophon Archiv LPs, recorded three years earlier in 1956.[222] Thus, in summarising all this received wisdom for the general reader, Dart was, to a considerable extent, writing about Cape's performances.[223] The influence of both Dart and Cape may be felt, too, in an article by the self-taught British scholar Gilbert Reaney, also published in 1956. It is hard to avoid the impression that Reaney is describing the concert programming techniques of Cape and his early imitators when he writes, 'A typical example [of an ensemble of contrasting instruments] is the group viol, shawm and horn, shown in Giotto's *Coronation of the Virgin* in Santa Croce. The attraction of such a colourful instrumental combination would be lost if new combinations did not soon succeed it, and this is no doubt what originally occurred. A vocal ensemble would be followed by an instrumental one, which would be followed by a vocal soloist accompanied by a lute, etc.'[224]

Similar principles were taught to students right up until the reinvention of the all-vocal hypothesis and beyond, as is illustrated in the compendium of advice published in 1978 by the Austrian teacher of performance practice Josef Mertin (and translated into English in 1986). As the translator remarks, 'In more than half a century as a professor [at the Hochschule für Musik in Vienna], he has taught thousands of students, among whom – because of the international role of the Vienna institution – Americans and other foreigners probably outnumber local students. Many performers now famous for their contribution to early music received their first and finest training from him'.[225] Mertin himself disclaimed scholarly credentials – 'Although I personally learned a great deal from Adler, Ficker, and Fischer, I am writing as a conductor and not as a musicologist'[226] – but that perhaps only serves to emphasise the lack

of rigorous scrutiny that any of this lore of medieval performance practice would have received; and in that respect Mertin, a pupil of Ficker
from 1924 (exactly when Ficker was most fully engaged in developing
his view of the musical Gothic),[227] was in excellent scholarly company.
Ensembles, he tells us, are small, and 'the professional musicians, the
jongleurs, are called in whenever needed'.[228] At Notre Dame there was
a group of jongleurs on hand 'who play instrumental parts in ever changing distributions';[229] words in the lower voices of homophonic pieces are
there only to aid co-ordination for players working from parts (a residue
of Schering's view), vocal performance would be 'musically wrong'; in
Machaut's Mass, 'Linear forces run ruthlessly over harmonic concerns',
demanding a 'split sonority' (i.e., contrasted instrumental colours on
different lines), and percussion might have been used to keep the ensemble together, while the make-up of the ensemble should change from
movement to movement:[230]

Machaut's ballades are specifically pieces favoring split sonority. A flute for the
triplum, a good tenor capable of falsetto in the upper range for the motetus, for
the tenor a viol, and in the contratenor a lute … will sound very good. This
arrangement will prove that there is no problem to playing E in one voice and
E-flat in another. Such apparent clashes are not offensive with parts assigned to
strongly contrasting timbres.[231]

The inference is clear: instrumental participation makes bearable
music that would otherwise be insufferable. A related distaste for aspects of medieval music is clearly implied in Schering, the apostle of split
sonorities, whose incomprehension in the face of medieval text-setting
underlies so much of this later teaching. And one can detect a similar lack of sympathy in the writings of many other scholars of medieval
music. There is a murky chapter of musicology that remains to be written
dealing with the extent to which medievalists' dislike of medieval music
influenced their findings. At any rate, it is clear that Mertin's teaching is
not scholarship, but it is what was taught and we can hear it sound in
recordings by Ruhland and especially by Mertin's pupil, René Clemencic. It descends in a clear line from Stainer and Riemann, and without
any new evidence for it having been found in the meantime.

The publication of Mertin's book in an English translation in 1986 is
interesting testimony to the continuing market for such advice, particularly in North America. The same market was tapped the previous year
by Timothy McGee's *Medieval and Renaissance Music: A Performer's Guide*,
which was published again in England in 1990. McGee is essentially a

Dart for our times, offering very similar advice but in much more detail. The text is peppered with phrases like 'We know that' unsupported, as in Dart and Mertin, by references to any primary evidence. Like them, McGee is describing a modern performance tradition, and that he can go into so much more detail is due in part to the greater space at his disposal (his was the first such book to deal just with medieval and Renaissance music) but also because the tradition is so much longer than in Dart's day. If Dart was describing performances by Cape, McGee can take on board Greenberg and Binkley, Morrow and Munrow, Vellard and Pérès and so many others. Like the pathologist-sculptors who rebuild early Man from half a jaw, medieval music performers feed back to scholars a lifelike reconstruction of a musical world from the few tiny fragments of evidence that earlier scholars dug up; and from those reconstructions – not the original material – missing evidence is guessed and new narratives are written. Thus McGee still passes on, eighty years later, Riemann's theory of instrumental introductions, interludes and postludes (though without mentioning Riemann),[232] together with much received tradition on plucked contratenors, contrasting lines, instrumental style and so on, but now adds detailed and lengthy advice on improvisation that corresponds well to the practice of medieval music groups since the 1960s.[233] As recently as the year 2000, a large collection of essays appeared, mainly written by American scholars and performers and published in cooperation with the popular magazine *Early Music America*, that – though it can add little new evidence – speaks eloquently of the desire for the instrumental tradition to continue to develop.[234]

COLLECTED EDITIONS

Several of the threads analysed above are woven into the introduction to one of the first 'complete editions' of a trecento repertory, Leonard Ellinwood's 1939 edition of Landini. From this distance it seems odd that, although Ludwig had transcribed very large parts of the surviving repertories of medieval music by 1905, and despite there being few technical difficulties of transcription after Wolf's *Geschichte* of 1904, and in spite of the rapid growth in scholarship surrounding medieval music, there were very few editions issued before the 1950s. One of those few was Gastoué's selection of pieces from the Apt manuscript, published in 1936. Gastoué seems to have been made aware of this source of fourteenth-century motets and mass movements shortly before his 1914 concert, for he used pieces from it there and refers to his recent knowledge of it in a footnote to the booklet (see above). In a section of his introduction 'Du rôle des instruments' Gastoué finds it self-evident that untexted passages were to be played on instruments, probably organs or a quartet of viols or wind instruments.[235] But this edition was one of few. Only the thirteenth-century motet was fairly fully published, mainly through editions presented alongside facsimiles,[236] and of course the complete music of Machaut, the only published fruits of Ludwig's astonishing transcriptions of almost all known medieval polyphony.[237] Ludwig would undoubtedly have published more, perhaps with profound results for study and performance, had he not been obsessed with total bibliographic control. Only in the case of Machaut did he feel confident that he had seen everything and could publish without fear of contradiction by later discoveries.[238] But Ludwig was an exceptional case. Quite why so little effort was put by others into providing the music is a question that deserves study in itself; but tied to it is the relatively late flowering of medieval music in the concert hall. This is probably not simply a question of the public being unready. The formalism, clear textures and lack of pictorialism in text-setting might have endeared medieval music to the neo-classicists, had they had easy access to it. But without editions there could be no performances, and editions were hard to find and laborious for performers to prepare until the collected-edition movement took off in the late 1940s with the first issues of the American Institute of Musicology. Thus the rise of the collected edition coincides fairly exactly with the rise of the full-time early music group, of early music in concert and on record – that is, with the rise of the early music movement as profitable business.

Not all editions included advice for performers, nor was it essential that they should, since work on performance practice was available, as we have seen, elsewhere. Of those that did, an early and thought-provoking example is Yvonne Rokseth's edition of the Montpellier codex, whose commentary volume, published in 1939, proposes vocal performance for the earliest motets and those with French song tenors, and an instrumental tenor for later pieces, with flexibility according to circumstances. More imaginatively, she proposes that certain motets – those with suitable texts – might have been dramatised, the singers acting their roles.[239] While Rokseth never addresses potential performers directly, speaking rather of plausible medieval performances, such means and contexts could hardly be imagined by a scholar with no interest in performance *per se* and inevitably speak to and guide readers who would perform – understandably, a common device among editors of medieval music who wish to advise without committing themselves.

While some editors clearly hoped that their editions would lead to more performances, others preferred not to be drawn at all into questions that could not be resolved through sufficient evidence. Ellinwood's Landini edition, one of the first musical publications of the Mediaeval Academy of America, falls into the former group, for it contains in its introduction a considerable amount of information on medieval practices that might be taken as defining the parameters of potential performances. A close (perhaps unfairly close) reading of his text suggests that Ellinwood's views have hardened since his article of three years earlier. He had no doubt in 1936 that the lower voices were instrumental, but argued effectively for the texted parts to be sung throughout, noting among other reasons the presence of text in some manuscripts despite its absence in others. Now he puts the argument the other way round, stating that while text was present in some manuscripts its absence in others points towards instrumental performance.[240] Previously he emphasised the familiarity of florid melismas to medieval singers as a reason for singing through the untexted melismas in Landini's music; now he finds that the parts without texts 'have intervals difficult or impossible to sing', that untexted passages between text phrases arc 'of an instrumental nature', and that the melismatic passages in the superius have 'many small figures ... that are typical of the possibilities of a simple wind instrument or a keyboard instrument'.[241] In other words, instruments play all parts, and play alone where there is no text, a view not far from Riemann's.

The response – almost a knee-jerk reaction – to largish intervals or melodic decoration typified by Ellinwood was strongly challenged in 1946 by Lloyd Hibberd.[242] Hibberd took Schering's categories of 'instrumental' style and demolished them one by one, and did so, some thirty years after Schering had published them, because he found so many musicologists still accepting them uncritically. It seems probable that he had some influence, for later statements by English-speaking scholars are on the whole somewhat less ready than was Ellinwood to characterise a line as intrinsically instrumental. But it would have had less influence on performers, for whom the introduction to the editions and the general surveys remained the main sources of information. This was, in effect, the front line between scholars and performers, and what was said there was crucial in shaping what was heard.

The introductions to the first volumes from the American Institute of Musicology need to be read in that light. The first issues of Guillaume de Van's Dufay edition (the Motets, followed by the *Missa sine nomine*)

appeared in 1947 and 1949, and the beginnings of a Machaut edition
also in 1949.[243] De Van's introduction to the Dufay mass firmly favoured
performance with instruments, even for these sacred pieces:

while the Kyrie, Sanctus and Agnus apparently permit of a vocal execution of the
lower voices (although the structure of these voices is distinctly instrumental),
the Gloria and Credo are indisputably conceived for a single voice with two
instruments. A third combination also suggests itself, whereby the *Cantus* and
Tenor of the Kyrie, Sanctus and Agnus be sung, and the *Contratenor* played. The
evidence furnished by the sources would indicate that all three combinations
were employed, as the mode of execution probably depended upon the resources
of each choir.[244]

It is not clear whether de Van imagined choirs, too poor to employ
enough singers, using instruments instead, or choirs rich enough to employ instrumentalists in addition to singers. His reliance on the evidence
of the sources, i.e., the manuscript texting, emphasises the lack of any
other evidence for instrumentalists playing in polyphonic masses. In
other words, de Van's proposal arises from his conviction that instrumentalists played untexted parts in music of this period rather than from
any specific evidence related to these sorts of pieces. In the Machaut
edition he starts from the same assumption, but allows the possibility of
all parts being sung:

The disposition of the text in these sources makes it impossible to affirm with certainty that any one of the four voices were intended for instruments only. There
is indeed a strong presumption, from the inherent character of the music, that
the *Ct* of the four isorhythmic numbers is to be played, while the corresponding
T can be either sung or played at will. . . . The reader can, if he likes, add or
suppress the text in these voices, because there was assuredly no uniform practice observed by the choirs of Machaut's time; it is altogether conceivable that
the same singers would have sung the Kyrie *Ct* and played the same voice in the
Sanctus, to mention but one possibility.[245]

Fourteenth-century French song other than Machaut received its first
substantial edition from Willi Apel in his *French Secular Music* of 1950,
whose advice to performers is not dissimilar from Ellinwood's:

The majority of the compositions have one vocal and two instrumental voice-
parts . . . a vocal part may well have been performed by a singer and an instrumentalist in unison . . . compositions with texts in all voice-parts [were], in all
probability, not performed *a cappella*.[246]

From Apel's introduction we also learn that 'wind instruments were
probably used in the accompanying parts', because of 'the fact that

in the fourteenth century wind instruments were more numerous than stringed ones'.[247] Apel's evidence for this deduction is that in the lists of instruments included in Machaut's poetic works wind outnumber strings by 2 to 1. This gives some idea of the desperation with which scholars latched on to any fragment that might conceivably be used as evidence for performance practice, and of the ease with which such a 'fact' might be taken to be one by unsuspecting readers and might find its way into performances. Apel also deals with Riemann and Schering,

who must be credited with having discovered [*sic*] the vocal-instrumental nature of mediaeval secular music, [though they] certainly have gone much too far in the application of their theory. To interpret all the numerous vocalizing melismas in French or Italian songs of the late Middle Ages as instrumental interludes, is a wholly untenable proposition and one that cannot be applied without arbitrary interruptions of the melodic lines. The situation is different, however, in the case of textless passages that without forcing can be considered as self-contained entities, particularly of those preceded and followed by rests.[248]

While seeming to distance himself from Riemann, Apel in fact accepts most of his argument, the difference between their positions hinging only on what may be considered as 'forcing'. And he has a new proposal of his own:

The most likely theory regarding the performance of a partly vocal and partly instrumental voice-part is that the singer had an instrument ready that he used for the instrumental passages.[249]

Gilbert Reaney offers similar advice to performers in the introduction to the first volume of his series *Early Fifteenth Century Music* of 1955.[250] Referring to Cesaris's rondeau *A l'aventure*, whose lower voices have brief texted passages in shorter notes, he comments:

One can imagine the instrumentalists singing instead of playing this bar in the tenor and contratenor. Evidently wind instruments are not in use here. If they were, the players would not have time to replace their instruments in their mouths after singing.[251]

One used to see this in concerts, a singer picking up a crumhorn and blowing it for a few beats between text phrases, or an instrumentalist singing briefly: a Medieval Ensemble of London recording of Dufay's *Resveilles vous* that simulates it is discussed below, and we have already seen de Van proposing that singers and instrumentalists were one and the same in the Machaut Mass.[252] In fact the influence of introductions to editions is easy for scholars (who generally pay them little attention) to underestimate. Apel cites Matheus de Perusio as a composer who needs instrumental introductions and interludes in the cantus line, exactly as indicated by Schering twenty years before,[253] and still practised thirty years later in the complete recording of his works made by the Medieval Ensemble of London in 1979 (see below). There is a long and very consistent tradition within which this sort of advice, however unfounded, must have seemed entirely natural. One can understand, then, that it would have been impossible for performers to do anything other than follow it; it was repeated wherever they turned, they had no reason to doubt it, so there was no reason for them to trace it back through earlier publications, which would have been their only way of finding out that it had no basis in evidence beyond text layout and the assumptions of a handful of scholars around 1900.

SOUND

Recordings of medieval music reflect and make into sound the guesses of earlier scholars; every feature of performance practice described by the scholars discussed here appears in early recorded performances, and many continue to be heard to this day. While this is not the place for a full history of medieval music on record, a few examples will show the continuing influence of Riemann and Schering as well as some of the broader trends in scholarship emerging later on record.

A good starting place is the Anthologie Sonore, a series of recordings initiated by Curt Sachs in 1933. Although there are interesting individual recordings from earlier in the century (including all-vocal performances of Dufay (in Columbia's *History of Music by Ear and Eye* series),[254] and Lambert Murphy's delightful *Douce dame jolie* (Machaut) with cod-Elizabethan accompaniment),[255] this French series set out to cover a wide repertory using researched editions and performance forces.[256] Like so many recordings from before the 1960s, the first disc to be issued, of trecento song,[257] makes very clear the Romantic understanding of courtly-love texts that, as we have seen, was promoted by Riemann and almost universally shared before the post-war avant-garde uncoupled textual and musical expression. Ficker's conception of trecento music as 'an individual, natural development of emotion paired with the highest pitch of soulful expression' and of 'the dolorous expression of hopeless love-torment [that] finds congenial expression in the music [of Giovanni da Cascia]'[258] is perfectly represented in these performances. Vincenzo's *Ita se nera* and *Io son un pellegrin* (attributed here to Giovanni) are sung slowly and with deep feeling by the tenor Max Meili using a heavy vibrato, accompanied with lighter vibrato by a vielle; while the anonymous Lauda *Gloria in cielo* is given Italian operatic treatment, complete with vocal sobs. In the first two pieces Meili sings through the melismas, but in the final item, Bartolomeo Brollo's *O celestia lume*, the melisma ending the second section is hummed, a novel solution to the melisma question, but one that surely reflects Riemann's insistence that melismas were not for setting text.[259]

Riemann is more faithfully followed in some of the later discs in the series. Anthologie Sonore 39 (issued 1936) opens with a performance of Arnold de Lantins' *Puisque je voy* (by the Brussels Pro Musica Antiqua directed by Safford Cape) in which the soprano Lina Dauby is accompanied by three vielles. Here the strings play the melismas at the end and between each text phrase, exactly as Riemann proposed. Similarly in Binchois' *De plus en plus* on side 2, the bowed string accompanying Mlle H Guermant plays the brief five-note end-melisma of the A section alone (as indicated in Riemann's *Hausmusik* edition),[260] even though she sings the other melismas. And a similar procedure is adopted in the last item, *Va t'ent souspir*, where the instruments alone play the brief melisma at end of penultimate phrase.

An extension of Riemann's and Schering's conviction that text disposition must meet modern criteria can be seen already on Anthologie Sonore 35 (1936), where instruments alone alternate with accompanied voices in Dufay's Kyrie *Se la face ay pale*, thereby removing all but the final melisma from the singers and ensuring that the words 'Kyrie eleison' are heard the 'correct' number of times. These sorts of treatments, like the alternation of voices with and without instrumental accompaniment in Dufay's *Alma redemptoris mater* on side 2, have been heard on disc in different forms countless times since the 1930s, but it is important to realise that they did not originate in Safford Cape's imagination (or in any evidence) but rather in views formed among scholars over several decades, handed on by the group's scholarly advisor, Cape's father-in-law Charles van den Borren.

Similar procedures were still being followed by Pro Musica Antiqua almost thirty years later when they recorded numerous discs for the HMV/Oxford University Press *History of Music in Sound*. Vol. III: 'Ars Nova and the Renaissance, *c*. 1300–1540', includes a performance of Giovanni's *Nel mezzo a sei paon*, the piece edited by Riemann as an example in the crucial passage of his *Handbuch der Musikgeschichte*. This performance could almost be of Riemann's edition, save only that the initial melisma is sung. The Mezzo and Tenor (Jeanne Deroubaix and Albert van Ackere) sing the opening and each text-line alone, but the remaining melismas are all played (on recorder and vielle), exactly as indicated by Riemann almost fifty years before.[261] The accompanying booklet, written by Gerald Abraham, says of this piece:

The extremely florid nature of the higher parts has given rise to various theories as to the method of performance; it has been suggested that all the florid passages are either instrumental interludes or instrumental embellishments of simpler vocal forms but, as this record shows, they can be sung without undue difficulty.[262]

Even here, Riemann and Schering are still present, though it is hard to see why Abraham might have written this if he supported so conservative a performance as Cape recorded, and in that case the edition provided in the booklet may have been edited to match what was on the recording. Certainly none of the five sources listed in the booklet (the *Historical Anthology of Music*, Pirrotta's authoritative CMM edition and three by Wolf) removes text from the melismas, so a deliberate decision was clearly made in this case to follow Riemann's theory.

In the History of Music in Sound we still hear the same romanticised approach to singing the texts as in the Anthologie Sonore recordings.[263] And though there are some performances for voices alone, the pitching is often so insecure and the vibrato so wide that the lack of interest in all-vocal performances during this whole period is easy to understand. It simply did not work well with the singing styles of the period.[264]

Similarly, the influence of Ficker's *Sederunt* is still strongly felt in the 1956 Pro Musica Antiqua recording for Archiv.[265] The scoring is restrained, using singers over a string cantus firmus, but the speeds and dynamic variations reflect very closely Ficker's 1930 edition. The opening section ends almost twice as fast as it began after the same gradual accelerando demanded by Ficker and reproduced in the early 1950s by Eugen Jochum and the Orchestra of Bavarian Radio.[266] In the same way, new sections tend to begin much slower, then speed up. The early music movement, for all its pretensions to historical authenticity – so strongly implied by the presentation of the Archiv series with its meticulous documentation (on separately typed record cards inserted in the foldout record sleeves) of times, dates, venues, producers and editions – is here simply joining in a modern performance tradition, bringing nothing of its own bar the reduced scoring.[267] Also clearly influenced by Ficker is Dart's recording from *c*. 1967 of Perotin's *Alleluya Nativitas* whose sleeve note presents the

music as analogous to the massive walls of Notre Dame:[268] the performance, by self-consciously virile tenors accompanied by an organ cantus
firmus (played by the organist of Notre Dame, Pierre Cochereau), proceeds at a rock-solid 48 beats per minute.[269]

More surprising is to find Riemann's theory still being performed by
early music groups in the 1980s and 1990s. The Ensemble Gilles Binchois,
in 1987, recorded Dufay's *Ce jour de l'an* with an instrumental introduction
and end melismas framing three-part voices with instruments strengthening the vocal parts, just as indicated in Riemann's edition of 1906.[270] The
Medieval Ensemble of London treated the piece similarly in their complete Dufay songs set of 1981.[271] As recently as 1999 Cantica Symphonia,
directed by Kees Boeke, were recording Dufay masses with instrumental melismas.[272] Riemann's assumptions about the nature of art song
are alive and flourishing and seem to be ineradicable from what is now
medieval music. On another track of their Dufay disc the Ensemble Gilles
Binchois play a contratenor on recorder an octave higher than written,
just as in the Anthologie Sonore in 1937.[273] In the Medieval Ensemble of
London's performance of Dufay's *Reveillies vous*, on the same set, a solo
voice is introduced and then accompanied instrumentally, except for the
words 'Charle gentil' (texted in all parts in the sources) which are sung
unaccompanied by three singers, a simulation of the practice supposed
by Apel in 1950 and Reaney in 1955 (see above).[274] In their 1979 recording of the songs of Matteo da Perugia, the Medieval Ensemble of London
perform *Pour bel acueil* after the manner of Schering's edition of 1931.[275]

The multi-coloured ensembles advocated by Schering, Ficker,
Geiringer and Mertin, among others, are so well represented in the
record catalogues to this day as to need little further comment. One
of the most popular advocates of that approach, René Clemencic, was
himself a pupil of Mertin in Vienna, and his orchestrations and dramati-
sations have a venerable tradition behind them, albeit a modern one. The
Oriental approach, likewise, has been widely adopted and developed.[276]
What is interesting, though, is that neither of these approaches began to
be realised in performance until some thirty years after they were first
espoused by Schering and Schneider. As well as the interruption caused
by German isolation in the 1930s, followed by the Second World War,
there seem to be two causes worth exploring. First 'medieval' instruments
in reproduction were hardly available until the late 1950s, when German
makers began to produce a range of Renaissance wind instruments with
which performers could re-create the exotic ensembles scholars had long
been describing from pictures. Most medieval music in the 1960s and

1970s was performed not on medieval but on Renaissance or Arabic instruments. And from this followed the second cause, which was the rapidly increasing demand for medieval music in concert and on record. The colourful bands of the New York Pro Musica, the Waverly Consort, Musica Reservata and the Early Music Consort of London were immensely popular, performing to packed houses in full-size concert halls. At the same time, and arguably as part of the same movement, recordings and concerts brought music of other cultures into Western musical life, and cross-fertilisation between these two highly attractive alternative new musics was inevitable. Both offered novelty without the challenge presented by modern music, and partly for that reason tended to attract rather similar audiences. The 'orchestral' and Oriental hypotheses thus flowered together, benefiting from (and on occasion feeding into) the not dissimilar values of pop culture in the 1960s.

In retrospect, none of this seems very surprising. The advice was there in the editions and the general histories, culled from scholarly articles and books stretching back to the early years of the century. What else could performers think than that it was well founded? What else should they have done? Once it became a run-away commercial success, what else could they have done? It was only the scaling down of medieval groups, as popular interest moved on during the 1970s with minimalism beginning to offer alternatives for the anti-avant-garde, that in due course made room for a new view of medieval performance to flourish and recapture the public's imagination. And in that process scholarship once again had a vital role to play. But scholarship would not on its own have been enough to get the all-vocal hypothesis off the ground. As David Fallows has remarked, and as we shall see in the following chapter, Christopher Page's original proposal of a medieval *a cappella* practice made little impression until he assembled his own group and showed how all-vocal performances might work.[277]

CONCLUSION

It remains to be seen how far research will vindicate the instrumental hypothesis. It was only a hypothesis, and one based initially on little more than an observation by the Stainers about texting in the Canonici manuscript. Other early fifteenth-century manuscripts, as they became available in Wolf, showed a similar pattern (though not consistently, as Adler pointed out). Pictures showed instrumentalists with singers. Archives showed that both were employed by courts and sometimes performed at the same occasions. The rest was speculation. Much of the modern performance tradition for medieval music thus rests on ideas invented, and presented (arguably misrepresented) as historical, by academics. The situation might seem less dire if more evidence had emerged in the interim, but it did not. The arguments that Fallows was rebutting in his seminal article of 1983 – the article that first provided the all-vocal movement with a broad basis in evidence – were the same ones that had been repeated over and over since the early days: texting, the Decameron, Il Solazzo, the Feast of the Pheasant, and so on. All that happened afterwards was that individuals continued to apply their imaginations to the situation they found, so that beliefs piled up one on another; and if one works back through them in search of their origins, one ends up back at Riemann in 1905.

For scholars that might be a matter for some concern. For performers, however, the lack of evidence for most of the features scholars proposed is not an issue. Invention is a necessary part of their work, so that maintaining a clear distinction between the provable and what is guessed or made up is pointless; what matters is the total result. We cannot therefore expect performers to be more meticulous than the scholars they read and consult: the responsibility for what they do is ours to a larger degree than, reviewing their work for example, we may appreciate. Having said that, one of the worrying things to emerge from looking at the relationship between scholarship and performance is the way in which some of the wilder ideas of the scholars continue to fascinate and be developed by performers long after they have been discredited in academic circles. It is easy to understand why. Performers thrive on variety and colour and surprise. It is much easier to make an effect with a performance in which voices and exotic instruments combine and alternate in changing groupings than with a voice and two viols, let alone three unaccompanied voices. And it is arguably more fun for the performers. So while it is easy enough to introduce a novel idea into the performance tradition it is much harder to get it out again. The way to bring about radical change is therefore not to try to stop groups doing things for which there is no evidence, but to persuade them to do new things for which there is evidence, or to set up new groups for oneself. For the moment, though, and despite the success of the all-vocal alternative, Riemann, Schering, Ficker and their colleagues are still a powerful force. The remains of their work are scattered all over our view of medieval music and are probably ineradicable from the public perception of a multi-coloured musical Middle Ages. It may be easier if history vindicates them, for we shall probably never remove them.

CHAPTER 2

The re-invention of the a cappella *hypothesis*

TOWARDS THE *A CAPPELLA* HYPOTHESIS

The modern literature advocating unaccompanied vocal ('*a cappella*') performance of medieval polyphony contains no suggestion that this view had been held once before. The assumption of vocal performance we've seen in writings before Stainer and Riemann seems to have been forgotten, even more so than the early history of the voices-and-instruments hypothesis. Consequently a certain amount of old research has been redone in recent times. To take but one example, Adler's 1909 article for the Riemann Festschrift, discussed in the preceding chapter, contained many points that were made afresh in the 1960s and again in the 1990s.[1] Adler's arguments, as we have seen, were drowned by the tide of opinion in favour of instrumental performance, and after so many decades in which instrumental participation went unquestioned it is hardly surprising that his contribution should have been, to all intents and purposes, lost. At least Adler was writing at a time when the assumption of vocal performance was still a recent memory. Theodore Kroyer was in a weaker position when in 1925 he attempted tentatively to revive the idea, and we have seen how his isolated dissent was in due course used by Schering for political ends. Support for Kroyer after the early 1930s would hardly have been possible. Thus Kroyer was long since forgotten by the time the idea of occasional vocal performance was floated again in the later 1950s.

Equally, we have also seen that vocal performances happened during the first half of the twentieth century, and that musicologists occasionally spoke in favour of them. Reviewing the Hamburg concerts in 1924 Besseler praised an all-vocal performance of Dunstable's *Quam pulcra es* and preferred the 1922 Karlsruhe vocal performance of *Der wallt hat sich entlawbet* to the instrumentally accompanied version heard in Hamburg.[2]

All-vocal performances of Dufay were recorded by Sir Richard Terry and the choir of Westminster Cathedral in 1930;[3] and in 1938–9 Louise Dyer's L'Oiseau Lyre label issued several discs of thirteenth- and fifteenth-century music sung *a cappella* by the Chorale Yvonne Gouverné.[4] The spate of medieval music recordings from the 1950s in the HMV and Archiv historical series contains a number of all-vocal performances and contrasting unaccompanied sections within pieces.[5] Perhaps not coincidentally, the Westminster Cathedral recordings, issued in the Columbia History of Music by Ear and Eye series, are the work of a British choir, steeped in the continuous tradition of unaccompanied singing that was to play such a vital part in the all-vocal movement of the 1980s, and they are singing sacred music, in which the question is less pressing and unaccompanied performance easier for a musicologist of the period to accept. The Anthologie Sonore discs, on the other hand, present almost exclusively accompanied performances, even of sacred music. Recordings from 1935/36 of extracts from Machaut's Mass and Dufay's Mass 'Se la face ay pale', conducted respectively by Guillaume de Van and Safford Cape, use brass and woodwind to reinforce and stabilise the vibrato-rich singing.[6] By the time of the 1950s discs, in the HMV History of Music in Sound and the Archiv series, Cape – who directed the performances on both – had changed his view enough to admit several examples of unaccompanied vocal performance. Almost invariably, however, they are pieces in which all voices are texted in the sources, so that this is a matter of historical accuracy rather than aesthetic choice. In defence of this overwhelming preference for instrumental performance, it is tempting to go on to say that the ensemble singing in these recordings, whether from the 1930s or the 1950s, is so execrable in imprecision of pitch and timing that it is hardly surprising that unaccompanied performance was not taken seriously as a general medieval practice; but to say that is to beg so many questions of period style and taste as to be almost worthless as an argument. We shall return to this question later, but for the moment it is more interesting to point to the coincidence of date between these later recordings (HMS II/III issued in 1953, Cape's Archiv discs recorded in 1953 and 1956) and the first suggestions in the scholarly literature since Kroyer that unaccompanied performance might indeed have been a medieval practice.

Of all the early examples of enthusiasm for *a cappella* performance the most interesting are Besseler's almost passing remarks in support of the Karlsruhe and Hamburg instances. Besseler would be especially concerned in his scholarship with the place of fifteenth-century music in

what he saw as the developing history of harmony, and this points to a recurring relationship to which we shall return. It is worth bearing in mind,
too, the coincidence of date between Besseler's 1924 review and Kroyer's
research favouring vocal performance, published the following year. The
defensiveness of Kroyer's article, prescient in view of the trouble he was
to have a decade later with Schering, is not hard to understand in the
context of all the other writing on performance practice from the first
quarter of the century supporting instrumental accompaniment. And
the brevity of Besseler's comments perhaps needs to be read in that light.
The extent to which he was struck by the Dunstable performance, in
particular, and the fact that he remembered the Karlsruhe vocal performance clearly enough to prefer it two years later, both indicate a more
than passing taste for voices without instruments in medieval music, but
a taste that he would then have found hard to justify other than on aesthetic grounds. Kroyer was perhaps more courageous, but to little more
effect. In his later work on the changing language of fifteenth-century
music, Besseler argued that already in Dufay's mature masses instrumental accompaniment was no longer used, and that the *a cappella* practice
assumed for later Netherlands polyphony was already being introduced,
which is more or less what Riemann proposed in 1909,[7] though few
would have agreed during the intervening years. For Besseler, Dufay
represented the beginning of modern music, encapsulating progressive
harmonic thinking. By imagining his mature music without instruments,
Besseler was invoking *a cappella* performance as another and desirable
aspect of musical modernity; in this sense it is clearly linked to the
a cappella ideal that so fired German musicologists of Ludwig's generation as they rediscovered Palestrina.[8]

But mass music was one thing, chanson entirely another, and Besseler
found the idea that songs might also be unaccompanied far harder to
accept, indeed impossible. His ambivalence is nowhere more evident
than in a paper delivered to the International Musicological Society at
its fifth congress in Utrecht in 1952. Here he provides a number of pictures
of music-making from the fourteenth and fifteenth centuries, all of them
showing a group of singers, without instrumentalists, clustered around a
copy of what is evidently mensural music. His earlier examples include
two from a Machaut manuscript and one from the Chantilly codex; and
Besseler naturally comments on this conjunction of music and pictures:

That in all three pictures only song is indicated, without participation of instruments, surprises us. . . . The surprise lies in this, that the main contents of the

Chantilly Codex, the three- and four-voice song compositions, was undoubtedly meant for voice with instrumental accompaniment. Were the accompanying voices of such music also sung from time to time, when it was really necessary? Or did the minstrels form a group by themselves that remained separate from the singers?[9]

Towards the end of his paper Besseler argues that women began to take part in the performance of chansons during the fifteenth century and that this provides the origin of the practice that led to the sixteenth-century madrigal.[10] What he cannot bring himself to suggest is that, since his pictures all show *a cappella* performance in this period, the *a cappella* performance of madrigals would also, following his argument, have had its origins here. For Besseler, the assumption of instrumental accompaniment was so deep-rooted that even clear evidence to the contrary must, he believed, be misleading.

Given Besseler's extreme reluctance to take his pictorial evidence at face value, it is easier to understand the tentative nature of Gilbert Reaney's proposal along similar lines, made four years later in an article from 1956. Reaney's view was at first hardly more enthusiastic than Besseler's; while Besseler asks whether unaccompanied vocal performance might from time to time have happened, Reaney takes a small step further and proposes that all-vocal performance was a significant medieval practice, although it is clear that he believes that it was exceptional, and that performance with instrumental accompaniment was the norm. Indeed he subscribes fully to the view that contrast was an essential property of medieval performances, both within and between pieces,[11] and he contributes to the Oriental hypothesis by offering further arguments for heterophonic instrumental decoration in the Arabic manner.[12] Nevertheless, he points to miniatures showing three singers around a lectern, in one case singing 'Presidentes',[13] the first word of a surviving three-voice motet in *Fauvel*, which he uses to argue for vocalisation of motet tenors. And he usefully quotes the description of *trumpetum* offered by Paulus Paulirinus of Prague, *c.* 1460, who describes lines in imitation of trumpets as 'for four voices',[14] thus calling into question the instrumental performance claimed for them by a number of earlier writers. But it is also clear that he is not entirely comfortable with the idea of unaccompanied performance, even in these special cases, apparently on account of the results in modern times:

An appropriate method of playing and singing has to be cultivated. Vibrato, both in voices and instruments, should be avoided, except in special cases. The tone of the voice should be as smooth as the unvarying tone of the cornett, viol or recorder. Otherwise, only chaos can result from the clash of constantly crossing parts[15]

which is very much the problem we perceive today in the recordings from the 1930s and 1950s. As Reaney realised, and as Page has since argued in detail, where the tuning is not precise and the voices absolutely secure, the result can be harmonically confusing.[16] Here we touch on one of the most significant beliefs about medieval music, one that profoundly influenced writings on it throughout the twentieth century. It was abstract music, not expressive of the texts it set; it was characterised by clarity of harmony and texture, features which, as we have seen, were until the 1980s thought to be best projected in instrumental performances. Here Reaney asks that, if there must be voices without instruments, they be as instrumental in sound as possible. We shall see that there is an important sense in which the proponents of vocal performance through the 1980s and 1990s were making exactly the same point.[17] For the same reason he preferred coun-tertenors to women singers: 'The purity of this kind of voice means that it is usually more effective than the typical soprano voice for performances of medieval music, though it is evident that women often performed secu-lar music in the Middle Ages, and of course sacred music in nunneries'.[18] The typical soprano voice in 1966, of course, was the problem, for it made use of a much wider vibrato than became customary during the early music boom of the 1970s and 1980s. In the end, though, Reaney simply did not believe that most of the music he saw could be anything but instrumental: Machaut's lower voices 'look so unvocal with their pas-sagework and leaps . . . ',[19] and although he wrote two motets texted in all parts which 'could very well have been for voices only', 'The important part played by instruments at this period and the melismatic charac-ter of much of the music suggests the support of even texted voices by instruments.'[20] For Reaney, then, *a cappella* performance had some histori-cal justification but was aesthetically problematic, and the aesthetic prob-lems tended to downplay the historical justification. Fifty years of almost unquestioned instrumental supremacy, in the sense that instrumental participation was taken for granted and seen as essentially characteristic of the musical language, taken together with the largely unrelated sounds of modern singing, left little room for an *a cappella* hypothesis to flourish.

Given the weight of existing assumptions about medieval music it is hardly surprising that the revived *a cappella* hypothesis had its first power-ful advocate in a student of documentary and not musical evidence. Nor is it surprising to find it first appearing in connection with sacred music, where the participation of instruments was easier to rule out. Edmund Bowles was at the time a Senior Program Administrator at IBM; his title comes straight to the point: 'Were musical instruments used in the liturgical service during the Middle Ages?' Bowles rejects archival evidence as sparse and, when concerning secular music, not transferable. As far as 'internal stylistic evidence' goes he is able to show, by switching between articles from different periods, that scholars cannot agree among themselves, which would seem to invalidate it as conclusive proof. He also rejects evidence from pictures because groups of musicians can have a symbolic purpose; visual arrangements are often influenced by mystery plays, he says, and for both reasons pictures are not reliably realistic; in addition we cannot be sure that they are performing liturgical music. Bowles prefers as evidence the wealth of prohibitions issued by clerics against minstrels in church and the inability of instrumentalists to read polyphonic notation. Only the organ, and in some special cases trumpets for fanfares, were permitted. By taking a more rigorous approach to the interpretation of the evidence, refusing any that is not specific, Bowles effectively excluded a large part of the evidence that had been used to argue for instrumental participation in sacred music during the preceding half-century. His conclusion shows a realistic anticipation that his findings are going to be unpopular:

Lest these conclusions should throw a blanket of gloom over the enthusiasts of medieval instruments, let it be urged that there is both intellectual and emotional satisfaction to be derived from coming as close as possible to an historically faithful performance. Even though the 'orchestral texture' may be denied, one should never feel that medieval church music is dead; or that in order to make it appeal to modern listeners, the sonorities of many instruments are required to bring it to life.[21]

One enthusiast for instruments who felt exactly that was the performer and scholar Robert Donington. Replying in the same journal, in a contribution ripe with colourful Huizingan generalisations, Donington pleaded on artistic grounds for retaining instruments in medieval sacred music: 'it is palpably not unhistorical to include a rich selection. The effect in performance becomes then incomparably richer and for that very reason more convincing as a medieval product.'[22] This is as nice an example as one could desire of the interdependence in a scholar-performer's mind between the colourful Middle Ages and orchestrated performances: the music is read so completely in that light that the two become inseparable ingredients in a unified view of the medieval world, whose unity is then taken as evidence. As Bowles remarks in his reply, 'Mr Donington deals mainly with inferences and hopeful suggestion, whereas I prefer to deal in what the record actually shows. He sees what he would like to see, more instruments; but I have reluctantly forced myself to look into the mirror of research.'[23]

The mid-1960s brought a new sense of urgency into the academic study of performance practice. Both Reaney and Frank Harrison begin their contributions to the Reese Festschrift, published in 1966, with comments on the need for new work,[24] and it seems possible that they were spurred on by the growing popularity of medieval music in performance and by seeing so much being invented by performers without the support of any substantial evidence. As Harrison writes,

The results of the absence of even the most elementary notions of performance practice may sometimes remind one of Angela Thirkill's headmistress Miss Sparling, who countered her history mistress's objections to anachronistic costumes in a proposed show with the words: '*Anything* looks nice in a pageant; why shouldn't Boadicea wear green tights and a yellow wig?'

Or in Reaney's words,

Strangely enough, it is too often left to the amateur who lacks the scruples of the musicologist and therefore assumes that any vocal and instrumental combination is acceptable, largely because of the variety and color of medieval instruments.[25]

Harrison's main purpose, therefore, is to specify appropriate medieval instruments for the surviving repertories of medieval music, so that, for example, the lower voices of songs would be played on instruments that in the Middle Ages would have had the necessary pitches, rather than on whatever a modern reproduction or Renaissance substitute happened to be able to do. Along the way, he considers the untexted lower voices of sacred pieces written in chanson style, produced in England and to some extent in France in the early fifteenth century. Given that there is no evidence for appropriate instruments in church,

The only possible hypothesis is that wordless tenor and contratenor parts in sacred music in chanson style were vocalized. This is a possibility that the musical traditions of the past three hundred years, with their bias towards instrumental music and an artificial style of singing, have made it difficult for musicologists to accept. But thinking has been moving that way, and it is now rarely held, for example, that the wordless *caudae* of vocal conducti were played on instruments.[26]

He goes on to offer 'the superb Bach performances of "Les Swingles Singers" and the jazz vocalizations of Annie Ross' as possible analogies. Nonetheless, instrumental participation in secular music is taken for granted, and indeed provides the *raison d'être* for the article and its title, 'Tradition and innovation in instrumental usage 1100–1450'. Harrison's conclusion points to a scholar's irritation with the increasing confidence of performers in their presentations of 'medieval' music:

The anything-looks-nice-in-a-pageant-ism that too often foists a rag-bag of sounds from pseudo-Renaissance instruments on the music of two or three centuries earlier is largely due to the failure of medieval musicologists to give a positive lead to would-be performers of the music they discuss.[27]

Reaney directed his own ensemble, The London Medieval Group, in the late 1960s and early 1970s, using a variety of instruments from different periods.[28] The thinking behind his scorings is set out in passing, but with some fascinating details, in this same article from 1966, showing how carefully he brought together evidence from medieval pictures and what seemed to be musical common sense. Yet even this scholar felt the need to go somewhat beyond the evidence from time to time, as suggested by his very engaging but telling apology for using bells in certain sequences and motet tenors: 'Even these [tenor parts] could be intended for voices imitating instruments, but surely the musicologist should drop his mask occasionally and display the musician behind it . . .'[29]

While it is certainly true that, in the 1950s and 1960s, musicologists often put on their own performances, on the whole, the most successful performers did their own musicology, maintaining an arms-length relationship with scholars. (To some extent this is still the case, although the close participation of scholars in the preparation of concerts and recordings by professional performers is more common now than when Harrison was writing.) While Cape relied on Charles van den Borren for advice, and Greenberg called on Gustave Reese and, for sacred monophony, Rembert Weakland, groups active in the later 1960s tended to produce performing materials and formulate interpretative strategies in-house. Thus the American-based Waverly Consort, popular for their arrays of early instruments and lively arrangements, relied on their own members, as did Capella Antiqua München and the Studio der frühen Musik in Germany (later in Switzerland), Musica Reservata in England, and – perhaps the most successful to the public eye – David

Munrow's Early Music Consort of London. With the single exception of the Studio der frühen Musik, whose instrumentarium was
restricted by economic constraints and the need to travel between
concerts in a single car,[30] all these groups made indiscriminate use of
medieval and Renaissance, and sometimes Baroque, instruments in
their performances of medieval music. To take just two examples from
hundreds on record, soon after Harrison's article Musica Reservata
recorded Adam de la Halle's late thirteenth-century motet *Au cuer/Je
ne/Jolietement* with two tenors and baritone accompanied by crumhorn
(invented sometime in the fifteenth century), tenor rebec (in the tenor
size probably a fifteenth-century invention) and nakers;[31] five years
later The Early Music Consort recorded Machaut's virelai *Douce dame
jolie, c.* 1340, which appears in the manuscripts as a monophonic song,
in a scoring by Munrow for tenor, chorus, sopranino recorder (which
first appears in Praetorius in 1618/19), cornetts (first appeared in the
fifteenth century), rebecs, citole (invented in the 1960s on the basis of
Tinctoris's description of *c.* 1487), and tabor.[32] Harrison had legitimate
grounds for complaint, therefore, but was nevertheless years ahead of
his time, for such practices continued to be the norm until the Studio's
pupils and followers became active a full decade later.[33]

One of the reasons that nothing much was done with Bowles' argument or Reaney's suggestion (let alone Harrison's call for a more responsible attitude) was simply that medieval music groups were becoming
so successful, and what made them appealing was not just, perhaps not
mainly, the music, but as much as anything the arrays of strange and
amusing instruments that they presented on stage and on the covers of
their records. Records were issued emphasising the instruments rather
than the music. Syntagma Musicum's 'Music of the Middle Ages and
the Renaissance' was typical of many in providing sleeve notes under
just two headings, 'Syntagma Musicum' and 'The Instruments'.[34] The
earlier of the two surveys by David Munrow, entitled 'The Mediaeval
Sound', was issued on the low-priced Oryx label, its cover festooned
with Renaissance instruments from Munrow's collection. Only its sub-
title, in very much smaller print, explains that this is only a survey of
early woodwind instruments.[35] Munrow's later, and much more ambitious survey, whose 'booklet' was published simultaneously as a book by
Oxford University Press's Music Department, begins its Preface,

In ten years of giving concerts of early music there is one question which I have
been asked with predictable regularity: please will you explain the instruments?

This book is a response to the hundreds of people who have asked me that question.[36]

But it also shows how scholarly concerns of the sort voiced by Harrison were at last, by the mid-1970s, beginning to filter through to the more aware among performers:

The division of the book into two parts (before and after *c.* 1400) is intended to show which instruments properly belong to the Middle Ages and which to the Renaissance, a fundamental point that, through the enthusiasm of early music performers (including myself), has sometimes been overlooked.[37]

Munrow's preface is dated November 1975. Fresh in his mind as he wrote may have been a scathing attack on players and makers of early instruments published only a few months earlier, in the July issue of *Early Music*, by Jeremy Montagu of Musica Reservata:

[P]layers are not willing to learn the proper instruments and will only play those that are easy... Players must realize that if they use cornetts and sackbuts, crumhorns, rauschpfeife, gemshorns and viols, all of which date from the end of the 15th century at the earliest, and recorders, which are only a century at the most earlier, in 12th to 14th century music, they might just as well use oboes, clarinets and violins.[38]

But few then had Montagu's specialist knowledge. A useful measure of general attitudes to medieval music performance can be found at any time in the pages of *Gramophone* magazine. In the later 1960s, the years immediately following Harrison's article, reviewers of early music there included Edward Greenfield, Mary Berry, Denis Arnold and Brian Trowell (and the first two are still contributing). Greenfield's review from May 1967 of Thomas Binkley's *Carmina burana* gives a good indication of what informed music lovers thought.

Some of the items... have a real kinship with modern 'pop' music. What the guitar is to Messrs Lennon, McCartney and Harrison, so the long-necked lute was to these anonymous medieval musicians... It is hardly going too far to say that Messrs Lennon, McCartney and Harrison might be just the ones to find fresh inspiration in this often oriental-sounding music, just as they have in Eastern music already.... Mr Binkley has relied considerably on oriental parallels, for many of these [accompaniment] techniques, and the instruments themselves are still in use in countries from Persia to Morocco. I am not at all sure what authority he has for his deductions in detail, but the results are always fresh and invigorating, and to a non-specialist like myself, they are nothing less than ear-opening.[39]

Greenfield was not alone. In the March 1968 issue of *Gramophone* even the musicologist Brian Trowell was writing of another Binkley disc, 'The last song alone would make the fortune of any pop group today'.[40] The pop parallel was enticing. The Beatles and Binkley, like so many at the time, were interested in learning and borrowing from non-Western music, on the face of it for different reasons but hardly so different that results could not seem similar to a listener with limited interest in one or the other.[41] Ethnic and Early Musics were both alternatives to the un-compromising modernism of the avant-garde, alternatives that so many hoped to find (including many avant-gardists), and it is hardly surprising to see them meeting from time to time. Machaut was reworked by pop musicians at just the same moment that 'early' musicians were re-creating North African habits of playing and decoration and Stockhausen was writing *Stimmung*. It may have seemed more natural to Greenfield in the late 1960s than it seems to us to suppose that Binkley was bringing a sense of the period fascination with Eastern-inspired alternative lifestyles to his view of the Orientalism of medieval music. The tradition started by Ribera in the 1920s and developed in Central European musicol-ogy by Schering and Schneider around 1930 finally found its home in performances now precisely because it at last seemed musically and spir-itually natural to combine Eastern and Western ingredients in art and thought, and in all spheres of life, even down to clothes and smells. It was a smaller step than one might now imagine (unless one lived through that time) from kaftans and jossticks to rababs and drones, and back again.[42] Consequently Greenfield is (unwittingly?) pointing to a circularity that included pop and early music and their common interest in alternatives, and one whose decline in the late 1970s – with a corresponding growth in purer and more literal readings of the musical text – coincided exactly with the new realism of the times.

But other currents are faintly present in these years too. Denis Arnold was clearly hoping for more from 'the medieval sound' when in 1969 he wrote of the Purcell Consort's Machaut Mass,

The other thing which is both effective and, presumably, historical, is the pro-nunciation of the Latin in what is said to be the fourteenth-century way. This gives something of the cutting edge to the voice that the Musica Reservata singers are obviously aiming at, without the unpleasantness of tone which often disfigures their performance, and may point the way towards a solution of a genuine problem.[43]

Musica Reservata, and Jantina Noorman's voice in particular, was a regular bugbear of Arnold's in *Gramophone* around this time, but nevertheless this very perceptive observation at least hints at a sense that medieval polyphony needed a clarity from singers that it was not getting in conventional performances. In general, though, during these years, multi-instrument performances of medieval music had the field to themselves and were enthusiastically welcomed by reviewers and public alike.

Consequently it is hardly surprising that voices were so little considered. It was the instruments that sold tickets and records, and incidentally provided work for a small army of players and instrument builders who would otherwise have had to find careers outside music. The economics of the early music revival offered little reason for any existing group to take *a cappella* performance seriously. Put together with the mass of written material provided by twentieth-century scholars supporting much of what these groups were doing – Munrow's Middle Ages of bright colours and sharp contrasts was, as we have seen, admirably supported in the scholarly literature[44] – and one may begin to see how unsympathetic all sides of the business would be to any suggestion that medieval practice might have tended in another direction. In this they were supported by most scholars. Just as Reaney, in 1956, had played down the importance of *a cappella* performance in the Middle Ages, so twenty years later Howard Mayer Brown began a large survey of fifteenth-century chanson performance with Besseler's evidence for vocal performance, plus some of his own; yet the rest of the article – all but two of its thirty-five pages (excluding footnotes) – could concentrate on instrumental combinations, which still appeared to be the norm.[45]

THE *A CAPPELLA* HYPOTHESIS REVIVED

Yet at the same time as the instrument-based early music movement was joining the European cultural mainstream, one scholar was gradually changing his mind. In a conversational article in the Plamenac Festschrift, published in 1969, Gilbert Reaney returned to the question of *a cappella* performance, and this time was markedly more enthusiastic. What seems to have led him to change his view was the experience of editing the repertory of *Early Fifteenth Century Music*.[46] Many of the songs he found himself transcribing had fragments of text in the lower voices, and in order to arrive at an edition he inevitably had to consider what this might mean. Noting that these text fragments tended to occur only where the lower voices were involved in imitation, he proposed that text was only written-in where it was not simultaneously declaimed in all voices. Supporting his hypothesis he was able to draw on pieces surviving in one manuscript with untexted lower voices and in another with the tenor texted, the longer notes broken up into short repeated pitches in order to accommodate the syllables. He began his article with perhaps the boldest suggestion of all, that since the only pieces fully texted in all voices were the polytextual motets and songs, where each voice had a different text, perhaps it follows not that all other lower voices were instrumental but rather that they were simultaneously texted with the text provided under the cantus. Text, in other words, was only indicated where it differed; text incipits indicated that the rest of the text was also to be sung. This was certainly the single most original suggestion since Schering, and, arguably, considerably more plausible. Yet Reaney never seems to have doubted that instrumental accompaniment was normal.

Needless to say, I am not trying to suggest that instruments did not perform the lower parts of late medieval polyphonic music. . . . I am convinced that the use of partially complete texts confirms a vocal performance, though I am inclined to agree with Professor Besseler that instruments may often have been used as well.[47]

The consequence of Reaney's view, though he never puts it quite this directly, is a performance practice in which all voices are sung, though they may also be accompanied by instruments. Were this view to be proposed today, many might feel it a cautious compromise between conflicting views, albeit one that required considerable editorial work (or improvisation in performance) adding texts to lower voices.[48] But there is little sign that it had any direct impact at the time. Yet, although he received little credit for it, Reaney's boldness was to be justified repeatedly over the next decade, as documentary evidence was presented to show that vocal performance of all voices of composed polyphony was a lot more normal than had been supposed.

A less compromising rejection of instrumental participation, albeit in monophonic, not polyphonic song, came just three years later – 1972 – in a study of the chansons of the troubadours and trouvères by Hendrik van der Werf:

Next to nothing is known about the circumstances under which the chansons were performed, yet there is a persistent theory that the chansons were always performed to instrumental accompaniment. I have been able to find neither the origin of this theory nor any substantial evidence for it. It may be true that 'the jongleur' [a concept van der Werf exposed in the preceding paragraph as partly modern] could both play on instruments and perform chansons, but assuming on this basis that the chansons were accompanied is scarcely logical; one may

just as well assume that the jongleur did a juggling act when reciting a chanson, or that his bear danced to it and his monkey climbed a tree.[49]
. . .
Considering the complete absence of documentary evidence of instrumental accompaniment, it seems unwise to maintain that as a rule the chansons were accompanied. Perhaps the chansons were accompanied but, in all truth, we can find no reason for this assumption other than our own wishful thinking.[50]

At the time this was a very striking conclusion, for it seemed to over-turn so many assumptions found both in the literature and on record. Although it applied only to monophony, it was a conclusion that, as I recall, stuck in the mind as more studies, through the rest of the decade, began to notice evidence for unaccompanied performance of polyphony.

The first of the document-based studies from the 1970s, whose accu-mulated influence considerably eased the task of the English *a cappella* enthusiasts in the following decade, was a doctoral dissertation on poly-phonic mass performance by James Igoe completed just two years after Reaney's article in 1971. After a survey of work to date, which offers a rather sketchy outline of the Riemann/Schering story, Igoe trawls the secondary literature, extracting evidence on performance practice. His conclusions are clear and thought-provoking: although instruments might on occasions be used at mass, and the organ was sometimes used to accompany or alternate with plainsong, 'all parts of the [polyphonic] compositions, i.e. discantus, tenor, and contratenor, were intended by the composer to be specifically vocal parts'.[51] Moreover, the singers of tenor and contratenor parts performed in a way that was different from the singers of the texted lines:

Almost never is the tenorista said to 'sing'; instead he 'says' the part, or 'does' or 'makes' the part, or 'pronounces' the part, or 'holds' the part. Never does the tenorista 'play' the part, although *ludere* is frequently used in connection with the organista. . . . From this reasoning and from other evidence, too, it seems that the tenorista must have sung *in a special way*[52]

and Igoe goes on to argue for partial texting or vocalisation of the un-texted voices. That conclusion could have been Igoe's greatest contri-bution to the debate had his work been better known, for the question of what was done with the lower voices remained the principal musical issue in any performance practice debate. As it was, he never wrote it up as an article, and consequently it appears to have been little con-sidered. So it was a contribution by Craig Wright to an International Musicological Society session some six years later that seems to have struck those present as the start of a significant reassessment of the evidence for vocal performance.[53] (I add the qualification, 'those present', because I have found in conversation with scholars that while those who heard the 'Euphony' session were struck by the novelty and importance of Wright's proposals, those who were not there remained unaware of them until the conference proceedings were published in 1981.) Wright showed that among references to the performance of polyphony from around the third quarter of the fifteenth century that were available to him, almost all described *a cappella* performance, the remaining few pointed to purely instrumental performance, and none to voice with instrumental accompaniment. Documentary evidence from the period shows no evidence that instruments played with singers in church; even the organ was probably unable to do so on account of its distance from the singers. Moreover, in Cambrai Cathedral there was no organ, yet the choirbooks still have untexted lower voices.[54] It follows that they were sung, 'despite the absence of words and no matter how disjunct the musical line', though how remains an open question. The core chansonniers lack lower-voice text because they were not performance sources at all but rather repositories or presentation manuscripts; performances, as shown in surviving pictures, used single oblong sheets. Thus the change that occurred in chanson manuscripts from texting only the superius in the earlier sources to texting all voices in the very late fifteenth- or early sixteenth-century manuscripts involved no change in performance but only in scribal habit. Here he was implicitly disagreeing with a proposal of Louise Litterick's, outlined in an AMS paper given in 1976 (footnoted by Wright), that this marked a change from instrumental accompaniment or vocalisation to fully texted singing. Litterick's paper was also published some years later, in 1980, and without referring back to Wright's (then still unpublished) IMS contribution; so that the chronology of papers and publications here is a useful reminder of the extent to which conference presentations influence the tone and detail of subsequently published work, making the historiography of the subject considerably more complex than the plain sequence of publication dates might suggest. (Perhaps I should add here that having entered musicology around 1976 I recall many of the discussions preceding and following publication of the work discussed from here on, and I am certainly drawing on this experience, often silently, in the remainder of this chapter.)

The title of the session to which Wright's paper belonged, 'Euphony in the Fifteenth Century', is significant, and his contribution needs to be read in the light of it, as an argument that was understood by him and his audience as leading to a more euphonious sound for medieval music than had been cultivated theretofore. In his introduction to the session, Leeman Perkins emphasised the Greek meaning of euphony as 'sweet-voiced', and asked 'What did the composer do – intentionally and purposefully – to *flatter* [my italics] the auditory nerves of his listeners? And did the performers devise or favor – just as intentionally and purposefully – practices that would throw the sonorous character of those works into sharper relief and make their euphony all the more evident to the hearer?' He speaks also of the experience of introducing undergraduates to early fifteenth-century music, celebrating that 'glimmer of recognition as the transition is made from the musical style of the late 14th century to that of Dufay and his generation. The student senses, almost invariably, that a threshold has been crossed, and that the sonorous realm attained is, at last, intrinsically familiar to the ear.'[55] Perkins' words seem to suggest a strong desire for a sweeter and fuller sound for fifteenth-century music, one appropriate to its comfortable familiarity, a sound that would evoke the warmth and relief of a long-awaited home-coming. And more than any other paper in the session it was Wright's that offered it.

Nevertheless, Wright was making proposals that were directly opposed to a long tradition, so that at the same time as he was providing welcome news for some he was of course raising difficult questions for many others. It is worth asking, then, what made it possible for Wright in 1977 to succeed in questioning assumptions made throughout the century, where those who preceded him had failed, for example the almost universally held belief that disjunct lines were by their very nature unvocal? Lloyd Hibberd had made the same point, a lot more forcefully, in 1946, yet had no discernable influence. The sense in which Wright was offering something comfortably familiar may have been one element but could hardly have been decisive. His success in appealing to a much wider range of preconceptions may have had to do with the extent to which his paper offers something for everyone: some radical suggestions about manuscript usage and about the treatment of ligatures (previously sacrosanct, except in the forgotten Adler 1909) alongside a new sound that would make fifteenth-century music seem more appropriately beautiful. Just as significant is the growing willingness among scholars of medieval and early Renaissance music through the 1970s to question universal assumptions, reflecting a growing trend towards seeing the Middle Ages as 'other' than anything familiar to us from more recent times. And musicological work in turn reflected larger trends in scholarship that preferred to emphasise difference and alienation, removing the object of study from its familiar surroundings and presenting it as unfamiliar and, to a larger degree than had previously been thought, unknowable.

It was thus attractively daring, yet in a larger intellectual context very much of its time, to propose that 'unvocal' leaps might belong to sung parts, that ligatures might after all be violable, and that parts that had previously appeared without question to be contrasting might in fact be euphonious – the first two points made by Wright, the third a clear consequence. This element in the development of scholarly arguments in general was certainly one of the factors that made it possible, at last, to question the instrumental hypothesis and be taken seriously. At the same time Wright was offering a sound that, far from being alien, was in fact considerably more familiar than fifteenth-century music had enjoyed in modern times. In this sense his paper, and a sudden rush of work along similar lines to be examined below, pressed a wide range of buttons, expressing an idea whose time had very clearly come.

Wright's paper appeared in print (and in a somewhat sketchy version) only in 1981, when the IMS conference proceedings finally emerged. In the meantime a new view of the iconographic evidence had appeared from James McKinnon, insisting on a far more rigorous distinction between realistic and symbolic representations of music-making than had been required by those, especially Schering, who had previously argued for instrumental participation in liturgical polyphony. McKinnon had little time either for Schering, or for those groups that had been performing mass music with instrumental support in the meantime and who had been citing 'iconographic evidence' as a blanket justification for whatever they preferred; as McKinnon dryly remarks, 'the vast majority of medieval musical iconography is biblical illustration, not depiction of medieval liturgy'.[56] In fact, the absence of instruments from the illustrations considered by McKinnon is so consistent that it merits only a passing mention.[57] His concluding section, however, presents a valuable overview of recent, and not so recent archival studies, emphasising the consistency with which they indicate the absence of instrumentalists from church and chapel choirs. Here lay the other essential, in fact the most essential ingredient required to persuade musicologists in general that *a cappella* performance, at least for sacred music, was unavoidably correct. Archival and art historical evidence was real evidence, in a way that supposition from the music never could be.

*

Christopher Page seems not to have known of Wright's still unpublished IMS paper, nor the spoken presentations by McKinnon preceding publication of his *JAMS* article, when he wrote his 1977 article for *Early Music* which for many is still seen as a turning point in the *a cappella* debate. That all these studies appeared at once was perhaps coincidence, perhaps a reflection of an idea that was so obvious, given Reaney, Igoe, and the previous archival work outlined by McKinnon, as to be unmissable. Drawing only on Reaney 1956 and Hibberd 1946, of the previous studies discussed here, Page offered a text and translation of a passage from Deschamps' *Art de dictier et de fere chancons* of 1392, preceded by a close reading of it that showed Deschamps describing the singing of three-voice chansons in all parts. Because Deschamps was a close follower of Machaut, perhaps his nephew, quite possibly his pupil, this was evidence of great significance; although mentioned briefly by Reaney it was given its due prominence only now. Page's background made his findings the more striking. As an undergraduate, reading English at Balliol College, he had directed The Early Music Group of Oxford, and wrote his first article, for *Early Music*, on the construction of medieval fiddles.[58] He worked as a lutenist with Musica Reservata in the mid-1970s, and at the time of the Deschamps article was directing an instrument-based group consisting mainly of university students, The Early Music Group of York, so he was well aware of the attraction of older assumptions:

The hypothesis that the tenors and contratenors of Machaut's polyphonic chansons were generally performed instrumentally in the 14th century has strong practical appeal. At this present stage of the early music 'revival', crumhorns, viols, sackbuts and other (anachronistic) instruments that can supply these lines at written pitch are readily available, whereas singers willing (and able) to vocalize them are not. Certainly there is no reason to suppose that the apparently entirely vocal performance envisaged by Deschamps was the *only* way in which Machaut's chansons were performed,[59] but this reference should inspire far more experiment with this method of performance. This would please the growing number of musicologists who believe that the question of instrumental participation in various forms of medieval music needs to be re-examined.[60]

The sense of an idea whose time has come could hardly be stronger. Page explicitly claims just that at the opening of his follow-up article in *Early Music* 1982:

We have reached a critical stage in our understanding of the role of instruments in medieval music, both sacred and secular. Few scholars and performers in the English speaking world now believe that instruments generally participated in liturgical music,[61] and lately some deeply entrenched views concerning the use of instruments in the secular repertories have come under scrutiny.[62] We have already reached a position where we cannot tacitly assume significant instrumental involvement in monophonic courtly songs, motets or polyphonic chansons.[63]

Page goes on to attack the multi-coloured strong-contrasts view of the Middle Ages, associating it with Huizinga, and emphasises instead the higher status given by medieval writers to voices over instruments. But the bulk of his 1982 article offers an edition and translation of extracts from a fifteenth-century romance, *Cleriadus et Meliadice*, concerning the composition and performance of polyphonic songs. The evidence is consistent: dancing is accompanied by professional instrumentalists or high-born, and therefore amateur, singers, but not both together. Polyphonic songs are sung in all parts without instrumental accompaniment, the lower voices 'held' more often than 'sung'; and a song is arranged for – 'put on' – a harp, and is performed on it as a solo, without singing.[64] Page's conclusion again points to his own activities as a performer:

We must imagine these pieces performed by equivalent resources, not a voice and several disparate instrumental timbres. It is possible, of course, that singers differentiated their sounds to individualize their parts, yet this still leads to what is, by the standards of an instrumentally accompanied performance, a remarkable homogeneity, as experiment shows. It is surely time to reconsider some very basic notions about the performance of late medieval chansons.[65]

When, in the extract quoted above from the Deschamps article, Page advocated experiment with vocal performance, he had not yet conceived the idea of a new group that would try it out. But it was in April 1977, when the article must already have been complete, that, taking part as an instrumentalist in the first York Early Music Festival, he heard Andrew Parrott's performance of the Machaut Mass with voices only, and was powerfully struck by its grandeur sung unaccompanied.[66]

Parrott had studied at Oxford with Frank Harrison and absorbed from him an awareness that there was far more to be learned about the original circumstances of performance for medieval liturgical music than had been considered so far. Another influential tutor was John Caldwell who had played the organ in the Purcell Consort's largely *a cappella* recording of the Machaut Mass, the recording that first aroused Parrott's interest in the piece.[67] Other Oxford expertise fed into this view of the Mass during the 1970s, especially views of French accentuation from C. A. Robson and of pronunciation from Eric Dobson (Harrison's collaborator in a key edition of medieval English song). Working with Michael Morrow and Musica Reservata Parrott encountered ideas about Pythagorean tuning. And as a research student at Oxford he was himself working on issues of vocal scoring, looking especially at the emergence of the countertenor voice, and coming to the conclusion that it was not a medieval phenomenon. So by the time he came to prepare the York performance, all the ingredients of a new view of the piece were in place; he used original pronunciation and tuning, solo voices without countertenors, and placed the polyphony in a liturgical context. And the performance took place in York Minster. Not surprisingly, the impact was huge, and the concert is still vividly remembered by early music specialists in the audience. As Parrott remembers it,

the whole festival was a heady event. That is to say, a lot of interesting people all pioneering these new ideas were there in the audience, and not just on that night. . . . They were part of the week and had had discussions, [attended] other concerts; so it was the focal point of that festival, and the building was the biggest building, . . . everything was going for [it].[68]

Parrott also attended The Early Music Group of York's concert, and offered to sing with them thereafter.[69] Fallows attended both concerts, and compared Page's instrumental improvisations with those of Binkley (with whom Fallows had previously worked); so that there were opportunities for all three of these key figures to think about the practical implications of vocal performance in the late 1970s. In fact, the development of the *a cappella* hypothesis in Britain from this time onwards owed, as I shall try to suggest, as much to personal contacts between the major participants encouraging one another's views, as it owed to the evidence they used. The same is true of many developments in musicology (and no doubt in most academic fields) and it may be that it is only the loss of so much biographical information on earlier scholars that conceals a similar process from us in examining the growth of the instrumental hypothesis. The teacher – pupil relationship of Riemann and Wolf in the first few years of the century, for example, must have been crucial. But the clustering of a few influential figures around one journal, in whose pages they were continually, and perhaps disproportionately represented, is especially noticeable and plays an important part in the story from here on. The role of the BBC was also vital: it was the BBC that gave Page his first opportunity to record medieval music without instruments; and later it was the BBC that created a further *a cappella* group – the Orlando Consort – precisely in order to provide more concerts of medieval music for voices alone.

Gothic Voices was assembled for a slot on BBC Radio 3's Early Music Forum, broadcast on 24 January 1981. A second broadcast followed on Valentine's Day, preceded by a talk in which – according to the Radio Times – 'Christopher Page sheds startling new light on the Language of

Flowers in the 14th-century garden'.[70] Their first concerts followed (in France) in July 1981, so that by the time Page's second '*a cappella*' article appeared, in *Early Music* 1982, he was already turning his hypothesis into sound, and indeed was already having some influence on the thinking of a number of British scholars. As we shall see, it was an accident that the very first Gothic Voices disc, recorded in September 1981, was of Hildegard and not fourteenth-century song: otherwise his Machaut recording, 'The Mirror of Narcissus', might already have been in the shops when the *Cleriadus et Meliadice* study came out. The article would then have been read somewhat differently, as more of a manifesto, less a further suggestion. But when 'Narcissus' did eventually appear, in late 1983, followed soon after by Parrott's Machaut Mass, their combined impact was very considerable. David Fallows' appreciative review in *Gramophone* is quoted later in this chapter.[71] Reviewing the Parrott Mass in *Early Music* I wrote:

There can be few medieval compositions that performers have treated so badly as Machaut's Mass. Few of the . . . recordings made since . . . the early 1950s have come anywhere near doing justice to Machaut's likely intentions, either historically or musically. Andrew Parrott's recording sets new standards in almost every respect . . . it breaks new ground in using for the polyphony four solo voices and nothing else.[72]

For those of us already enthusiastic about the possibilities for vocal performance it was impossible to doubt that a new age in the performance of medieval music had begun.

At the same time that 'The Mirror of Narcissus' was issued a collection of *Studies in the Performance of Late Mediaeval Music* appeared from Cambridge University Press including what arguably remains the most significant article on the performance of fifteenth-century music, David Fallows' 'Specific information on the ensembles for composed polyphony, 1400–1474'. The crucial word here is the first; Fallows restricts his study to evidence that definitely concerns the sort of music that survives, excluding more general descriptions or illuminations in which the nature of the music being performed is uncertain. With such a high entry standard for admissible evidence most pictures of music-making are excluded from consideration, simply because they fail to tell us what kind of piece was being sung or played. Likewise, archival evidence of payments to musicians also needs careful sifting, accepting only those records in which a particular type of music, and the forces required for its performance (not just the forces available to the institution), can be inferred. Literary descriptions must be similarly specific. Also to be considered is how much can safely be inferred from specific evidence about general practices:

the issue is surely not whether a particular kind of performance could conceivably have taken place in the middle ages so much as what was then considered the best performance. The social historian may be interested in all kinds of music making, but the student of the music that happens to survive needs to know what was thought to be the ideal performance, the one that is worth emulating in an attempt to revive the music today.[73]

There may be a case to be made for seeing this as a perfectly formed period view for the early 1980s. With the authenticity movement at its peak of influence, shortly to be deflated in a long series of publications by Richard Taruskin, the question of the composer's ideal seemed crucial. But no proponent of medieval instruments had yet argued that authenticity was irrelevant, on the contrary, authenticity was the reason for using them, and equally no scholar or performer was yet so postmodern as to argue that evidence of a patron's or composer's wishes could legitimately be ignored. If Fallows could show that their preference was for performance without instruments then the whole voices-and-instruments hypothesis was in jeopardy. And that is exactly what he did.

Fallows showed that the minimum performing ensemble for the Burgundian court chapel in 1469 consisted of six high voices, three tenors, three basses and two contratenors, all of them grown men, and no instruments. Like many other documents of the time they show that tenors and contratenors were distinct, despite their similar ranges (a point that has yet to be properly explored by scholars or performers, incidentally). According to Dufay's will, a similar balance in favour of the top line seems to be required by his Mass for St Anthony of Padua and also for his four-voice motet *Ave regina celorum*. The scoring of a number of other fifteenth-century sacred pieces can be determined in the light of Wright's work on the arrangement of voices in the choir of Cambrai Cathedral. Fallows allows that instruments were occasionally used, citing the known references, but since in the ideal conditions specified by a major patron and a major composer they were nowhere to be found, his article can only be read as indicating that the use of instruments was exceptional and normally unnecessary. Fallows (following research, then recent, by Alejandro Planchart and Fallows' student Gareth Curtis) proposes that the tenor in cantus firmus masses was sometimes sung with the cantus firmus text, that sometimes the lower voices applied the mass text, dividing long notes and ligatures where necessary, and that sometimes they were vocalised or played. None of the evidence set out in the article encourages the last thought, but to exclude it as a possibility might have seemed to be tempting fate.

Turning to the song repertory, where *a cappella* performance was harder for many to accept, Fallows points out that there is 'very little' conclusive evidence for performance with instruments and that pictures are not to be relied upon unless the music can be clearly identified as polyphonic song,[74] a far higher standard of proof than was required by the main contemporary proponent of instrumental accompaniment, Howard Mayer Brown, whom Fallows rather mischievously quotes in support of all vocal performance. In his most concrete statement, Fallows writes: 'voice and instruments in the polyphonic song repertoire is without clear documentation. I do not wish to state that this never happened, merely that most of the evidence offered so far can be interpreted differently – as being concerned with monophonic and improvised repertories.'[75] He then offers the specific evidence for the performance of known songs, all of them describing unaccompanied singing and those that go into detail about the voice types specifying girls' or boys' voices on top accompanied by men's. And finally he looks at descriptions including instruments and voices, concluding that none is demonstrably describing a performance of composed polyphony.

Fallows' article offered a strong documentary basis supporting Page's view of the music, and it was providing that documentary basis that, on top of Wright's archival work from Cambrai, definitively turned the tide of scholarly opinion. As Roger Bowers argued at around this time, archival records of payments, and the obligations of those paid, had as their sole purpose the accurate recording of fact,[76] and for a historian that made archival evidence the most valuable and reliable of all. If ordinances and payment records indicated that polyphony was sung without instrumental accompaniment then, for most scholars, that is what happened. For Fallows, though, powerful as they were, the documents were not the only consideration that weighed: with a remarkably brave, because unacademically personal, final one-sentence paragraph, Fallows concluded:

the evidence for all-vocal performance of secular polyphonic songs in both the fourteenth and the fifteenth centuries is far greater than has been supposed.
I also now think that much of the music sounds better that way.

and his footnote to that last sentence pays tribute to Page's BBC broadcast with Gothic Voices. Page recalls seeing Fallows' article in typescript at around the time he was working on *Cleriadus et Meliadice*, and remembers

Fallows advocating vocal performance already at the first York Early Music Festival, mentioned above, so that it is clear that the influence worked both ways. The mutual influence of Page's research and experiments, and Fallows' research and thinking, is considerably deeper than this simple paragraph might suggest.

By the time 'The Mirror of Narcissus' appeared in the shops, therefore, the critical ground had been very well prepared. But it had been prepared not so much by a concerted plan of action as by several years of increasingly enthusiastic discussion among a fairly small group of scholars and performers whose ideas started to filter through into print from Page's 'Deschamps' article onwards. Yet that 'critical mass' can hardly have been great enough to generate the phenomenal success of the revived *a cappella* hypothesis. True, there was evidence brought together that would have been hard to ignore – by now everyone agreed that lower parts were sung in the Middle Ages, at least on occasion – but without persuasive performances it seems impossible that this information could have brought about any substantial change in outlook. To understand the scale of the vocal revolution we have to look at the performances. For it was music-making, not scholarship, that changed medieval music history.

GOTHIC VOICES

It is no exaggeration to claim, and easy to show, that nothing since Riemann has so much reshaped the performance and perception of medieval music as the work, and above all the recordings, of Gothic Voices. Giving concerts worldwide, and issuing on average one disc a year since 1983, Gothic Voices has, at the time of writing, set down over 300 pieces on twenty discs, stretching from Notre Dame conductus to late fifteenth-century masses – statistically a tiny proportion of the surviving repertory, but nonetheless a very substantial sample that adds up to an exceptionally large and representative survey of medieval music.[77] This in itself would make the group impossible to ignore in any consideration of medieval music today, whatever performance practice they promoted. On top of that they offer a radical presentation of the all-vocal hypothesis. This in turn is supported, and to some extent made into scholarship, by the series of articles Page has written over the years, developing his understanding of the music in relation to medieval evidence. Put all this together and one can easily see why Gothic Voices has to be considered at length. There is a sense, indeed, in which the issues examined in this book would seem far less pressing, and the book hardly worth writing, without the strength of the Page/Gothic Voices evidence. This remark needs some glossing. By evidence I mean both the writings of Page, exploring the documentary evidence and penetrating its implications with considerable daring, and also the very different kind of evidence formed by the performances themselves, the latter not, of course, evidence from the past (or not directly so) but very much of the present, 'sounding' the medieval evidence and Page's understanding of it. The nature of that 'sounding' has changed over time, yet it continues to persuade a large body of modern listeners, and has become so much a part of our contemporary perception of medieval music that it seems strong enough to stand against the decades of instrument-based performances that followed from Riemann.

To put it at its simplest, Gothic Voices made the all-vocal hypothesis of medieval performance into modern fact and straightaway turned Page's first small article on Deschamps from an interesting and thought-provoking presentation of a possibility into the trigger for a revolution. As we saw David Fallows remarking in the previous chapter, 'Page's original proposal made little impression until he assembled his own group and showed how all-vocal performances might work'. Fallows speaks there from personal recollection, of course, for he was himself a key player in the group of scholars and performers discussing all these questions at the time. These discussions have left no record, for they happened in conferences outside the paper sessions (as often as not in the bar) and in informal meetings of like-minded musicologists organised privately. It is not necessary to document these here in any detail, but it is important that they happened, for they served to strengthen the sense of mission and common purpose that many of us felt and that was one of the factors lying behind the reviews and articles cited above. The sense of an idea whose time had come has been recalled above, and nowhere was it more strongly felt than in the circle around Gothic Voices. Within that circle, and increasingly – as the recordings appeared – far beyond, it was the results of Page's experiment that convinced, rather than simply the argument: to quote Fallows once again, 'Nobody took [the evidence for all-vocal performance] particularly seriously until the publication of recordings that virtually dispensed with instruments. At that moment many listeners were astonished by how much more convincing and eloquent the music sounded in a purely vocal performance. It was the musical impact, not the nature of the arguments, that convinced so many musicians that the music can be better without instrumental participation.'[78]

And that is how I remember it, too. Like many scholars thinking about these issues in the early 1980s, and intrigued by the possibility of unaccompanied performance, the first Page broadcasts and then 'The Mirror of Narcissus' came as a revelation, converting interest into belief, making the musical language comprehensible for the first time, no longer thin and quirky but rich and lyrical. This is a heady and, for the scholar, a dangerously volatile mixture of emotion and research, and one that can only be fully explored when we come, in chapter 4, to look at this whole phenomenon as an interaction of personalities and social structures. Suffice it to say, for the moment, that there is nothing new about that. Exactly the same forces were at play in the minds of all those scholars whose work we have examined so far and who wished to imagine how medieval music sounded, and in some cases went so far as to try to make it sound that way again. In introducing a personal note here, therefore, I am attempting to place my own reactions to Gothic Voices, and those of many of my contemporaries, in the same frame, open to scrutiny of any who care to look, as those I've been writing about so far. It would be incredible to try to place myself as the author of this book outside that frame, to pretend that I could in some way stand apart from the issues being discussed here, an impartial observer of the sort traditionally, but implausibly aspired to by Scholarship with a capital S.

At the time of the first broadcast Gothic Voices was nothing more than a few singers brought together to make a programme. Page wrote and read the introduction and continuity (the BBC announcer, incidentally, was Nicholas Kenyon, from 1983 editor of *Early Music*), and the programme consisted of four *ars subtilior* songs. Page's introduction used Deschamps (as in the 1977 article) to argue for all-vocal performance, but went a step further by proposing how the results might be perceived: 'ideally, this should encourage a broader, smoother approach to the music, unruffled by instrumental articulations . . . I also find that the sustained sound of voices makes more of the dissonance in the music, while providing more of the lower harmonics that most medieval instruments seem to lack.' This was exactly what seemed so important to those of us who heard it. Listening to a tape of the broadcast now, more than twenty years and twenty Gothic Voices discs later, it sounds imprecise and insecure, and rather flabby; but at the time, and coming after decades of what seemed by comparison too often to be warblings accompanied by buzzings and scrapings, those performances were a delight, and seemed to reveal to us an essential but long-hidden truth about the nature of medieval song.

The programme opened with Philipoctus da Caserta's *En remirant* sung by Margaret Philpot, Rogers Covey-Crump (tenor) and Colin Scott

Mason (baritone), the first two of whom were to form the sonic core of Gothic Voices in its first incarnation. (Rogers Covey-Crump's previous experience with Andrew Parrott has been mentioned earlier, and he was already an important figure on the medieval music scene, having recorded previously with the Landini Consort, the Medieval Ensemble of London and the Hilliard Ensemble among others. Margaret Philpot was introduced to singing medieval music by Michael Morrow and John Beckett in Musica Reservata in the early 1970s. So both brought a wealth of useful experience to Gothic Voices.) In *En remirant* all parts were texted, breaking up ligatures as necessary, and all three stanzas were sung, something which had practically never happened before on record, so that one for the first time got a live sense of how long these pieces are. Then came Baude Cordier's *Amans ames secretement* and Anthonello da Caserta's *Amours m'a le cuer mis* (only one stanza). The programme ended, in another move that would become characteristic of Gothic Voices discs, with Baude Cordier's *Se cuer d'amant* sung (by Margaret Philpot) to the accompaniment of a harp (played by Page) in order to demonstrate one of most popular medieval instruments but one little used at the time. A second broadcast, three weeks later on 14 February 1981, used male voices only and included Machaut's *Rose, lis* and *De toutes flours*, both sung in three parts without the triplum.

For scholars already interested in the all-vocal idea these broadcasts, once heard, were impossible to forget. The notes were the same notes we'd read on the page and had heard in other performances (of the Machaut songs, at any rate; the *ars subtilior* items were less well known); yet the relationships between the notes seemed to have changed. Most obviously different were the lower parts, not least because they could both be heard at the same volume as the cantus, so that one became aware for the first time how well these pieces worked as harmony at the same time as being (as we'd always known) collections of lines working within a contrapuntal framework. Another important consequence of the new homogeneity was the much finer coordination it made possible. These sorts of singers – people who worked together in small choirs, often as students first of all and later as professional early music singers in London – have to communicate well with one another; they are used to listening closely to their neighbours, blending and coordinating precisely with them: these are the fundamental techniques of their trade. The same is not true to anything like the same degree of mixed groups, combining one or two singers and one with two instrumentalists. Aside from the occasional work on medieval music, the need for that kind of cross-border coordination simply was not there, and consequently matching vocal and instrumental styles was a constant problem for medieval and Renaissance music groups, and one that had no ideal model before Les Arts Florissants emerged with a new style for Baroque music, also in the early 1980s. There is an interesting comparison to be made here between the early Gothic Voices and their immediate predecessors, the Medieval Ensemble of London. MEL also used Rogers Covey-Crump and Margaret Philpot at exactly this time, but the standard of ensemble is not as high; the sense of a single musical body articulating and shaping the music that Gothic Voices achieved so early on, even in their first disc, is simply not there and was probably not possible. The voices and instruments are not really speaking the same language. Of course that can be a virtue if you want to emphasise the linear qualities of this music, but Gothic Voices' contribution was to show that it could also work from the opposite perspective. Using only voices, exploiting the particular skills of these London jobbing musicians, made that possible.

Gothic Voices, phase 1: texted Tenor & Contratenor

The first Gothic Voices disc, recorded in September 1981, was of Hildegard of Bingen,[79] and proved to be a runaway success. In fact it was chance that led them to begin with Hildegard rather than with the late medieval polyphony that was to be their staple diet thereafter. Ted Perry, owner of the recently founded record company Hyperion but still driving a London cab to make ends meet, happened to hear Page's early broadcast of Hildegard on the radio, and when, by coincidence, Page sent him a tape which had the *ars subtilior* broadcast on one side and Hildegard on the other, it was the Hildegard that Perry particularly wanted to recapture. Its unexpected success guaranteed the group's future.[80] Consequently it was only in 1983 that Page finally recorded the first disc of unaccompanied Machaut, 'The Mirror of Narcissus'.[81] By then he had already been experimenting for some time with untexted lower voices, a solution to the lower-voice problem already tried in the group's first concerts, in Senanque and Villeneuve-les-Avignon, in July 1981 when the singers vocalised tenor and contratenor to 'oo'.[82] But the singers were unhappy without text to articulate note attacks, and for the recording Page prepared editions with as much of the text as possible fitted to the lower voices. The motets were relatively unproblematic since they could adopt the chant or song text proper to the tenor. For the songs Page chose to break ligatures in order to fit in the text, but not to split long notes, despite some early fifteenth-century manuscript evidence for that practice,[83] so that in extremis the lower voices omit text rather than change note lengths.

Another possible influence here may have been Fallows' discussion of texting in the Chansonnier Cordiforme, which, although not published in full until 1991, was written in 1979 and circulated in typescript for some years thereafter,[84] before its essentials appeared in 1989.[85] Fallows argued that since text underlay was so imprecise in the manuscripts, singers would have to learn the melodic line before they could apply text to it; thus applying the additional strophes (invariably laid out as a block of continuous text after the end of the part) was a simple matter, as would be the application of the text to the untexted voices, assuming, of course, that they or the text were equally well memorised. 'In practice, therefore, the omission of text from the lower voices in most French chansonniers of these years is irrelevant to the question of whether these voices were sung.'[86] He goes on to argue that pieces have to be judged individually, some being suitably texted in all voices (the criterion being that there should be distinct musical phrases to correspond to the text lines), some being more sensibly treated as texted in cantus and tenor but instrumental in the contratenor. A footnote in Fallows' collected essays points out that Fallows 1983b supersedes that latter proposal.[87]

So Page was not working in a vacuum. On the contrary, as Fallows' *Gramophone* review of 'Narcissus' indicates – recounting the Gothic Voices singers' unhappiness with vocalisation – there was constant discussion between all the key scholars and performers, providing mutual support and encouragement and contributing to a palpable sense of mission:

Christopher Page seems to have been the first to argue that there is considerable evidence for the performance of this music without instruments. That was over six years ago. Since then his suggestion has received increasing support, from performers who are beginning to find that the music works better that way, from listeners who find much of the music more powerful without the distraction of varied instrumental timbres, and particularly from other researchers who are currently making two important points: that there seems to be virtually no evidence that instruments and voices performed together in the polyphonic repertory of the fourteenth and early fifteenth centuries; and that any of the instruments found in pictures of that time would have been incapable of performing a line of polyphony with any coherence. . . . It is a complicated discussion which will doubtless continue for some years; and there are unlikely to be simple answers. But the point at issue here is that Page's record offers the most persuasive advocacy of his position.[88]

Lower voices continue to be texted through the following three discs,[89] the main development being towards a cleaner sound and more strictly enforced Pythagorean tuning. Those two features work together with medieval French pronunciation (rather as Denis Arnold had half-imagined, some fifteen years before, that they might)[90] to produce a bright and sharply focused tone which enables lines to be followed within a homogeneous texture. In other words, Page was working towards a re-conciliation of the arguments for vocal and instrumental performance, while remaining faithful to the core beliefs of the '*a cappella* group' which had coalesced around him.

It is also important that from 'The Garden of Zephirus' onwards Page almost always included some items using instruments (the only exceptions being discs devoted to sacred polyphony). The possibility that hard evidence for instrumental participation would eventually sur-face has never been far from the group's collective mind. And Page's own research with *Cleriadus et Meliadice*, together with Craig Wright's demonstration that at least one *ars subtilior* composer was a harpist,[91] leaves little doubt that the harp, at any rate, had a role to play in poly-phonic song, if only in its composition or later arrangement.

It was only with 'A Song for Francesca', recorded in 1987,[92] that Page finally tried vocalisation on disc, having the lower voices of the anony-mous *Confort d'amours* sung to 'oo' (International Phonetic Alphabet sym-bol [u]). Page has said that on the early records he chose only pieces whose lower voices he could plausibly text; so vocalisation was to open up a much wider repertory, and it may be that the need to branch out played a part in his decision to push ahead on record with a technique he had been trying out in concerts for years. [u] was a cautious choice: already in about 1983 he had tried the French 'u' [y], getting Colin Mason and Peter McCrae round to record the lower voices of Solage's *La Basile* on [y], then playing it back to himself while singing along with the cantus to see if it worked, and he thought it did.[93]

The issue was set aside during the next GV disc, 'Music for the Lion-hearted King', recorded in 1988,[94] but that disc nevertheless marks the start of a very significant change in the Gothic Voices sound, leading into what I am here calling 'Gothic Voices, phase 2'. For the moment, the question of what to do with the lower voices does not arise, because the disc is devoted to monophony and conductus where the text beneath the original score notation can reasonably be assumed to apply to all voices;[95] but Page's note on performance points to a newly focused view of vocal sound which in due course was to lead to a substantially new treatment of untexted parts. In this note Page stresses the importance of precise tuning, of avoiding any vibrato and of a straight vocal tone; and this works together with the first realisation on disc of Ernest Sanders's then-recent reinterpretation of conductus rhythm (arguing, in effect, for an isosyllabic setting of texted, *cum littera* sections, confining modal rhythm to *caudae*), producing an even flow of vowels precisely and uniformly sung on each beat, so that the changing text-sounds provide the principal element of variety and articulation in the surface of the music. The effect was enhanced by a change of recording venue to the church of St Cross, Winchester, which was used also for the two discs following.

By the time 'Lion-hearted' appeared in the shops, Page was already working on the later repertory of *ars antiqua* motets, initially for two BBC broadcasts of Robin and Marion motets, and then for the next disc, 'The Marriage of Heaven and Hell'; and in the May 1988 issue of *Early Music* he published a much fuller treatment of these ideas, as applied to that repertory. 'The performance of ars antiqua motets' argues for singing all lines (and several other details of performance, informed by his experience with Gothic Voices so evidently looking towards the next CD) and for either vocalising the tenor on 'i' or stretching out the chant text to indicate structure. He advocates original pronunciation (to make articulation crisper without having to change the length of notes), original tuning (varied tactically according to context), above all for precision and strong straight tone, 'clear and fresh sounds being combined with perfect accuracy'. The article amounts to a uniquely detailed description of a group's practice and its director's decisions.

At the same time he must have been working on his chapter for Howard Mayer Brown's volume of the New Grove handbook on *Performance Practice*, published in 1989, which sets out the same ideas but does so both more fully and with wider applicability; and this remains Page's fullest and most closely argued presentation of the ideas, and their basis in research, that lie behind the Gothic Voices sound.[96] He starts not with evidence for vocal performance (which he approaches indirectly later on) but with tuning, arguing that one common factor in writing on medieval polyphony is its interest in precise measurement. On the one hand, he sees this as a rhetorical ploy, aiming to present music as an intellectual discipline on a par with its fellows in the quadrivium and deserving its place alongside them. On the other he proposes that it relates to a practical concern with precisely judged intervals in performance, and supports this view with telling quotations from theorists that point to the tactical adjusting of intervals in performance in order to emphasise the directed progression from imperfect to perfect consonances, the progression that drives all late medieval counterpoint. Once it is accepted that precision of tuning is essential to the performance of medieval music (that it was 'their' concern and for a good reason), then to Page the other details of the Gothic Voices sound follow inevitably. There can be no vibrato, because vibrato is wider than the differences between tuning systems; similarly there can be no more than one voice per part, since small differences in pitch would make precise tuning impossible; pronunciation has to be medieval and, in conductus, identical, because the position of vowels in the mouth effects pitch and thus tuning – something that only a performer could know, incidentally, which again emphasises how essential Gothic Voices is to Page's research; and tuning has to change according to the repertory, tending towards meantone (pure thirds) for English music but Pythagorean (pure fifths) for French and Italian. As another aspect of the medieval concern with precise measurement, tempo has to be strict, albeit with judicious use of final ritardandi and pauses as described by the theorists. This striving for precision is one vital feature of Gothic Voices that puts it at odds with other modern traditions – it would have been anathema, for example, to the Studio der frühen Musik, for whom the non-coordination of parts was an essential corollary of the linear conception of medieval polyphony that (as we shall scc) so many performers and scholars have ascribed to medieval musicians: the parts were conceived separately, as independent melodies, and must therefore be performed and heard as individual lines. By contrast, the Gothic Voices sound brings with it the necessity of considering all parts as a unity, precisely coordinated and balanced, a point implied by Page whenever he advocates a well-blended sound, as he does here, drawing on Jerome of Moray in support.

Up to this point Page is describing the sound of Gothic Voices as achieved on the 'Lion-hearted' disc. But at the end of his essay he makes a point that would surprise anyone who had followed the earlier Gothic Voices recordings – unless they had listened very closely to 'Francesca'. The single example of 'oo' vocalisation that Page had offered there is here justified by the conclusion that the lack of text for tenor and contratenor in the manuscripts probably indicated not that the parts should be texted but rather that they were either played or vocalised. And that was to be Gothic Voices' practice from now until the end of 'phase 2', and the subject of a later article. Page's final proposal is in favour of the harp as an instrument appropriate for polyphony, which as we have seen he had been promoting since the first broadcast. In the chapter that follows in Brown's New Grove handbook, Fallows argues also that harp and lute are 'the only instruments that can confidently be included in the performance of a polyphonic song'.[97] It is much to Brown's credit that he should have made space for views with which he disagreed so profoundly. In his own contribution he continues to support instrumental accompaniment and attempts as far as possible to restrict all-vocal performance to no more than a legitimate option. And this contrast is symptomatic (as we shall see) of continuing tension among medievalists with a lively interest in performance.[98]

Gothic Voices, phase 2: vocalisation

Finally in 'The Marriage of Heaven and Hell', recorded in 1990, Page put down [y] in lower voices for the first time on disc.[99] The sleeve note says that 'brightness of vowel timbre' was sought, and there is certainly a much cleaner sound than on earlier discs. St Cross provides a strong ambience which blooms around the very precise sonority of sharply focused voices singing markedly dissonant motets. Similar qualities are found in the following 'Medieval Romantics', mostly recorded later in the same year, while in 'Lancaster and Valois' of 1991 Page extends the distinction between English and French music, already made by tuning on 'Venus and Mars', to a different vocalisation syllable.[100] Here the Old Hall Credo by Pycard has its upper-voice melismas sung to vowels that vary widely, perhaps according to the sounds in the text, while the lower voices are sung on 'eh' [e], a vowel that, lacking the bite of the French [y], perhaps seemed to work better in the meantone temperament that English third-rich harmony seemed to require. There are a lot of 'seems' here because, like everything that Gothic Voices was doing with details, there was no evidence beyond Page's arguments for the medieval appreciation of precision. His practice was consistent with that and with observations about French and English musical styles, but in the end could reflect nothing more than an imaginative response to a limited amount of information. The justification came from the results which, to most of us then (and now), seemed musically plausible. Of course 'musically' means musical in current terms – all it can ever mean.

To a great many early music critics, though, and especially to those outside Britain, the Gothic Voices style lacked essential ingredients of fantasy and emotion. Page quotes a number of them, drawn from the Hyperion archives, in an *Early Music* article of 1993. Vocal precision was so foreign to listeners used to the Studio der frühen Musik, the Clemencic Consort or the Ensemble Organum that it seemed cold and disengaged. This fundamental difference of values would be worth exploring here at length if Page and Don Greig had not already raised many of the issues from the angles (respectively) of taste and anthropology.[101] For these are not really arguments about medieval music at all, but simply about the need for medieval music to fill gaps in current music-aesthetic provision. For Page the music is sound in motion, and therefore the quality of that sound is absolutely crucial, more important than anything else. But for listeners brought up in a tradition stretching unbroken from the Anthologie Sonore through the Studio and on to Sequentia and Mala Punica, what medieval music must do above all was to express its text, and the texts are about love. For that approach nothing works better than a single voice expressing the text it sings as intensely as possible over an accompaniment whose job it is to support but not to share. There has been little reconciling of these views in medieval performance up till now. Some ideas of how to do it may be gleaned from the success of Renaissance groups on whom the need for a solution has been forced by the nature of the music: fully (and emotively) texted chansons and madrigals have come to seem to demand an emotionally charged precision that was very obviously absent from performances from before the 1990s. But none of this was evident in 1993. At any rate, it may be nothing more than coincidence that 'The Study of Love', recorded at exactly the time that Page must have been conceiving this article, offers performances that are noticeably more emotional.[102] Page's own view is that this was not a cause, and that the ebullience of the tenor Andrew Tusa was a more significant factor, a view perhaps supported by a similar trend emerging through the mezzo Catherine King in Gothic Voices discs made at the end of the decade, especially 'The Masters of the Rolls' of 1999.[103]

*

While Page was facing up to his record critics, on the scholarly front articles were beginning to appear from other authors, all from a younger generation of scholars, offering further evidence for unaccompanied performance. Dennis Slavin, in the May 1991 issue of *Early Music*, showed that texting or partial texting of tenor and contratenor was much more common in manuscripts of fifteenth-century song than one might think from looking at modern editions, which more often than not suppressed the manuscript evidence (presumably because they did not believe it) – and also far more common than Brown had suggested in his notorious 'heresy' review of Gothic Voices' 'Castle of Fair Welcome', to which Slavin ties his title: 'In support of "heresy"'. (Brown's contribution to the debate will be discussed more fully below.) Slavin's argument led to the conclusion that texting lower voices, breaking ligatures and splitting long notes as required, was a fifteenth-century practice and one, alongside vocalisation – clearly required in certain other songs – that performers today were justified in adopting. In the same issue Lawrence Earp argued, on a slightly different tack, that since the texting of the cantus in fourteenth-century songs was so meticulous the absence of text from the other voices clearly indicates that they were to be vocalised, not texted, and he went on to criticise Page and Gothic Voices for adding text to the lower voices of their recordings. His article (first presented as a conference paper in 1989) may have been complete before the appearance of Page's recantation in the 'Lion-hearted' booklet, and certainly before release of the 'The Medieval Romantics' which first puts vocalisation in chansons into full-scale practice – indeed Earp only cites recordings up to 'Francesca' – so that in effect this part of his text was outdated by the time it appeared, but it must have provided Page with some recompense to see his recent practice so eloquently supported.[104] Earp and Slavin agree that partial texting should be sung as written, again Page's practice since 'The Medieval Romantics'.[105]

In the following year, 1992, Page contributed a brief essay on 'The English *a cappella* heresy' to the Dent *Companion to Medieval and Renaissance Music* edited by David Fallows and Tess Knighton. This idiosyncratic, and therefore unusually interesting, volume, was compiled (at least as I recall) with the aim of getting scholars and performers to write about their subject in a way they would not normally risk in print. Page took up Brown's taunt and attempted to place the all-vocal movement in a wider context. The first three pages of the article summarise an important part of the story told here in the previous chapter, identifying an aesthetic favouring colourful and contrasting sounds that emphasise the linearity of medieval polyphony, an aesthetic stretching from Ficker and Schering (showing the influence of Huizinga) through the early music groups of the 1950s and 1960s. He contrasts this with the work of the Medieval Ensemble of London, notable for their more responsible use of only medieval instruments, and not many of them.[106] And then he runs through the main kinds of evidence in support of vocal performance, concluding that 'The English *a cappella* heresy . . . is not, in short, a heresy'.[107]

The heresy image appears yet again the following year in the title of Knighton's article, 'The *a cappella* heresy in Spain', which finds on the basis of literary evidence that performing groups in Spain were not unlike those in France, to the extent that the normal options were 'all vocal; all instrumental; and vocal soloist accompanied by a plucked instrument such as lute, vihuela or harp'.[108] A notable player in the then younger generation of British musicologists and already an influential figure in the

British early music scene, Knighton had been editor of *Early Music* since volume 20/2, May 1992, and although she had been supportive of vocal performance in reviews since 1985 she had in fact been an important member of the *a cappella* circle since the beginning.[109]

Page next turned, in an article appearing in *Early Music*, August 1992, to the nature of the vocalisation Gothic Voices were using.[110] One feature of this piece that is remarkable, and deserves recognition, is that it is the most detailed and technical analysis of the sound of a group yet written;[111] that it was written by the group's director, and not by a commentator, is noteworthy, for it emphasises the extent to which Gothic Voices is not just a group of singers but represents a body of research and thought, and to that extent is a scholarly and intellectual as well as a musical enterprise. This should be apparent from the way it has been possible in this section to interleave discussion of the recordings with discussion of Page's contemporary articles. There is no other medieval music group of which this is true to anything like the same extent. The separation and incompatibility of scholarship and music-making is so much a given of traditional thought (the one concerned with recovering fact, the other with recreation in both senses of the word) that it has sometimes been hard for specialists to credit the extent to which Page has succeeded in marrying the two.[112] That said (and at the risk of falling into exactly that camp) the article allows us an honest but exceptionally telling sight of the gap between what the most intelligent research can recover and what the best informed performers must still invent.

The preliminaries to this article are rather longer than the main argument, but they are valuable, adding significant extensions to the *a cappella* hypothesis. Page raises further questions about the possibility or (for medieval writers) the desirability of performing Gothic polyphony on instruments, emphasising doubts about the ability of medieval instruments to play low enough, and pulling together quotations from medieval writers that seem to exclude instruments from sacred or contrapuntal music. He examines in rather more detail than before some less well-known cases of partial texting in the manuscripts; and he brings his philological training to bear on the possible terminology for vocalisation in descriptions of musical performance, investigating the possibility that several of the terms used as alternatives to 'chanter' or 'cantare', including 'tenir', 'dire' and especially 'bourdonner', indicate vocalisation.[113] To this point the article is typical of the way in which the *a cappella* hypothesis was developed, during the years following the Deschamps article and the emergence of Gothic Voices, in small steps, contributing to an impression that a fully formed hypothesis existed and was simply being refined: yet it had (and at the time of writing still has) never been presented whole, in the way that, outstandingly, McGee was willing to set out a thorough description of instrumental practice.

Nevertheless, the second part of Page's article is remarkably bold, for it crosses over from written evidence from the period, a category of evidence any scholar of a humanistic discipline would respect in principle, to unchanging, but until modern times undocumented, acoustical fact, a kind of evidence guaranteed to make humanistic scholars nervous. Everything taught to aspiring medievalists today serves to persuade them that modern perception is no basis for deductions about medieval people. To accept that the laws of acoustics are applicable in the fourteenth century in exactly the same way as today, however reasonable, goes against that grain, and encourages doubt as to the plausibility of any argument that depends on it. Few, therefore, could be expected to take this part of the argument seriously as evidence, on a par with that summarised in the preceding pages. Page's argument runs as follows. The vocalising parts must not obscure the texted voice. Therefore, the vowels singers use for vocalising their lines must have a harmonic spectrum that covers as little as possible the spectra of the changing text syllables. Using spectrographic analysis of vowel formants Page argues that [y] is an ideal candidate, for its formants are sufficiently widely spaced to leave room for the changing vowels of the text to sound without interference from the accompanying voices. Almost as good are 'ih' [ɪ] and [e], the latter, as we have already seen, used in the Credo by Pycard on 'Lancaster and Valois' and reappearing in similar pieces later. Page concludes with a list of tracks from 'The Medieval Romantics' and 'Lancaster and Valois' illustrating the results, for as usual he is writing about his existing practice, not offering proposals that performers might try – another sense in which the Gothic Voices project needs to be seen as, if not circular at any rate spiral: from research to performance and then from performance-as-research to print.

There are a number of respects in which 'Going beyond the limits' is exactly what Page is doing here. In the first place, however reasonable his argument, he sounds as if he is transgressing the (impossibly idealistic) dictum, invoked above, that modern perception is no basis for deductions about medieval people. There is no period evidence at all for [y] or any other vowel as preferred for vocalising untexted voices; nor for that matter is the evidence very strong that they were vocalised at all. Both these are reasonable deductions, albeit of different kinds, the option of vocalisation almost unavoidable given the literary evidence for singing these parts and the manuscript and musical evidence against full texting, but partial texting remains at least one alternative possibility, and there may be others that have not yet occurred to us, or at least have not been tried (for example, the different kinds of vocalisation for the different untexted parts suggested in passing in Page 1982 (449), which would explain why singers of tenor and contratenor parts are differentiated in some documentary evidence, and would appeal to those who favour contrasting lines, and a linear approach to performance). As far as [y] goes, not only is there no evidence from the period, but it could also be argued that the acoustical facts might have gone unrecognised in many performance practices, that other vowels might have been preferred for reasons of tradition or association or their more effective interaction with the particular colour of medieval voices, which can reasonably be assumed to have been quite different from our own and to have differed substantially from place to place and time to time. And finally, one might question the fundamental assumption on which Page's argument rests, which is that the text must be clearly audible: Page takes this as axiomatic, and few scholars would consider disagreeing, for the primacy of text has for centuries been an inviolable truth of musical performance, teaching and criticism; but it would not be difficult to argue, using medieval evidence, that 'they' thought it less essential.

All these alternatives are offered not, as may seem so far, to undermine Page's hypothesis, but rather to point out how unusual it is. If pressed to give a personal view I would say that it is the most detailed and rationally argued proposal for the sound of medieval music that anyone has yet made:[114] at the very least, I would say, it is a well-grounded attempt to take the performance of medieval music beyond the limitations of the surviving evidence while remaining within the bounds of deductive scholarship. But the point that really needs to be made, and the reason for emphasising its uncertainties, is that it is the same kind of argument – based on reasonable deduction, as it seems to us – that Stainer and Riemann were willing to make when confronted with the Canonici songs: there is a certain amount of evidence, and then there is reasonable deduction, and what is reasonable is a matter of opinion and may change. It is this that makes it so unusual in its context: for arguments of that sort are now so unfashionable and so suspect. Yet as Riemann realised, any conception of what medieval music was like can only be formed by making these kinds of deductive leaps. In this sense the dilemma faced by musicology has not changed: either one works minutely, assembling fragments of evidence that some day in the future may accumulate to such an extent that a picture becomes visible; or one takes what one has and guesses the rest. Only the latter can lead to performances. One of the beauties of Gothic Voices, from a research point of view, is that they seem to add so little to the evidence and yet manage to achieve what seem to many today to be near-perfect performances. The evidence for all-vocal performance removed at a stroke all the problems of which instruments to use, in which combinations and how to play them: voices are (we tend to think) voices, and all one has to do (it might seem) is to book some good singers and put the notes in front of them. There seems (again), compared to the work of any of the great instrument-based groups, to be so much less intervention between the notes and the music in an all-vocal performance. The key guesses, as we have seen, concern the untexted voices, and here Page has been able to find a rational reason for doing one thing rather than another. But it is only a guess, and does depend upon quite an accumulation of assumptions, and in that sense it is qualitatively very similar to the deduction made by Stainer, that untexted material was instrumental.

This is a detail, however, compared to the weight borne by the fundamental assumption, of all assumptions the least secure, that voices today sound anything like voices of the Middle Ages. Again, Page has addressed this by reasonable deduction, above all in the chapter for the Brown *Performance Practice* handbook, arguing that the fine tuning that was so important to theorists, and can tie in so logically with the contrapuntal language (imperfect intervals straining for resolution), requires a straight tone (no vibrato, except as occasional ornament), and that their interest in measurement, again so apparent in the language (and some would argue in the construction) of their pieces, requires a straight tempo (no rubato, except at major pauses); put that together with the argument for a particular quality of vocalisation, and something like the Gothic Voices sound is hard to avoid. And yet . . . anyone who has followed the history of singing on record, which is essentially the history of changing vocal styles through the twentieth century, understands that what is considered essential to the voice changes more over time than, at any one moment, one could imagine was possible. Gothic Voices is as much a part of that process as any other group of musicians. Indeed, the change in their own style from 'Narcissus' to, say, the 'Spirit of England and France' discs we shall look at in a moment, mirrors rather well changes in general performance style during the 1980s and 1990s. In fact, in their very next disc, of Spanish song, although in using voices only they go right against the modern Flamenco-inspired tradition of early music performance in Spain, Gothic Voices nevertheless take on something of that very idiomatic vocal sound, brighter and more nasal than anything on their French discs.[115]

All these issues lie close to the surface of Page's next article on the Gothic Voices project, and his last for seven years, 'The English *a cappella* renaissance', which appeared in *Early Music* for August 1993.[116] Page presents an 'English discovery' theory that leads on directly from the arguments presented in the Brown volume for what I have just called the Gothic Voices sound:

the English discovery theory . . . begins from the premiss that English singers performing *a cappella* are currently able to give exceptional performances of medieval and Renaissance polyphony from England and the Franco-Flemish area because the ability of the best English singers to achieve a purity and precision instilled by the discipline of repeated *a cappella* singing in the choral institutions is singularly appropriate to the transparency and intricate counterpoint of the music. From that premiss we proceed to the theory that, in certain respects, and especially in matters relating to accuracy of tuning and ensemble, these performances represent a particularly convincing postulate about the performing priorities of the original singers.[117]

This is of course treading on extremely dangerous ground, for while it may be no more than a happy historical coincidence that English singers have achieved exactly the qualities that independent research suggests medieval music required, it may also be possible that there was significant influence in the opposite direction, namely that the abilities of the singers, and local English taste, were what made medieval music seem to require those skills. Page addresses this, from various angles, in the remainder of the article. First he emphasises, with a degree of well-merited irony, the shared background of most English early music singers and most English scholars and critics, a background in Oxbridge colleges and cathedral choirs. Compared to continental critics, the English seem to require more adherence to period evidence (because English critics are generally scholars and continental critics are not) and are likely to expect that evidence to be realised with the values promoted by their shared musical and education background, like English singers and choirmasters, admiring precision and purity of tone. At this point in his argument one is fully armed to conclude that the English *a cappella* tradition in early music performance is nothing but the product of peculiarly English tastes and assumptions, inculcated in a few peculiarly English institutions. As Page points out, this is an argument I proposed in a number of reviews from the early years of Gothic Voices,[118] claiming that Machaut's 'extraordinary music originated in 14th-century France, worlds away from the Oxbridge tradition'; yet for Page – and this is where his article takes such an unexpected turn – that is far from clear. In fact, he now goes on to argue,

The collegiate and cathedral tradition in which many English singers received their training is comparable in some respects to the context in which medieval (and Renaissance) singers received theirs. It is one in which a repertory with a large *a cappella* element is cultivated on a daily basis by men and (usually) boys, all of them relatively young, who hold positions in a cathedral or chapel (often for a relatively short time) for which there is much competition. They are singers for whom singing and rehearsal are constant duties that are not always (to say the least) touched by concerns of high art. The prevailing notion among them is one of a versatile, professional competence, constantly kept in trim by *a cappella* performance, that can readily be turned to music more ambitious and enjoyable when liturgical duties are over. The process of rehearsal draws upon a training which often reaches back into the singer's boyhood, which provides him with the directed quickness of mind and the vocal stamina he requires, and which ensures that the choral results are generally quite passable – and are sometimes excellent – despite the constant absences, deputizations, hirings and firings that always threaten the homogeneity of what can be achieved. It is a tradition where instrumentalists – apart from organists – are apt to seem like a different breed of musician altogether.

I tentatively suggest that this is, in some measure, the world of the medieval and early Renaissance singer of polyphony, and the implications of this resemblance, whatever they may be, deserve a reflective study to themselves.[119]

Page then relates to this tradition the particular qualities we have already identified as belonging to the Gothic Voices sound, borrowing the fourteenth-century English word *clanness* or cleanness. Although the article is worded with infinite care, what this amounts to is very simple, and certainly very bold. The quasi-medieval training that English singers receive contributes to their ability to produce the most appropriate sound for medieval music. There is something almost Fickerish about this heartfelt and vivid evocation of a world of medieval musical training that Page conjures up. English singers (and so Gothic Voices) are called upon to make this sound because the evidence supports it, and they can make it because they were trained in a similar way to medieval singers. There is a sense, in other words, in which the English, singers and scholars, have a hotline to the Middle Ages. If only it could be true: but I must say that I remain unconvinced. It seems to me, as it seemed when writing those reviews Page cites, that the Gothic Voices sound has grown from the skills of English singers honed and shaped by Page's research filtered through a very fine ear and an unusually focused musical imagination, and made communicable by his quite exceptional ability to explain in words what it is he wants his singers to do.[120] Whether the background of the singers, or what Page brings to the process (which, I am trying to suggest, is much more than is usual for the director of a British ensemble), takes their sound any closer to that of medieval singers than is the sound of other groups seems impossible to know, not because of any shortcoming in the use made of the evidence but simply because singing styles change so much more than one imagines or, without the evidence of recordings, than one could ever be induced to believe. Music-making is so varied and so changeable with changes in general taste that there seems to me no realistic chance of stumbling on the sound of medieval singing by design, nor by accident.

A similar point was made by Donald Greig in a subsequent issue of *Early Music*. What makes Greig's contribution particularly apt, aside from his training in film studies which brings an appropriately modernist perspective to the subject, is that he is himself a professional singer working within the tradition Page describes, indeed on occasion sings with Gothic Voices. For Greig, Page's article

sets up a sort of unconscious of the English early-music world, a set of drives and desires which are rarely overtly expressed but which underlie and motivate a particular aspect of the performance of early music.[121]

and his view of Page's invocation of what one might loosely call 'the analogous English tradition' is as sceptical as mine:

I contend that the similarities are mostly a happy coincidence, and that the particular skills of the British early-music singer can prevent a full appreciation of the demands of the music and inhibit forms of expression yet to be explored. I suggest too that modern *a cappella* performance may tell us more about modern cultural conditions than about the original performance.

Greig goes on to argue that *a cappella* performances tend to dematerialise the performers, to remove the sense of them as bodies at work, a tendency that is strengthened by the 'cleanness' and purity of the British early music sound, so that the singers seem more angelic than corporeal. At the same time, the CD, as the dominant medium for early music performance, offers another representation of cleanness, purity and technical perfection, and one that – again – keeps the body of the singer invisible, disguising their physical reality. In both respects, purity of sound and purity of medium, *a cappella* performance sounds quintessentially of our time.

To argue that Page is attempting to bring Gothic Voices into a special relationship with the Middle Ages is of course to offer a very much more specific reading of his article than he would himself have wished to present, and indeed his wording is always more subtle than I have allowed. Nevertheless, to the extent that this book tries to relate many different views of medieval performance to assumptions, tastes and wishes of the people who have proposed and promoted them, Page's must also be considered closely as a product of its time. As a long-time sceptic in matters of historical performance, much as (on personal grounds) I regret it, it is impossible for me to join confidently in Page's conviction that Gothic Voices has re-created sure features of the sound of medieval music. And yet I can say that for me the group has come closer than any other to making this music live. There is more to this than musical excellence, over-ridingly important as that is. The Gothic Voices project as a whole – Page's scholarship and its practical translation and elaboration into music – is an outstandingly successful combination of research, technique and imagination: three elements at work in both the project's scholarly and musical manifestations. In some respects, as we have seen, the scholarship follows on from the performances, and learns from them. Page deserves respect for having the courage to allow that. We have seen Ficker allowing something similar, with remarkable musical results but with absolutely no discernable gain for scholarship. In Page's case there are perhaps scholars who would make a similar judgement, and reject performance absolutely as being too hopelessly contaminated by modern taste to have anything to offer as evidence. I do not believe that it is right to view the achievement and contribution of Gothic Voices so harshly. So many of their performances, and increasingly so from the mid-1990s onwards, border on the miraculous that one would have to be immune to musical beauty to maintain that no sense of the music as it was conceived can plausibly be supposed to have been re-created. But how much is something we cannot ever know. Whether there is any sense in which *a cappella* performances, by Gothic Voices or any other group, can be objectively shown to improve upon the results of the instrumental hypothesis is a question we shall come back to.

*

Between 1993 and the end of the decade the Gothic Voices project continued in concert and on disc only, but it is not difficult to see where it led. The first of the series of discs begun in 1994 and globally entitled,

'The Spirits of England and France' is notable for a new recorded sound, much clearer than before and tending therefore to emphasise exactly the values of *clanness* Page evoked the previous year.[122] At first Page continued to work with [y] vocalisation, broadened to [e] for the English Gloria by Cooke; but in volume 3, from 1995, some changes are noticeable: in the Binchois chansons the [y] sounds a little closer to [u] than on previous discs, and in *Adieu mon amoureuse joye* (track 3), a more reflective example, it has clearly moved back to [u]. Again an English Gloria, by Power, uses [e], the Dunstable song-style motets take an intermediate [y/u], reserving [y] for the earlier Machaut. It seems entirely reasonable to play with different kinds of vocalisation for different repertories: Page has told me in conversation that vowels are often modified after first playback, when the singers have a chance to hear the interaction of vowel, tuning and balance. But in fact since that disc (and are we now in Gothic Voices, phase 3?) there has been almost no vocalisation, for thereafter Page began a series of three discs of fifteenth-century mass music,[123] only returning to the Middle Ages with 'Jerusalem' in 1997 which revisits the conductus of 'Lion-hearted' but – and the comparison simply emphasises the group's continuing achievement – still cleaner than before.[124]

How might we summarise the view of medieval music that Gothic Voices and Page offer us? It is interesting to look back at Reaney's call for an appropriate singing style for medieval music, dating from 1956 and quoted early in this chapter:

An appropriate method of playing and singing has to be cultivated. Vibrato, both in voices and instruments, should be avoided, except in special cases. The tone of the voice should be as smooth as the unvarying tone of the cornett, viol or recorder. Otherwise, only chaos can result from the clash of constantly crossing parts.[125]

As I remarked then, Reaney was tapping into a persistent belief about medieval music, that it was – to a greater degree than music from the Renaissance onwards – abstract music, not expressive in any modern sense of the texts it set; it was characterised by clarity of harmony and texture, features which, until the *a cappella* revolution begun by Gothic Voices, were thought to be best projected in instrumental performances. Reaney asks that if there must be voices without instruments they be as instrumental in sound as possible. There is certainly a sense in which Gothic Voices has achieved just that. What Greig characterises as sexless and incorporeal about modern English *a cappella* singing might also be seen as quasi-instrumental, at least in its textless precision, 'smooth and unvarying'. There is a sense, then, in which the Gothic Voices sound brings us back to instrumentally accompanied performances, *except* – and this is crucial – that the principle of contrast has been abandoned. The only contrast to survive is that between text and no text; aside from that the sound is homogeneous, emphasising progression of harmony to a rather greater extent than continuity of line. The main achievement of the *a cappella* revolution, then, concerns its view of musical texture rather than the colour of the lines that make it up. It offers a euphonious medieval music of the sort implied by Wright in placing his 1977 paper in a session on euphony, and extends backwards the observations of Perkins in his introduction to that session. What Perkins thought was new about early Renaissance music, Page/Gothic Voices argue is already there throughout the polyphonic Middle Ages. It is a view of medieval music as consistent with some recent work on the language of polyphony as it is profoundly at variance with other thought on the topic, and the way in which these divergent views developed, and where they stand in relation to each other today, will be considered in the next chapter. Until then, the significance of Gothic Voices' achievement for a wider view of medieval music may be left only partly revealed.

THE CONSEQUENCES OF SUCCESS

In the preceding section I have tried to show how Gothic Voices developed alongside Page's research, so that the two become inseparable, each an aspect of the other. And I have suggested that it was above all the outstandingly persuasive musical results that led so many to be convinced that the *a cappella* hypothesis was far more than just that, a mere hypothesis. But while the performances surely carried more weight than any amount of scholarly support, we have also seen the very close links among the scholars encouraging Page and inspired by him. For, in a peculiarly British arrangement, they were also the principal reviewers of his work. The senior figure in the informal alliance of scholars that I've loosely called 'the *a cappella* group' (and that Page called 'the forum') was unquestionably David Fallows. Born in 1945, he was the oldest and, in the late 1970s, the best established, already a leading light in British early musicology. With a Ph.D. from Berkeley he was broadly trained, already knowledgeable across a wide range of later medieval and Renaissance music, energetic and charismatic, fascinated by issues of musical sound and structure. His work on Dufay had led him through many of the major archives that preserved data on fifteenth-century musicians and most of the sources of music, and along the way he had acquired a lot of information about performance practice. Alongside Howard Mayer Brown he probably knew more of the evidence than anyone else in the later 1970s. Page himself was trained as a scholar of English, read medieval Latin and French fluently, and of all musicologists was the best equipped to read and interpret references in medieval literature to music and performance. (Indeed, it is tempting to argue that it was precisely his training outside the musicological establishment that made the originality of his contribution possible.) Towards the end of the 1970s he was working his way through the corpus of late medieval French romance seeking out descriptions of music-making, and it was this that led him to Deschamps and then to *Cleriadus et Meliadice*, and later through the Latin sermons, manuals for confessors, treatises and French narrative poetry which provided so much material for his second book, *The Owl and the Nightingale.*[126] Page and Fallows between them could access the two bodies of potential information about performance that seemed likely to prove the most fruitful. Also deserving special mention, although his work is strictly speaking tangential to the issues discussed here, is Roger Bowers, trained as a historian but, like Page, choosing to make medieval music his area of expertise. Bowers' archival and deductive work on performing forces and on pitch in England offered powerful support for the sense, shared by all these scholars, that *a cappella* performance was fundamental for medieval polyphony.[127]

Clustering around them were a number of slightly younger scholars just starting out on their careers at the end of the 1970s. Apart from myself there were Tess Knighton, John Milsom and Nick Sandon, all of whom were to figure in the pages of *Early Music* advocating *a cappella* performance. They and others, including Lawrence Wright, Ronald Woodley, Andrew Wathey, Ann Lewis, Mark Everist and Gareth Curtis met from time to time, usually in Oxford where Page was then based at New College, for informal 'conferences' at which issues of performance practice scholarship were vigorously discussed. Several of us were close to the *Early Music* editorial team,[128] where Fallows was the book- and music-reviews editor. Fallows also wrote for *Gramophone*, and Page was already becoming a regular voice on BBC Radio 3. Knighton, as we have seen, became editor of *Early Music* in 1992. It is not hard to see why Gothic Voices was so favourably received. Everyone who reviewed their discs positively, or instrument-based discs negatively, understood from the inside the importance of what Page was doing and of his motivation in doing it. All shared the same underlying values.[129] There seems little room for doubt that the reviews produced by these scholars from around 1980 were cumulatively of considerable influence on the futures of performers and instrument-makers in Britain.[130]

Phase 1: anti instruments

Discontent with medieval music performance began to surface in reviews in the late 1970s, soon after Page's first article. We have already seen Harrison complaining about indiscriminate mixing of instruments as early as 1966, and David Munrow responding ten years later with a more cautious separation of medieval from Renaissance instruments in his book of 1976. By that time there was a considerable sense of distaste among scholars for the everything-but-the-kitchen-sink approach to scoring medieval music in concert, reflected in a review by David Fallows in *Gramophone* in 1978 of René Clemencic's recording of Dufay's *Missa Ecce ancilla domini*:

My disagreement with Dr Clemencic lies rather in his general approach to the work. He makes a passionate argument for a large festal performance and composes his own relatively intricate trumpet and drum parts for several sections of the work. These have the disadvantage of obscuring much of Dufay's writing, and they also fly straight in the face of most recent scholarly work on the composer which leaves little room for doubt that the two late masses were both conceived for Cambrai cathedral choir without any instruments at all. . . . These things do matter: it is all very well to refer to a viewpoint as 'puritan', but it simply will no longer do to consider all early music as so much potential fodder for shawms and sackbuts. . . . Music of this importance and quality deserves the finest possible performance and I am certain that better can be achieved relatively easily.[131]

Two years later, reviewing Alexander Blachly's recording of the same work (and referring silently to Wright 1978), Fallows wrote:

Taking note of what we now know about performances at Cambrai Cathedral, for which the Mass was evidently composed, Alexander Blachly has recorded the work with just 10 singers: no instruments, no messing around.[132]

Similarly in 1980 a review by Page in *Early Music* (one of his last – he ceased to review after forming Gothic Voices) was scathing about Clemencic's three-record set of *Cantigas de Santa Maria* for its apparent lack of interest in the texts and spurious instrumental improvisations:

'the perennial curse of medieval music performance today – *variety*' ...
'destroying the pieces' ... 'outrageous gimmick' ... 'Clemencic is an
indifferent composer of music for (pseudo-)medieval instruments' ...
'concealing the music in a veil of gimmickry'.[133]

In the following issue, in my first record review, I adopted a similar
tone:

> Les Musiciens de Provence ... have few ... redeeming features – unless one's
> view of redemption includes the novel perversion of playing a trouvère song on a
> combination of fife-and-tabor, recorders, flageolet, and tromba marina. ... The
> public wants new sounds but it is suspicious of new music, and for the time
> being, at least, certain early music groups seem happy to resolve the problem.
> What will happen once the tromba marina and tenor kortholt have become
> as stale as the harmonium is anyone's guess; but in the meantime one may be
> forgiven for wondering whether contemporary music is really so unacceptable
> that records such as these can provide a profitable alternative.[134]

The tone of both these reviews now seems quite vicious (mine inex-
cusably so), and this is something one would never find today, but it
accurately reflects the intensity of feeling at the time. We felt medieval
music was being raped; and we wanted justice for it.[135]

In the following issue Lawrence Wright, a colleague of Page's in French
studies, carried on the theme in a review of René Jacobs' performance of
Machaut's *Le Voir Dit*: 'Unaccompanied singing must have been the com-
monest way of performing music in the Middle Ages, yet in the present
revival it is a rarity'. And he called other aspects of the performances
'dishonest ... insult ... unreliable'.[136] Here we see the hostility to instruments crossing over, surely under the influence of Page's Deschamps
article, into advocacy of unaccompanied vocal performance.

Phase 2: pro voices

Certainly, my own pro-voices reviews in the April 1981 issue of *Early Music*
were strongly shaped by my enthusiasm for Page's *a cappella* proposal.
In an enthusiastic review-article on the Consort of Musicke's record-
ing of the Cordiforme chansonnier (for which Fallows was consultant)
I nevertheless called for more *a cappella* performances and criticised
the colour contrast of instruments and voices; and in a review of the
Medieval Ensemble of London's first disc, the complete works on
Matteo da Perugia, I called for vocalisation, citing Page 1977, 'a solution
for which trials are long overdue'.[137] (Incidentally, the following review, by
Shaun M. Tyas, describes a record of fourteenth- and fifteenth-century

songs from Ensemble Ricercare de Zurich using Baroque bassoons, oboes and viols, which perhaps shows why we felt so strongly that there was much still to be done.)[138]

At the end of 1981 Fallows provided the first challenge to instrument-based performances in the pages of the more widely read *Gramophone*. This was part of a topical feature on early music assembled by Stanley Sadie, to which Fallows contributed a section on 'Medieval Instruments'. After telling the story of the modern invention of the douçaine, the *Early Music* correspondence about it and the consequent collapse of the market for douçaines and cornamuses (of which more below), Fallows concludes:

It is my firm belief that we are coming closer to a proper understanding of various aspects of medieval performance practice. . . . I find myself in agreement with many of the findings offered in recent research, . . . I have changed my own views accordingly, and . . . many performers have done the same. But to me the most important feature of that progress is that more and more works are being performed for their own intrinsic qualities, not subjected to a colourful razzmatazz of pseudo-medieval jollity. . . . In fact, some people would now argue that most of the reconstructed instruments were used only for that lost improvised music. . . . One thing that these people are saying is that much of the music sounds best in the simplest performances with voices alone. There is increasing evidence that much fourteenth-century music, for example, was intended for purely vocal performance. The available documentation says the same for most of the fifteenth century and suggests that the mixing of voices and instruments in composed polyphony was an invention of around 1500. . . . My own feeling is beginning to be that performances of medieval polyphony might do well to eliminate instruments wherever possible. But it is not yet time to say that the *douçaine* should never be used.[139]

It is tempting at this point to write, 'and so it went on', but to leave it at that would be to fail to show how intensive was the propaganda bombardment. Indeed, I cannot think of anything comparable before or since. Thus the following month I advocated unaccompanied vocal performance in reviewing Thomas Binkley's 'Cantigas de Santa Maria'.[140] In the April issue Mark Everist, reviewing a one-record reissue of parts of Munrow's 'Music of the Gothic Era', wrote that 'Completely vocal performance rediscovers so many musical subtleties which are lost when parts are taken by instruments with limited control of timbre and intonation . . . '[141] In the October issue, in which Page's 'Cleriadus et Meliadice' article appeared, I reviewed the Medieval Ensemble of London's complete Dufay songs, maintaining that their use of instruments was 'a fundamental error of judgement', that sung phrases in the middle of instrumental parts were 'ridiculous', that 'the weight of evidence overwhelmingly favours vocal performance'. And the review goes on to set out an early overview of the evidence for all-vocal performance and for harp accompaniment, offering support for vocalisation over texting, and for partial texting when shown.[142]

By February 1983, when Iain Fenlon reviewed the Medieval Ensemble of London's *ars subtilior* record 'Ce diabolic chant' in *Gramophone*, he could write:

More controversial than any of the vocal performances is, as readers of GRAMOPHONE hardly need reminding, the Medieval Ensemble's approach to the use of instruments. There is neither need nor space to re-rehearse the arguments here – suffice it to say that well over half of the performances involve instrumental participation.[143]

Fallows spoke appreciatively of this same disc's *a cappella* performances when he came to review it for *Early Music* in October 1983, a broadly favourable piece that reflects Fallows' continuing sympathy for older-style instrument-based performances, perhaps acquired during his time working with the Studio der frühen Musik in Munich, a sympathy which marks him out as a far more reasonable reviewer than many of his followers.[144] His January 1984 review of 'The Mirror of Narcissus' has already been quoted at length, for it makes the collegiality of those concerned with these questions so evident, but it is worth emphasising here its warmth. No regular reader could fail to distinguish his support for instrument-based performers from his intense commitment to Page's alternative approach:

its importance lies in ... [the fact] that this is the first record to present fourteenth-century secular music without any instrumental participation whatsoever. ... Page's record offers the most persuasive advocacy of his position ... the record is not only extremely fine to listen to but also extraordinarily thought-provoking.[145]

I published warm reviews of the Hilliard Ensemble's *a cappella* 'Medieval English Music' and of 'The Mirror of Narcissus' and Andrew Parrott's Machaut Mass (quoted earlier in this chapter) in the August 1984 issue, praising Parrott's use of Pythagorean tuning (something that Fallows advocated in the pages of *Early Music* as early as 1975)[146] and noting critically only Gothic Voices' less consistent medieval tuning and more familiar 'Oxbridge' sound:

Previous recordings of Machaut's songs – and almost all writings on Machaut's style – have stressed the dissonance and eccentricity. The performances by Gothic Voices suggest, absolutely convincingly, that these are the works of a composer with a masterly grasp of harmony and part-writing, and with a fine sense of sonority.[147]

Over the next few years in *Early Music* these themes are continued. In a review of recent recordings by Gothic Voices, the Hilliard Ensemble and the Medieval Ensemble of London in February 1986 I questioned the influence of the English choral tradition and the incestuousness of London medieval music groups, calling for more variety, but added an unnecessarily vicious anti-Clemencic postscript.[148] In the February 1988 issue, alongside an appreciative review by me of 'The Service of Venus and Mars' appeared a critical review by John Caldwell of Philip Pickett's instrument-dominated 'Carmina burana'.

Tiresome as it is to go through all this in such detail, it does show just how much pressure was brought to bear by reviewers from the circle around Page and Fallows in order to change the way medieval music was performed. We wanted to influence the performers, the record-buying public and through them the record companies, and (with the notable exception of Fallows) we spared none of the instrument-based groups whose records came our way. The tone may be scornful or patronisingly sorrowful, lofty or irritated, but the message was unmistakable: buy Gothic Voices, the Taverner Consort, the Hilliard Ensemble, and leave the rest. And I'm sorry to say that it made a difference.

Many groups changed their practices. None, so far as I know, that were instrument-based became entirely vocal, for instrumentalists were invariably their directors, but almost all began to introduce a noticeable quantity of *a cappella* performances. The Ensemble Gilles Binchois and the Ensemble Organum in France, Sequentia in Germany, Ensemble Project Ars Nova in the USA, and many others, all began to offer un-accompanied singing as a regular option. At the same time new vocal groups were founded, the Orlando Consort in the UK, Anonymous 4 in the States preeminent among them. But there were losses too, by far the most serious that of the Medieval Ensemble of London.

MEL, jointly directed by instrumentalists Peter and Timothy Davies, began giving concerts in London in the late 1970s and made their first record, of Matteo, in about 1979 (Decca Florilegium records at this time offered no information about recording dates; it was issued in 1980).[149] Perhaps influenced by Page's first article, perhaps by the few vocal tracks on Florilegium's Cordiforme set later the same year, per-haps by reviews of Matteo, when MEL came to record the complete

Dufay songs they included a few unaccompanied performances, corresponding to pieces fully texted in Besseler's edition.[150] Their next set, the complete Ockeghem songs issued in 1982, offered five *a cappella* tracks out of thirty.[151] By the time they made 'Ce diabolic chant', probably in 1982 (it was issued in 1983) the influences of the *a cappella* group was such that six out of sixteen tracks were unaccompanied, including the first and last.[152] Their 1983 record of two Machaut lays was perhaps the first to offer vocalisation of lower voices on record.[153] 'Mi verry joy', recorded and issued in 1983,[154] had a majority of its tracks unaccompanied, and the seven instruments of 'Matteo' had become but two, one for each of the brothers. Their final records were of Josquin masses and songs, in the first case with no role for instruments, and in the second secular music from a period where there was at last some historical justification for instrumental accompaniment.[155] In conversation outside (though not broadcast in) a radio interview with Christopher Page many years later Peter Davies explained that they genuinely wanted to do medieval music the right way, and tried in 'Ce diabolic chant', but that the brothers had nothing to do themselves, and in the end preferred to give up rather than go on getting it 'wrong' or not being involved.[156] The group folded in 1985. In retrospect it is impossible not to regret the loss of MEL deeply. They put on concerts and made recordings of coherent repertories at a time when most other groups were still mixing indiscriminately music from different countries and even centuries; they restricted their instrumentation to medieval instruments when most others were combining medieval, Renaissance and even Baroque instruments for the sake of spurious variety; they sang all stanzas when most groups were still cutting ruthlessly; they hired outstanding singers and scholars to advise them; the musical results were often excellent and occasionally, as in *La harpe de melodie* on 'Ce diabolic chant', wonderful (and that track is still unsurpassed). While some of the pressures on them to fold came from within the group, one can only regret the part played by changing tastes, and deplore the part played by hostile reviews, in their demise. It is a salutary reminder of the way that special interest groups, even in early music, can twist a consensus to suit their own narrow agenda.

A happier, but also striking example is that of the Ensemble Project Ars Nova, whose practices changed markedly during the later 1980s and early 1990s, gradually including more vocal performances and with ensemble getting increasingly tight, in other words moving steadily towards the

Gothic Voices model and away from their origins as students of the
Studio der frühen Musik at the Schola Cantorum of Basel.[157]

*

At the same time as Page and Fallows were transforming views of
'correct' performance practice for medieval music other changes were
being felt, changes that interacted with the *a cappella* revival to cause a
marked shift in interest away from medieval music and towards later
repertories. The new orthodoxy cannot be entirely blamed for this, but
it was certainly a factor. During the later 1960s and for much of the
1970s early music was medieval and Renaissance music. After the harpsichord and recorder revivals earlier in the century, it was in medieval
and Renaissance music that the new sounds of old instruments first came
to seem essential. Through Cape, Hindemith and Greenberg, and the
many groups they inspired, it came to seem normal, even essential that
'original instruments' should be used in concerts and on record. This was
authenticity: historical support, original instruments, new sounds. Thus
the aims of the authenticity movement were fully accepted for the earliest
music when for Baroque music they were still considered experimental
and academic, and for Classical music (in the shape of the fortepiano)
thoroughly misguided. But the very fact that so much of early music's
appeal lay in its novelty and its offering an alternative to New Music,
made it inevitable that when audiences became familiar with rackets
and crumhorns their attention would drift towards innovations in other
repertories. Clearly, once you have got used to the idea of authenticity,
as it was then conceived, there is no problem in principle about looking
for it in later repertories; and equally clearly, performers of Bach, then
Mozart, then Beethoven, had far more controversial and novel possibilities to offer an audience eager for new old music, for their music
was 'real music'. It was one thing to make funny sounds in Machaut or
Praetorius where no one, beyond a handful of academics, really believed
the music was of lasting worth; it was quite another to mess about with
the sound of the great composers. Performing Bach on Baroque instruments was challenging, performing Beethoven on instruments of his time
was extraordinary. It is hardly surprising, then, that as soon as significant
numbers of concerts of great works on original instruments began to
happen attention would shift rapidly away from early repertories.

Exactly the same process happened in musicology. During the 1970s,
musicology was dominated by scholars working on the Middle Ages
and Renaissance; it was there that the most respectable and technically
demanding work was being done. Yet by the end of that decade there

were already clear signs of a drift towards later music. Analysis, which until then had mainly concerned itself with modern music, was returning with new techniques to apply to canonical works. And scholars trained in source studies and textual criticism on medieval and Renaissance topics were beginning to apply those same techniques with missionary zeal to eighteenth- and especially nineteenth-century music, rescuing it, as they saw it, from mere biography and criticism. Perhaps that was another reason why the *a cappella* hypothesis seemed attractive: it offered a way of revitalising an area of study that looked to be on the wane.

Thus while medieval sounds were still flourishing a new field was being opened up, above all by Nikolaus Harnoncourt, in the revival of Baroque instruments and their application to Bach. As his Vienna Concentus Musicus issued high-profile and challenging recordings of some of the Western canon's most sacred musical cows – the St Matthew Passion, the Mass in b minor, the Brandenburg concerti, the cantatas – the attention of the musical media, the record companies, their markets and, as a result, the attention of performers shifted towards the Baroque, where the most exciting developments were now occurring.[158] This in itself might not have greatly affected medieval music, for at least as far as instrumentalists were concerned the Baroque revival spawned a new generation of performers rather than poaching from medievalists, and anyway required outstanding professionals, where medieval groups could still manage to a considerable degree with performers who in any other field might have been considered amateurs. Moreover, as the early contents of *Early Music* imply, there was a large supporting cast for medieval music in the shape of genuinely amateur players and singers making music locally.

A glance through the first decade of *Early Music* reminds one just how popular medieval and Renaissance instruments had become. The first three years of the journal (twelve issues) contain three articles on the crumhorn, two on medieval percussion, and one each on the medieval fiddle, the dulcimer, hurdy-gurdy, cornett, and medieval recorder. All were aimed at amateur players and makers.[159] Jeremy Montagu's 'Early percussion techniques' begins, 'Having chosen and built some drums for medieval and renaissance music, what are we going to play on them?', which gives a neat snapshot of the mood of the time.[160] Windows on this extensive amateur market are offered by 'The Register of Early Music', published as a supplement to the first few years of *Early Music*. This began as a listing of players in the UK and abroad, aimed at facilitating contacts and the formation of ensembles. From the second issue (April 1973) it included a note of players' level of ability, as 'a great saving of embarrassment'.[161] It is a fascinating series of documents. After recorder and keyboard, the most popular instrument is the crumhorn, and considering how difficult it is to play in tune there are a surprising number of cornett players. Some examples will give the flavour. Flight Lieutenant R. N. Armstrong, from an RAF base in Cambridgeshire, plays the recorder, crumhorn and sings;[162] Dr R. H. S. Carpenter, from Cambridge, plays the recorder, crumhorn, cornett, keyboard, kurtal and sings; the third issue reveals that he's a member of the Susato Consort, and that he's a beginner on cornett and rebec, but competent on keyboards, singing, percussion and Renaissance woodwind;[163] the Rev. F. H. Mountney from Hereford plays viol, recorder, crumhorn, rauschpfeif and keyboard;[164] A. C. Baines of Oxford plays 'all wind instruments', which one can easily believe, for this was Anthony Baines, curator of the Bate Collection and author of several books on early wind instruments, which usefully emphasises the heterogeneous mixture of amateur and professional that was so characteristic of medieval music at the time;[165] N. Wilkins (the musicologist and Machaut specialist) of St Andrews plays viol, recorder, crumhorn, rebec and harp, all at professional level;[166] Dr B. Woods, who in the first issue played recorder and crumhorn, has by the third dropped the crumhorn but taken up shawm, cornamuse, sordun, rackett, dulzian and flute;[167] The Medieval Consort, from Milwaukee, offer keyboard, recorder, singer, Baroque violin, viol to professional level, and cornemuse, crumhorn, guitar, harp, percussion and kortholt as competent amateurs.[168] By the time the cumulative 1975 Register appeared, listing names received up to October 1974, there were over 750 UK entries, and close on 200 from the USA, as well as substantial numbers in Belgium, Canada and The Netherlands, France, Germany and Australia. All these were individuals or ensembles offering themselves as players of early music keen to meet others in their vicinity, and the instruments they list are overwhelmingly medieval and Renaissance.

To a surprising extent this amateur market survives today. The Register of Early Music is still published by the UK's National Early Music Association, and still lists lots of people playing the same kinds of instruments. The 1998 register included 152 players of the crumhorn (52 of them professional, the rest competent amateurs or beginners), 59 (16 professional) of the cornamuse, 35 (16) rauschpfeife, and so on, though many of these are the same people playing a variety of early instruments. (It is also striking, judging by the surnames, how many families seem to play Renaissance music together.) Medieval instruments, however, are much less well supported: there are only 18 medieval fiddlers, most (12) of them professionals; 27 (11) players of the rebec; 21 psaltery players; 3 gitternists, an instrument that used to occur often on disc; and – perhaps the most telling comparison – 21 (16) medieval vocal and 17 (11) instrumental groups. 'Vocal Ensemble (Medieval)' was a category that did not exist in the registers from the 1970s, but even so, in both that and the instrument-based category ('Medieval Chamber Ensemble') the numbers are small, showing how far interest in medieval music has declined overall.[169] The ratios of amateur to professional – high in the Renaissance instrument categories, low in the medieval – indicate the way that the centre of gravity in early music has shifted. To an extent the vocal revolution, which in its early years so scorned instrumental performance, disenfranchised amateur medievalists, withdrawing scholarly encouragement and leaving them to manage as best they could.

In this atmosphere it is hardly surprising that the market for medieval and Renaissance instruments began to decline. *Early Music*'s 'Register of Early Instruments' first appeared in 1974, listing available models with prices. It includes 3 makers of violins, but 9 of medieval fiddles, 2 of cello (presumably Baroque cello) and one of viola, but 22 of viols, also 8 makers of hurdy-gurdy, 15 of rebec, 10 cittern, 9 psaltery, 8 dulcimer, 7 orpharion, 5 tromba marina, one rote, and 37 makers of lute. In 1998 the figures looked very different. In a list perhaps eight or nine times as long as that of 1974 there are 65 makers of Baroque and Classical violins as against 19 of medieval fiddle, 47 makers of cello, 46 of viola, still a huge number of viol makers, but only 16 makers of rebec, 16 of psaltery, 12 of crumhorn, 8 of cornamuse, one of tromba marina. Perhaps most tellingly indicative of the influence of scholars on instrument-makers, for reasons that will become apparent below, the list includes two makers in the new category 'Mary Rose Pipe (Douçaine, Dulcina, Still Shawm)'.

The decline in advertising by instrument-makers tells a similar story. The October 1977 issue of *Early Music*, in which Page's Deschamps article appeared, carried 79 advertisements from instrument-makers, 46 selling medieval and Renaissance instruments, 12 of those specifically medieval.[170] Over the next decade there was a gradual decline, surely due in part to the Thatcher recession, but by the time the figures stabilise again in the later 1980s the proportions have significantly changed. In the May 1988 issue (carrying Page's article on the performance of ars antiqua motets) 24 makers advertised, but of these only 9 dealt in medieval and Renaissance, and only 2 specifically in medieval instruments. A decade on, in May 1999, 17 advertise, 7 medieval and Renaissance, and one medieval. So while (advertising) instrument-makers as a whole have fallen to 22 per cent of their 1979 level, makers of medieval and Renaissance instruments who still think it worthwhile to advertise in *Early Music* have fallen to 15 per cent, and makers specifying medieval to 8 per cent.

Of course the factors that caused this general decline must have been several. Recession has been mentioned. We've also seen that there was a gradual shift from identifying early music with medieval through Baroque to Classical and more recently into Romantic music. And it is obvious that advertising has shifted in tandem. But the message coming again and again from articles and reviews must have had an effect. Makers, players, enthusiasts can hardly have failed to take away from *Early Music* after 1977 (and especially from 1980 onwards) the message that the way medieval music had been imagined up till then was 'wrong'; performers and record companies selling the public a colourful instrumental Middle Ages that they used to love must have felt increasingly threatened by the inevitability of unfavourable reviews; amateurs who had taken up one of the many quite easy early instruments to play with friends must have been increasingly embarrassed by the message repeated again and again in their trade journal.

David Fallows offered an early and telling example of the process I have been outlining in *Gramophone* for December 1981. The story begins a few years before, in a letter he wrote to *Early Music*, January 1979.

Early in 1969, when I was employed by the Studio der frühen Musik, Munich, as Thomas Binkley's assistant, Binkley sent me instructions to assemble the available useful documentation on the dulzaina and its cognates . . . he felt that there could be some value in attempting to build an instrument on the basis of the available information, even if that information was not sufficient for accurate reconstruction. I think he felt, as I did, that an answer of some sort might be right, but no answer at all would certainly be wrong. That, I now see, was a dangerous attitude in an atmosphere that makes people so eager to grasp new ideas.

I gathered some material. . . . On the basis of that material Binkley made some plans and then disappeared for a weekend at the workshop of Günther Körber in Berlin. Shortly afterwards Körber produced a set of the now-familiar instruments, constructed like a crumhorn but straight and end-stopped with a pepper-pot.

This was a wild hypothesis, but one that seemed compatible with the available data; yet the important and stunning feature of the new instruments was that they were infinitely more stable than the crumhorn and far easier to control and tune. . . .

When an instrument works so well, historical considerations have a tendency to fade into the background; and the 'dulzaina' very quickly gained a popularity that far outstripped its hypothetical origins.

The July 1979 issue contained a pained response from Herman Moeck, representing the largest maker of cornemuses, who clearly felt that Fallows' revelations could have a damaging effect on sales, followed by a pessimistic endorsement of Fallows' scepticism by the crumhorn scholar, Barra Boydell.[171] What happened in consequence is related by Fallows in the 1981 *Gramophone* article, as he retells the story:

> I was once present at the invention of a medieval musical instrument. It was an attempt to represent the *douçaine*, an instrument mentioned in several descriptions of music from the fourteenth century onwards.... Various assumptions were necessary. In particular we had to assume that the instrument remained fairly constant in shape and performing characteristics over a period of about 300 years; and we also had to assume that all mentions of *douçaine* or its cognates (dulzaina, etc.) referred to the same instrument. But even then... several enormous leaps of faith were necessary to create our *douçaine*.... As things turned out, the newly invented *douçaine* was a tremendous success.... In the 12 years since this instrument was invented it has had a distinguished career in the concert hall and the recording studio....
>
> Now the story of the *douçaine* took an interesting turn three years ago. I outlined the history of its invention in a brief letter to the magazine *Early Music* – which is perhaps the central forum today for discussions of early performance practice. By then several makers were selling the instrument with considerable success; but apparently as soon as the instrument's true history was known the bottom fell out of the *douçaine* market. An instrument hitherto thought to be 'authentic' was seen to be largely hypothesis and was therefore shunned. This was surely absurd. Much of what we do in performing medieval music is based on hypothesis; and without these hypotheses nothing would be possible. The only important issue is that people should be aware of where the areas of hypothesis lie.
>
> Moreover the bottom fell out of the market for a related instrument, the cornamuse. This is firmly a late-renaissance instrument, and is described in a seventeenth-century treatise with enough detail for there to be some confidence that it has been reconstructed more or less accurately. But the reconstructed cornamuse is practically the same as the 'invented' *douçaine*; indeed... it seems possible that the reconstructed cornamuse was developed in the light of our *douçaine*'s success. In any case, the opprobrium of 'inauthenticity' which tainted the one affected the other as well. This is surely even more absurd... [172]

Well, yes it is. But it is also perfectly obvious that the early music public would never have taken a scholar's word so seriously if music historians had not for generations been claiming that their answers were the best that could be achieved and thus, for all practical purposes, were correct. It is very hard not to conclude that scholars got themselves into this situation: they insisted (and still insist) in reviews, articles and books, that their expertise be trusted by their readers (so many of those readers performers and listeners); they have no one but themselves to blame if people came to believe them. Among modern writers Fallows is outstandingly good at making clear the weaknesses and uncertainties in the evidence, but scholarship in general has built up such a façade of impregnable expertise that the public may be forgiven for a strong reaction to the discovery that the scholarly edifice is quite literally made of paper.

The wider suspicion generated by Fallows' honesty is hard to measure, but it must have fed into the dissatisfaction with instrumental participation that became so apparent in the early 1980s, so that by 1985 he could write:

In universities throughout the world, those crumhorns, shawms and even renaissance recorders so eagerly purchased during the 1960s are now gathering dust, virtually relegated to the limbo of a musicological past.[173]

The situation today is not quite that bleak. The douçaine has since recovered some of its reputation following the recovery from the wreck of the 'Mary Rose' of a sixteenth-century instrument claimed by a scholar, again in *Early Music*, as a genuine douçaine.[174] Since that claim, as we have seen, instrument-makers have begun to offer a 'Mary Rose Pipe', the cautious name an all-too-clear indication of sensitivity to opprobrium attached to 'douçaine'. 'Douçaines', along with most of the instruments that had their heyday during the 1970s, are still available and selling in modest quantities: a recent catalogue from the Early Music Shop in Bradford, Yorkshire, one of the world's largest suppliers of early instruments, lists them all, many of them also in kit form (including the cornemuse, now made with plastic reeds).[175] But when in 2001 the same shop cleared their warehouse of 'undocumented and long forgotten items that we have decided must go regardless of cost', the largest category was of medieval instruments.[176] 'The Register of Early Music' shows that there are still players at amateur and professional level, if (proportionally) a lot fewer than before. Yet if one looks on the internet now for medieval instruments it is striking how many are presented as no more than accessories on sites selling medieval costume and equipment for 'mediaeval fayres', or as folk instruments, and how few are aimed at mainstream classical musicians. The 'merrie' Middle Ages live on in popular life, but among musicians who cluster around the scholars and their journals they are hanging on by a thread.

One final point about all these changes remains to be made, but it is as symptomatic as any. *Early Music* started as a journal for amateurs and enthusiasts first and foremost. Today it is above all else scholarly. Scholars in Britain, as nowhere else, have taken moral control of early music. Gothic Voices made the *a cappella* revolution happen, but scholars got the credit for it. Continental Europe, and to a large extent North America, has kept scholarship at bay: most groups outside Britain do their own musicology, most critics are not academics, and the making of medieval music is still seen as an artistic activity before it is historical. It is no coincidence that *a cappella* performance is, even now, largely a British phenomenon. It is as well for the British to remember that.

CONTINUATIONS AND REACTIONS

Just as the voices-and-instruments hypothesis went almost entirely unchallenged by scholars at the beginning of the twentieth century, so at the end of it the *a cappella* hypothesis has received almost no criticism on historical grounds. Many record reviewers beyond the shores of the British Isles have objected on grounds of taste, as Page has pointed out, criticising especially the coolness of British vocal groups. And Page went on to propose that the survival of instrument-based groups on the Continent was related to the non-academic background of continental European and American record reviewers, as well as to the lack of sympathy abroad for the English choral and Oxbridge traditions in which British scholars are mostly steeped.[177] No doubt he is right, though I am arguing here that more immediate than those cultural pressures (to which they were certainly subject) was the sense of community among a very particular group of younger scholars who knew one another well and met often. In the end, though, their perceived strength as a group came not so much from their common culture, or their sense of community, as from their ability to point to evidence and (and here the social factors do matter) from their agreement on what it meant. The evidence was the key, for it provided the single respect in which they could claim to be on stronger ground than their opponents. Thus however groups or reviewers elsewhere chose to object, whether on grounds of taste or simply by insisting that instruments must have been used, there could be no significant academic challenge without new evidence or new interpretations of the old.

It was these two routes to saving instrument-based performance that were taken by the only scholar to mount any attempt at an academic challenge in the early years. Howard Mayer Brown was a professor at the University of Chicago, but had spent two not entirely happy years (1972–4) as King Edward Professor at King's College, London, and seems to have returned to the States with some distaste for British musicology. Brown had long been fascinated by instrumental music of the Renaissance and was the author of a distinguished book on instrumental embellishment; he had a wide knowledge of sources, and among earlier topics that fascinated him were musical instruments in fourteenth-century Italian pictures. He himself played the recorder well; and he therefore had a heavy personal and professional investment in instrument-based performance of medieval music. Though he could be charming in the company of like-minded Europhiles, he was extremely sensitive to disagreement and was prone to waspish put-downs as an instant response. A challenge to a set of beliefs about early music that were so integral to his tastes and abilities, worse still a challenge coming from younger British scholars, he clearly found very hard to accommodate.[178] As Gothic Voices went from strength to strength, Page's success, as well as David Fallows' role in providing for it a wealth of documentary evidence (for Fallows was a scholar he could not but admire for his other work in fields so close to Brown's heart), clearly caused him increasing bitterness. It spilled over in his review of 'The Castle of Fair Welcome' in *Early Music* for May 1987:

Certainly the evidence supporting what I call the 'new secular *a cappella* heresy'[179] – a heresy propounded not so much by Page as by his groupies[180] – is almost all ambiguous in ways the true believers do not always acknowledge.[181]

Brown's metaphors are revealing. In the previous issue of *Early Music* Richard Pestell had cited 'the Puritan view' in his denunciation of the *a cappella* hypothesis.[182] Like Donington, both Brown and Pestell clearly feel deprived of legitimate pleasure by the elimination of instruments, and both use metaphors of religious intolerance (though interestingly from opposite points of view: heresy is presumably anti-authoritarian, Puritanism definitely not). 'Heresy' perhaps merits further decoding. Brown writes as if he saw instrumental participation as a matter of faith to which one must adhere; reading him one almost feels that he would have cheerfully sent his heretics to the stake. Pestell's argument, though insubstantial, depends on his taste for highly decorated medieval art and his belief that music must have been similar; a sort of specialised Huizingian or Fickerisch multi-coloured view that again brings him close to Donington. For Brown in the 'Fair Welcome' review 'Page's groupies', though also heretics, are 'the true believers'; and he ends by presenting the instrumental and vocal views as two interpretations of the evidence, one of which one 'chooses to believe'. However contradictory his metaphors, it is clear that it all comes down to faith and that he sees himself as upholding the true religion. For Brown such metaphors are inevitable, reflecting his frustration at being unable to prove his position; it is very clear from this review that he has no evidence that meets the standards of Fallows, and admits as much when dealing with the Pheasant description, working hard to argue that the duchess's lady accompanied by two fiddles is likely to have been singing polyphony, and to escape the trap of the Fallovian view that since the description is not specific it must be discarded. It must have been immensely frustrating for him. It also may have been just too bloodless. One of his first points is that Gothic Voices' interpretations are too cool, referring to Page's remark in the booklet/sleeve note that the words are like the marginal foliage in manuscripts. A little further on, when discussing a song whose text is heated and mentions sex, it becomes 'a flasher among all that medieval foliage', as if what really turned him on was hot-blooded expressive performances with strong contrasts. Page's performances are 'a bit too perfect, slightly without individual personality or nuance'. Brown's fundamental objection, felt so strongly that he was compelled to strike out in any direction that seemed threatening, was exactly the same as Donington's. Both had derived enormous emotional satisfaction from playing medieval and Renaissance music in ensembles. Both saw the new evidence threatening not just to end those opportunities for 'authentic' music-making, but – far worse – to render them meaningless. For while a performer needs no more justification for their performance than the pleasure it gives, a scholar has to know that they are working out the evidence in sound. And when the evidence turns against your performance, it becomes worthless, so much wasted time. No wonder they defended their beliefs with such passion.

Brief as they were, Brown's contributions had a striking effect. Much of the writing that promoted and refined the *a cappella* hypothesis over the next five years reacted explicitly to him. We have already seen how Dennis Slavin faced up to Brown in his 1991 article for *Early Music*, 'In support of heresy', accusing Brown of inaccuracy when he claimed in the 'Fair Welcome' review that 'scribes almost never added texts to the lower voices' and implying that Brown allowed himself to be misled by the lack of text in modern editions (no light charge to make to a specialist, though it is only fair to add that Brown's expertise was in later repertories). And we have seen how in the same issue of *Early Music* Lawrence Earp looked at 'Texting in 15th-century French chansons' in the light of the evidence of fourteenth-century practice, of which he had acquired unrivalled knowledge working on Machaut. They read the evidence somewhat differently, yet neither seems to have much doubt that the lower voices in chansons were to be sung.

Although they published in *Early Music*, which may have served to suggest (not entirely incorrectly) that they had been in close contact with the British *a cappella* circle, with Earp and Slavin the *a cappella* hypothesis crossed the Atlantic, for both were American scholars of a younger generation who had made early reputations for meticulous work on music manuscripts of their respective centuries. They in effect broadened the base of the supporting evidence, adding source studies to Page's work with literature and Fallows' wide cull of 'specific information'. We have also seen how Tess Knighton, in the same year, broadened the evidence-base geographically by showing support for 'The *a cappella* heresy in Spain', and how Page responded to Brown in 'The English *a cappella* heresy' of 1992. This extreme sensitivity to Brown's attack – which after all was insubstantial enough from an academic point of view – can only be understood in the light of the close relations between so many of the American and British scholars, and a smaller sampling of continental Europeans, working in this field: they met regularly at conferences, not just the huge annual meetings of the American Musicological Society, the less frequent congresses of the International Musicological Society, or the UK's (then) annual Medieval & Renaissance Music Conference, but also at much more intimate gatherings arranged by invitation on both sides of the Atlantic where more or less guarded conversation would be taken to indicate the direction of a potential competitor's thought. Brown's standing as one of the world's leading Renaissance music scholars empowered his view of the *a cappella* revival way beyond the value of his published contribution.

RETURNING ARGUMENTS FOR INSTRUMENTAL PARTICIPATION

If this book were being written ten or – who knows – perhaps only five years from now there might be another chapter here called 'The reinvention of the voices-and-instruments hypothesis', for there is clearly a gap in the story between the realisation that all-vocal performance was an important, perhaps for a long time the most important medium of composed polyphony, and the evident fact that by the end of the fifteenth century instrumentalists were taking part. How that came about has still to be unravelled.[183] There is ample evidence that by about the middle of the fifteenth century instrumentalists were beginning to see the ability to read music as an essential skill; and from that point on one of the most obvious impediments to their participation with singers in composed polyphony is removed.[184] Similarly during the fifteenth century the ability to read polyphony extends from small groups of specialists to larger choirs.[185] Also from the fifteenth century comes the first substantial evidence of instrumental participation in sacred music. And work on Flemish and German archives of the period has shown that civic wind bands and polyphonic music-making increasingly overlapped.[186] It seems beyond question that practices gradually changed during the second half of that century, so that by Josquin's time the intermingling of voices and instruments in composed polyphony was widespread. How this happened has yet to be shown in any depth, and when it is the relative significance of the two modern movements outlined in these two chapters is going to look different.

This has been evident throughout the period of the *a cappella* debate. And it is not hard to see how that might have made the major promoters of the *a cappella* hypothesis occasionally uneasy. Perhaps that helps to explain the rhetorical strategies of Fallows' subsequent article on 'The performing ensembles in Josquin's sacred music', a follow-up to his 1983 'Specific information' which looked at the changed situation at the end of the fifteenth century. The bulk of the article concerns vocal ensembles which 'must . . . be considered to some extent paradigmatic'.[187] But Fallows also reminds us that instruments often played in churches in the later fifteenth century, and that range can be used as an argument in favour of at least one line being instrumental in certain works. He finds this undesirable for pitch reasons – potentially instrumental tenors often enter long after the start of other parts and the pitch may have wandered (though this seems a somewhat weak argument if the singers were competent). And he also argues against 'analytical' scoring, bringing out the cantus firmus, which leaves using instruments on all parts preferable to using them only on one. Nevertheless, he argues, vocalisation is more likely. Thus

The preceding pages are offered partly as a corrective to some disturbingly rigid views in recent literature. But if it is accepted that the position of instruments in church polyphony around 1500 was simply to double the lines and add to the magnificence of the occasion, it follows that the vocal ensemble not only remains more or less unaffected by the presence or absence of instruments but is the fundamental group for which the music would have been conceived in the first place.[188]

Yet one can sense, in his enthusiastic summarising of the arguments for instrumental participation right at the beginning, a degree of ambivalence, perhaps a wish not to identify too closely with the evidence for continuing *a cappella* practices, despite their being the main conclusion of the article.

Howard Brown's New Grove Handbook, also from 1989, offered Fallows a larger opportunity to look over the whole question of performing secular music in the fifteenth century. It includes (in a footnote) a useful list of the evidence then available for instrumental performance of composed polyphony, but notes that recent thought has favoured the idea that we should 'aim at the kind of performance the composer might have had in mind'.[189] And working through the various problems that arise when trying to use instruments in fifteenth-century song, he arrives at the conclusion that 'the role of instruments in the performance of the 15th-century song repertory now seems considerably smaller than was once assumed'.[190] Nevertheless, the chapter as a whole is coloured by moments of uncertainty, warnings against rigid conclusions, possible counterarguments for instrumental participation, problems with the assumption of radical changes towards the end of the fifteenth century. It reflects very well the awareness that any scholar is bound to have, especially now that the *a cappella* position has been so long and so firmly established, that the balance of evidence in any argument concerning medieval music is always changing.

A more direct challenge was mounted by Sylvia Huot in a 1989 article 'Voices and instruments in medieval French secular music . . .' which revisits and augments the literary evidence mined by Page in his 1987 book *Voices and Instruments of the Middle Ages*. Huot finds in thirteenth- and fourteenth-century French literature a wealth of references to playing and singing. Interpretation is of course very difficult, and Huot avoids definite conclusions. It is clear to her that minstrels played and sang lais, possibly at the same time (though it is by no means easy to relate this to surviving music). Instruments involved are commonly fiddle or harp. When aristocrats performed they seem to have sung, confirming Page's previous proposal that instrumental performance was the domain of the professional minstrel. Composed polyphony was sung in all parts, but other references could be read as describing combined vocal and instrumental performance, including self-accompaniment on a small organ. In the end, Huot takes away from her encounter with a wide range of literary sources the impression that there was a similarly large variety of performance practices (exactly the conclusion reached by Handschin, and offering the same escape from the whole problem). Yet, as always, the literary descriptions are so easily read in different ways, according to the punctuation one provides or the emphasis one prefers to place on one or another meaning of a word, that it is hard, reading Huot's article, not to conclude that one could use literary evidence to support many different arguments while proving none.

More recently, and yet again in *Early Music,* Jon Banks has pointed out that the amount of polyphony copied without text around 1500 is far greater than has generally been supposed.

In fact, texted chanson sources from around 1500 are actually outnumbered by those which the compiler considered complete without text.... Textlessness is the normal condition of much of the chanson repertory, and as such can be seen to represent not so much an anomalous incompleteness as an alternative authenticity. If we accept that textless sources were intended for instrumental performance, then it seems that much of the chanson repertory was heard as often on instruments as voices.[191]

Of course, not even the most zealous *a cappella* enthusiasts had been proposing that instrumentalists and singers, and instrumental and vocal music, remained separated as late as 1500. As we have seen, there was always plenty of evidence that they mixed increasingly from the earlier fifteenth century onwards.[192] Thus the implication that recurs through Banks' article, that his findings offer a challenge to the *a cappella* hypothesis, is eloquent testimony to its effectiveness and to the length of its reach. Banks surely knows that it was never thought to have more than limited application beyond the middle of the century, but he takes it for granted that many of his readers will suppose that it applied everywhere and throughout the Middle Ages and early Renaissance. He concludes,

If lutenists knew the parts of this music, did they ever join with singers in a mixed consort? ... The thriving instrumental practice evinced by the Segovia Codex also raises the question of whether it was a radically new phenomenon, or whether it can be extrapolated backwards to an earlier part of the 15th century.[193]

and it would be surprising if the answer to these questions were not just as he suggests. The more interesting question is how much further this argument will go. Once it is widely understood, once again, that most fifteenth-century music is fair game for instrumental participation, how long will it be before scholars and performers extrapolate backwards from there into the fourteenth century, and so on? We will surely not be content with *a cappella* performances for ever.

APPENDIX: SELECTED EARLY RECORDINGS OF UNACCOMPANIED
VOCAL PERFORMANCES OF LATE MEDIEVAL MUSIC

1930s

Columbia 5710, side 1
'Columbia History of Music by Ear and Eye'
Veni sancte spiritus, dir. Sir Richard Terry
Comments: solo chant alternating with choral organum in fourths

Columbia 5711, side 1
'Columbia History of Music by Ear and Eye'
Dufay, *Christe redemptor omnium, Conditor alme siderum*
Singers from Westminster Cathedral choir, dir. Sir Richard Terry, 1930
Comments: All male choir, including falsettists, notable today for their
    use of portamento

Anthologie Sonore 59
'Musique française au quatorzieme siècle'
Pro Musica Antiqua of Brussells, dir. Safford Cape, artistic direction Curt
    Sachs
Discs manufactured May 1937 (based on the Pathé factory codes stamped
    on the disc; information generously provided by Jerome Weber)
Comments: notable for the realistic barking dogs in the anonymous chace
    Se je chant

Anthologie Sonore 91
'Musique de Jongleur et Musique savante du Moyen-Age'
Side A (matrix AS 137, rec. 27 May 1937, soloists dir. Safford Cape): *En
    mal la rousée* (solo harp); *Anima mea / Descendi / Alma* (Montpellier)
Side B (matrix AS 204, rec. 28 March 1939, soloists dir. Guillaume de
    Van): *Congaudeant turbe* and *Ad regnum / Noster* (Engelberg 314); *Je voi /
    Fauvel* (Fauvel)
Comments: Issued 1939. All four motets unaccompanied, side A
    lovelorn, side B vigorous (note different recording dates and per-
    formers)

Editions de L'Oiseau Lyre OL 62
'Les Musiciens de la Cour de Bourgogne'
Side 1: [Ockeghem], *Déploration sur la mort de Binchois*
Side 2: Binchois, *A solis ortu candine; Sanctus*
Chorale Yvonne Gouverné
Recorded soon before 18 October 1938

Comments: the Ockeghem uses vocalising accompanying voices; very slow, deeply felt, with much portamento.

Editions de L'Oiseau Lyre OL 109
'Motets du XIIIe Siècle: MS H 196 Montpellier'
Chorale Yvonne Gouverné
Recorded soon before 16 January 1939
Comments: women's voices only. Two-part motets, Rokseth numbers 64, 146, 184, 189, 239. (Error on label: 236v should read 263v. Again, my thanks to Jerome Weber.)

Parlophone R 1017
'2000 Years of Music', parts 3 and 4
Side B 'Early Polyphonic Music': *Congaudeant Catholici* (Cod. Calixtinus)
Soloists from the Choir of the Gregorian Society of the Berlin State Academy of Church and School Music, cond. Prof. H. Halbig
Comments: three baritones

1950s

HLP 4
History of Music in Sound, volume II: 'Early Medieval Music up to 1300'
Comments: the LP is almost wholly vocal, emphasising that for Dom Anselm Hughes, at least, instrumental accompaniment became common only after 1300. Here only a viol or regal is used on the tenor of thirteenth-century motets.

HMS 20, side 1 = HLP 5, side 1, band 1
l'Escurel, *A vous douce debonaire*
Pro Musica Antiqua, dir. Safford Cape

HMS 22, side 5 = HLP 5, side 1, band 9
Piero, *Cavalcando*
Franz Mertens, René Letroye (tenors, dir. Cape)

APM 14019
(Archive Production: History of Music Division of the Deutsche Grammophon Gesellschaft) 'Research Period III, The Early Renaissance [NB], Series A: The Florentine Group: Madrigale e Caccie From the Codex of Antonio Squarcialupi.'
Pro Musica Antiqua, Brussels, dir. Safford Cape
Side a (dated 24 June 1953) (no bands), item 4: Giovanni, *Nascoso el viso*

Comments: Mezzo & Tenor soloists. No instruments. Singing more
secure than on the English set.

APM 14063
'II. Forschungsbereich, Das zentrale Mittelalter, Serie D: Ars Nova
in Frankreich. Guillaume de Machaut La Messe de Nostre Dame,
10 Weltliche Werke.'
Mass, side a (rec. 31 Jan./1 Feb. 1956); Songs, side b (rec. 2/3 Feb. 1956).
Pro Musica Antiqua of Brussels, dir. Safford Cape.
Comments: Won a Grand Prix du Disque. Insert card says editions are
Ludwig, revised by Charles van den Borren & Cape. Side a, bands 2,
5 & 6 (Kyrie I, Agnus I & III, Ite) are *a cappella*. Side b, band 7 offers
a very unsteady unaccompanied performance of *De triste cuer/Certes
je di/Quant vrais amis* by René Letroye, Franz Mertens and Willy
Pourtois.

1960s

Expériences Anonymes EA 83
'Music of the Middle Ages: Volume IX – The Fourteenth Century'.
Capella Cordina, dir. Alejandro Planchart (rec. Jan., May, June 1966 at
Yale University).
Side 2, band 6 (NB labels and matrix marks were on the wrong
sides on the available copy): Landini, *Sy dolce non sono chol' lir' Orfeo*.
Comments: Amateur all-vocal performance.

CHAPTER 3

Hearing medieval harmonies

The stories offered in the preceding chapters suggest a variety of conclusions about what the sound of medieval music has done for people in modern times. But before these conclusions can be drawn in adequate detail, two sets of issues need further investigation. First, how has the effect of medieval music in performance interacted with views of the Middle Ages drawn from other kinds of evidence? And secondly, what can we learn from everything we have seen here about the way people study early music history? These are the subjects of this chapter and the next.

What other kinds of evidence are there that suggest ways of understanding this music? In a sense everything is relevant, so that the whole range of evidence touching in any way on medieval music could belong in our story: views of chronology, manuscripts, biographical details, cultural and political contexts all have a bearing on how we tell it. But I want to restrict this study to the question of how we hear those sounds as music, and to take in aspects of the music in its broader cultural role only in so far as they affect the sounds that are made and the conclusions that are reached about their musical interrelationships. So while I recognise that, for example, the modern construction of Perotin the composer out of the remarks of the thirteenth-century theorist Anonymous IV has a significant impact on the way we hear the four-part organum *Sederunt*, to investigate that properly would call for a far larger study (in every sense) than this aims to be. More pressing, to my mind, would be the question of how we hear the notes of *Sederunt* change in relation one to another according to the way it is performed. Certainly I would want to go into the construction of Perotin just far enough to argue that the image of 'the great composer of Notre Dame' encourages us to hear grander long-term relationships in the music than we would think appropriate in two-part organa or early motets, even though they belong within the same broad repertory. But I would not wish to press this further by investigating, for instance, the extent to which our notion of Anonymous IV's extended modal theory (if we have one) colours our perception of the music in performance as more or less convoluted today. It is not that any clear line can be drawn between one kind of evidence and another; simply that the level of insight required to show perceptible, let alone audible relationships between such indistinct concepts is way beyond my sensitivity as a listener or writer.

But even with such liberal exclusions, one area remains very clearly within our reach, and that is the relationship between performance and an understanding of the musical language, above all the harmonic and contrapuntal language of medieval music. Exactly what those terms might mean may be unwise to specify too closely: one can easily get lost in the maze of different medieval and post-medieval uses of each word, and to make any claim about what they should mean would be out-of-keeping with the spirit of this book (which is, I hope, essentially anti-legislative). The difficulty here is in distinguishing 'harmony' from 'counterpoint'. Any definition one might offer of each drops one into the middle of the debate that I wish to analyse. For example, I might offer as a starting-point the following: a harmony-led view of the music hears a sequence of vertical sonorities (chords)[1] made up of rhythmicised pitches proceeding in a linear fashion, while a counterpoint-led view hears lines of rhythmicised pitches that proceed through changing vertical relationships. Put like that, it is not easy to see the difference. But it is in fact a dichotomy that has been perceived between these two views – or, if you prefer, an insistence on perceiving a difference between them – that lies at the heart of the century-long debate about the hearing of medieval music, and that relates with striking ease to the performance practices we have been examining.

HARMONY

When nineteenth-century musicologists made their aesthetic response to medieval music clear, it was to the sound of the vertical relationships between pitches that they drew attention. For Fétis, whose research into the musical past, it has been proposed, develops the theme that 'art does not progress, it simply changes',[2] an exception had to be made for medieval music:

The monks Hucbaud de Saint-Amand and Odon de Cluny, writing in the tenth century, are the first to speak of [diaphony or organum]. Gradually people grew bold and had harmony in three and four voices which was called triphony and tetraphony, but what harmony, great God! Everyone knows that successions of two parallel fifths or octaves are forbidden today because of the hard and dull effect they produce. The French ears of our ancestors were more battle-hardened than our own, for their tetraphonies consisted in strings of fifths, fourths and octaves which were heard throughout the duration of an antiphon or a litany. They were moreover so fond of this cacophony that those who caused masses to be sung consented willingly to pay the singers *six deniers* for having the pleasure of hearing it, instead of the two deniers due for plainchant.[3]

A related, but ultimately more sympathetic view was held by Fétis's older contemporary (and the source of much of Fétis's knowledge of medieval music) François Louis Perne, who worked extensively (though without published results) on late medieval notation and the music of Machaut. For Perne 'The true friend of art knows neither ancient nor modern music . . . he sees practical music for what it is in itself, just as the customs of the times and the degree of civilisation bring it about'.[4] But not all civilisations are equally expert, as Perne's view of Machaut's harmony makes very clear:

There is no denying that the harmony of this Mass offers no charm to a practised ear. Its effect is hard and savage; at every turn the sound is betrayed by false relations, by parallel fifths and octaves and by passing tones that proceed by skip. The foundation of this harmony is composed of nothing but fourths, fifths and octaves. Rarely a third or a sixth appears to soften the harshness – if I dare to call it thus – that results from such a bizarre assemblage. Let us add that the rhythm of this composition is worth no more than the harmony. Thus must moderns judge such monstrosities. But if we look back to the time when this composition was made, should we not be astonished by the amazing degree of genius required to succeed in composing on plainchant an entire Mass in four parts without employing anything but fifths, fourths and octaves, and in forming in each voice a melody analogous to the principal chant?[5]

Kiesewetter's view, however, was no more sympathetic than that of Fétis:

Even Hucbald must have renounced the organum, if he could ever have listened to it with his own ears. . . . [A]mong the penances . . . of the order, one of a nature so painful to the senses could never have been inflicted.[6]

Kiesewetter's much-cited annotation to Machaut's *Dous viaire*, 'O tempora! o mores!', arises, it is true, from an understandable difficulty with the unusual parallel sevenths leading into Machaut's final cadence, exacerbated by Kiesewetter's failure to suggest B-flats, but his labelling the entirely normal parallel fifths in the same passage suggests that his reaction to more conventional passages may have been only slightly more favourable.[7] An extract from the Gloria of Machaut's Mass, published by Kiesewetter on three occasions, shows mistranscription helping to form an unfavourable view of the music. His source was Kalkbrenner 1802 which contains numerous gross errors producing dissonance and undirected progressions.[8] Kiesewetter 1831 improves considerably on this, emending Kalkbrenner apparently by instinct rather than from seeing any of the sources (which speaks well of his instincts). He improves it still further for Kiesewetter 1834, this time so well that contact with the original seems likely (though the emendations would not be impossible to arrive at alone with careful thought). Perhaps it was his gradually improving transcriptions that allowed Kiesewetter to describe Machaut in 1843 in rather more favourable terms as 'a bold, albeit incorrect contrapunctist'.[9] For Fétis a little later, 'The mass and motets of Guillaume offer numerous passages full of bad harmonic progressions, the remains of the diaphony that had long been in use during the Middle Ages'.[10] For Ambros in 1864, borrowing his uncle Kiesewetter's *Dous viaire* transcription, 'Guillaume Machaut, a graceful melodist, as a contrapuntust stands no higher than Adam de la Hale',[11] and his view of Adam must to modern sensibilities seem thoroughly offensive:

Here in the lower voice lies a pretty but deformed melody; the harmony is again horrible. As in [Adam], the 'Hunchback of Arras', a fine soul lived in a misshapen body, so his fresh melodies are stuck in a crippled, misshaped harmony.[12]

Kiesewetter offered an early statement of a view that was to become widespread later:

It is further to be regretted, that the composers and theorists of this period, and those who came afterwards in direct succession, trusting to their erudition, considered their works or examples perfect as soon as the mere labour of writing had been completed; and, as if they toiled only to please the eye, they disdained to sit down in the stillness of their study, and try the effects of such works upon their senses by means of the spinet (should it have then existed), the psalterium, or any other suitable instrument, whereby many a false relationship (*mi contra fa*) of the harmonic progressions would have become manifest, but which otherwise continued to be unnoticed by them when represented only on their parchments.[13]

In other words, medieval composers could not hear their music in their heads as they composed it, that is to say, they couldn't imagine accurately how it sounded, and were sufficiently unconcerned with the results to try it out afterwards, which is why it sounds so bad. Composition was an activity for the eye, putting down notes on parchment according to simple rules, rather than for the ear.[14] Hence:

That music is an aesthetic art, the essential aim of which is to please and to affect, had been made clear at that time neither to teacher nor pupil, both of whom in their theories believed themselves to be possessed of its sum and substance. But the theory, or (as we might rather say) the grammar of the music, could not flourish so long as there was no perception that theory must be united with practice, to which it should give precedence, according it even a reasonable freedom and self-activity; nay, in fine, also condescending to be instructed by it.[15]

And yet, writers from this period were far from unsympathetic to medieval counterpoint theory. For Kiesewetter the counterpoint teaching of Johannes de Muris – so easily assimilable to one brought up on Fux – was admirably far-sighted, 'as pure as can be desired even at the present day';[16] yet when he came to look at Machaut's subsequent music:

I have always regarded it as the work of a presuming dilettante, who, being adept at versification, and having a superficial degree of knowledge in regard to most things, was bold enough to try his skill in a musical composition. But we are told by M. Castil Blaze . . . that this mass was performed at the coronation of Charles the Fifth of France (1364) by the choir of the chapel royal. Such was the state of music in the country where forty years previously a Johannes de Muris had been a teacher.[17]

And for Heinrich Bellermann modern counterpoint (though he does not realise it, for his date for Franco's treatise was over a hundred years too late) has an even earlier origin:

Our modern interval teaching is almost entirely Franconian, only with the difference that we in certain cases must treat the fourth as a dissonance, and that we further consider the sixths, like the thirds, as imperfect consonances. This modern teaching comes already from the 15th century.[18]

The error in dating helps Bellermann explain why fourteenth-century music falls short of Franco's counterpoint theory:

The 14th century made considerable progress in this respect. The voices, as one had been assembling them up to then, were, of course, shaped in quite a random manner and were very different from one another in character; they lacked anything in common, an artistic unity. This one still sought to achieve in order to make the melodies of the different voices similar.[19]

Wooldridge may be thinking of this passage when he writes, in a review of *Early Bodleian Music*,

it is clear that the musicians of this generation [the fourteenth century]..., possibly... awaking to some perception of the frequent cacophony of the earlier works, were beginning to apply themselves to the evolution of a more sober and more agreeably sounding style.[20]

The gap between counterpoint teaching, which deals almost exclusively with more-or-less consonant two-part progressions, and musical compositions whose harmonic world is often considerably more adventurous, lies at the heart of all discussions of medieval harmony; explaining away the dissonances in real compositions has been the aim of writers from Kiesewetter right up to the present day. Kiesewetter's answer – that the composers didn't know what they were doing, or didn't care – inevitably became too crude as ideas of progress in music history came to seem less reasonable. But we shall see later that the problem he perceived continues to be felt to this day.

Of course, all these nineteenth-century writers just quoted are looking for sixteenth- or eighteenth-century ideals in medieval music, and are failing to find them.[21] That almost goes without saying. But what is interesting for us is the reasoning they use to explain the inability of medieval composers to hear what to modern writers seemed so obvious. The composers clearly lacked basic musical skills, which had either been lost or developed only later; music in other words began as a paper (or parchment) exercise, and only gradually became artistic.[22] Yet for anyone surveying music history as a whole, from the ancient world onwards, it was evident that that had not always been so. Testimonials to the power of Greek music left scholars, trained in the Classics from their earliest years, with no doubt that music there achieved a power it later lost and had hardly recovered since. So reasons had to be found for the inability of medieval musicians to hear the obvious. On the one hand it was easy to look, with Burckhardt, to the Renaissance and the recovery of ancient learning and to find the beginning of adequate music there, as Kiesewetter had already done in his work on the Netherlands school, and as generations of scholars of fifteenth- and sixteenth-century music have done ever since. Another strategy became Ludwig's, once he had seen manuscripts of trecento music during the first three or four years of the twentieth century; the same strategy, at exactly the same time, became Riemann's, as he encountered trecento song in Wolf's transcriptions. For Riemann, there *were* great medieval composers, but they were Italians, composing from nature, in stark opposition to the French who composed from the book:

the Florentine Ars nova of the trecento did not take up the laborious studies of the Parisian school . . . , but rather appears with a whole new fundamental form and further with such security and natural liveliness that any suspicion of a theoretical starting point is out of the question. No, this Florentine New Art is very much an authentic indigenous offspring of Italian genius . . .[23]

And we have seen how Riemann explained the harmony of a trecento song in terms of simple, thoroughbass-like progressions.

Similarly for Ludwig:

It is an extremely difficult task, to try aesthetically to approach one of the more complex Ballades, for example from the Codex Chantilly, with regard to its melody and rhythm; how disappointing is the kernel that hides behind the shell![24] With its array of well over a dozen simple note forms – quite apart from the various colours of those note forms, often two of these colours next to one another in the same note – it is, fortunately, unique in the entire history of music . . . What a different effect, on the other hand, the Italian Trecento has on us![25]

Even for Riemann, however, it was necessary – as we have seen – to move the text around in order to produce syllabic declamation suitable to the Renaissance.

Until this point, then, medieval harmony is measured against later models and is read as more or less competent, and more or less significant, according to the extent to which it anticipates them. But it is essentially a harmonic reading. Just as, until about this time, its performance was assumed to be *a cappella*. The two views are not unrelated. Since Rameau music had increasingly been conceived as a harmonic art, and never more so than during the second half of the nineteenth century as composers and theorists assimilated the innovations of Wagner. At the same time, the Palestrina revival had generated an '*a cappella* ideal' much discussed in German writing on music.[26] It must have seemed perfectly reasonable to judge medieval music by its harmony, and to find it lamentable. But the introduction of instrumental accompaniment was to change all that, for it would liberate medieval harmony from the demand for vertical coherence. By making it easier to conceive it as a collection of lines – a conception that could easily be related to medieval theory – it became possible to transfer musical attention somewhat from the combination of those lines back to the integrity of their individual melodic profiles. The transformation of theories of performance practice thus made possible a transformation in understanding of the music's logic. Riemann had no idea of this, of course, for Riemann was above all a theorist of harmony; his aim in overturning old views of performance practice was to bring medieval song (especially Italian song) into the historical mainstream, by showing that it was in its essentials already modern. That one might go on from there to explain even French music as collections of well-formed lines, accessible to the modern ear through appropriately linear performance practices, surely never occurred to him. His view, however, made that step possible, indeed easy.

For Riemann the heart of the relationship between performance practice and musical language is to be found in the functions of the voices. It is the accompanying nature of the lower voices, as much as the upper-voice melismas, that suggests instrumental performance, but not any linear view of the music. On the contrary, for Riemann vertical construction is crucially bound up with musical excellence:

The Caccia is often a hunting scene and indeed a canon for two voices with or without a fundamental bass voice. The musical construction of the Florentines in this time thereby breaks clearly with the Parisian school in that almost without exception it lacks a self-standing cantus prius factus; thus successive voice invention is abandoned. Even in the cases where a low voice proceeds in long notes it appears not so much a cantus firmus as a *fundamental bass*. The canonic voices cannot have been made one after another, but rather are worked out together.[27]

Here we can see already crystallised the either/or view of vertical vs. horizontal construction that has dominated discussion of medieval harmony ever since. From Riemann's nineteenth-century perspective, simultaneous composition of all voices is essential to the quality of the result, and is therefore to be identified especially with trecento pieces. (The fact that canons are to be found in French repertories as well is passed over silently, and was very probably not yet known to Riemann.) For Riemann then, brought up on an assumption of *a cappella* performance, and as the pre-eminent theorist of harmony concerned above all to understand this 'new' music in harmonic terms, there is no obvious association between the contrasting sounds of an instrumentally accompanied performance and the linear quality of the music. Ludwig, writing at the same time, had much less difficulty making this association. For him, the fifteenth century is characterised by the disappearance of a contrast between melody and accompanying voices, and the loss of the distinctive vocal and instrumental characters of cantus and lower voices, at the same time as 'vocal spirit and vocal life penetrate all voices equally'.[28] Less bound to explain the history of harmony than Riemann, Ludwig saw clearly that there was an obvious correlation between performance practice and musical language.

For Schering, Ludwig's reading presents no difficulties. Schering belonged to the first generation of scholars trained on the assumption of instrumental accompaniment. And for him it is much easier to imagine a more linear conception of the music: counterpoint before harmony. Here is his commentary to a Machaut ballade provided for the 1912 annotated reissue of Riemann's anthology:

His ballade 'Ploures, dames' one imagines sung in the upper voice and in the two lower voices played on instruments, probably low viols. In the difficult rhythm of the voices and in the harmony, in many ways still tainted with the ashes of an older conception, it shows a certain relationship with the work of the Florentine trecento composers. One observes here, as in similarly made polyphonic pieces, that the attention is not so much on the sounding together of the voices as on their horizontal stretching-out and their natural running along beside one another. For at the time of Machaut chords are not bound one to another but rather only 'voices', a peculiarity in which the compositional technique of this time in many ways touches that of the present.[29]

Similarly, in his updated edition of Dommer's music history, published two years later, Schering explained that in Adam's music (as found in Coussemaker's edition of 1872),

the era itself gives, with the practice of combining different melodies and different texts in a single piece, an indication that it takes pleasure principally in the independent melodic movement of the voices and gives consideration to the harmony only as a secondary factor.[30]

Although [pseudo-]Johannes de Muris sets out rules for note-against-note counterpoint in two parts it is far from clear to Schering that they are followed by composers. Thus in Machaut's music (as found in Wolf 1904),

it becomes apparent how around this time free expression in polyphony is striven for. Of course here too the way the pitches work [das Tonleben] is no longer comprehensible to us. The voices certainly move with extraordinary freedom, and the change between polyphonically entwined and homophonic passages, for example in [the] . . . Kyrie and Credo of a Mass [*sic*; this of course predates any overview of Machaut's work], points to increasing historicity, using the means of the multi-voice polyphony for the characterisation of expression; but on the whole the compositions seem completely strange and antiquated, especially on account of the parallels and innumerable harshnesses that arise from the reckless voice leading. Thus it was seen as in no way insufficient to leave the third voice dissonant against the two-voice core [den zweistimmigen Satz], so long as it was consonant with at least one of the two other voices.[31]

Given that the harmony is so unsatisfactory, it is possible for Schering to argue that the fourteenth century is significant not so much for the worth of its music *per se* as for its new approach to performance:

Probably the significance of the 14th-century *Ars nova* is above all to realise that it brings on a time of the most tremendous upturn of instrumental playing, and that the merits of Vitry, Machaut and the older Florentine masters consisted principally in the brilliant tracking down of the possibilities, and in the written fixing, of the new instrumental art-practice.[32]

These passages, written for a general audience and reflecting views that Schering might not so freely have expressed in an academic study, clearly show a link between his dislike of fourteenth-century counterpoint, his understanding – from reading medieval theory – that parts were added to a two-voice core, and his beliefs about performance practice. A view of successive composition, contextualised here for the first time, is used to explain what seemed to him to be crudities in the harmony. Composers were not concerned so much with the overall sounding result as with the correctness of counterpoint between pairs of voices. This is not so different from what Kiesewetter had been saying eighty years earlier, except that now it is possible to see a correspondence between this layered approach to composition and a layered approach to performance. And the fact that there is a correspondence begins to suggest that the harmony may not be so careless and accidental as Kiesewetter's generation would have supposed. It seems possible, therefore, that the new view of performance, emphasising through contrasted colours the different lines running along beside one another, encouraged scholars to see medieval counterpoint as intending to operate, and thus as correctly to be perceived, in a linear rather than a vertical fashion. Schering played a key role in this process. Kevin Moll points to earlier hints at successive composition (a two-part, 'dyadic' core, plus other voices added one at a time) in Ludwig and Ambros and also, in the case of fifteenth-century music, to Schering's other 1914 publication, his Studies in the Music History of the Early Renaissance.[33] There Schering proposes two fifteenth-century approaches to three-voice composition, one successive, the other simultaneous (i.e., all three voices conceived together), supporting the first with a reference to the thirteenth-century theorist Johannes de Garlandia on the addition of a third voice to a two-part core. This only emphasises Schering's willingness to apply conclusions from one century to another. Looking at both these publications, it is not hard to see how, by putting together hints from different periods and repertories – Garlandia, Adam, de Muris, Machaut, the fifteenth century – the idea of dyadic/successive composition could grow into a single view of late medieval music.

Consequently, as Rudolf Ficker began to form his view of Gothic music during the second decade of the century, expressed in publications from the 1920s onwards, many of the ingredients were already in place.[34] Even Schering had an inkling that fourteenth-century music was not being properly understood:

Nearly all these polyphonic compositions are so far removed from our feelings that a judgement of their sensory value seems impossible.[35]

Yet in his early publications Ficker seemed to follow Schering's harsher views quoted above, even to the extent of echoing some of his phraseology, as in these comments on the apparent crudity of the music he found himself editing for the Denkmäler der Tonkunst in Österreich in 1920:

The basically harmonic formation of this compositional technique makes itself felt also in the numerous parallel octaves and fifths which arise in the polyphonic development of the lower voices. [He lists them.] Liebert therefore appears not to have been a notable musical artist [Satzkünstler]. Even though these parallels, the repeated doubling of the leading note, and other compositional freedoms and harshnesses appear unbearable to the polyphonically educated ear, they were not emended in the edition since they constitute characteristic features of the compositional technique.[36]

For Ficker, approaching this music as a classically trained musician, Liebert is not much of a composer if he writes parallel perfect consonances, despite (one might add) such parallels being the foundation of all polyphony up to his time. Five years later, though, Ficker's view had considerably changed. 'Problems of form in medieval music', of 1925, takes a noticeably more sympathetic approach to the difficulty of understanding this music in terms of its historical context:

Today we are beginning to recognise that all theoretical laws are conditioned by their time and have no universal validity.[37]
The fact that it is not possible, with the help of the musical terms and notions familiar to *us* today, for us to recover as correct an attitude to the musical products of the Middle Ages as we adopt, more or less, towards the music of the sixteenth century, also proves that even that notion of the 'musical' that we feel today as natural and innate, the perfect balance of the melodic, chordal and rhythmic components, did not exist at all in the Middle Ages.[38]

Rather, the balance between these components varies, and Ficker therefore divides the period into three phases: the chordal organum-conductus phase, the metric-rhythmic phase that produced the modal compositions of the Gothic period, and finally the melodic phase of the late Gothic and early Renaissance. In the first period chant is brought north with Christianity, but is transformed under the 'special musical disposition of Nordic man', stripped of its (Southern) melodic qualities so that, as a cantus firmus, it 'becomes the substratum for the foundation of a new, sonorous [klanglichen] world of ideas' typical of Nordic man.[39] In the second, Gothic phase, the top voice becomes melismatic in Notre Dame organum, and a stronger contrast between the melodic-sensuous duplum and the intellectual-ideational tenor develops.[40] In the third phase Italy offers a new emphasis on sensuous melody but now supported by, and organically related to a sonorous-harmonic foundation, and it is this that provides the foundation for the perfect balance of musical components that characterises later music:

Thus, in this true Ars Nova [as opposed to the French], a new notion of the 'musical' developed through fusion and concentration of the three musical driving forces, melos – rhythm – harmony. The basis of this notion has remained unchanged through the course of time until today, despite all modifications.[41]

In seeing the Italian ars nova as crucial to the development of modern music Ficker follows Riemann, but aims to integrate Riemann's vision into a scenario that allows Nordic/Gothic tendencies to dominate through the originality of Nordic man and his ability to mould, with the intellect, material formed only instinctively in the South. It is a wholly masculine vision, dependent on the power of the will to shape nature. Four years later, in an article of 1929, Ficker links up his view with other German scholarship (of an even more speculative character) aimed at finding an origin for music itself.[42]

A number of keywords appear again and again in Ficker's work: Nordic, Gothic, chordal/sonorous (klanglich), concepts belonging to an ideology with deep roots in Germanic writing. Ficker was far from alone in this. Chapter 1, reporting Pamela Potter's work, noted how in the 1930s a range of popular beliefs about the nature and superiority of German music became respectable in musicological research.[43] SS officer Richard Eichenauer in his 1932 *Musik und Rasse* (Music and race) 'ascribes an inborn Nordic racial tendency to Leonin's and Perotin's innovations in polyphony',[44] while Albert Wellek in 1936 argued for 'a pattern of "linear" music perception in the north and "polar" music perception in the south', accounting for 'northern composers' tendencies to write "polyphonic" (contrapuntal) music'.[45] Pushing these beliefs only one step further produced, as reported by Potter,[46] an unpublished essay by

Reinhold Zimmermann from the early 1940s entitled 'German music in the French-speaking areas', music that for Zimmermann included the works of Leonin, Perotin, Philippe de Vitry and the Franco-Flemish masters of the Renaissance. The essay was written for a collection edited by Hans Joachim Moser and 'initiated by Goebbels's ministry . . . that aimed to demonstrate Germany's long history of musical hegemony in territories recently occupied by German troops'.[47] As I shall argue in more detail in the next chapter, it was the attitude fostered in work like Ficker's that ultimately led to this sort of distortion, contributing to an ideological environment in which territorial expansion became no more than a recovery of what was rightfully German. While Ficker never contributed directly to those kinds of arguments in print he shared in the ideology that led to them, even drawing attention to his early exploration of Nordic qualities in music in a letter to the Dean of his Faculty in 1939.[48] In fact, the assumption which resonates through Ficker's writing in the later 1920s, that linear counterpoint was in some deep way Germanic, is so pervasive in writing on music, not just during the Weimar and Nazi periods, that it may be hard today to realise how much we still depend on it.[49]

Throughout Ficker's pre-war writings the consistent musical thread is his conception of *Klang*, or (crudely) 'sonority'. For Ficker it embraces vertical and horizontal, providing the origin for both the melodic and harmonic aspects of polyphony; and it is produced in sound by the interaction between them. It offers a way of avoiding a black-and-white distinction between successive and simultaneous approaches to the construction or the perception of polyphony. And it offers a justification for the particular balance between them that composers, and particularly Northern composers, can be argued to have achieved in various ways throughout the history of Western music. It is in this context that his later ideas about the composition of medieval polyphony, when we come to them, will need to be read.

At the same time that Ficker was finding a way of assimilating medieval music into a wider vision of German musical thought, Heinrich Besseler was also attempting to construct a coherent story of the development of medieval and Renaissance music, drawing on the massive collection of transcriptions made by his teacher Friedrich Ludwig. Like Ficker, Besseler wished to shape the ingredients of medieval music available to him into a grand narrative. But unlike Ficker, Besseler had a much greater and more representative range of music to study: he did not need to fall back on general concepts in order to fashion a quasi-historical narrative. Moreover, where Ficker was above all interested in what one might broadly call spiritual concepts – the expression of Germanness and religious feeling in early music, which he aimed to evoke, even re-create in his dramatisation of Notre Dame organum – Besseler's interest was much more down-to-earth, and ultimately more modern. He was less interested in fantasies of medieval man's musical spirituality than in the essentially philological question of tracing the development of musical language towards modern times. While for Ficker medieval music offered a key to medieval man, for Besseler it was a step towards something better. One could argue that Ficker's view was more sensitive to the period context of medieval music, and that in that sense it ties in more readily with more recent views promoting 'authenticity' in performance and in musical discourse. And one could argue also that Besseler was continuing to work with the attitude of Fétis and Kiesewetter (and arguably also Ludwig), seeing medieval music as a form stumbling towards Palestrina, and that Ficker was therefore, from our point of view, the more historically minded thinker. But that would be to misunderstand entirely their motivations. Ficker, in his pre-war writings on the language of medieval music, was a fantasist not a historian, using his imagination to create an unknown and unknowable past. Besseler, on the other hand, had the evidence in front of him, and used it, within the constraints of his time, to form a narrative, based on calculable features within the music, that could explain the known and observable early Renaissance future.

Besseler studied philosophy with Martin Heidegger, and it is possible to understand his particular concern with the development of music towards tonality in the light of Heidegger's belief in the overriding significance of humans unfolding themselves through time, becoming rather than being.[50] In his musicology Besseler shows an unusual concern not only with music-historical processes but also with perception. And this reflects too his practical involvement in the German *Singbewegung*, with its emphasis on singing and communal involvement in traditional 'folk' music-making,[51] and his enthusiasm for *Gebrauchsmusik*.[52] The interaction of these interests helps to explain why Besseler believed, to a greater extent than most of his colleagues, that musicology had to deal with the history of performance and interpretation, and it goes some way to explain why so much of his work dealt with how to 'hear' medieval and early Renaissance music and thus with the workings of its harmonic language and the procedures of its composition. For Besseler medieval music was practical and functional within everyday life, rather than (as for Ficker) profoundly spiritual, and thus the study of its manufacture – its crafting – offered a direct route to understanding it historically.

The introduction to his review of Gurlitt's 1924 Hamburg concerts offers some useful clues to Besseler's interests and beliefs. On the whole he seems to be sceptical of, or at least non-committal about, overarching theories concerning the unity of medieval life and thought, as discussed in Gurlitt's introductory lecture; he is more interested in details of individual pieces of music in relation to their performance. In particular, he comments again and again on matters of tonal construction and on the different perceptions of singer and listener:

[The details of *O Maria maris stella*] are not meant for listening, but rather for singing or following from within. That is to say: they do not demand to be passively accepted by a listener as an integrated sound-structure. Rather, their musical sense is fulfilled in the live interaction between the performers. Even though, with the modern dissolution of a sense of tonality, comprehending by pure listening no longer presents any difficulties (as I often find confirmed), the misunderstanding of presupposing here the usual external listening focus must urgently be pointed out. This [focus for listening] lies, rather, in each of the equally empowered voices, which above all perform themselves and only incidentally refer to the others. A listening process of such intense involvement is directed above all towards a regularly felt, clear interval-relationship to the neighbouring voice. It is in this way that the thirteenth century's governing interval-consonances – unison, fourth, fifth, octave – are to be understood, as an actual performance will immediately show.[53]

This is the voice of a scholar concerned, like Ficker, to hear the music as it was, but – for Besseler – to understand it in purely musical terms. He is interested in how it worked, and in how it was experienced at a practical level, rather than in what it signified; in how to listen through following its working rather than through experiencing its meaning.

The kind of collective performing/listening required by the thirteenth-century motet seemed not to work for the innovations found at the end of the century, nor for the ars nova which followed. The virtuoso melody plus accompanying lower voices, that Besseler saw in the last fascicles of the Montpellier manuscript and thereafter, seem to him to go together with functional chord progressions to require a different kind of hearing:

It is all set down with such artistic sureness that one must no longer assume mere hearers for such masterworks but rather already a knowledgeable public.[54]

And Besseler quotes Grocheio on the need for an educated audience to appreciate this kind of motet. Medieval music, in other words, as it takes on elements of functional harmony, is starting to become art music, a position that Riemann would have been able to recognise without too much difficulty. A new approach to hearing is thus tied up with a new approach to harmony. With the ars nova, 'voice and instruments combine in sonorous splendour that together with full three-part writing and extensive musica ficta give French music a fantastic colourfulness'. And so we come to Machaut, whose late four-voice motet *Christe/Veni* we have already seen Besseler hold up as proof, refuting Riemann, that French ars nova music is at least as fine as Italian. Besseler admires 'the new colourfulness of sonority, the splendid spacious rhythms streaming along and the new formal principles'. But above all he is fascinated by the harmony:

For the audacity of the chord-leading, which results from the strong linear construction . . . just one example: in the Triplum at *Nec tueri se poterant* comes, precisely signed in all voices, in modern terms a g-minor chord led, via the diminished triad on e, immediately to f-sharp minor and then through g major and e minor to c major – executed by four instruments and two voices in strict polyphonic leading, a downright amazing effect of sonority, yet one that is by no means unique in this music. The age of Dufay still preserves a weak reflection of it.[55]

And it is above all around developments in harmony that Besseler begins to shape a history of style-change through the late Middle Ages and early Renaissance. One can see him moving pieces around in his mind as he seeks a set of relationships that makes sense of both the manuscript and the sounding evidence:

We find the same attitude [as in the Dufay mass movements] in Dunstable's wonderfully fresh-sounding *Quam pulcra es*, performed vocally in all three voices.[56] The chordal writing of such pieces points, more clearly still than to fauxbourdon, to the vocal conductus technique of Italian trecento madrigals, in whose two-voice form the harmonic underlying bass-leading had priority above all else. In these surroundings the sung three-voice *Ave regina* of Leonel came as a strange surprise: one almost believed one was already hearing a Netherlandish choral sound. In any case this piece leads far more definitely to the soundworld of Ockeghem and Josquin, than for example [does] Dufay's *Alma redemptoris mater*, that likewise was performed purely vocally – correctly in the chant-decorating upper voice, but by contrast, for the extensively ligated tenor and contra, instrumental performance is at least as permissible, especially as both sources (Trent 92 and above all the careful Ms Modena lat. 471) underlay no text.[57]

The relationship in his mind between chordal writing and vocal performance is very obvious, and we have already seen that later in life Besseler argued for *a cappella* performance as early as Dufay's mature masses on precisely these grounds, that the new chordal thinking of composers went hand in hand with vocalisation of the previously instrumental lower voices.[58]

Taking his Hamburg review as a whole we can see Besseler already beginning to form the history of medieval and Renaissance music that he was to publish in full less than a decade later. But it arises out of an attempt to relate what could be seen to what could now be heard. And what was heard depended on a negotiation between what could be inferred about medieval thinking on the one hand and modern ideas about musical form on the other, the former filtered through the latter even while contrasted with it. Besseler brought clear conceptions of musical form, shaped in the study of much later repertories, but he brought too an acute ear and an unusually open mind. He was aiming all the time to see medieval music as both different from and yet analogous to modern music, so finding in it procedures (especially harmonic procedures) that were comparable to those he knew, yet seeing them operating with medieval constituents. It was a delicate balancing act, and one that subsequent generations of scholars continued to practise, for precisely the same reasons, up to the present day. The continuum from Besseler to Sarah Fuller, for example, is easy to see when one considers it in these terms. Besseler's horizon was rather more tonal than Fuller's, but they are both engaged in essentially the same enterprise. (We shall come to Fuller later in this chapter.) For Besseler, however, this was virgin territory, uncrossed by musicologists before him. To consider music this early as plausible, even in its own terms, was a brave step, and he must have been very aware of the need to bring his views into a recognised intellectual context. Even more daring was to try to tie this new understanding of the workings of medieval polyphony into its sound in modern performance. His final sentence needs to be read in this light:

Musicologically, performance (apart from its special meaning for the Middle Ages) certainly deserves the credit for emphasising that music history also embraces a history of sounds and hearings, and that it is not least a part of the history of ideas.[59]

All these ideas come into sharper focus in Besseler's contribution to the multi-volume *Handbuch der Musikwissenschaft*, the first large-scale treatment of *Die Musik des Mittelalters und der Renaissance*, issued in parts between 1930 and 1934.[60] What is new here, for Besseler, is the greater emphasis on German values and on the concept of *Klang*, both crucial features of Ficker's work during the previous decade that have clearly rubbed off on Besseler, a process that can only have been made easier by the rise of nationalistic sentiment in Germany during these years.[61] Besseler is concerned, too, with the relationship between art music and the *Volk*, which for him becomes a problem for the first time with the ars nova motet, the form in which Besseler finds the beginnings of art music.[62] The early thirteenth-century motet is still *Umgangsmusik*, colloquial music, music for participation rather than listening or contemplation, craft rather than art. But with the innovations attributed to Petrus de Cruce, and the ars nova that grows out of them, we arrive for the first time at *eigenständige Musik*, music for its own sake, to be listened to, aimed at an elite.[63] Yet all the while Besseler emphasises the need for modern listeners to be educated in medieval modes of listening in order to avoid misunderstanding. This, above all, is his higher purpose in the book, to lead readers into his way of hearing medieval music so that as well as knowing facts about it they may also learn how to listen to it.[64] And that listening crucially involves hearing the gradual shift from melodic to harmonic thinking between the late thirteenth and early fifteenth centuries, culminating in the achievements of Dufay.[65] Reading *Die Musik des Mittelalters und der Renaissance* one could still see medieval music as striving towards something more sophisticated, but nevertheless as having an integrity of its own that, with an effort to direct one's listening via medieval modes of thought, one could recover and appreciate today.

Like most German academics, Besseler survived denazification almost unscathed, but the details that came to light during his trial made it impossible for him to find work again in the West.[66] (Unlike Ficker, Besseler was heavily involved in Nazi organisations and in the implementation of Nazi policy.) Consequently his post-war work was carried on mainly in East Germany, and was largely confined to fifteenth-century music; it has been well surveyed by Kevin Moll,[67] and will only be summarised here. Yet it is relevant. If their pre-war work laid down the outlines of the modern view of medieval harmony – its difference from and yet its analogies with tonality – the lengthy debate between Besseler and Ficker during the late 1940s and 1950s essentially laid the tracks from which scholars have viewed medieval harmony ever since. For Besseler the emergence of modern tonality can be traced to the early fifteenth century, above all to the contratenor writing of Ciconia and Dufay and the consequent emergence of a true bass line that directs harmony, rich in triads and focused towards V–I cadences, from the bottom up.[68] For Besseler, Dufay was essentially a tonal composer and his music could be accurately described in terms from Riemann's theory of functional harmony. It is possible to see how this view might develop out of the ideas with which he was juggling in the Hamburg concert review, particularly his taste for triadic writing and full sonority in Machaut and Power, and later in *Die Musik des Mittelalters* in his reconciliation of medieval hearing (as he saw it) with the first stirrings of tonal procedures. By the 1950s Ficker's views had developed as well. His mystical and ideological understanding of a Nordic medieval soundscape, reflected in his writing and performing in the 1920s, and his inclusive and necessarily fuzzy conception of *Klang* has in the meantime focused into a much narrower concern for intervallic usage and compositional procedure. Concepts that in the 1920s could be discussed impressionistically, even poetically, now in the harsher reality of post-war Germany needed to be pinned down and analysed.

Although they differed on a crucial issue of interpretation and hearing, Besseler and Ficker shared important ideas in common. Both saw the origin of tonality in the late medieval use of thirds and sixths within directed progressions. To both, as for Schering, it was obvious that late medieval pieces had a two-voice contrapuntally self-sufficient core formed by the discant and tenor parts. But the meaning of that 'self-sufficiency' was quite another matter. We have already seen how for Schering this view formed, in part, as an explanation of what he (and all his contemporaries) perceived as crudities in the music, and we have seen how it related so conveniently to a linear view of performance practice. By 1950 the inadequacy of fifteenth-century music was much less obvious. That neither Ficker nor Besseler revisits Schering's work may be because neither shared his unfavourable view (though both had been closer to it in the 1920s). Indeed, it is absolutely clear from everything he writes that for Besseler, at any rate, Dufay was a very fine composer; and it was precisely his taste for Dufay's music that led Besseler to insist on its tonality. He loved it because for him it was tonal. Dufay therefore had to be a crucial innovator. To see him as nothing less than the creator of the most effective organising technique in Western music must have been intoxicating. Ficker – and this is just as clear from the way he writes – identified much less personally with early fifteenth-century music; for him it was a question of evidence, of what could be learned from the theorists and from the relationships between the voice-parts. While Besseler brought a deep need to justify his musical reaction, Ficker did not; for him it was more a matter of history. Consequently, their difference of opinion lay not so much in their ability to see the relationships between the notes and the existence of a cantus–tenor pair, as in their understanding of the musical imagination that underlay such an arrangement of voices. For Ficker 'the primary element of contrapuntal function' (to borrow Moll's useful phrase) was this cantus–tenor duet. For Besseler, in certain progressive kinds of early fifteenth-century music, it was the contratenor lying beneath which directed the harmony made by all voices together. Ficker's view encourages a linear hearing of the music, Besseler's a vertical hearing, and this for our study is the key issue. They imagined the music differently.[69]

'Hearing' and 'imagining' in this context need a further gloss. I have used both terms because hearing in the narrow sense (whether in concert or mentally) is only one ingredient. We cannot possibly know in any depth how these two men perceived Dufay in performance. It is easier to guess how it seemed to Besseler because we know that he brought later models of tonality to it, and it is reasonable to assume that to him it sounded not entirely unlike later music, at any rate in broad terms, for example in having a melodic line supported by harmony. Ficker's aural impressions are, at first glance, much harder to gauge because there is nothing to which one can relate his more linear view. But that must have been the case for him also. There are no models: what it means to hear this music as a duet with filling voices remains uncertain still; it seems doubtful that many listeners, however expert, can separate out a cantus–tenor duet and follow it as such, at the same time perceiving a contratenor individually, as a coherent independent melodic line, even when the parts are performed on contrasting instruments. There seems no reason to assume that Ficker did either. Reading him one can easily discern a harmonic hearing of progressions of thirds and sixths leading to octaves and fifths ($\frac{6}{3}$ to $\frac{8}{5}$); in other words, to judge by the way he writes he heard the standard three-part progressions harmonically. The difference, therefore, seems to reside not in the hearing but only in thinking about the formation of these progressions. For Besseler a composer imagined them together, for Ficker they were conceived as a duet first, with other voices formed in relation to it. The difference, in other words, comes down to compositional procedure, but a procedure reflecting a significantly different way of thinking. Thus for Ficker, fifteenth-century composers continued as before, for Besseler they changed over to something new. For Ficker there was continuity with the Middle Ages, for Besseler there was a radical change of approach.

Given examples like this, it is not hard to see how beliefs about performance practice, compositional procedure and musical quality are tied up together in complex personal views of medieval music. Besseler instinctively loved early fifteenth-century music; as an expression and justification of that love (at a time when it was not widely shared, even among specialists) he needed to see these pieces as 'works', to promote them to the level of great works from later times; he needed to make them (in the modern sense) canonic. Part of the reason he loved the music was that he heard it tonally, and showing its tonality was the surest way of proving its quality: if he could show that Dufay actually created tonality his place in music history was assured. And 'his' means Dufay but also Besseler: as ever in humanistic research, author and subject tend to fuse into one. Bound up with this is Besseler's ambivalent attitude towards vocal performance. He cannot believe in it, yet (as we have seen) he is sympathetic when he hears it (in Karlsruhe in 1922)[70] and sufficiently intrigued to show some of the evidence for it (in Utrecht in 1952),[71] because vocal performance would emphasise the richness of the full sonorities that play such an important part in his view of tonality. In the end, this is more surely about Besseler than Dufay. But that is true of every scholar, including Ficker. Ficker must have felt that his view of the music was fully endorsed by contemporary performance practice (and again, contemporary embraces 'them' and him). And to present him as the objective observer of the medieval facts is to overlook the personal investment that speaks so clearly from his stance towards Besseler. Ficker's 1951 article 'Towards a history of the genesis of fauxbourdon', far from being, as its title implies, a careful step towards a determination of what happened in the past, is rhetorically dominated throughout by the need to attack Besseler, and one needs to ask why.

Crucial to Ficker is his belief in lost English improvisation practices providing the basis for compositional developments. There is perhaps a sense in which this imagining of a lost world relates back to his more imaginative pre-war view of medieval music, but at any rate Ficker is concerned to see the musical past as different and partly unknowable. Besseler, as we have seen, is more interested in seeing the past in modern terms, in collapsing the gap between then and now. Similarly Ficker is content to imagine medieval counterpoint as quite unlike that of later centuries, while Besseler wants to push back modern counterpoint as far as possible (at least, as far as his musical tastes require). But Ficker also identifies personally with his view, and Besseler's alternative is perceived as dangerous and liable to undermine it. So while, as I have suggested, Besseler's passion springs from his love of the music and his need to promote it, Ficker's springs rather from a need to imagine the past as different and yet reconstructable: he has a vision to promote, but it is of a mental world rather than a musical style, it is based in ideas rather than in sounds, in concepts rather than in sensations. These two approaches are incompatible, and they illustrate two strands of thought that one can trace in constant opposition generating and sustaining musicological disputes throughout the past hundred years.

In an article that started as a kind of sketch for this book I illustrated these two approaches with examples, seeing Riemann as a 'familiariser' – perhaps the most influential of all, finding the origins of tonality and of art song in fourteenth-century Italian music – and Schering as a 'defamiliariser', who saw the same repertory as organ music decorating simpler originals, now lost.[72] One can see some of the same yearning for a lost past, recoverable today only via one's own insights, underlying Ficker's work. Schering's, of course, was crazier, requiring more faith and obedience from the reader; but given their not dissimilar ideologies in other respects it may be that we are looking in both these cases at the mentality of a prophet, setting out a new vision, claiming a higher authority (in this case, historical truth), and insisting on its acceptance. Such a mentality is not unknown in academia; indeed it is the very nature of humanities subjects that they allow the formation of idiosyncratic visions, and give their creators the power to teach and examine, to award or to withhold approval, funding and employment. We shall consider this further in the next chapter. For now it is enough to be aware that in cases such as the Besseler/Ficker dispute there is more at stake than simply the correct interpretation of evidence.

Kevin Moll has suggested that through their writings, and then through the writings of their pupils, Ficker and Besseler set up and sustained two parallel readings of medieval and early Renaissance harmony that continue to be promoted today.[73] By placing in sequence most of the crucial articles from before 1970 and publishing them together, his point has been very well made. On the one hand, he shows Besseler's pupils and admirers continuing to argue for a proto-tonal, vertically constructed harmonic language; on the other, we see Ficker's successors promoting a linear procedure built around a two-voice core, as implied by early counterpoint theory. Enough has been said here of both views for those articles to be read now in a slightly wider musical-ideological context. Rather than go over the same ground here, and before considering developments since 1970, I should like instead to look at some other writers, working slightly outside these two schools but very clearly influenced by them, writers who were especially concerned to apply to medieval music views that Besseler and Ficker, and Schering too, had developed to handle the music of the early Renaissance.

Willi Apel trained as a mathematician and pianist and was largely self-taught in musicology, gaining, by a somewhat unusual route that excluded him from a major university music department, a doctorate in 1936 on 'Accidentals and Tonality in Musical Sources Fifteenth and Sixteenth Centuries', following which he immediately moved to the USA. His first article written after emigration offered a view of 'The partial signatures in the sources up to 1450', arguing that theorists were not to be trusted, but that scholars should pay heed, rather, to the accidentals written in the music. Partial signatures (for example none in the cantus, one flat in tenor and contratenor – a pattern common throughout the later medieval and early Renaissance periods) he saw as implying a kind of bi-tonality. Written accidentals in general were to be read literally and not supplemented by supposing that unwritten ones would also have been sung. What made this view possible was the assumption we have already seen again and again that this music was to be considered only horizontally, without heed for vertical relations. Apel's is one of the most uncompromising statements of this belief:

No notions of the vertical relation – neither approving or disapproving ones – should be applied to a passage where there are no vertical relations at all.[74]

In dealing with vertical clashes,

No rules can be considered as satisfactorily solving the problem unless they are of a strictly horizontal character, and enable the singer (as well as the modern transcriber) to judge 'a parte ante', that is, from the consideration of the voice in question exclusively . . . [75]

His views on the value of medieval music surface momentarily here and there in his classic textbook on the notation of polyphonic music (1942), which he must have begun soon after arriving in the States. The book – the first substantial study of notation since Wolf 1904, and much wider-ranging – was brilliantly timed, meeting a need in the American university music departments that were being so suddenly propelled into advanced musicology by the influx of refugees from Germany and Austria. For all his fascination with the principles and practice of notation, Apel clearly dislikes 'mannerist' music. Echoing Ludwig in 1902–3, Apel writes:

It is in this period that musical notation far exceeds its natural limitations as a servant to music, but rather becomes its master, a goal in itself and an arena for intellectual sophistries . . . [76]

Yet Apel's view moderated as he got to know the music better and as time went on. In the introduction to his edition of late fourteenth-century songs published in 1950 – another seminal work used by everyone – he quotes that same passage and goes on: 'Today, after more extended studies in this field, I should prefer a somewhat more cautious statement'.[77] We shall see that a similar gentle conversion towards a genuinely musical response to medieval pieces was experienced by other musicologists around the middle of the century. No doubt a number of factors came together at the same time: the availability of more music, the fading away of Romantic harmony as the background musical language of the time, and its replacement by neo-classicism and serialism, the beginnings of a widespread early music revival, but also an increasing determination to see the music in the terms of its time rather than in the light of later developments. Here Ficker's approach was the more useful, for it corresponded to a more general desire after the Second World War to set aside traditional (in this case proto-tonal) views of the past and take a more objective look at the evidence. The rise of modern music made this much easier, for it provided an example of the way in which an unfamiliar musical language might be learned and understood without falling back on the recent past for comparative models. A great many writers, however, made comparisons between medieval and modern musical procedures; indeed, it is one of the most commonly recurring themes in medieval music reception, and we have already seen examples here.[78] Apel makes a similar point in talking of the texture of late fourteenth-century songs:

It is a texture of utmost subtleness and refinement, consisting, as it were, of extremely loose threads which from time to time only, frequently at wide distances, are bound together in full coincidence and consonance, while in between they move with a considerable degree of independence, rhythmic as well as harmonic . . .
   Again one cannot help noticing the similarity of this method to present-day practice. Stravinsky has used the term 'polar attraction' in order to describe a phenomenon characteristic of his own style, and essentially identical with that to be observed in the style of the late fourteenth century.[79]

And Apel goes on to talk of the 'shredding' of texture in some pieces where the parts almost never coincide save at a cadence. It will come as no surprise that he goes straight on from here to discuss 'valid' analysis and successive composition, for of course that provides an irresistibly obvious explanation for the shredded texture:

Turning now to a consideration of the harmonic idiom of the manneristic period,[80] it is essential that such a study should be undertaken with the proper tools of analysis. It is hardly necessary to say that the methods of our present-day books on harmonic analysis cannot be applied without reservation. A valid result can only be expected if the analysis proceeds along the same lines as the creative process of composition, and in the fourteenth century this process is entirely different from that of the sixteenth or of the nineteenth century. The music of our period represents the final stage of that early method of composition which is known as 'successive counterpoint' which is based on the principles of *discantus*. . . . [T]here can be little doubt that the composition starts with the upper part (*superius*) or, to put it more accurately, with a two-voice texture, superius–tenor, in which the superius receives primary attention. . . . The addition of the third voice, the contratenor, is made by connecting this with the tenor in another *discantus* combination. The most frequent vertical combinations . . . are 8/5/1, 5/3/1, and 6/3/1 (1 being the lowest note). However, our compositions contain not a few examples of combinations like 7/5/1 or 7/3/1 in strong positions. In spite of their dissonant quality, these chords conform to the principles of three-voice *discantus*, since in all these cases the tenor is in the middle, forming an upper third (or fifth) with the superius, and lower fifth (or third) with the contra. Therefore it would be more correct to indicate these combinations as follows: 3/1/-5 or 5/1/-3, where 1 stands for the note of the tenor. This representation also helps to clarify the 'consonant' character of these chords, which may well be termed 'discordant consonances' or 'consonant discords'.[81] . . .

It appears that the harmonic idiom of our period rests on the principles that were developed during the thirteenth century. However, our composers did with them what Richard Strauss and Max Reger did with the system of nineteenth-century harmony: without abandoning the basis they pushed on to the outmost frontiers. It is the extreme application of the system of *discantus* which characterizes the music of the late fourteenth century. By combining a freely elaborated superius–tenor texture with an almost independently conceived contratenor–tenor texture, the composers arrived at a musical style much more daringly and deliberately dissonant than ever before and, indeed, ever thereafter until the advent of the twentieth century.[82]

This is worth quoting at length because it contains so many points that were to be repeated and elaborated from here on. Although Apel is drawing on Schering and other pre-war work in assembling this rationale for late fourteenth-century harmony, his statement – in the introduction to the only substantial edition of fourteenth-century song (apart from Machaut) issued before 1970 – could hardly have been more prominent, and must have been read by every medievalist and every performer for the next twenty years and more. Late fourteenth-century song was mannered, it was discordant, it was to be compared to modern music (not necessarily a recommendation in 1950 and even less so over the next ten years as integral serialism came on stream), and it was like this because the composers worked on the parts successively and thought of dissonances as consonant provided that each was consonant with the tenor. Since this is not consonance as we know it, it is essential to study this music in medieval terms in order to understand it. Part of the attraction of this view is that it is both different and logical: understanding comes through strictly following the theory of the time, unmoderated by more conventional views – just like twentieth-century music. One is not required to like either, but simply to understand that this strange music arises from clear procedures rigorously followed.

OBJECTIVITY

The influence of views like this is clear in the work of one of the most interesting barometers of mid-century opinion, the Machaut scholar Gilbert Reaney. Reaney was a student at Sheffield University in the later 1940s, concluding with a Masters thesis in 1951. During the 1950s he researched at the Sorbonne, at Reading and then at Birmingham universities. Only in Paris did he encounter any professional medievalists; so that throughout his student years, and for much of the following decade, he was necessarily working independently. As a result his views were formed from what he read and saw rather than under the influence of a supervisor, and his early writings, in consequence, present a valuable insight into the view that a widely read independent scholar would form around the middle of the twentieth century. Reaney is above all a pragmatist, aiming to derive common-sense conclusions from clearly relevant evidence. Consequently he is less interested than Besseler or Ficker in forming global views within which details might be interpreted, and more interested than either in relating detailed points in treatises to specific moments in compositions. Indeed, his 'Fourteenth-century harmony', from 1953, is very deliberately restricted to cross-referring counterpoint teaching and Machaut's practice which, he argues, is based upon it yet both goes beyond and falls short of it in related respects. Machaut's taste for rhythmic figuration, producing displacement and decoration of the underlying correct counterpoint, for Reaney produces a level of dissonance that fails to meet the theorists' requirements, requirements met more successfully in the following century. Here one can clearly see Reaney sharing earlier doubts about the competence of fourteenth-century composers: he speaks of four-part consecutives that 'become really embarrassing', of parts constructed 'without regard for relations between them', of 'intolerable clashes' (in Machaut's earlier four-part writing) and 'bad effect'. All these he explains as the product of 'successive counterpoint' as specified by the theorists: Machaut began with the tenor, then wrote the cantus, then the contratenor and finally (where there was one) the triplum, and so long as each voice was consonant with the tenor 'that was what mattered most'.[83] It is hardly possible to read this together with the disapproving adjectives and not to conclude that Reaney found this approach inadequate, though characteristic of its time. So for him, too, later music provides the ideal towards which Machaut and his contemporaries were taking significant steps, without ever quite arriving.

Yet although Reaney brings a view to the fourteenth century that would later on be considered anachronistic, he is in most respects following a methodological route that was to become eminently respectable. For in restricting himself, like Apel, to the theorists and the notes he is evidently taking a step back from the more imaginative arguments of pre-war scholars, aiming instead at providing the spadework that – for a historically minded musicologist – needs to precede any larger view. In this, too, he is very much in line with Apel, and indeed his view of the harmony and its creation is clearly indebted to the passage just quoted. What Reaney does in this article is essentially to apply Apel's view to Machaut and work it out in more detail. For Reaney, as for Apel, a 9/5/1 chord is consonant because the superius and contratenor lie a fifth either side of the tenor. This, and numerous other details, are to be understood in terms of 'successive counterpoint'.[84] Following Apel, Reaney offers a descriptive, theory-based approach to Machaut's harmony that is only momentarily disfigured by discomfort with its dissonance. In many ways, then, this early article has worn remarkably well. Precisely because he offers relatively little interpretation, and that easily excisable, there is not a great deal in Reaney's work with which historical musicologists today would be inclined to argue. Of course that also reflects the stability in their ideological approach over the intervening half-century. What the theorists say and what the pieces consist of are still seen as the only stable points in a constantly shifting landscape; tying one's approach firmly to them remains for many the only guarantor of safety. One way of looking at Apel's and Reaney's work, then, is to see them reining in those earlier scholars who aimed to understand medieval music in as complex a light as later repertories, insisting rather on a cautious approach based in the surviving evidence. This is to see them as the godfathers of what, by analogy with authentic performance and in full recognition of its impossibility, one might call 'authentic analysis'. We shall return to the difficulties with this concept below.

Fifteen years later (though perhaps writing earlier, since the new text begins, 'Ten years ago . . . ') Reaney revisited his early article with notably more tolerance of Machaut's dissonance usage:

But evidently Machaut sought out these collisions, which are admittedly some-what experimental, though interesting in their results. I believe that they are not merely arbitrary but were considered acceptable by Machaut in much the same way that we accept the various dissonances in traditional harmony.[85]

The 'traditional' is revealing, of course, but this altered emphasis illustrates Reaney's sensitivity to changes in the general view of musicology. By the later 1960s it was at least clear that Machaut made more intentional use of dissonance than his immediate predecessors, and thanks to the thesis of Ursula Günther, of 1957, it was possible to see this as a stage in the development of late medieval harmonic thinking rather than an aberration. In general, though, there is something very comforting about Reaney's writings: medieval music emerges as a little strange, per-haps, not quite fully formed, yet knowing its own mind and susceptible to rational examination by modern musicians. Medieval composers were really not so unlike us, and given a willingness to put ourselves in their situation it is not too hard to understand what they were up to. To an Englishman, it all seems quite reasonable.

Günther acknowledges a very considerable debt to Reaney,[86] who was one of the only Anglo-Saxons writing about fourteenth-century music during the years in which she developed her thesis,[87] though admittedly the alternatives were not inspiring. The 1950s in France saw the publi-cation of Armand Machabey's book on Machaut (1955), and one does not have to examine it for long to see why it was hopeless as a model anywhere else. Machabey, using the standard French labels of tonality, offers a résumé of each of Machaut's compositions, pointing to odd fea-tures of interest but working systematically only in the sense that he goes through the same motions for every piece. Machaut is here the French composer in microcosm, idiosyncratic certainly, but with a taste for har-monic twists and parallels that shows him clearly as the predecessor of Berlioz and Debussy. Machaut becomes familiar for the French, just as through Reaney he became familiar to the English.

Ursula Günther's achievement is characteristically national too, but working in the tradition of Ludwig and Besseler she has less need to prove the value of her subject. Indeed, prevented from travelling to the manuscripts by post-war restrictions, and having instead to work in Göttingen with Ludwig's transcriptions (just as Besseler had worked with them in the 1920s), Günther had a better grasp of the whole range of late medieval music than any scholar with the single exception of Besseler, whose interests had now shifted to later periods, leaving the field wide open. And unlike Besseler she came to the subject with a much cleaner ideological slate. Partly this was due to the extraordinary obstacles placed in her way as a woman working for a doctorate in medieval music in Germany. The disapproval of her supervisor, Heinrich Husmann, forced her to form her own view and spared her (exceptionally for a German student at that time) the close supervision of a senior scholar with a line of his own. Consequently she had no choice but to work from the ground up, taking the materials to hand – above all the music and the published work on it.[88] It is understandable that, as a sympathetic, non-partisan scholar in the same field, Reaney should have provided reliable support. In these difficult but bracing circumstances Günther developed a commonsense approach ideologically close to Reaney's, but carried through with the systematic thoroughness that only a German scholarly education could instil.

Günther saw herself as turning back (like Reaney) from the cultural-historical approach, attempted by Besseler, in order to continue the scientific approach of Ludwig, re-examining the origins of the manuscripts, but going on from there to look systematically at the music itself, at its formal, notational and stylistic characteristics and at the way those changed over time. Above all she was interested in style-change and its potential for filling out the meagre documentary evidence for datings and influences between Machaut, his contemporaries and followers. Her approach was rigorously descriptive. Rhythms, intervals, form-schemes, metres provided the details on which stylistic distinctions were based. How they worked together was not an issue that could reliably be determined. That composers did attend to vertical considerations, even with their essentially linear approach to composition, was clear, but in the absence of guidance from medieval theory on how to label progressions, there is only a limited amount that can be said without falling back on modern terminology. Consequently, questions of larger-scale harmonic function lie beyond the reach of an objective investigation. It is not hard to see, in this approach, a determination to avoid the subjective judgements that were so crucial to Besseler's or Riemann's attempts at a synthetic view of the nature of medieval music, attempts now seen as grossly premature.

Here, then, is post-war realism: the grander views of the older generation failed because they were based on wishful thinking; what is needed now are facts; only by going back to what can be known for certain, and adding gradually to that, can historical knowledge about the past be gained. 'Back to Ludwig' becomes the unspoken motto for Günther, and it was one adopted, more or less consciously, by many medievalists of her generation and that which followed. Yet at the same time, the pupils and grandpupils of Besseler and Ficker were prolonging their controversies partly because of an understandable, and perhaps even laudable unwillingness to abandon the ideal of achieving a wider view of the subject.[89]

Ernst Apfel studied under Thrasybulos Georgiades, who was himself a pupil of Ficker in the 1930s. Georgiades's doctoral thesis, on fifteenth-century English discant treatises, owed a large debt to Ficker both in its concept of *Klang* and in its insistence on the crucial role played by England in the development of tonal harmony. Emphasising that the treatises deal with progressions of sonorities, not with the formation of lines, Georgiades sees the sonority as the fundamental unit of medieval polyphony, arguing for a principal line of development from thirteenth-century organum across to England, where sonorities are enriched to produce a language that could then be fully developed on the continent in the fifteenth century, arriving at its full realisation in Netherlandish polyphony. Fourteenth-century French and Italian musics are thus a distraction, a temporary elaboration of linear writing tangential to the onward march of sonorous (and by implication still Nordic) thinking.[90] Georgiades is even able to make room for Ficker's *Sederunt* orchestration, arguing that although medieval pieces are notated within an octave, this is simply a matter of recording the sonorous constituents in the most economical form; 'it was up to the performance to realise, by the spatial expansion of these sonorous components, the large soundspace intended'.[91] Apfel, too, shows clear signs of a developmental view that looks towards Palestrina, and beyond that to the development of major–minor tonality,[92] but his methodology is very clearly a product of its more objective time. Apfel's characteristic procedure, followed again and again in minutely detailed studies,[93] is to count, list and categorise the interval-teaching of treatises, and then the intervals used between voices in pieces, in order to argue that the contrapuntal function of a voice indicates its place in the composition-process, and also to show a gradual development of sonority-progressions towards the classic procedures of the sixteenth and early seventeenth centuries. Apfel's almost obsessively cautious approach is both admirable and maddening for, aside from the point about composition process – whose underlying assumption (that voice-function proves composition process) is never questioned, the meaning of his data remains largely unexplored. The theorists imply, and the pieces seem to support, several approaches to assembling multi-voice pieces; interval-usage changes over time from the progressions described by medieval theorists to those of the Baroque. This is objectivity taken to a point where little is argued that is not already obvious.[94] Its purpose within its period context it is surely that, by rejecting interpretation, it avoided – unlike the work of Besseler or Ficker – disfiguring the pristine evidence with modernist accretions. In this sense it is comparable to, but more fundamentalist than, Günther's work with sources, notation and forms; her *Back to Ludwig* is conceptually related to Apfel's (and Apel's) *Back to the Theorists*. For German scholars in the 1950s Ficker and Besseler, not to mention Riemann and Schering, had gone much too far, and it was clear that a new respect for fundamental research was necessary.

To anyone who has studied the growth of 'historically informed performance' over these same years, all this will seem familiar. At exactly the same time in Germany scholars and performers were beginning to look critically at the way they had been playing Bach, in particular, aiming now to strip away the remaining traces of post-Romantic interpretation, leaving as far as possible the bare notes of the score to speak for themselves. Mengelberg gave way to Karl Münchinger, Schweitzer to Helmut Walcha. In these same years, the American Institute of Musicology and L'Oiseau Lyre were starting their series of collected editions of early music; the new journal *Musica Disciplina* was publishing descriptions and inventories of the principal manuscripts – all the work Ludwig had done, in other words, was finally being redone by others and now published – and theory treatises were beginning to appear in critical editions. Musicology was starting again, setting aside the hasty conclusions of the generation after Ludwig, aiming this time to get it right. And inevitably that meant not discussing harmony. Because nothing was clearer from reading early musicology than that any talk of harmony invariably led towards tonality and thus to anachronistic conclusions. This idea of anachronism is quintessentially 1950s. The belief that one could keep modernism and romanticism out of the picture, returning to medieval views uncoloured by modernist interpretation is, in fact, pure modernism, the same kind of modernism that insisted on clean editions and clean performances. Interpretation was bound to be wrong, and so to avoid interpretation was the only way to avoid anachronism. That the results were then assumed to be 'correct' shows a failure of common sense that seems hard to credit now. But at the time the shadow of Romanticism was still so deep, because Romanticism lived on so strongly in mainstream cultural practice (consider Klemperer, notwithstanding his authenticist claims), that its exclusion from historical work was a *sine qua non*. Nothing infected by it could be scholarly.

Common to all these writers after Besseler and Ficker is thus a disinclination to engage with the music in any kind of relationship that depends on perception. To a large extent this is precisely because Besseler, his contemporaries and nineteenth-century predecessors, were perceived as so anachronistic. Indeed, 'anachronistic' became the strongest critical term in medievalists' vocabulary, sounding the death-knell of any work that could be accused of it.[95] Thus the generations of Apfel and Günther and their pupils studiously avoided issues of harmonic function, viewing with disdain those attempts by non-medievalists such as Salzer, Schachter or Perle, to see medieval music in any but historical or objectively descriptive terms.

One can see how instrumentally accompanied performances made this relatively easy. By downplaying vertical combinations and emphasising linear thinking, the modern, smooth solo voice accompanied by the utterly different, relatively thin sounds of reconstructed medieval and Renaissance instruments positively discouraged a harmonic hearing of medieval pieces. Apel, in the introduction already quoted, argued for wind instruments precisely on the grounds that they were better able than strings to make the parts separately audible. He adds in a note his debt to Hindemith's Yale performances, and in such a way as to suggest that he had perhaps not heard the music before:

Actual performances would help greatly to clarify these questions [of scoring]. I had the pleasure of attending the performances of music of the thirteenth, four-teenth, and fifteenth century given under the direction of Prof. Paul Hindemith at Yale University in 1946 and 1947, and I hope to be permitted to express to Mr. Hindemith the sincere gratitude of the whole clan of musicologists for his splendid and highly successful efforts.[96]

As we saw in chapter 1, Hindemith's performances, for which he borrowed instruments from the Metropolitan Museum in New York (a thought that must send shudders down a curator's spine now), were closely modelled on those advocated by Schering in 1931 in their attitude to scoring, so that again one can see in operation the very clear continuity from pre-war Germany to post-war America, brought by so many exiles from National Socialism.

Performances like this, with their unfamiliar and sharply contrasting instrumental sounds, meant that the question of how to understand the harmony as functioning was not pressed upon scholars by hearing the music. The way the music sounded in concerts and on record tended only to emphasise its strangeness, the impossibility of knowing it with one's modern musical tastes; indeed, for many the thought that one might have a view of the music as music, that one might value one piece more or less than another, that a performance might leave one feeling 'what a wonderful piece of music', seemed out of place among scholars. The new objectivity of scholarship thus found no challenge in the rapid growth of medieval music performances after the war. Furthermore, the very strangeness of the music as it sounded then seemed to confirm the objectivists' suspicion that nothing reliable could be said about its language beyond description of the facts. The Middle Ages were not approachable through artistic recreation but only through historical investigation. Performance was amusing, fascinating, even thrilling, but it was not scholarship.

Only from this perspective can one understand what otherwise seems an extraordinary lack of discrimination among scholars when faced with a huge range of competence among performing groups. Standards in recordings from the 1950s are often quite rough. Yet that seems not to have elicited much comment. I have myself seen on a number of occasions distinguished medievalists applaud enthusiastically (and comment warmly afterwards on) performances of late medieval songs that failed even to synchronise the parts, not through choice but because one of the players got a beat out and stayed that way. The music is meant to sound strange, and unless the score is very familiar nobody knows that anything is amiss. It is not, on the whole, a case of cloth ears, but simply a lack of familiarity with the notes: they are not, for most musical medievalists, the subject.

It is necessary to appreciate this environment in order to understand fully why the early attempts at harmonic analysis, which we must now examine, were so frowned upon. First, it was not considered appropriate to examine the music other than through the eyes of medieval theorists; secondly it was not music in the full sense in which the kind of music for which analysis was devised was music, and so to analyse it was to treat it as a fully formed art work rather than a craft object (a slightly more sophisticated variant of the 'primitive' argument); thirdly to emphasise its vertical aspect was to misunderstand it fundamentally, to concentrate on an incidental feature and treat that as essential; fourthly, to look for long-term harmonic planning was to seek something that had not even been conceived at this time. It is not hard to see how many unsupported assumptions underlie this set of beliefs. Nevertheless, they were widely held until at least the mid-1980s, after which, as we shall see, theory-based work in harmonic analysis (Fuller's in particular) finally undid them. It is worth remembering, too, that analysis itself, as a discipline aiming to do more than just describe the score, had developed relatively recently, and continued to be distrusted by musicologists until quite late in the twentieth century. Analysis of early music was therefore on the fringe of a practice to which many were already hostile. Add this to all the other objections from medievalists and it is hardly surprising that the first systematic analyses of medieval polyphony were offered by professional analysts rather than by medievalists.

ANALYSIS

Paul Hindemith's fascination with medieval music can be understood in the light of his neo-classicism, more precisely his anti-romanticism, and his interest in *Gebrauchsmusik*. For Hindemith, going back to an earlier age, when composers seemed more interested in construction than expressivity, offered one way of reacting against the continuing hold of Wagner over early twentieth-century musical taste. Coupled with that, it was easy to imagine that medieval music, anonymous and apparently simple, was produced by craftsmen for daily use rather than by egotistical geniuses (Wagner again) with an eye on posterity. All this accorded with Hindemith's own view of the function of composers. *The Craft of Musical Composition*, his analytical textbook for composers, speaks of this in its very title:[97] composers needed to work within a clear framework of rules and tricks of the trade, passed on from master to pupil, not write according to whim.[98] His inclusion of an example from Machaut must, in part, be intended to demonstrate the continuity in compositional technique from the Middle Ages to his own time. His analysis of Machaut's ballade *Il m'est avis* is notably sensitive to the balance of linear and vertical, which he analyses separately but in alignment (Illustration 3.1). His comment on the relevance of this is revealing:

There are the boldest oblique accumulations of non-chord tones, as well as parallel fifths, sevenths, and seconds – all features which can only today

[204]

3.1 Paul Hindemith's analysis of Guillaume de Machaut, *Il m'est avis* (1942: 204)
(Reproduced by kind permission of Schott & Co. Ltd.)

again be felt as correct and beautiful, because we again have the ability, common in Machaut's time, to separate harmonic and melodic elements while listening, and to weigh one against the other.[99]

Hindemith speaks for himself, of course, for hearing contrapuntally was exactly the skill he developed so acutely as a composer and required in his listeners. His music goes perhaps further than any, in this period, towards exactly the interaction of apparently separate domains that he hears in Machaut, and both composers are notable for their ability to lead voices through apparently chaotic dissonance that, just as one despairs of resolution, turns a corner into a perfectly prepared cadence. (It is tempting to suspect that Hindemith's and Machaut's compositional procedures were not unalike.) There is no better, because no more fully documented, example than this of the way a medieval piece was heard in modern times; and to dismiss it, as at least one scholar has,[100] for failing to respect medieval theory is to miss everything about it that matters. In important respects it is more faithful to the implications of medieval counterpoint theory as seen by Apfel, and later Bent and Leach, than any of the harmonic analyses to be considered below.

Hindemith's work was disrupted by National Socialism and its consequences. When he moved to the USA in 1940 he entered an academic environment where the understanding of medieval music was far less sophisticated than in pre-war Germany; and his teaching and performing at Yale, while it left some fascinating recordings, must, in the more positivistic post-war period in the States, have seemed anachronistic. A comparably sophisticated sensitivity to the interaction of the linear and the vertical was not achieved again until the very end of the twentieth century.[101]

Felix Salzer had studied in Vienna with Guido Adler and Heinrich Schenker before moving to America in 1938 where he set about disseminating his teacher's ideas, writing the first textbook of Schenkerian analysis, *Structural Hearing* (1952). But while Schenker used his understanding of tonal structures to limit the canon of great music to a small body of pieces from Bach to Brahms, Salzer – once he reached America – saw no reason not to apply the same insights to a much wider range of music, including music from before and after the common-practice tonal period. Thus at the end of *Structural Hearing* he offers analyses of polyphony from right through the medieval and Renaissance centuries. His purpose is not to show that these pieces are tonal in the (then) generally accepted sense, but simply that, contrary to assumptions based in medieval theory, which dealt only in note-to-note progressions, medieval pieces also ordered harmony and melody over longer spans. Salzer insisted that this was not to say that such pieces were composed chordally, but simply that composers were aware of longer-range direction as they worked out the counterpoint.[102] Moving on into the fourteenth century, Salzer begins to search out V–I progressions but, perhaps not surprisingly, remains baffled by Machaut's harmonic practices, only regaining some confidence as he reaches the fifteenth century. Hence,

this author can not conceal his personal conviction that the fifteenth century is a musical period exceeding the fourteenth century in creative achievement. The expressiveness of the music is certainly no less strong, and the power for creating tonal direction and coherence is much greater. It can be said very definitely that a larger percentage of compositions of the fifteenth century, in fact larger than of any previous period, can be explained.[103]

For all his care to accommodate what was known of medieval composition, according to the theorists, Salzer needed to see a more modern tonality in this music before he could understand it. Of all the pre-tonal music he analyses, it seems to be the Notre Dame organum that he finds most fascinating, perhaps because its necessarily clear harmonic structure was the easiest to follow without reference to later practice. And it is this music to which Salzer returned, fifteen years later, for a much longer and more detailed attempt to apply structural hearing to medieval pieces.

In 'Tonality in early medieval polyphony' (1967) Salzer begins by stating a view powerfully felt by many over the next ten to fifteen years, namely that medieval music, though edited, contextualised and known through description of its style, remained almost wholly unknown at any deeper level. Setting up in opposition 'description versus analysis', Salzer maintained that almost all work on medieval music came into the former category, almost none into the latter; and it was this that he aimed to rectify.[104] What he meant by description was essentially everything that had been written about the music over the previous twenty years by medievalists. He was reacting against the ideology of the back-to-the-sources generation, and advocating instead the application of principles of melodic and tonal analysis that could get beneath the musical surface to reveal underlying melodic and contrapuntal structures. This was the justification for early music analysis that *Structural Hearing* had lacked, a fight-back against those musicologists who felt that Salzer's earlier analyses had nothing to do with their subject. For Salzer, musicology had failed to reveal anything about the music that was not already obvious. What was needed was a genuinely analytical approach, derived from Schenkerian principles, but more carefully shaped to fit medieval music than the examples in *Structural Hearing*, an approach that looked not at historical-musical questions – style change – or at compositional matters, such as form or chant use, but rather at 'the music itself'. This is the phrase Salzer uses again and again and that became the principal slogan for analysts in the 1960s and 1970s. 'How the music works' was the issue that needed now to be addressed above all else, and the thought that how it works today might be different from how it worked then, though never entirely absent, was pushed aside in the belief that the musicologists' assumption that a modern technique of analysis could allow no access to a medieval perception of the music could not be accepted without challenge. With such powerful analytical techniques now available, who was to say what we might learn about the music if only we were to apply them?[105]

As for medieval theory, Salzer saw it as simply unconcerned with such questions:

The more familiar we become with the trends of Medieval musical thought, . . . the less we can expect that the theorists could present anything resembling a theory of composition or analysis. This would have been foreign to their way of thinking and could not have entered the range of their immediate interests.

Does this, however, mean that we must resign ourselves to the description of visible facts, just because the theorists of the time divulge so little about the meaning of their contemporaries' compositions? Are the writings of Medieval theorists the only legitimate avenue through which analytical access to the music can be gained? I do not think so. For, if such opinions had any validity at all, our chances of understanding Medieval music would be next to hopeless. Contrary to a still widely held view, there is no reason why meaningful analysis necessarily depends upon temporal proximity between composer and analyst or the absolute correspondence between a composer's theoretical outlook (or the writings of contemporary theory) on the one hand, and the type of analysis presented on the other.

Moreover, in evident reaction to the supposed objectivity of early music research, he continues:

By and large, we have become so afraid of being accused of 'interpretation' that the last vestiges of the bold adventurousness of early musicology seem to have all but vanished. 'Historical objectivity' has become not only a slogan but an obsession that all too frequently has resulted in a completely neutral, unimaginative, musicological reportage.

Salzer's answer to the problem of inappropriate tonal hearings – the chief reason for medievalists' dislike of analysis – was to go back a step and look for,

the one elemental factor which has been common – until fairly recently – to all Western music regardless of style and period: the factor of motion. . . . The musical utterance of the West is largely characterized by the constantly recurring phenomenon of directed motion. . . . I believe that any investigation of the actual music of Medieval polyphony will have to come to terms with these basic problems of motion and direction. Out of the solution to these basic problems, an analytical approach will evolve that, far from merely describing and enumerating facts, may open the door to hearing the details as parts of a larger whole; this kind of hearing, in my opinion, characterizes the essence of musical understanding.[106]

For Salzer, prolongation and directed motion both begin in what we now think of as 'Aquitanian polyphony' and are quickly and greatly developed by 'Leonin'. Salzer is far more sensitive than in *Structural Hearing* to lack of a single tonal focus in much of this music, finding it in some pieces but not in others; on the whole he is more concerned with local prolongations and their juxtaposition during the course of a piece, not necessarily adding up to an organised tonal scheme. Only the three-voice *Alleluia Posui* (by Perotin?) shows large-scale tonal structure, and then tonal not in the modern sense but as an accumulation of prolongations of a single sonority, interspersed with sonorities a step away. In many respects, then, this is a new approach to the analysis of medieval music, one that recognises both the nature and the (greater or lesser) extent of its tonal coherence.

Salzer's attitude to performance is revealing. His view seems not to stem from performance at all, but rather from an internal imagined hearing, perhaps without particular instrumental or vocal sounds attached. This is 'the music itself', in a pure imagined state, not imperfected by any particular set of real sounds imposed upon it, but simply a sequence of pitches in motion, propelled by rhythm and directed progression. In other words, it is a hearing that grows from an analytical approach, not the other way round. Salzer brings the ideology of Schenkerian hearing to the notes of medieval music, and finds that he can hear them that way. *Ergo*, that is how they 'work'. Performance, therefore, is something that needs to be informed by analysis, not analysis by performance:

Without this knowledge, performances can only result in a rhythmically monotonous and mechanical note-after-note rendering. What can still be grasped instinctively in much music of later periods must here be arrived at by analytical understanding.[107]

For Salzer, performances failed to realise the music as he heard it in his mind. Performers needed to hear it his way in order to know how to do it.

Immediately following Salzer's article, his co-author on another (related) project, Carl Schachter, published in the next issue of *The Music Forum* a detailed study of Landini's contrapuntal practice, using a similar analytical approach, but this time slipped in gradually during the article and without any special comment.[108] Presumably he intended, like Salzer, that it would become the normal mode of analysis for medieval counterpoint, and more quickly the less attention was drawn to it. But in fact it did not. There was almost no further neo-Schenkerian analysis (and little analysis of any sort) published during the next decade and a half and, by and large, medievalists continued as before. The chief, though radical exceptions were two unpublished Ph.D. dissertations, one on Dufay by Frederick Bashour (1975), the other on Machaut by Terry Zipay (1983). Zipay's aim was to show how linear and vertical aspects of Machaut's motets interacted and combined to produce closure. His method was to provide prolongational (though not reductional) analyses of each voice separately, pointing to closures within it; then to do the same for all together; a rhythmic analysis is factored in; and the results are summarised in a reductional graph notated so as to show, by stem direction, which part each pitch belongs to. Zipay's initial assumption, therefore, is that each voice functions individually as well as in combination with others. Considered from a performer's point of view that seems not unreasonable, for clearly the voices happen individually. But it may be at odds with a theory-grounded view in which the voices make sense only according to their contrapuntal relations, cantus and tenor forming a duet, contratenor added to work with them. Zipay thus sits at one extreme of the linear–vertical spectrum, where every aspect of the music functions alone as well as through interaction. Frederick Bashour, by contrast, aimed to reconcile reductive analysis and counterpoint theory by reducing the cantus–tenor duet on one staff and the contratenor on another. As a demonstration of the fact that prolongation operates in Dufay's songs it was notably successful, charting a middleground level that Zipay's (later) approach overlooked, and managed not to violate the apparent principles of successive composition. Yet even this failed to persuade the wider community of early music scholars that analysis was a legitimate form of research. Musicology was simply not ready for analysis.

Bashour's thesis was possible because of an article published by another American scholar over a decade earlier. Richard Crocker's classic study, 'Discant, counterpoint, and harmony' from 1962, could have been written at any time in the previous sixty years or more. Indeed, as Crocker himself says,[109] it was all obvious since Riemann published his history of theory in 1898. Crocker, inspired by Georgiades's 1937 thesis, goes back to the counterpoint treatises, describes their teaching, and observes that they thought in terms of a two-part core, not one melody at a time. For him, this is not linear counterpoint, the simultaneous sounding of two melodies, but rather a sequence of progressions of two-note entities. It follows that medieval musicians would have considered third and fourth voices as belonging to vertical collections too, so that there is only a limited sense in which they can be thought of as independent. Progressions, of however many voices, are functional in that they progress. Thus all that changed in later centuries, resulting in classical 'functional harmony', was the harmony.

What is most striking about this article now is how obvious it is, and therefore how confused an understanding of medieval theory (not to mention practice) scholars must still have had in 1962 to make it worth writing. In large part, this sense of confusion can be attributed to the unresolved questions – tonal or non-tonal, linear or vertical – disputed by Besseler and Ficker, which Apfel in Germany was still in the process of trying to nail. Crocker's text is punctuated by asides directed at traditional but erroneous beliefs about medieval music and by remarks such as 'It is frequently said that ... ', all reflecting the legacy of confusion created in Europe before the war and still unresolved in the States. His solution is along the lines of Apfel's, but expressed more economically and, in its general admission of vertical hearing, more adventurously. By showing how medieval musicians could think in terms of a two-voice core and yet hear three and four voices in the same way, as all engaging in directed progressions, Crocker was bringing together theory and common sense, potentially clearing the ground for an analytical approach to the music that begins from medieval writing yet goes far beyond it. Yet Bashour remained one of the few to step further and propose an analytical method. Why?

One reason must be that performances still tended to stress the horizontal rather than the vertical, contrasting lines rather than sonorities. But still more powerful was a methodological reason. To musicians familiar with the principles of reductive analysis, whether they were broadly Schenkerians like Salzer and Schachter, or were simply sensitive to a functional distinction between decoration and structure, like Hindemith or Bashour, it seems to have been evident that medieval music was not fundamentally unlike the music of later times. To put it another way, experience of reductive analysis made one inclined to hear medieval music in a broadly 'Schenkerian' way. This is perhaps because, more than any other analytical view of music, reductive analysis is tied up with hearing, with the perception of music in time and so in performance (even if only mental performance). It is impossible to be at the same time a neo-Schenkerian and a 'defamiliariser', however much one's view is rooted in medieval theory. To perceive prolongation at work is to be absorbed in the music in real time and to follow harmonic and contrapuntal processes as they unfold; it is, by its nature, a process of understanding, not one of categorisation or comparison. Hence the suspicion with which proponents of objectivity must view it. To accept a reductive analysis, it is first necessary to accept the way of hearing music that it demonstrates. This is exactly the sort of circular preconditioning that objective scholarship is determined to avoid.

The medievalist trained to be objective who yet remains passionate about the music is thus caught between two opposed forces; either they have to be kept separate, as for example in the scholar who remains objective at work but listens or performs enthusiastically after hours, or they must somehow be integrated, but, for reasons that will now be very obvious, that is a route fraught with the danger of disapproval. Only by very strictly limiting the role of musical judgement in one's work can one allow it space at all. A scholar with a sense of larger-scale musical forces at work, and a desire to use that sense in elucidating the music, has to be extremely cautious in order to avoid being dismissed as unreliable or 'anachronistic'. It is in this light that one may begin to understand the range of approaches adopted by scholars who wished to use their music-analytical judgement and yet stay on the right side of the law, if possible pushing the boundaries of what was legal just a little further. Bashour was one of these. Another, from the previous generation of American scholars, was David Hughes, also the author of a remarkable but largely disregarded thesis.

For Hughes, writing in the mid-1950s before Günther's and before most of Reaney's work and making early use of Apel's edition of *French Secular Music* (1950), it was necessary first of all to speak up for the fourteenth century, to treat 'the late Ars nova not merely as a predecessor, to be invoked only when necessary and convenient, but as an established style in its own right'.[110] Considering that it offers the earliest extended analysis of late fourteenth-century melodic and contrapuntal practices, Hughes' study is an astonishing achievement. Taking linear and successive thinking as a given, and rejecting Salzer out of hand, he nevertheless develops a reductive method that, like Fuller's but thirty years earlier, is grounded in the teaching of the counterpoint treatises and designed to reveal underlying contrapuntal structure. Hughes' method is to discard the contratenor (as a later-added voice) and then from the cantus–tenor duet remove passing-note decoration, syncopation and dissonance in order to leave a two-voice contrapunctus skeleton which, though not necessarily composed as such, would have been used by the composer as a core that the musical surface elaborated. For Hughes, the contrapunctus skeleton was very definitely not dynamic:

It has, apparently, no long-term objectives of its own: its sequence of perfect and imperfect consonances is not essentially different in different parts of the piece. Composers seem to have used it as a continuing, uninflected substratum, related to the final product rather as plaster or bronze is related to a work of sculpture.[111]

But the melody was dynamic. Cantus lines, Hughes believed, were elaborations of well-formed melodic skeletons; and to show this he introduces prolongational graphs, using a primitivised Salzerian notation. With the benefit of hindsight it may seem odd that Hughes never considered the directed cantus core as the top line of a directed contrapunctus, especially as Apel had pointed clearly to exactly that conclusion in the text quoted earlier,[112] but, approaching the music with a successive model of composition fixed in his mind, it seemed clear to Hughes that the tenor could function only as a support.[113] The contratenor could take on various roles but was above all an instrumental part requiring contrasting tone colour to set against the cantus and its accompanying tenor.[114] His hearing of late fourteenth-century French song was therefore a strictly melodic one: one concentrated on the cantus, which did all the work, hearing the other voices as no more than accompaniment and decoration. In Italian song, on the other hand, Hughes saw superius and tenor (often both texted) working together much more readily, and the reason for the difference in national habits seems to him clear:

It is not difficult to assign an immediate cause to this peculiarly Italian concept of voice-relations: the mere fact that the tenors were performed vocally seems adequate enough. For an instrument can perform with equal ease a cantabile melody and a wholly discontinuous accompaniment, while a singer (and dare I say, projecting the aura of the days of Verdi back into the *trecento*, especially an

Italian singer?) must have something with continuity and sense – something, as it were, for him to get his larynx into.[115]

Moreover, as Italian counterpoint develops through the late fourteenth century, Hughes sees in it, rather than in the French style, the origins of classical vocal polyphony, and not just in scoring but in tonality and structural imitation as well. So for Hughes, just as for Riemann and so many others in the meantime, the hearing of musical functions was inextricably tied up with assumptions about performance practice.

And yet, despite a view of the unimportance of harmony in fourteenth-century France that made sense in relation to his reading of the theorists and to previous work, Hughes was not quite able to leave it at that. Given that everywhere he looked he saw details to be admired, and given that he was dealing with some of the most dissonant music of the Middle Ages, he could not resist facing head-on the question of French composers' control of vertical combinations. To Hughes, linear and successive composition seems so strongly supported by theory that a lack of vertical control must be a possibility, but it is not one with which he is comfortable:

It is generally agreed that this liberality in the use of dissonance was largely due to concentration on the individual lines, without much concern for vertical combinations. We ourselves have tentatively attributed one form of dissonance [the unprepared appoggiatura] to this attitude. We must also admit, however, that these composers must have *liked* the dissonant results, for it is perfectly possible to concentrate on lines without being ignorant of their clashes. We do not ascribe the sometimes quite acute dissonances found in the later works of Brahms – to say nothing of twentieth century composers – either to ineptitude, nor to 'indifference to vertical combinations': it is hardly wise to assume that composers are indifferent to any aspect of their music. No: we regard those sounds as indicative of the expressed personal preferences of the composer. Let us extend the same courtesy to the composers of the *Ars Nova*.[116]

That scholars were still making this point almost thirty years later, and only then were setting about developing a more fully theorised method of reductive analysis, reflects the lack of interest in Hughes' work in the interim. Only Crocker, whose 1962 article redid Hughes' elucidation of the counterpoint treatises in more detail and with a slightly more nuanced view of vertical thinking, took his work further. He was, by and large, overlooked: he was jumping too far ahead of current thinking; and to reach beyond him it would be necessary to go over the ground much more slowly. As things stood, medieval music studies had, as yet, no use for his approach or for the idea of analysis that went beyond description.

Thus, by the early 1970s there was a sense among medievalists, for all the reasons we have seen, that analysis of early music was desirable but not yet possible, or at any rate, not in a form that medievalists could accept. Crocker had cleared some space, but only in general terms, and to make acceptable progress it was going to be necessary to go through medieval counterpoint teaching in much more detail. Bashour attempted the synthesis this implies, but never followed it up with articles or a book; it is possible that even in his case the treatment of theory was too cursory to be perceived as a solid foundation. Hellmut Kühn, preparing his study of ars nova harmony at the end of the 1960s,[117] was working in the more systematic German tradition but with a far larger body of work on medieval harmony looming behind him.[118] Indeed, Kühn's first task was to review the literature from Riemann to Apfel, telling very much the story that Kevin Moll has illustrated. But having done that, Kühn's real purpose, like Crocker's, was to start again by going Back to the Theorists. Taking counterpoint treatises as a starting-point, Kühn could then follow composers' working-out of interval progressions in similar terms, classifying sonorities as more or less perfect or imperfect and showing how sonorities with different degrees of perfection could be placed in sequence to create larger units. Kühn's was an extremely cautious piece of work, but given all the precedents, and his position, that is understandable. What it achieved, though, was to show how much further one could get towards an understanding of the music as process – in other words an understanding true to the perception of every musical listener – without actually going beyond what was written in medieval theory. And once Kühn had shown that, it became considerably easier for others, particularly for those working in the somewhat more liberal tradition of American musicology, to take one crucial step further, and to devise an analytic notation, not unrelated to that used by reductional analysts, to show the relationships between the sonorities that made up each directed phrase. In other words, it became possible, at last, to do reductive analysis without frightening off the medievalists. This was the achievement of Sarah Fuller.

It is impossible to read her first article on the subject, published in 1986, without being aware of Fuller's determination to ground her approach so firmly in medieval terms that there could be no accusations of anachronism later on. Even the language speaks to it: 'To establish a *bedrock* of terms and concepts *appropriate* to discourse about sonority in fourteenth-century music' (my italics). With considerable rhetorical skill, Fuller establishes a system of interval labelling that works from the bottom up (by no means uncontroversial, but managed by careful reference to fourteenth-century practices); extends medieval terminology to include doubly-imperfect, inflected imperfect and dissonant sonorities, alongside the authorised perfect and imperfect, as recognisable within an underlying contrapuntal structure; teases out from the treatises medieval support for hearing directional tendencies in the progression of imperfect towards perfect intervals during a phrase; and then for reducing out melodic and motivic decoration in order to reveal an underlying structure. Thus, with the medieval teaching lined up behind her, she lays out almost all the vital ingredients for a reductional analytic method. When it comes to the examples, she introduces the remaining crucial concept, that of prolongation, which entirely lacks medieval authorisation, so cautiously and with such simple and obvious instances that no reader could possibly disagree. She is extremely careful to use none of the terms guaranteed to ring alarm bells – chord, triad, tonal, Schenker, Salzer. Yet only in one respect does she depart significantly from Salzerian principles, namely in insisting that duration is a factor in the perceived significance of a sonority. This can produce some curious analyses, as for instance a sequence in which the f′ at the top of a g–b–f′ chord is held to be more important than the g′ to which (for a Schenkerian and almost anyone else) it resolves, simply because the f′ occurs on the first two pulses of a mensural unit whereas the g′ comes only on the third.[119] But again, it was clearly necessary to establish a principle that medievalists, versed in the overriding importance of mensural theory, could accept. A powerful tactic that runs throughout the article is Fuller's willingness (almost over-willingness) to label and categorise, since these are such characteristic procedures of the readership she aims to persuade. Types of sonorities, types of progressions, types of termination are all set out and labelled, even when the labels are not used again.[120] With this powerful alliance of musical hearing, musicological method and rhetorical ingenuity, Fuller succeeded where all others since Riemann first tried had failed: she provided an approach to understanding and mapping tonal functions in medieval music that specialists in medieval music could accept and even adopt.

Fuller's graphs were clearly not Schenkerian, or even Salzerian. The underlying sequences of perfect sonorities she exposed were just that, sequences of sonorities, not melodic/harmonic background forms complete in themselves. She was not aiming to find a well-formed *Ursatz*, indeed deliberately avoided doing so,[121] but simply to follow the processes at work just beneath the surface. Principally this was because, unsupported by medieval writings, she was not willing to enter into that circle of analytical hearing that, as we have already seen, a traditionally (neo-)Schenkerian view imposes on its adherents. Although to perceive prolongation over more than a few beats without some knowledge of Schenkerian analysis would be unlikely in the 1980s – reinventing a wheel that was already universally known – it was certainly the case that to hear local prolongations in medieval music (and that they exist and play a crucial function in the shaping of a piece she demonstrated beyond question) could be managed without raising a Schenkerian banner, whereas hearing and notating a single directed structure running the length of a piece could not. Others were less cautious. My own study of a Machaut rondeau, published in 1984, took a determinedly Salzerian view, and was militantly (and I now think, quite unnecessarily) disinterested in a medieval-theoretical perspective which, for all the reasons identified above, placed it clearly beyond the pale. While it has been much used to provoke debate, its prolongational rather than strict *contrapunctus* view of structure (reducing to a voice-led rather than a necessarily consonant core) has left it seeming too much indebted to post-medieval models of musical process to be widely emulated.[122] Musicology was not willing to be pushed into analysis, and an approach like Fuller's, fully grounded in medieval teaching yet ready to go somewhat further, was the only kind that could succeed. It is her achievement that, by the end of the century, reductional analysis had come, at last, to seem normal.[123]

It took a century, more or less, from the point where scholars ceased to condemn medieval harmony as incompetent for it to become generally accepted as a functional tonal system in which vertical collections – one might even say chords – were arranged in progressions directed towards goals. In other words, it took a century for it to be accepted as harmony. Fundamental to this process was the contribution of Schenker, for the underlying process of prolongation that he made visible (and, for the initiated, made audible) allowed twentieth-century musicians to explain what they perceived instinctively about medieval polyphony from the earliest performances, namely that it was not, as Fétis and Kiesewetter supposed, arbitrary and accidental, but rather worked according to principles of decorated structure, exactly as implied by the counterpoint teaching that Kiesewetter so easily admired. That it took so long was partly due to the haste with which earlier scholars, Besseler in particular, had jumped to conclusions; partly to the extreme caution of scholars determined not to lose touch with medieval writings; and partly to the insensitivity of analysts to musicologists' concerns.

Machaut: R13

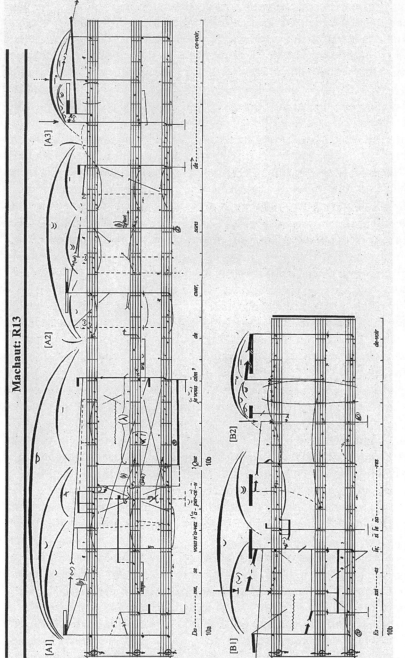

3.2 Guillaume de Machaut, *Dame, se vous n'avez aperceu*, analysed by Kimberly Connor (1999: II, n.p.)

But it was also due to changes in the conception of performance. Once the instrumental hypothesis was adopted it became far easier than before to hear this music as a collection of contrasting lines and more difficult than before to hear it as harmony.[124] It was unfortunate, perhaps, that the change came before scholars found some sympathy for the musical language: had *a cappella* performance survived another thirty years or so the story might have been very different. For it seems highly likely that the coincidence of date between the *a cappella* revival and the final acceptance of reductional analysis is not coincidence at all. In my own case, I know it is not, for it was a recording of the early Gothic Voices broadcasts, and a rough edit of 'The Mirror of Narcissus' that Page gave me some months before its release, that confirmed my instinctive belief, supported up till then only by reading Salzer and the scores, that much medieval music was conceived with vertical considerations firmly in mind, and that led me to work on the harmonic aspect of Machaut's *Rose, lis* in 1983.[125] I have no reason to think that Sarah Fuller was influenced by Gothic Voices in the same way; though of course it was formed out of hearing harmonic order in the music,[126] her view was much better prepared. But I certainly want to suggest that the acceptance of her work, after so many disregarded attempts by earlier writers,[127] was significantly eased by the transformation in everyone's sense of the sound of medieval song after 1983. Once everyone, at the drop of a stylus or the touch of a button, could hear medieval harmony working through time in a single blended sonority it was impossible to continue to maintain that it was essentially linear or only dyadic in intention. However it was composed, it was now heard as a whole, and if the *a cappella* hypothesis was correct, it was heard as a whole then too. Harmonic analysis became appropriate and inevitable once the Gothic Voices recordings began to appear.

LATER TRENDS

Performance practice will change again, needless to say, indeed is changing right now; but what will happen to analysis in response? It is possible to imagine a reductive analysis less tied to a vertical hearing of the music. Bashour attempted one by removing the contratenor to a separate staff. Illustration 3.2 shows a page from a 1999 Ph.D. thesis by Kimberly Connor which offers a more subtle approach, one that requires more commentary than can be reproduced here but that arguably reflects much better the interaction and interplay of vertical and horizontal that has always been sensed in this music. In Connor's understanding of Machaut, the kinds of tendencies illustrated by Fuller are teased out in greater detail and are often perceived as overlapping or contradictory, recognising the multidimensional quality of our interaction with the music. This is, again, a view of the music that is formed from inner listening rather than under the influence of any one performance practice. If it has a correlative in performance it is perhaps in some more recent styles developed by groups using instruments but cultivating a much smoother sound than was customary before the *a cappella* revival (Mala Punica, for example). It is not impossible to imagine that if the instrumental revival grows in strength some fusion of performance styles that were previously separate may occur, with consequences for analysis that Connor's approach perhaps heralds.

None of this, needless to say, does anything to relieve the scholar's deep-seated suspicion of performance as a securely grounded, historically accurate, potentially informative practice. The range of *a cappella* sounds, from the freshly cleaned Anglicanism of Gothic Voices to the rasping Corsican bawling of Ensemble Organum, only emphasises the impossibility of attaining a medieval performance style (or of knowing that one has attained it). And the possibility of a revived instrumental hypothesis grows ever stronger. Historical musicology 'knows' it should not rely on performance to dictate its approach to the music. This is one of the reasons (though certainly not the main reason) why, despite the gains of analysis and hearing (better, the analysis of hearing) as a musicological technique, scholars remain devoted to the search for systems. More significant, of course, is the hopeless instability of 'the evidence'. The surviving evidence for medieval music, as we have seen again and again, is patchy and fragmented; interpretations, and pictures formed by arranging it, change from scholar to scholar, from place to place and from generation to generation. The attraction of a global system that explains how the pieces must fit, and what must come between them to join them up, remains, and will always remain, irresistible to many.

The 1980s and 1990s saw a resurgence of interest in such systems. Building on work from the early 1970s by Andrew Hughes (1972) and Gaston Allaire (1972), Jehoash Hirshberg in 1980 proposed that by identifying the hexachords in which medieval singers would have conceptualised the notated lines in front of them one could correctly determine the intervals they would have sung. The problem of when to use musica ficta, previously dealt with by a few rules of thumb applied according to taste, would be very considerably eased: provided that the singer is in the right hexachord the intervals are, in principle at least, fixed. Of course, determining the hexachord is not so easy. Christian Berger, working on a similar hypothesis, came to quite different conclusions in a study published in 1992; for him, medieval musicians thought modally and only then hexachordally. Again, the argument is too intricate to go through here, but one intriguing consequence is that # signs could produce, in modern terms, a lowered rather than a raised note. Clearly, when a system is applied rigorously but produces results that contradict all previous beliefs some serious questions have to be asked on both sides. Berger has, in effect, followed a hypothesis so far that it has changed his hearing of the music. For an author that is a thrilling result, but for most readers it will be far easier to reject his initial hypothesis – that medieval musicians conceived polyphony modally – than to relearn the musical language. Nevertheless, it is reassuring to find that a radically revisionary approach is still possible and publishable.[128]

In the mid-1980s (though unpublished until 1995), building on work by Bernhard Meier on Renaissance music, Peter Lefferts proposed a method for classifying medieval pieces according to 'tonal types', defined by scale (determined by signature) and final. This in turn formed the basis for an analytical approach developed by Yolanda Plumley (1990, 1996) which drew also on reductional analysis, considering fourteenth-century songs as decorated structures, working within a number of closely related tonal systems and according to a fundamentally linear conception of tonal order. Although growing out of a system of classification, this approach turns back into analysis, using the features of the tonal systems defined by Lefferts to explain features in the music. Plumley traces the interaction of counterpoint, line and motive, among themselves in individual pieces, and as workings out of fundamental tonal types and compositional strategies. This leads to a view of later fourteenth-century song as elaborating a limited range of conceptual models, growing out of the characteristics of the available tonal types. Once again, openness to a greater range of compositional procedures than were conceivable by Apel, Hughes or Reaney (though perhaps not Apfel nor Ficker) allows a more complex view of the interaction of linear and vertical.

In this respect Plumley's, like every recent method, reflects the strong sense among musicologists that somehow this music has to be seen in two ways at once. Yet this brings new problems with it, for, having devised ways of talking about the music as an interaction of the linear and the vertical, presumably we need now to find a comparable way of listening. This is an idea so foreign to our training as musicians that there is no obvious way of doing it. Thus, for the moment at least, it seems necessary to suppose either that medieval musicians heard very differently, almost in an extra dimension, so that the parts were perceived together and separately at the same time, or that in leaning over backwards to turn medieval counterpoint theory into a way of hearing we have lost our balance and fallen over, ending up in an intellectual heap in which, for a while, nothing seems to be quite the right way up. With so much uncertainty and methodological insecurity the attraction of a system that explains everything can be hard to resist.

No system depends as faithfully on the teaching of medieval counterpoint as that proposed by Margaret Bent (1998) and worked out in practice by her then student Elizabeth Leach (1997). Indeed, its starting-point is the belief that counterpoint treatises provide not just models or frameworks but rules which composers follow. To determine the composer's intention at any moment of textual uncertainty (including those traditionally dealt with by ad hoc application of musica ficta) one has only to make the underlying cantus–tenor progression agree with the rules of progression in the treatises to arrive at the correct reading. In cases where music and theory are at odds with each other, the working assumption is that it is the music that is wrong and needs to be emended editorially. Only if the music can be shown to be intentionally exceptional can a departure from theory be permitted, though how that could be shown strongly enough to override the 'default' assumption of error is hard to see. Thus the scholar's preference is to line up behind the theorist against whoever is responsible for the manuscript reading (scribe or composer) and pronounce him wrong. For a modern scholar this is very attractive, offering an escape at last from the inevitability of not-knowing, and replacing it with the reasonable certainty of being right. It depends hardly at all on hearing, in the sense of making subjective judgements about the balance and interrelation of sounds as ordered by a listener or reader. Only in order to find the underlying two-part core at any moment in a piece must one make any decision not sanctioned by a medieval source, and even there, the assumption that composers do as they are told by the treatises strongly predisposes one to choose readings that accord with them.[129] Hearing is as nearly as possible banished from the investigation, for as we have seen it is inherently unreliable. There is thus no relation to performance practice, existing or proposed. Like many systems, it chooses to find insignificant any contraindications, which in this case might include human nature (the possibility that a composer, even a medieval composer, might often want to do something not covered by theory),[130] the less than total agreement among theorists, not just about intervals and progressions but also about approaches to elaborating a contrapunctus core,[131] the possibility that theorists are legislating for beginners,[132] not attempting to define every practice, as suggested by the let-out clauses offered in the more specific treatises allowing (apparently willingly) that one may do other things than are specified,[133] and those extra-theoretical progressions found in pieces that theorists excuse.[134] But one need not be surprised to see such points argued away, or at least, as far away as possible. Given sufficient uncertainty (and we have seen more than enough of that), a strict system can be overwhelmingly appealing.

The idea that medieval composers worked entirely systematically, without wanting the kinds of artistic licences that for us are so characteristic of a creative mind, has another interesting consequence. It stresses, indeed it depends for its force on, the medieval musician being a stranger to us, thinking in a fundamentally different way about the business of composing. Pushing the Middle Ages away from us, seeing the time gap that separates them from us as a chasm rather than a process, makes them necessarily strange, indeed, absolutely requires that they be so.[135] Shock thus becomes a defining feature of correct research findings. The more different one's story looks from everything with which we are familiar, the more likely it is to be right. Scholars thus acquire a licence to startle, and at the same time become essential as intermediaries who can explain and guide us through the alien landscape that at first only they understand. It is the Musica Reservata or Ensemble Organum approach to research, attractive for its very difference.

HEARING/LISTENING

Looking back over the twentieth century's attempts at understanding medieval harmony it is easy to feel that an inordinate amount of effort and debate has been required to reach broad agreement on just a few very simple points, most of which were staring us in the face (from medieval treatises) all along. The same might be said of work on performance practice. But to see it that way is to fall into the trap of assuming that where we are is where we ought to end up, and that others could have got here long ago if only they had not been so blinded by the views of their time. In fact we can be sure, just as with performance practice, that what we think now will seem just as deluded a generation hence. It seems unwise, therefore, to believe that definitive solutions are finally beginning to emerge. On the contrary, some key questions remain entirely open, not least how we should encourage our minds to follow medieval polyphony as we listen. We have seen several variants of the vertical approach, and several hints at something more multiply linear, encouraging us to try to follow several lines at once; and we have seen, inevitably, a growing number of attempts at reconciling the two,[136] at least in analysis. But what kind of literal hearing (listening to a performance) can we really expect to achieve that differs in any appreciable way from our usual mode of listening? Plenty has changed in the way we understand medieval harmony, so that when we hear it now we are not, on the whole, horrified by it, or amused, but rather follow its workings, if not as 'they' did then at least with a sense of understanding, however mistaken. But none of this quite addresses the vertical/horizontal issue. We may understand the rules of interval progression without that necessarily changing our attitude to the texture of the polyphony. Hoping to make a noticeable difference, the Studio der frühen Musik used to try to play their lines independently, avoiding precise synchronisation; they and other groups tried hard to contrast the colours of the lines; and to an extent it worked, though at a cost; for the dividing lines between non-synchronisation and sloppiness, and between contrast and incompatibility, were very hard to recognise, even if one understood the intention. Gothic Voices, on the other hand, have been accused of ironing out the independence of the individual lines, rendering the texture in bland monochrome. We do, I think, hear these different approaches to sounding texture a little differently; in one it is a little easier to hear the lines, in the other the harmonic progressions. But it requires enormously different performance practices to make a very small difference to our ability to hear vertically or horizontally. Analysis and performance, then, have less impact on hearing-during-performance than they do on the way we think about music in the abstract.

This is likely to be to do with the way the brain processes music. There is experimental evidence that people today can differentiate up to three voices heard simultaneously (depending on the similarity of their timbres), but can follow only one voice fully, even though they may be aware of others sounding with it.[137] Of course we cannot know if this was true also in the Middle Ages, but on balance it seems more likely than not. Page points to a passage added to Johannes de Garlandia's treatise which suggests that some listeners in the Middle Ages switched their attention from one part against the tenor to another, which is just what we would expect today when any attempt is made to follow lines within a larger texture.[138] It is conceivable that exposure to different music would train people in different cultures to hear more or less polyphonically,[139] but it seems likely that the ability to follow separate strands of sound is harder-wired than that. Thus, on the whole it seems more reasonable to suppose that most listeners at any time in musical history, in so far as they are listening at all (a point to which we shall return in a moment), are listening either to one part (sensing a fundamental part against it) or to the whole, rather than separating that whole into two or more parts and following them equally. The thought that we perhaps ought to be listening in some more polyphonic way to polyphonic music therefore seems misguidedly theoretical.[140] Encouraged by a dispute almost a century in the running but arising solely out of the problem of how to talk about the music, have we perhaps been missing the point in trying to turn analysis into perception? Analysis can relate easily enough to performance practices, as we have seen again and again, but perhaps not so easily to different kinds of perception. Perhaps, then, knowing how music was composed and understanding the functions of the voices in relation to one another are quite separate matters from listening to the sound of their performance. However much we 'know' (or believe) about music, it seems probable that our brains respond to music in performance by concentrating on what seems most enriching. That may be a line, or a texture, or a harmonic progression, or a quality of tone colour, or (more likely) some more complex combination heard as a whole but a whole in which the balance is weighted in favour of some features over others. Exactly what it is at any moment is well-nigh indefinable. In due course, something of this process may be understood through research, but it will be research into the brain, not by research into history, and it will provide an understanding of what we do (which may or may not be what people have always done), not a statement of what we ought to do. Hearing music is simply too complex for the advice of historical musicology (as, for example, 'listen horizontally here') to be taken seriously.

Performance, obviously, may be historical only in so far as history can recover information about it. Hearing may be historical only in so far as history can tell us about performance and help us understand the language. There is very little more that we can know. We cannot even say, with Gilbert Reaney, that this (he is writing of the fourteenth century) was 'a period when individual, contrapuntal parts were valued more than unity of texture' because that is to come to conclusions about a process of hearing that has necessarily left no trace and that must, like ours, have varied from person to person and moment to moment.[141] Historically informed hearing, despite the very clear links that scholars have tried to make (or have failed to avoid making) between performance practice and analysis, is a chimera.

Exactly the same has been said by Shai Burstyn of 'historical listening' in the context of an article reviewing the problems inherent in trying to recover a historical listening practice.[142] Listening practice, which has recently become an issue of interest among musicologists, is not quite what I mean in this book by hearing (which is to do with the understanding and envisioning of the music through performance and analysis in modern times). Listening practice is, as yet, mainly concerned with the circumstances in which people listened to music in the past, their behaviour while listening, and their written responses to hearing music in performance. In other words, it involves applying the values of historical musicology to listening to music in an attempt to discover how it was for them, and to make it so for us. To put it less sympathetically, it extends the historicist project in order to bring more of our response to the sound of music under the control of historical correctness. At the time of writing (2000) it has hardly begun as an identified branch of early music studies (though it has a longer history for later periods),[143] but what has been published so far is worth considering.

As Burstyn says, 'even the restriction to contemporary theoretical musical concepts does not ensure a direct line to listening habits',[144] but the reasons for this he sees in insufficient detail in medieval writings rather than in our limited ability to read them historically.[145] Burstyn's aim is to stimulate thought about the possibilities in, and obstacles to, the recovery of a historical listening practice, and his view is therefore shaped by the belief that it is to some degree possible. To what extent it might be is suggested in two studies by Christopher Page, one dealing with trouvère song (Page 1997), the other with some remarks by the fifteenth-century theorist Johannes Tinctoris.[146]

In the first study, Page identifies a listenership for trouvère song that is secular, literate, articulate, learned in grammar and discerning. They assemble in hall or chamber – the two spaces Page identifies as locations for performance – at the invitation of a host, typically of high social standing, higher than most of the guests whose duty is thus to attend first and foremost to their host rather than to the music. They are principally men: though women may be present trouvère song is essentially concerned with men's experience of love. There may be some spoken introduction; during the performance silence may not be maintained unless it is commanded by the host, so that close listening of the sort we expect may not have been practised other than at moments felt by a dominant individual to be especially important; we cannot assume that a musical performance would have been thought to contain any. The song may not be perceived as having a fixed state, but rather a performance may be a new realisation of a much looser notion of 'the work' than we tend to have; and that too may imply a less reverent attitude to music than is ours. After the performance there may be some discussion among the men present, but if so it is conducted with deference for the host's opinion. Any discussion is likely to be conducted formally and to concern the text more than the performance, and the music least of all.[147]

This is thought-provoking, for again it emphasises difference. In such an environment listening to a trouvère song would have been a very different experience, and would have involved different kinds of thought, than we expect from or bring to musical performance today. And of course the evidence deals only with external circumstances; the rest we infer. How the notes were processed by the mind in this environment we can get nowhere near to sensing even faintly, let alone understanding. Listening practice, in this case, is about circumstances, not processes.

The problems involved in trying to recover listening experience have been well summarised by Leon Botstein.[148] They include, naturally, the lack of evidence, but also the fluidity of the musical text (whose notes, scorings and manner of performance might vary from day to day), the variability of experiences among period listeners, the difficulty for them of expressing their experience in words even when they tried, the need to appreciate the acoustic environment (performance spaces) and the social environment (the function of music). Yet the longer the list, the more evident it becomes that this is traditional musicology as it has always been practised. What is new is simply the sense among some scholars that it is desirable to take as one's conceptual starting-point the experience of hearing the music of the period one studies. In other words, it is a new variant of the desire that lay behind the rise of early music analysis. Where before, some desired to take the musical text as a conceptual starting-point for research of all sorts, now some (mainly others, interestingly) desire to take the musical sound. In listening practice, just as in analysis, a division will soon emerge between those who believe that historical work is possible in this area and those who do not but wish rather to explore our own responses. And some will try, at least, to bridge the two. As in Fuller's analytical project, with its reconciliation of counterpoint theory and post-Schenkerian hearing, it seems likely that the most successful will be those who manage to bring the evidence for period practice, such as it is, into alignment with listening strategies that are possible now. But what is so interesting about this comparison is that this time a wish to think from the music has come from within historical musicology, not from outside.[149] The desire that analysts felt so strongly to direct musicology towards the notes seems, at last, to have found a willing response, redirected towards something that, while its questions look historical, will prove far harder to do than analysis. It will be fascinating to see how or if it develops.

For all the reasons discussed a moment ago, however, listening practice cannot realistically be in the business of legislating for hearing today. There is no problem in principle with reusing the original listening spaces, indeed performers have tried to do that since early music performance started up again. But attempting to re-create the chatter of a period audience will be self-defeating if the listeners are trying to listen to it. And there is no point at all in even imagining that we might be able to perceive the music at any deeper level in the way that they did. It is hard to see, then, how listening practice can ever produce more than descriptive historical musicology. This, of course, explains its appeal. For all its ambition, listening practice is not nearly as radical as analysis. Analysis did encourage us to think about the music in different ways, and even, to the limited extent that this was possible, to hear it in different ways, ways that students of medieval theory did not always approve. It had the power to tempt us into non-historical views, and that was what made it dangerous. Listening practice, on the other hand, for all that it deals with hearing the music, is perfectly safe, for by its very nature, as currently defined, it is about then, not now. Of course, that could change.

CHAPTER 4

Evidence, interpretation, power and persuasion

INTRODUCTION

The preceding three chapters outline a story that is to an extent complete in itself. They show how medieval polyphony has been thought about, as music, since it began to re-emerge about 200 years ago. Along the way many recurring themes and attitudes have been identified; for while the subject moves onwards in some respects, in others it simply circles. Partly this is because the evidence has been asked to produce clear results: instrumental or vocal, linear or vertical, successive or simultaneous, all arising, as I have tried to show, out of the single unresolved issue of how polyphony ought to be understood as a set of functioning voice relationships. Partly it circles because musicologists themselves tend individually to adopt one of a few sets of attitudes towards the subject as a whole. And partly it is due to the relatively stable structure of academia, and of the power relationships that characterise it. All three of these issues – the moral obligations of musicology (note the 'ought' above), the psychology of historical research, and its anthropology – need to be addressed. They are necessarily interrelated. The discipline itself (in common with other research subjects) maintains a group psychology that shapes, through the interplay of professional expectations and rewards, the way questions are framed, investigated and answered. These issues are rarely discussed by scholars of early music, yet a good case could be made for including the study of this process in all graduate training programmes, for it shapes everything academics do. From this angle, the reinvention of medieval music in modern times is simply an instance, and a very telling one, conveniently delimited in time and topic, of these processes at work.

To show this properly requires, at the very least, the existence already of wide-ranging investigations of the psychology and anthropology of humanities research, followed by a similar study of musicology as a particular instance. That might not be impossible to attempt now. There is enough literature in the philosophy and the sociology of history, in group psychology and in the anthropology of institutions to offer a framework around which to build a study of musicology. But it would need many instances like this one to serve as illustrations or case studies. So while I have given much thought to approaching the topic from that end, I have come to feel that the most useful way to present this story, and certainly the safest given the present state of understanding of musicology as an activity, is as a story in itself, one which needs further discussion, perhaps leading to future studies (by others) of different areas within musicology. Then in due course we may be in a better position to look at the activity as a personality- and institution-driven process.

What I want to do with this chapter, before drawing together the threads of my story in a conclusion that is necessarily nothing of the sort, is to outline some of the forces that I see as contributing to musicology as a process and that we can see at work in this example, intending by this only to offer some thoughts on the kinds of issues that might be discussed as we work towards a better understanding of why we do musicology.

It may be helpful, first of all, to say a little about what musicology is. It almost goes without saying that it cannot be defined with any precision. The safest definition, in my view, though almost comically non-committal, is that musicology is whatever musicologists do as musicologists. Despite the vagueness of that definition I don't myself see that it needs to be delimited more narrowly than that. If one wanted to be a little more specific one could add that it seems likely to include study and music in some kind of relation, though of the two the study is obviously the stronger element since it is always present, whereas music needs to be defined very broadly, as anything that touches on music, rather than as music per se. Thus writing the history of institutions that sponsor music, without needing to discuss the music they sponsor, is musicology if we want to think of it as such. Typically such a study would be considered musicology if the author were professionally a musicologist, or as history if they were professionally a historian, emphasising that musicology is what musicologists do, rather than a particular set of procedures and subjects. It is worth emphasising, in the context of this book, that musicology need not be historical: it can be about us and our relation to music too. Thus analysis, perception, psychology, culture (popular, high or anything in between), journalism can all fall within musicology if we want them to (or even if one of us wants them to). The other fairly constant feature of musicology to bear in mind is its status as a humanity rather than a science. There are areas of science that can come within musicology if we wish – anything that involves the physical constituents of music for a start – but on the whole musicology is about ideas and opinions, not about demonstrable facts as usually understood. (Of course all these are imprecisions, but I am not aiming for absolute definitions here, just acceptable approximations.[1])

A broad definition of musicology, perhaps something along these lines, is both realistic and allows us to concentrate, in trying to understand it as a process, on musicologists rather than on the 'discipline'. In fact, the more one examines it, the less that word seems appropriate, and the more it seems like a defence against the uncertainty and openness of the subject, an attempt to empower certain areas or procedures at the expense of others. Medieval music studies provide a particularly obvious example, as must by now be evident. Throughout this study we have seen writers arguing above all else about the correctness of one another's hypotheses, and all these hypotheses concern what happened in the past. That has always been insisted upon as the absolute requirement for studies of medieval music, that they be historical, that is, concerned with recovering the past as it was then. Discipline here tends to mean protecting that view from challenge. Medievalists, almost without exception, have acted as guardians of a historical ideology, policing the work of their colleagues in search of ideas or views that might not be historically correct, and in the process building up a body of common law that forms the generally acceptable story of music in the Middle Ages. There is no branch of musicology in which 'discipline' has been a more apt term.

But it must also be obvious that the knowledge of which this edifice consists is in fact a body of opinions, opinions that for the sake of a viable subject are accepted for all practical purposes as facts. That is inevitable, and hardly needs special comment, except that the vehemence of some of the disputes we have seen appears to be out of all proportion to the security with which any of the opposing views can be established as preferable on any objective grounds. And that is the whole point. They are hotly disputed precisely because they depend on opinion, and so on personal grounds, rather than on proven fact with which there could be no argument. Even within this tightly circumscribed society, therefore, there is a ferment of competing personalities, each offering a slightly different take on medieval music, a take that is generated in each case by who they are.

The main procedure that characterises musicology, therefore (and let it be assumed that I am speaking from now on particularly of the musicology of early music), is the presentation of views within a rhetorically calculated argument. The key word here is rhetorical. Musicology is about persuasion. Individuals have to persuade as many of their colleagues as possible, and in particular the most influential of their colleagues, that their views are correct. Naturally, they must also be novel, for it is a fundamental requirement that each study offers something new. Musicology is therefore also about creativity. The essential tasks are to think up, or discover, something new – and to present it persuasively.

CERTAIN KNOWLEDGE

Hundreds of thousands of documents survive that contain some evidence of medieval music-making, but perhaps not many hundreds of thousands: too many for any one scholar to know them all, but too few for many of them to connect up into a continuous narrative. If one is to do anything more than compile a photographic archive of them all (which would be useful), one inevitably has to make guesses about their meaning, their relationships, and about what is missing or – and this is the category that must cover most of what we would wish to know – what was never recorded. To do historical musicology is therefore to make guesses into arguments.

There is nothing against which to measure or check the correctness of one's conjectures. They may be strengthened or weakened by the chance discovery of more evidence, but there are no 'controls'. Too many things might have happened at any point for one to know what did. Put this together with the tiny amount of surviving evidence and you have a situation in which the chances of arriving at an accurate reconstruction of 'what actually happened' are extremely poor.[2] Knowing for certain that it is accurate is to all intents and purposes impossible. Whatever the evidence, part of the process of historical recovery is interpretative: what is evidence and what it means are matters of judgement that can be shaped by the way we view the world. Here we face the difficulty, so much stressed in recent thought, of escaping from the preconceptions of our own culture. To pursue the analogy developed by J. M. Balkin, as historians we face the problem of setting aside our own cultural software and using instead an earlier, in this case a far earlier, version, which has first to be reconstructed from code left behind and which can then run under the current version without causing conflicts.[3] Unless we can do that there is no possibility of arriving at an understanding of how any surviving data were originally processed or of the results that the data produced. Put together all these obstacles that lie between us and 'their' understanding of 'themselves' and historical musicology looks like an ideal so fantastical that it's hard to imagine why anyone pursues it, still more why anyone would fund it. It is very tempting to say that despite all this we can come to some understanding of 'how it was'. But realistically we cannot, and if by chance we did we couldn't know that we had. To do musicology honestly, therefore, one has to let go of any claim to, or any belief in, being right when one offers a hypothesis as a result of one's research. This is very hard to do. After months or years of sifting evidence, trying out and weighing up different ways of understanding it, arriving eventually at an arrangement and interpretation of it that seems to work in relation to what is already believed and that seems to offer possibilities for further development, it is not easy to admit that, though one may seem more right than anyone else, one is nevertheless undoubtedly wrong. The best one may allow is that one is offering a view that will need to be scrutinised but that should be accepted until shown to be less right than another yet to emerge.

It is easy to see how compromises come to be taken for granted in such a situation. When a musicologist writes 'we know', or 'X has shown', or treats as equivalent to those the more modest 'I hope to have shown' or 'I would argue', the uncertainty of all the conclusions that follow is silently recognised yet rhetorically denied, because to spell out all the uncertainty is to weaken one's case and to keep constantly at the forefront of the reader's mind the dubious worth of a strongly historical approach to studying the distant past, an approach that measures its success by what it is able to 'show'. Compromises therefore seem essential, otherwise few positive conclusions could seem to be reached. The temptation to accept them as so normal that they are no longer seen as compromises is very great. Compromises of this sort, because they are so necessary for any kind of findings to be reached, become invisible. And so musicology builds up a culture of its own in which certain attitudes and assumptions are taken for granted, are no longer even seen, let alone seen as problematic. Moreover there is very little to be gained by asking fundamental questions about this. Asking questions just makes the whole thing harder to do. And the more strongly historical the musicology – the more insistent that its job is to recover facts – the harder they make it. Questions of this sort are not useful to the kind of historical musicology that medievalists have, for the most part, come to practise.

Whether this is a sensible way to treat 'knowing' and 'showing' what happened in the past might be a matter for debate: it has been in almost every other area of the humanities; medieval studies in music is among the last to face up to it. But most would agree that, at the very least, from time to time the process needs to be checked. We need to be reassured, for example, that the number of hypotheses built upon hypotheses is not now so great that the whole edifice is in danger of collapse; we need to feel confident that those at the bottom remain strong enough to bear the weight of those above, and that those above are equally sound and necessary. The voices-and-instruments hypothesis offers one of the most disturbing examples, for we now see that it has so slender a base that nothing built above can be considered safe. Yet that superstructure continued to grow through the greater part of a century precisely because it was not convenient to ask questions: the advantages – academic, musical, commercial – of preserving the illusion were too great. Now that we have asked the awkward questions, how much of the work done over those eight decades between 1898 and (say) 1977 still seems worthwhile?

If, to take a concrete example, we read what Reese had to say about the performance of medieval music and consider his influence on people who played and recorded it, what can we say is its value? The answer need not be 'very little'. It will be if we insist that all this work is measured by its demonstrable historical validity (demonstrable according to current standards, needless to say). But if we ask instead how productive it was in its time, how interesting or how useful it was the answer looks very different. Reese's teaching, through his students and his writings, had a very considerable influence on the sound of medieval music during the second half of the twentieth century; it was extremely useful to a great many people for a long time. The fact that it now looks 'wrong' need not invalidate it. Indeed, to say that it is wrong would, according to a historicist methodology,[4] be to fall into exactly the same trap that medievalists so often warn against, that of reading a text anachronistically, measuring it against values of another time. Read according to the values and beliefs of his own time, Reese was of course right. Unless one wished to argue that there is to be one rule for reading medieval writers (only in their terms) and another for modern ones (only in ours) it must, to the historicist, seem inappropriate to evaluate past research in terms of its apparent correctness today. But that is exactly how it is often evaluated. One might typically say that Reese was right then but he's wrong now, and because scholarship moves on we can, while admiring what he did at the time, now look beyond him, leaving his work to take its place in the history of the discipline, no longer contributing to research. That seems a reasonable view. But, if we believe that scholarship improves knowledge about the past, there must still be a nagging doubt about the value of his work. If it seems wrong now it follows that we believe that it was also wrong then, even though nobody was able to see that at the time.

A pessimist might conclude from this that knowledge about the distant past is so hard to come by, the correctness of views so uncertain, views themselves so changeable, that we can safely conclude nothing at all. If one insists on the 'safety' then that is unfortunately a reasonable conclusion. But it misses the point. The scarcity of the evidence, both for facts and for the way those facts were understood 'then', is something we have to be able to accept in order to do anything with the study of medieval music. We accept it and then work with it. But that also means that we accept that almost no findings are really 'safe'; even the simplest observations about the evidence (for example that one part is texted and the other two not – in the manuscript) may lead to questionable interpretations (for example that the other two were not texted – in performance). And this applies to everyone's work, our own as well as the work we now think discredited. Any scholar, like Reese, who lives a long and productive life inevitably lives to see at least some of their work devalued by subsequent 'findings' (by which I mean the whole complex of found data and changed views). On a personal level this is well understood; the estimation in which scholars are held generally declines less quickly than belief in the correctness of their findings, and this is precisely because we recognise that although they seem wrong now they seemed right, and usefully so, at the time, and we admire them for it. But while this moderates in an admirably sympathetic way the harshness of the relentless changing of views that characterises scholarship of all sorts, it hardly alleviates the essential problem, which remains that each generation persists in believing that it is closer to the truth that its predecessors, despite all the evidence that only a rather small amount of knowledge is actually accumulating – only a few things are being established and are then remaining accepted by most people thereafter: most of what is accepted at first is sooner or later discarded. On the whole then, because there are so many possible readings of the evidence, most of them lying outside current paradigms and therefore not currently conceivable, we cannot know if we are getting significantly nearer to finding out what really happened in the distant past. There is therefore, it seems to me, an argument to be made for moderating claims to correctness, even claims hedged about with the kinds of provisos discussed above, and for valuing scholarship more by its usefulness or by its interest than by any supposition of its increasing accuracy.

IMPROVING KNOWLEDGE/IMPROVING UNDERSTANDING

This sense of increasing accuracy is always with us. During most of the twentieth century it would have been hard to find a medievalist who was not certain that knowledge about the performance of medieval music was continually improving. What that improvement consisted of was the continuing development of the voices-and-instruments hypothesis through the reconstruction of medieval instruments and playing techniques, the latter discovered by doing it and by learning from other cultures. From our vantage point it looks far from clear that there was a substantial increase in historical knowledge. Of course the same cannot apply to all aspects of the study of medieval music. It is perfectly obvious that by rediscovering most of the manuscripts that we know today Ludwig and Wolf improved our knowledge of medieval music, at least to the extent that they made it possible for us to see examples of it in notation. In the same spirit so did everyone who made known a new document, whether music manuscript, theory treatise, payment record or whatever. This continues today, though now almost exclusively in the area of archival research which has taken over from manuscript studies as the main site of discovery in early music.[5] But seeing these documents is one thing, interpreting them is another. Moreover, for the Middle Ages performance practice and analysis are not being enriched by newly discovered documentation to any very great extent. In neither field has a large amount of new evidence emerged in recent years; innovation here has been in interpreting material already available (if overlooked).

It is when we look at changing interpretations over a long enough timescale that the notion of improvement in the musicology of medieval repertories begins to seem most suspect. Each step along the way naturally seems to offer some improvement over what went before. But almost every step forward involves also taking steps backwards, undoing 'knowledge' that now seems wrong and on which we hope to persuade readers that our new view improves. Over a long enough time-span, as we have seen, almost every interpretation ends up either rejected entirely or so much modified that it becomes fair to credit its current form only to its most recent author. Inevitably this will be repeated with our own work, but we are skilled at finding ways of reading progress into process, of persuading ourselves that despite the relentless replacement of one view by another we are nevertheless, indeed thereby, getting closer to verisimilitude.[6]

This is particularly clear, but on a particularly shaky basis, in our approach to the language of medieval music – to 'hearing medieval harmonies' as chapter 3 put it – where there is a very strong sense that we are getting closer all the time to a correct understanding. This seems to arise from two beliefs. First, our view is thought to be getting closer to 'theirs'. At first glance this might seem reasonable, for so much work on 'their' view is always being done, and it is so easy to argue that medieval music is likely to make more sense heard through medieval ears than not. But medieval writings on music, which provide the main evidence for a medieval 'hearing' of the music, have been available since the theory treatises were first published in substantial quantity in the 1780s, and their relationship to the music has been evident since music became available in reasonable quantities at the start of the twentieth century. By the 1930s, at the very latest, musicologists were able to see how the music exemplified, albeit in more complex form, the basic principles set out in the treatises. Understanding of medieval counterpoint theory has not changed significantly since at least Crocker, arguably since Schering. Therefore if this understanding of medieval theory offers a reliable route to the correct hearing of the music then it should have been heard correctly, and thus in the same correct way, throughout the past seventy years. Evidently it has not. This is of course because of the prior understanding of music that scholars brought to understanding the theory. But any argument that scholars of previous generations were blinded by preconceptions of their own time can be countered by asking why scholars of later generations should suddenly become immune to that.[7] The belief that by getting closer to 'their' words about music we are getting closer to their hearing of it is exactly the belief that underpinned the authenticity movement from the 1960s through to the early 1980s and is vulnerable to exactly the same rebuttals.[8] We hear what we believe; we cannot know that it is what they heard.

Secondly, and this is the more interesting issue, there seems to be a belief that we are getting better not just at understanding the music intellectually but also at understanding it as we hear it: we're getting better at listening to it because, knowing what we know about it, we hear it better than earlier generations did. But is it reasonable to suppose that our hearing of a medieval piece is more rewarding for us than Besseler's was for him? It really cannot be maintained that modern knowledge gives modern listeners a richer experience than 1930s knowledge gave 1930s listeners. There is no way of telling, of course, but judging by the enthusiasm Besseler shows in his Hamburg review it would be unwise to claim that his experience was any less rich than ours. In what sense, then, can we be getting 'better' at listening? Certainly it is possible that what we 'know' about music may affect the way we hear it, but what we 'know' will be shown to be wrong by the next generation, and, further, we hear the music not just in relation to what we 'know' about it but also as a sequence of sounds more or less familiar from other *music*. The familiarity of the sounds is, I would suggest, much more influential in our experience of music than things known intellectually about it.[9] We learn to make sense of medieval music above all by hearing a lot of it, and by hearing music that seems to us to be like it.

Returning to the persistent claim among scholars that knowing things about music brings understanding of its sound, one may observe, finally, that there is more than a whiff in this of the perennial *musicus/cantor* debate – the *cantor* simply sings, but the *musicus* understands – which has been used since the Greeks to enforce a class distinction between performers and scholars. Modern musicology has made a profession out of re-establishing it, and then buttressing its claims to a monopoly on understanding by attempting to collapse into a single concept the separate notions of learning (nurturing existing knowledge) and intellect (analytical thought in search of understanding). But you don't have to know about music to enjoy it, or even to find it intelligible. Nor, as I have argued (and as is anyway perfectly evident from daily experience), is there any way of maintaining plausibly that people who do not know about music enjoy it less than people who do. It is hard to maintain, therefore, that the best access to medieval music is via current learning. We must accept, rather, that we study medieval music, or any music, because it is interesting, not because of any further application our findings may have. And this, in turn, offers another reason to value scholarship not by claims to its absolute correctness but simply according to its interest for whoever reads it. This is the only sense in which the understanding of medieval music is certainly 'improving'.

MECHANISMS

It is hard to say how consciously the scholars covered by this book have worried about the limitations of absolute knowledge. On the whole, one may suppose, those limitations seemed clear enough that (in a classic compromise of the sort discussed above) they could be ignored for all practical purposes, and musicology could continue to do its best to recover the past, offering hypotheses that could be accepted as best guesses, to all intents and purposes as descriptions of what happened. At any rate, all the scholars discussed here in detail were significant figures, to their contemporaries and in retrospect; all were capable of producing thought-provoking narratives piecing together fragments of evidence; all had command of the musicological rhetoric that enabled them to be persuasive. How, then, did some hypotheses succeed and others fail? The crucial requirement is that new hypotheses are seen to fit with what is 'known'; from there they get taken up, adopted and used as a basis for – or in constructive relation to – subsequent work. They prove to be useful, in other words, and their merits are measured according to their usefulness, albeit usefulness disguised as correctness (the more correct they seem, the more useful they are, and vice versa). They must, of course, seem plausible, which (except on the very rare occasions when a new hypothesis provokes paradigm change) will mean fitting within the boundaries of what seems plausible already. Plausibility is culturally dependent, both within musicological culture and beyond, and it changes over time. Instrumentally accompanied performance seemed likely because the manuscripts had untexted lower voices, which made an acceptable argument within the conventions of musicological culture at the beginning of the twentieth century, and also because, in including all those instruments, it made an attractive picture of the Middle Ages, one that could accommodate existing, nineteenth-century images (wandering minstrels and so on). The *a cappella* hypothesis then failed, and continued to fail for over half a century, because it was less plausible and less useful. Judgements about history, therefore, depended on assumptions specific to a particular group at a particular time. Evidence (of which there was only a little) played only a small part in the process, and what it meant changed.

From here it is easy to see how the story outlined in the three preceding chapters makes a beautiful example of Thomas Kuhn's theory of paradigms. Kuhn sees a process underlying scientific developments in which problems with existing conceptions, or paradigms, increase until, in a piece of 'revolutionary science', a new paradigm is proposed. The paradigm succeeds by solving the most serious of the accumulated problems, causing the field around them to look quite different. This he calls a paradigm shift. What follows is then 'normal science' once more, but working within the new paradigm, and consists of 'mopping up operations' that fill in the details and that occupy most scientists throughout their lifetimes.

The same descriptions can apply almost as well to work in musicology. Normal musicology consists in refining our 'knowledge' of, in this case, medieval music, using existing approaches but using them more precisely or on new material.[10] Examples from recent musicology could include the increasingly meticulous work on sources done so well since the 1970s (since Bent's and Hughes' work on the Old Hall manuscript), or the text-critical work of the 1970s and 1980s (since Allan Atlas's Cappella Giulia chansonnier edition), or the archival studies that have improved (and continue to improve) so much since the early 1970s (especially since Roger Bowers' Ph.D. thesis of 1975).[11]

It may be hard to imagine how some of these approaches could be questioned, but that is the nature of paradigms; living within one makes it extremely hard to see how one could live outside it. In order to show that this applies more widely than just to views of performance practice and analysis it is worth looking for a moment at one of these other areas. Text-critical work, for example, takes for granted that establishing a text is an essential step before performance or analysis can be considered. In turn it originated within (although it now strains to escape) a view of the sanctity of the composer's written text that shaped almost every branch of musicology during the second half of the twentieth century. But there are several perspectives from which that might now be questioned, perhaps enough that if anyone had the courage and imagination to propose a new paradigm they would fall into place in a new and more plausible relationship to one another. These perspectives in search of a paradigm include work on orality and literacy; arguments for the superiority of the original notation over modern editions; the variability of the text in its various medieval states; the failure of the work-concept through the impossibility of identifying the piece with any one possible (never mind surviving) set of pitches and durations and syllable placements; the minimal difference that new editions generally make to the notes, for all their meticulous reconsideration of each one; the huge loss of other information about music's sound. Putting together all these views it might not be so hard to develop an acceptable view of the medieval composition quite different from one based on the notion of a 'text'. At present this is happening slowly, but rethought thoroughly and imaginatively enough, the textual criticism, editing, performance, publication, analysis and conceptualising of medieval music could change radically and suddenly, in which case it would look more like a Kuhnian paradigm shift. Critics of Kuhn, especially in the more subtle, recent commentaries, by writers young enough not to feel threatened by his

work, have argued persuasively for a continuum of change between normal and revolutionary science.[12] The changing notion of the musical
text, which I see happening gradually, well illustrates that: in the end
we will have reached a position quite different from the older paradigm,
but we will have got there without any sudden revolution in thinking.
Paradigm shifts as Kuhn described them remain rare in musicology –
normal musicology, like Kuhn's normal science, has attractions enough
to sustain most careers – but the rapid and almost universally accepted
switch to instrumental accompaniment after 1905 provides a very clear
instance; the shift between the voices-and-instruments and the *a cappella*
hypotheses comes close, I think, to being another, and at least some of
the changes in thinking about the analysis of early music may offer other,
smaller examples.[13]

Certainly Kuhn's analysis of the ferment of competing views typical of
a period leading up to paradigm change has many points of contact with
our subject. The increasingly tortuous adaptations of existing theory in
order to account for anomalies within the existing paradigm have their
parallels in Besseler's successive attempts to understand medieval harmony as tonal,[14] and it is easy to see, on both sides of his argument with
Ficker, two scholars unable to step outside their competing paradigms
in order to demonstrate the efficacy of either.[15] No less interesting are
the examples of unsuccessful attempts to overturn a paradigm. In Kuhn's
view it is necessary to have accumulated enough anomalies for it to seem,
at least to young or new members of the research community, desirable
for a new paradigm to be developed. Without a widespread perception
that the existing paradigm is inadequate, attempted changes will fail.
Thus the development of ideas from Salzer to Bashour, or from Hughes
to Crocker, could both be seen as questioning the prevailing paradigm,
but neither was successful in overturning it, partly, perhaps, because there
were not enough other indicators being observed simultaneously.[16] Had
vocal performance started in the 1950s, for example, had Besseler in his
1953 article taken a different view of the evidence mentioned there, the
climate could have felt different for all these theorists. Only when vocal
performance and harmonic analysis received boosts simultaneously, in
the early 1980s, and following further work leading towards a new view
of medieval harmony, did the paradigm switch.

We can see, too, in the work of Hellmut Kühn on the theorists' classi-
fications of vertical sonorities, an important contribution to change that
(unintentionally) helped to loosen the grip of the existing paradigm. As
pointed out in chapter 3, once Kühn had shown that it might be possible,

without transgressing medieval theory, to understand ars nova harmony as process, it became possible for others, working in the more liberal intellectual environment of North America, to take a step further and devise a reductional analytic notation able to show how that process worked.[17] One could hardly ask for a clearer example of the dependence of paradigm change on a combination of enough widely recognised problems, enough pointers towards a solution, and a research environment in which it was possible to think afresh about a subject.[18] Another example of incipient paradigm change may be emerging in the recent work on musica ficta, some of it touched on in chapter 3 above. In Kuhn's words, '[The] proliferation of versions of a theory is a very usual symptom of crisis'.[19] And we could certainly be said to be facing just such a proliferation, with competing views from Margaret Bent, Christian Berger, Karol Berger, Thomas Brothers and Elizabeth Leach all currently under consideration by the research community. Of course these are all relatively small examples (so far: they may yet blow up into something much more significant). The paradigm shifts that marked the origin of the voices-and-instruments hypothesis, and then the *a cappella* hypothesis, are far more visible instances in the wider musical world.

What is so fascinating about the first of these shifts is that it was so radical and yet was achieved so quickly; indeed it is its speed and extent that makes it such a beautiful example of how the process works. The Stainers had already begun to show how manuscript evidence could be read to indicate instrumental participation. But just how anomalous manuscript texting was within the existing (*a cappella*) paradigm only became apparent when Ludwig started to copy, and Wolf started to publish, pseudo-facsimiles of a wide range of sources. By switching paradigms, Riemann, Ludwig, Wolf and their circles could see immediately how to make sense of the great variety of instruments, of which pictures and literary descriptions had been appearing with increasing frequency over the previous three-quarters of a century. For Riemann medieval song suddenly seemed comprehensible as the origin of modern song. Later, from Schering onwards, the new paradigm began to seem appealingly compatible with a theory-led view of the musical language. Also from Schering onwards it began to be possible to link different kinds of writing with particular instruments. Links made through the instruments allowed connections to be made with 'Oriental' music and, especially by Ficker, with colourful images of the Middle Ages derived from other sources. And so on. Once the new paradigm was adopted all sorts of new hypotheses became possible within it. Note that Riemann's main reason for switching paradigms – that the new one made the trecento madrigal into a *Kunstlied* – was soon rejected because the others seemed so much better. It is probable that the paradigm would not have survived without the other theories derivable from it, though the reach of Riemann's view, through the huge circulation of his own publications, is another crucial factor in this example. But put together his influence with the paradigm's ability to stimulate and then accommodate so many useful hypotheses, their interaction generating still more in a chain reaction continuing for decades to come, spreading outwards to encompass a whole complex of interlinked ideas about performance, analysis, history, the soundworld, even the very nature of the colourful contradictory Middle Ages, and it is easy to see why it so rapidly became unstoppable. All these aspects worked together to form and sustain and continually reinforce a paradigm based around instrumentally accompanied performance.[20]

The eventual switch to the *a cappella* paradigm shows some of the same characteristics, but on a smaller scale and with less wide-ranging consequences. The new paradigm had been approached on a number of occasions in the past, as we have seen, and increasingly so in the years leading up to its acceptance. The switch came following Wright's and Page's proposals because enough reasons had accumulated by the early 1980s for them to overcome the ever-weakening hold of the instrumental paradigm. Critics were increasingly dissatisfied with the indiscriminate use of instruments, and increasingly aware of the compromises with the evidence that had to be allowed in order to produce instruments capable of playing the lower voices. Evidence was also increasingly clear that instrumentalists were occupied with other kinds of musical activity than composed polyphony. The new hypothesis used an important body of evidence that had previously been ignored because it didn't fit, turning what seemed anomalous under the old paradigm into a fundamental principle of the new. This appeared as specific medieval evidence at a time in musicology when medieval texts were rising above suspicion, a tendency to see them as inadequate mutating into a tendency to see them as beyond reproach. As a result, the evidence of medieval documents was now worth more than the texting in music manuscripts or the presence of instrumentalists and singers together in pictures. On top of that, Page showed in his performances how the new hypothesis could sound good (in relation to current norms of vocal excellence) and how it could emphasise aspects of the music that had been deliberately downplayed. But equally – and this too is characteristic of paradigm switches – the problems it created were, in turn, downplayed, above all how to understand the notation of the lower voices, a problem perfectly solved under the old paradigm; and secondarily the implausibility (from a modern viewpoint) of instrumentalists not often playing in composed polyphony. Both cases involved turning a blind eye to new problems;[21] and some of the 'normal musicology' that followed – Kuhn's mopping-up operations – involved finding ways around them. I am thinking especially of the work of Fallows on lower-voice texting,[22] and more recently, particularly in the work of Banks,[23] the rehabilitation of instruments as partners in the performance of polyphony.

In the light of Kuhn's work it becomes easier to understand the difficulties we continue to have with the concept of continually improving knowledge. Although we have tended to assume that if knowledge is not continually improving it is only because human frailty sometimes leads to mistakes, in fact 'cumulative acquisition of novelty is not only rare in fact but improbable in principle. Normal research, which *is* cumulative, owes its success to the ability of scientists regularly to select problems that can be solved with conceptual and instrumental techniques close to those already in existence.'[24] However, a paradigm that recognises anomalies cannot accommodate the new paradigm that recognises them as law-abiding, and therefore steady cumulation of knowledge is not what is happening when a paradigm changes. With paradigm change the continuum is broken, and the world looks different afterwards. To an extent this aspect of Kuhn's theory – the aspect most hotly disputed by his critics, understandably – is also illustrated by the argument over instrumental participation in polyphony. The emergence of the *a cappella* hypothesis, because it was based in literary and documentary evidence from the Middle Ages, made it possible to see the evidence for the instrumental hypothesis – based on texting patterns – as inadequate, which is not how it looked until then. Similarly, the literary and documentary evidence, already known during the 'instrumental' period, looked then to be insignificant compared to the overwhelming quantity of music notated without lower-voice texts. The world was the same, in fact, before and after the paradigm change, but it looked quite different.[25] Thus, within each paradigm knowledge appears to be improving, but looking back over a long-enough period of time one does not see continuous improvement but rather periods of steady progress ending in sudden change, following which scholars affected by that change must, to some extent, begin again.

For those who made the switch to *a cappella* thinking this is substantially true. The music sounds different and, as I've argued, it is conceptualised differently as a consequence. But the *a cappella* paradigm has not been universally accepted by any means. As a result the gradual replacement of the old paradigm by the new has not happened. We remain stuck in the revolutionary phase, with camps acquiring permanence on both sides, because there is not enough evidence to prove either hypothesis to the satisfaction of adherents to the other. This is, therefore, a rather particular instance of the impossibility of improving knowledge. What we 'know' is what we agree we know, and agreement here has not yet been found. But perhaps what is surprising about this is that there are not more instances of this kind of stand-off in early music studies. Considering the paucity of evidence for almost everything, one might expect that agreement would be harder to reach almost everywhere. How, then, is agreement so often achieved?

GROUPS

Most research in musicology is done by individuals working alone. But alone does not mean cut off. On the contrary, both by working within widely shared and universally taught paradigms, and by taking close account of the views of other scholars (for mutual support and defence purposes), musicologists form hypotheses in contact with the views of many others in their field. By 'defence purposes' I mean protecting their arguments from objections that can be anticipated from the known views of competitors. 'Mutual support' involves acknowledging and connecting up new ideas with those already favoured by colleagues with whom one is or wishes to be in intellectual alliance. Thus there are invisible groups operating all the time, influencing the form taken by new work.

Visible groups are much less common, precisely because on the whole musicologists are in competition and benefit from seeming to be independent of one another. The most effective groups are those formed through contacts between individuals who occupy a sub-discipline within the institution. Obvious examples would be specialists in archival work, analysis, codicology, theory, and so on; they form sub-cultures, defined by specialised skills and also by particular views of what is significant, leading them to have shared attitudes towards other fields and to those who work in them. None of this, however, necessarily leads to a sense of shared purpose or of belonging, since the members of such groups, even more than in groups defined by an interest in a particular period, are in continual competition to find the best document, reconstruct the making of the most important manuscript, develop the most powerful analytical approach, and so on. Groups of this sort have real power through their influence on the wider academic community, not because their members are working together as a conscious group, but rather through the collective attitude fostered by their shared methodology. Thus it is not the expertise in archival work (for example) that forms a group of the kind I am identifying here, but rather the sharing – openly or privately, admitted or concealed – of underlying views of a subject, of ideologies, but more particularly of the constitutive components of ideologies. This kind of exchange within disciplinary groups becomes most clearly visible when scholars form consciously into seminar groups or small conferences meeting from time to time specifically in order to exchange ideas within a shared intellectual space. Here these units of ideology – Richard Dawkins' memes, Dan Sperber's cultural modules[26] – are, as it were, released into circulation from presentations and comments, and are absorbed or rejected in unpredictable mixtures peculiar to each person present according to their sense of what is useful in their work, but in a density and variety that is hard to find in any other kind of exchange. The proceedings of the Berkeley IMS session on euphony give us a faint sense of such a group working powerfully to shape a new view of their subject. A session like that can leave behind, at least for a while, an invisible group formed from those who continue to ponder and develop ideas exchanged there.

To these kinds of groups we can now, thanks to email, add 'virtual' discussion groups and ad hoc networks. Discussion groups, where a list is held centrally and every member receives every communication, function exactly like a meeting, except that documents (including references to publications) can be exchanged and absorbed and can feed back into the discussion much more readily. With ad hoc networks – the unorganised result of one person emailing another – the pattern of communication is a little different, ideas moving for the most part from person to person around a network whose membership is variable, dependent on who communicates which ideas with whom. No one member of such a shifting network will be aware of more than a few of the others. They can nevertheless be surprisingly effective routes for the dissemination of new angles on old problems. This book, for example, has been considerably influenced by this kind of network, spreading out via email through some of those listed in the acknowledgements, and no doubt beyond each of them to correspondents unknown to me. These kinds of virtual groups might be thought of as (semi-visible) variants of the fundamental types outlined above, encouraging more frequent if still fragmentary communication. An email discussion list is visible to the extent that its membership can be known at any moment, but in fact it is the informal network that is more conscious of its homogeneity, for the members of each pair (or, if messages are copied at source, each sub-group) of correspondents are linked strongly enough by shared values and interests that they trust each other to pass on certain types of information only to correspondents with similar values. Rightly or wrongly (wrongly in that networks by their very nature leak in torrents), members of the network feel that they belong to a strongly characterised and semi-closed group of like-minded thinkers.

This sense of intellectual collegiality helps to explain why invisible groups are so much more important, promoting much less tangible but far stronger influences than the visible. The classic example from the wider world of humanities scholarship is the spread of postmodern thinking during the past twenty years. Taking again the instance closest to home, there is a lot of influence from postmodern thought in this book, much of it absorbed rather than sought out and deliberately adopted. In this sense *The Modern Invention of Medieval Music*, like so much writing in the humanities, offers an example of Balkin's notion of cultural software.[27] Units of cultural information spread by a variety of mechanisms,[28] many of them informal, but when enough are held in common by individuals in contact with one another a culturally coherent group will have formed. Likewise the links that this book will seem to make to an ever-growing quantity of books and articles on musicological historiography, many of them written at the same time as this and by colleagues with whom I am in regular contact, are typical consequences of the operation of networks and invisible groups.

The musicology surveyed in earlier chapters offers innumerable examples, innumerable because there is too little evidence left with which to identify and reconstruct them all. As far as Riemann's hypothesis goes, much of the relevant information has now been lost through the death of all the participants, though it is not hard to guess at some of the groupings that must have been crucial. Looking at who taught whom, and at the groupings evident in concert series, conferences and publications it is possible to get a faint sense of some of the alliances that fostered particular views through the first three decades of the twentieth century.

Riemann was, of course, heavily influenced by Wolf, and no doubt vice versa. Wolf provided Riemann with materials he had not the time to collect for himself and developed skills of transcription that Riemann may well have lacked. Riemann offered Wolf a hypothesis for both the development of styles and for performance practice, both of which Wolf was able to modify in the light of his own findings. Ludwig's relationship to Riemann, though distant personally, must have been rather similar to Wolf's intellectually (especially in their shared disagreement with Riemann over many details), since Ludwig and Wolf were not only finding and transcribing the same sources but seem to have been arriving at rather similar views of them (which partly explains Ludwig's extreme irritation at Wolf's book). Later, Gurlitt, also a pupil of Riemann, worked directly with Ludwig, using transcriptions he provided, indirectly with several others via their published editions, and less visibly as a member of a now widespread and extensive circle of writers about medieval music, all of this feeding into the content and presentation of his seminal concerts in Karlsruhe and Hamburg. Indeed, these concerts can be thought of as a point of convergence for sixty years' work on late medieval polyphony (since Coussemaker's motet publications), a realisation in performance of the product (useable editions) of the largest possible invisible group of musical medievalists, namely all those who had contributed to the recovery of performable music and of knowledge about it.

Looking at other networks with teacher–pupil relationships as their nexuses, it is probably not coincidence that Kroyer, later cast as the maverick, studied with Sandberger rather than with Jacobsthal or Riemann, who were the teachers of Ludwig, Wolf and Gurlitt, nor coincidence that there should be a separation in training between Ficker, who studied with Adler, and Besseler who studied with Ludwig and Gurlitt.[29] The teacher–pupil descent through Adler, Ficker, Georgiades, Apfel clearly indicates a somewhat separate tradition of thought. Schering, too, developed independently, studying with Kretzschmar before becoming a colleague of Riemann. None of these teacher–pupil relationships could be indicative in itself but, in the light of patterns made by these scholars' activities and their published work, they look intriguing. Again, the Karlsruhe and Hamburg concerts used Ludwig and his student Besseler to provide editions and advice, a grouping that certainly reflects shared interests and opinions. Handschin, too, was a pupil of Riemann, and there seems no reason to doubt that it was in Riemann's Collegium at Leipzig that both he and Gurlitt developed their interest in performing medieval music. Similarly Riemann's enthusiasm for making popular editions of early music may have sparked Wolf's interest in amateur performance and practical editing, already evident in his earliest edition of trecento songs which he completed while still studying with Riemann.[30]

In these rather crude examples (necessarily crude because so much can no longer be known about their intellectual contacts) we can, however, see cases of one of the most interesting types of visible group, namely groups formed by chance through the coincidence of individuals being students or (less often) staff together. At the student level this is particularly intriguing, since ideas that will shape a career are being formed partly through the interaction of members of a group, colouring in particular ways the paradigms they are all being taught. Groups formed at this point, though they will break up within a few years, can continue to function invisibly but effectively for many years afterwards.

There is a clear case in the *a cappella* group already identified by Page 1993 and discussed in detail in chapter 2 above. There I argued that 'the development of the *a cappella* hypothesis in Britain ... owed ... much to personal contacts between the major participants encouraging one another's views' and I named several of those who made up what was then a clearly visible group of young scholars fascinated by the new approach.[31] The group produced many of the early reviewers of Gothic Voices discs, and I have tried to show how their favourable view of *a cappella* recordings, and unfavourable view of groups continuing to work around an instrumental core, contributed to a shift in general attitudes towards the performance and hearing of medieval music. What held them together as a group was above all their shared experience of entering musicology at the same time and via the same institutions, an experience that encompassed absorbing and questioning the same paradigms through studying similar repertories and the same body of secondary literature, regularly exchanging information and, as a consequence, exchanging views. In Balkin's terms there was a great deal of cultural information being shared. Add to this the opportunities for spreading their views via the pages of *Early Music* and it is not hard to understand how effectively they could contribute to the growing pressure for paradigm change. Brown perceived this more clearly than anyone – certainly more clearly than the members of the group itself, who I would say were more aware of their individuality than their coherence – and in his bitter phrase, 'Page's groupies',[32] came uncomfortably close to an important truth about the way that academic groups at postgraduate level can function. The extent to which these young scholars have continued to function as an invisible group through their subsequent careers is, of course, much harder to measure. It seems reasonable to suppose that sharing those formative experiences creates links that to some extent survive the very different directions that individuals' research may subsequently take; but taking different directions inevitably means that as individuals grow away from their training they shift allegiance away from student groups towards groups defined rather by a shared ideology of method.

What is the effect of shared ideology on the work of individual members in an invisible group? Every member of such a group – and perhaps it is this that defines membership most clearly – has a strong awareness of the constituency for which she writes;[33] it is that collection of colleagues whose judgement of her work matters most to her, whose approval she most seeks and whose disapproval she most fears. Writing ostensibly for publication to the widest possible audience, it is this much smaller group she is really addressing. To gain their agreement with whatever her argument may be she adopts perspectives they will find interesting and views they can share; she puts in signals to them, using current 'hot words' – terms that evoke a particular complex of values – and citing authors approvingly or disapprovingly according to the ideology of the perceived group. Scholars who successfully establish themselves at the cutting edge of a discipline will unwittingly attract an invisible group to form around them, made up of those (often younger scholars) who admire their approach and who aspire to be perceived as sharing their ideology. A body of literature will begin to form defined by its shared values which are, in turn, signalled by shared codes and citations. Aspiring members will be hoping for alliances with those they cite and for the citing to become mutual. Gradually an increasingly visible group forms and with it a new complex of values, in extreme instances even a new paradigm, in which case the group will grow to include the larger part of the disciplinary community. The process is fuelled by a volatile mixture of intellectual excitement and the need to belong, and what it forms, besides new orthodoxies, are centres of power.

POWER RELATIONS

Power accumulates. A research student has very little to begin with, but he starts to acquire it quite early. A sense of it may be felt while reading existing work and seeking a gap to fill or a field to develop, and it may take the form of dissatisfaction with existing work, a sense that he can improve on it. It thus germinates as a sense of his ability in relation to others, particularly in a competitive relation to them. Another important process is that of growing beyond his supervisor. There comes a point where the student realises that he now knows more about his subject than the person who, at first, was teaching him. That gives him an early taste of being the best in his field. That sense may be enhanced when he starts to give conference papers and realises that others find his work interesting, original and impressive. Of course there may be knocks here too. There are few more competitive environments than a research students' conference, where everyone is hoping to stand out from the crowd, especially in front of those senior scholars present, and some will always seek to achieve that not only by their own presentation but by the critical questions they can be seen to be able to ask of others. Everyone here is aware that grants, fellowships and jobs may be won later on by those who already have a reputation for a sharp mind.

Once in full-time employment power accumulates in two directions, one administrative within the employing institution, the other academic within the disciplinary community.[34] The former can contribute to some extent, in that rapid promotion within the institution can feed back into a perception of accumulating power outside; but much more depends on developments in a scholar's research, above all in the effectiveness with which it inspires the formation of invisible groups or, failing that, the effectiveness with which it taps into influential groups already existing.[35] It is not hard to see how, when a scholar's perceived power reaches a high level, their hypotheses gain credibility by association and are more likely to be accepted, at least for a time, simply by being theirs.[36] Research success, defined in this way, leads rapidly to power of a slightly different sort, as the scholar is increasingly asked to referee, examine, and report for journals, publishers, programme committees and grant awarding bodies on the work of others. Much of this – typically all the reporting just listed – is done anonymously by the reader, sometimes of anonymous submissions but by no means always, so that the reader is in a doubly powerful position, able to promote or suppress work by others without being accountable. Anonymity allows readers to exaggerate, misrepresent, suppress and promote on grounds other than the merits of the proposal, and it may be especially tempting to do so when other applicants for the same positions or opportunities may be closer intellectual allies. Even with the best will in the world, a great deal depends on the relationship between the submission and the reader's particular ideological orientation, and publishers and awarding committees cannot be expected to filter that out in assessing readers' reports. It is hard, therefore, to see that anonymous reporting offers any advantages other than concealment for the reporter, and if the report is properly defensible there should be no need for that. For all these reasons, and also because in small sub-disciplines reporting tends to be done by the same few specialists, power in these situations is both concentrated and easily abused. Schering's treatment of Kroyer offers an obvious and a particularly unpleasant example.

With power goes patronage, which again tends to promote disciplinary alliances. Patronage can take many more forms than simply the promotion of approved work; it can function through bestowing or withholding information (for example, about newly discovered sources, bibliography, ideas), through appointing to research or teaching assistantships with no or limited advertising, through passing on work (especially reviewing, which allows shared values to be promoted while sparing the patron the labour of writing the review), as well as through references and recommendations. Taking into account the workings of ideological groups and of power relations it is not hard to see how the success or failure of research hypotheses can be determined by factors other than the details of the argument.

Power comes too from the status of one kind of study in relation to another, and this factor is particularly relevant to the work studied here.[37] One of the characteristic aspects of work on performance practice, and one that does not hold for analysis even when the two are as closely related as here, is its unusually direct effect on the perception of medieval music beyond academia. Riemann's hypothesis, and Page's, have both had a profound impact on the musical public's view of these earliest repertories. Yet the public influence of a scholar's work has a rather double-edged correlation with her power within the profession. The public dissemination of her knowledge seems, if anything, to weaken the academic's position; conversely, the more abstruse the research, the greater the power it generates. There is a high degree of snobbery underlying this paradox. Just as in the sciences pure research has traditionally had a higher status than applied, so here the analytical work on musical language described in chapter 3 has a higher status than the views of performance practice described in chapters 1 and 2. With a single exception – his chapter in the New Grove Handbook on performance practice, aimed at a similarly wide readership – Page's key articles all appeared in the low-status but widely circulated journal *Early Music* which has a large non-specialist readership concerned with performance and listening, while most of the work from chapter 3 appeared in specialist low-circulation journals and books with an exclusively academic readership. There is thus a simple inverse relationship between public power and professional power.

PERSONALITY

Intertwined with the factors outlined so far is the tricky issue of personality. We have seen how the success of a hypothesis depends in part on the perceived position of its proposer within the disciplinary community. But that in turn depends to a very considerable extent on personality, both as perceived on paper and as experienced in the flesh. Personality on paper is easier to analyse, for it can be reduced to habits of rhetoric; I shall be looking at aspects of that in the following section. Personality in the raw is much more difficult, but it is inevitable that to understand musicology one has to understand something of the psychology of its practitioners.

At the most constructive level, personality determines what interests the scholar. I have suggested already, and shall be arguing again later, that interest to the community (as narrowly or as widely defined as you like) is one of the defining qualities of worthwhile musicology, and since it is hard to be interesting without being interested we must allow that personality rightly plays a vital part in determining the topics and methods that musicology evolves. In a preparatory study for this book I illustrated this notion by pointing to a distinction between scholars who sought to make medieval music familiar to us, and those who sought to emphasise its otherness.[38] Both seem perfectly defensible strategies, on the one hand an attempt to emphasise aspects that have analogues in more familiar contexts, and especially in later music; on the other a determination not to downplay the foreignness of the medieval mind or the very great differences of approach to using and to thinking about music. Pursuing this contrast of approaches I tried to see one group of scholars as bringing the music to us, the other as taking us to it. Riemann, it seemed to me, was crucially a familiariser, the obsessive author of guides through every branch of musical knowledge. It is entirely in keeping with his passion to explain that he should seek to bring medieval music as close to modern music as possible, seeing in it the origins of tonality and adjusting it as necessary in order to conform to modern views of text-setting and performance practice. Schering, by contrast, I saw as having 'a far more radical imagination, both for musical sounds and for historical hypotheses' and thus as, by nature, a defamiliariser, someone who revelled in striking hypotheses (as anyone familiar with his work on later composers will agree). This makes it easier to understand why Schering should have been ready to imagine medieval instrumental ensembles well before anybody attempted to reconstruct them, and to reconceive the music as elaborating lost melodies. Looking back over other work considered here it seems reasonable to see Besseler as a committed familiariser, Ficker as more determined to adjust our view to theirs (as he perceived it), a contrast clear in everything these two scholars did, even down to their different editorial policies, Ficker later preferring original note shapes without barlines while Besseler continued to use a lightly adapted modern notation.

We saw too, in chapter 3, how a need to attack Besseler seemed hard not to discern in Ficker's responses to his work, and I proposed there that this arose as a defensive response to a fundamental incompatibility between their responses to the musical past:

Ficker is concerned to see the musical past as different and partly unknowable. Besseler, as we have seen, is more interested in seeing the past in modern terms, in collapsing the gap between then and now. Similarly Ficker is content to imagine medieval counterpoint as quite unlike that of later centuries, while Besseler wants to push back modern counterpoint as far as possible (at least, as far as his musical tastes require). . . . [W]hile . . . Besseler's passion springs from his love of the music and his need to promote it, Ficker's springs rather from a need to imagine the past as different and yet reconstructable: he has a vision to promote, but it is of a mental world rather than a musical style, it is based in ideas rather than in sounds, in concepts rather than in sensations. These two approaches are incompatible, and they illustrate two strands of thought that one can trace in constant opposition generating and sustaining musicological disputes throughout the past 100 years.

A related distinction might be drawn fairly safely between generalisers and collectors, with Riemann and Besseler again lining up very clearly among the former, both of them scholars with a mission to explain and thus willing to risk taking an overview despite the lack of a full set of supporting evidence underpinning their narrative at every stage. By contrast one might see Apfel, and perhaps also Ludwig, as examples of scholars for whom detail was everything, an essential foundation without which nothing could safely be concluded. These are crude distinctions, but useful in enabling us to see how personality can be crucial in forming a set of beliefs about what scholarship should be. Bringing scholars still active into this picture can be awkward (as I learned in correspondence arising out of that earlier article), but it seems safe to say that this book is the work of someone who is by nature a generaliser.[39]

The extent to which personality conflict interferes with scholarship is so obvious that one may perhaps be allowed to make one's excuses and avoid providing live examples. An illuminating comment *post facto* comes from Richard Hoppin looking back after thirty-five years on his acrimonious exchange with Edward Lowinsky over the proper understanding of conflicting signatures:

First, I must beg those who read [our] articles to disregard as much as possible the sometimes acrimonious tone in which they were written. In his letter to me about this return, Edward wrote that he was certain 'we shall now be able to discuss our differences of a generation ago more amicably. Indeed, had we known each other before you wrote your critique of my *Musical Quarterly* article, I am sure that already then we would have written in a different tone.'

Of this I too am sure. When we did meet for the first time, some two years after the 'critique' was published, we had a wholly amicable discussion over beers in a Santa Monica hotel. Shortly thereafter, Edward sent me an offprint of another article that I shall always cherish for its inscription of an 'old antagonist and new friend'. I am thus most grateful to our ancient controversy for bringing about the formation of a firm and lasting friendship.[40]

Perhaps the proper response in situations like this is to have the beer first and publish later. But the extent to which scholars identify with their research, and more particularly with the subject of their research, is not always appreciated, and it is this, I would argue, that gives rise to most of the acrimony that surrounds public disagreement. I suggested in chapter 3 that there is a tendency to collapse scholar and composer, author and subject into one, so that criticism of findings tends to be perceived (by both sides, I suggest) as personal criticism of the finder. This tendency is not confined to humanistic scholarship, but it is more serious there precisely because there are no absolute measures by which correctness can be determined; everything depends on perceived balances of probability, perceived because humanistic scholarship almost invariably lacks the firm statistical data from which probability might be calculated.

Writing of these matters, and no doubt reading of them, is an uncomfortable process. Yet scholars argue as scholars are. They write themselves into their work, just as (and perhaps to a similar extent as) performers perform themselves. A scholar's argument cannot be evaluated without considering who they are. For anyone who has met a good selection of the people they have read (and that is the most valuable thing about conferences) there is no question about this. And yet we never discuss it. It surfaces, often in a rather nasty way, when individuals argue in print; but even then it is too embarrassing to mention. Yet one is bound to ask, if we want to claim that we are working as objectively as possible to recover the past as it was, how we can refuse to look at the most significant influence that shapes our findings. We write the way we do first of all because of who we are, only after that because of what we find.

Continuing to work from the general towards the specific we come to a final level on which hypotheses are shaped and promoted. There is always, one must suppose, at least a semi-conscious awareness among expert readers of the role of ideology, power and personality in the shaping of hypotheses. And there is certainly an acute awareness that because there are so few facts no single hypothesis can speak for itself – facts could always be pieced together differently, very differently if one could escape existing paradigms. For both these reasons, rhetoric plays an especially important role in the writing of medieval studies, and medievalists therefore are particularly adept at using a repertory of standard ploys to persuade readers to accept their story. These ploys need to be identified and investigated to see how they work to distract a reader's scepticism from weaknesses in an argument. I shall do no more here than air the issue: musicological rhetoric deserves a book in itself, not so much as a guide to research students on how to be persuasive but more in order to make it harder to wrap up possibilities in the language of certainty and thereby to inhibit new thinking and change.[41]

Writing musicology – choosing the words and their arrangement in text, footnotes and documentation – is about appearing to be right and about continuing to appear to be right for as long as possible. The key strategies are finding strongly persuasive phraseology and covering oneself against anticipated objections. The needs of those strategies often clash, since one of the most common protective measures against contradiction is to soften one's proposals by hedging them around with 'let-outs', words and phrases such as may, perhaps, on occasion, generally, often, usually, for the most part, to a considerable extent (and there are plenty of those here). More elaborate let-outs may extend to clauses, sentences or paragraphs, typically pointing out exceptions but playing down their significance or 'notwithstanding' work of others that points in a different direction. More daring is to present evidence for alternative findings but to leave it looking weaker than that for the findings one prefers. More subtle is to use keywords characteristic of opposing arguments but in support of one's own. And so on. Examples of all these, and many more, may be found throughout this book, both in my writing and in writing quoted from others. It is tempting but, I think, unnecessarily provocative to point them out again here. The aim is always to use language as a rhetorical flak-jacket, leaving one's own hypothesis alive after all the others have been shot down. The will to live powerfully underlies academic writing, and can lead to just the same kinds of aggression as in real life.

One tactic, however, deserves special mention because it plays so large a part in promoting or condemning work on medieval music. The charge of anachronism has become one of the most favoured weapons in the medievalist's armoury. Although it generally works well, doing considerable damage when aimed carefully, its basis in reason is not entirely sound. The insistence that comment on music should be restricted to the sort that could have been made 'at the time' (though what 'at the time' means is hard to define) depends on a set of interlinked beliefs, first that it is possible to understand music now in the way it was understood then, secondly that to do that would bring some added benefit and thirdly that there is special moral value in historically authentic commentary, the same value, presumably, as is thought to lie in historical accuracy of all sorts.[42] To be more realistic – because one obviously cannot experience anything as it was experienced by others in the past – there is at least an assumption that if we today could place 'their' view, or as near as we can get to it, alongside our own, and allow it to interact with and modify our own as far as possible, submitting our own to it, then we would experience an understanding whose value would be greater than any other,[43] and that that value would consist both in the greater richness of the experience and in the fact of its historicity. Actually, it is hard to see why a historical view should be any more rewarding than any other for the person experiencing it, so in the end this argument comes down to a moral principle, that to be historically accurate is virtuous in itself. Why should it be? One reason might be a sense that we owe something to the past, presumably to the people of the past, since one can hardly owe anything to a concept; in other words that it is a duty to be true to the people of the past by seeing them as they were. But how can we owe something to people who no longer exist? It is hard to see, therefore, that there is anything self-evidently wrong with, for example, Salzer or Besseler seeing tonal progressions in medieval music. One might wish to argue that those progressions are not there, but since they clearly are for Salzer and Besseler that argument could only be made by claiming that they are not there unless they were deliberately put there by the composers. Which brings us back to the moral value of historical authenticity. But what we are really dealing with here is a conflict of paradigms. Neither side can see the question in the same terms as the other. If you feel that history has special claims then it is impossible to agree that it does not, and vice versa. Only by switching paradigms will you be able to see the other side: both cannot be seen together.

The charge of anachronism, therefore, belongs exclusively within the historicist paradigm. There is no point in aiming it at a non-historicist argument, for it has no effect there. Its effectiveness within the historicist paradigm is nevertheless striking, even the suggestion of it can do damage, and as a result there is a tendency among the more strictly historical musicologists to use it as a scarecrow, set up at the weakest point in an argument to frighten off potential critics. This points to the principal function of 'anachronism' as a weapon. I said above that 'facts could always be pieced together differently, very differently if one could escape existing paradigms'. What the charge of anachronism is trying to do, above all, is to protect the historicist paradigm from attack; it is trying to prevent the piecing together of the evidence differently to make a new picture.

In writing the preceding paragraphs I have made special use of metaphors of war and survival. They seem appropriate because of the highly competitive character of so much work in these areas. Where evidence is thin, as it is for performance practice, and where so much hangs on ideology, as it does in analysis, beliefs held by the individual scholars are going to be providing much of an argument's foundation, rhetoric is going to have to do much of the work of making an argument seem plausible, and the promotion and defence of an argument are going to overlap more completely with the promotion and defence of the individual than in areas more self-sufficient in medieval materials (for example in archival or manuscript studies). The scholar thus perceives greater need to fight for or to defend her work because it is more nearly herself. Only the strongest will survive. It is for these reasons that metaphors of war and survival are used so freely in historical musicology. One defends a hypothesis, knocks or shoots down an argument, makes a well-aimed criticism, fires off a letter to a journal, has a competitor in one's sights.

Prevalent too are metaphors of power, carrying, as usual, all their traditional masculine associations. We read of a masterly overview, a magisterial put-down, an authoritative treatment, a commanding view, a powerful counter-argument, a scholar who dominates the field, as well as control of the sources, of the literature, of the data.[44] Arguments themselves can invoke power: a characteristic example is the insistence that one's hypothesis must be accepted as correct until proved wrong, or superseded by a better hypothesis, a claim that arises from a patriarchal view of the process of scholarly argumentation: the king remains king until deposed. The thought that there need not be a king lies entirely outside this paradigm.

Fundamental to scholarly work in the humanities, both modern and postmodern, is (in the well-worn phrase) science envy. Musicology, in developing out of German Musikwissenschaft (with 'wissenschaft' also meaning 'science'), has perhaps believed too much in the scientific quality of its methodology.[45] Hypotheses are said to be 'tested', although in fact no testing as understood by a scientist is done at all. Probability is assessed, though it cannot be measured. Measurements, when taken, are more precise than can ever be useful, as when a parchment sheet is measured to a millimetre despite its ability to expand and shrink by more than that with a change in the weather.[46]

THE EVOLUTION OF HYPOTHESES

If paradigms, groups, power relations, personality, rhetoric, and no doubt other factors one could isolate and analyse, all work together to shape hypotheses, how do some hypotheses (and indeed some scholars) rise to the top, taking on more influence and shaping the conclusions of the rest? The best way to understand this, I think, is to use a Darwinian metaphor. Hypotheses survive and breed not because, as historians might wish to claim, they reach back over many generations to take on the form of things as they were in the past, but rather because they provide the best fit with their current environment.[47] It is a case of survival of the fittest, the best adapted to their surroundings.

Those hypotheses that fit best with what is believed at the time and that show the best potential for producing offspring (new hypotheses derived from them) are the ones that are held up as excellent, and whose progenitors are, for a while, the most honoured. The more productive of well-adapted and fertile hypotheses a scholar seems, the more successful they will be. Increasing power, and with it esteem, enables scholars to protect their offspring more effectively from attack; and to that extent it is possible for a while for weaker offspring to survive and breed alongside the stronger, weakening the stock overall. Equally, if their offspring turn bad and prove not to be good breeding stock, the respect for their progenitors falls away.[48] In scholarship this happens far more predictably than in the evolution of life. Precisely because scholarly arguments are to such a large degree invented, and to such a small degree demonstrably correct, and so are to an extent reflective of personal and period taste rather than absolute truth, each new generation has greater need and greater opportunity than in the evolution of life to impose its own stamp, which is to a large extent the stamp of personalities. In a sense, then, we are seeing not the evolution of organisms, but rather of psyches. The strongest personalities impose their beliefs most ruthlessly on their weaker colleagues, and the stronger they become in position and influence, the more it is in the interests of the weaker to ally themselves with them, and to follow in their footsteps. Because there is so little that can be done to prove any argument, it is difficult to depose such an accumulation of power, and thus the direction of a field of study can be turned permanently.

On the other hand, there are dangerous challenges always arising, whether from upcoming contenders for power or from dissident groups importing ideas from outside (new musicology, for example). And inevitably, individual contenders and dissident groups succeed in at least some areas of a subject. Previous theories are overturned and new ones set up in their place. Paradigms change, but within the new paradigm the process starts again and continues as before.

The lessons of this metaphor are exactly those we take away from observing the role of natural selection in the evolution of life. The strongest will survive and their genes will be passed on, so that although individuals all die the genetic information of some lives on in their descendants. In musicology the struggle is to produce hypotheses sufficiently powerful that they will be able to pass on, and pass on widely, the units of ideology from which they are formed. Successfully arguing for power depends not only on strong units of ideology and strong evidence or ideas, but also effective skills of persuasion (rhetoric), influential protection (patronage), persistence (personality), and the good luck to avoid accidents. There is more to it than just 'pure scholarship'.

PERVERSIONS AND DANGERS

It may be easier to understand now why scholarship can be perverted. To the extent that being able to do research depends upon funding, and success as a researcher depends upon power, the kind of research that gets done, and its successful promotion, can depend upon political forces originating outside the academic community. For scholars working in Britain, this became particularly clear during the 1990s when a nationwide process for evaluating and rewarding research was imposed on university staff. Since then each researcher has been required to submit a specified amount of work for evaluation, and each has been given a rating reflecting its perceived quality. Departments are then funded in proportion to the ratings awarded. Senior staff have allowed themselves to collaborate in the process by providing the evaluations. Collaboration was ensured by letting it be supposed that without it a worse system would be imposed from outside the community, although there was in fact little reason to believe that such a system could be devised without collaboration. The fear of one nevertheless proved sufficient. So far, the kind of research that is valued most highly has continued to be determined by the ideology of the academic community. But it is easy to see how, with no more than carefully worded suggestions of possible sanctions, government would be able to take a hand in encouraging or discouraging particular kinds of work.

What is so revealing and frightening about this example is that it was not necessary for government to bring any legislative pressure to bear on the community in order to get its way on peer evaluation. The rumour of a worse alternative was all that was necessary to ensure compliance. Examples of exactly this kind of pressure are to be seen in the story of the German Musicological Society's capitulation during 1933 to the will of the Nazis. The first step was the removal of Alfred Einstein, a Jew, from the editorship of the journal. As Wolf wrote to Einstein, notifying him of the decision, 'The board . . . came to the conclusion that it is impossible to run against the current, especially since the enterprise must request a subvention from the state'.[49] As Pamela Potter reports, no instructions appear to have been received that the Society should reform itself along Nazi-approved lines. The perception of a wish that academic organisations should do so, coupled with the expectation that with approval would come funding, was sufficient to fuel a thoroughgoing restructuring by its president, Arnold Schering, who as a result of adopting Hitler's *Führenprinzip* now enjoyed absolute power, with complaints against his decisions banned under the society's new charter. As a result the society was in a better position to look for projects that would help the Nazi cause and thereby gain funding. The reorganisation involved setting up new task forces to promote regional studies, folklore, comparative musicology (including race), preservation and other topics directed towards specifically German nationalist concerns. To oil the wheels of patronage (presumably) Schering trumpeted the reorganisation in a letter to the propaganda minister Joseph Goebbels, announcing the Society's 'joyful will to work together to build a new German culture with all its strength'.[50]

Schering was not just concerned with the promotion and funding of the Society, nor with the health of German musicology under the new regime. We have seen too how his promotion of his own views on performance practice, and his suppression of Kroyer's strongly worded disagreement with them, was facilitated by the sacking of Einstein;[51] and also how Schering prevented Wolf's promotion to Ordinarius and forced his resignation from the Berlin faculty, while promoting younger National Socialists.[52] He offers an all too clear example of a scholar shamelessly using political circumstances to enhance his own power and promote his own work. Given those political circumstances it was not hard to do.[53]

The perversion of research on a much wider scale is equally clearly illustrated by the ever-growing promotion through the 1920s and 1930s of a Germanocentric, 'Nordic' view of medieval music. We have seen Ficker already in 1925 attributing the development of 'Gothic' organum, with its marriage of 'sensuous' upper voice and 'intellectual' tenor, to Nordic man's characteristic transformation of southern melody. Later in the same article he contrasts 'the sensuous-naturalistic air of a southern race', as seen in trecento song, with the development of an organic relationship between melody and tonally ordered harmony in the Nordic Gothic.[54] During the Nazi period he was to claim credit for his early appreciation of the contribution of the Nordic race in Western music history.[55]

Besseler in his seminal history of medieval and Renaissance music, issued in parts between 1930 and 1934, was thinking in similar terms of a musical evolution dominated by Nordic values. In what now seems an absurd argument, but one that was entirely in keeping with scholarship in Germany in the early 1930s, and using keywords of the time, he finds the origins of modal rhythm in Germanic languages: 'The powerfully hurled forth accents of old Germanic verse provided a rhythmic primeval form that had an effect wherever German people as a unified class determined the new combinations of race'.[56] And we saw in chapter 3 how SS officer Richard Eichenauer in his 1932 *Music and Race* (in Potter's words) 'ascribes an inborn Nordic racial tendency to Leonin's and Perotin's innovations in polyphony'.[57] Further, for Besseler 'those regions in which a broad flow of Germanic settlers fused with the indigenous population into a new, unique being always step forth leading'.[58] In the language of his place and time this meant very much more than might appear today, drawing on notions of race and power and of a greater Germany extending beyond the nation's existing borders. Though a party member,

Besseler was not a thoroughgoing Nazi – Potter reports that he provided some protection for his Jewish students – but he shared much of the nationalist ideology and clearly played along actively, working the system in order to promote musicology. In the same year that his history completed publication he delivered a speech '("Musik und Nation") endorsing plans to forge a bond between music and the Nazi state and to isolate German music from unsavoury influences'. As Potter further reports, 'Besseler learnt how to use politics to benefit musicology and strengthen its relationship with the state and the public, a skill which served him well in dealing with the authorities of the Third Reich and [later] the German Democratic Republic'.[59] We can see Ficker following exactly the same strategy when 'In 1938 he proposed setting up a musical instruments museum . . . and cited its importance . . . in areas of *Volk* and race studies'.[60]

Playing along with Nazi obsessions in order to protect one's disciplinary community may be seen as not just understandable but even, presented in the right light, as honourable. But it cannot be seen only in its relation to musicology. It functions too, whether we like it or not, in relation to Nazi ideology and policy. When Reinhold Zimmermann, in an unpublished essay from the early 1940s entitled 'German music in the French-speaking areas', covers the works of Leonin, Perotin, Philippe de Vitry and the Franco-Flemish masters of the Renaissance,[61] it is clear to everyone who would have read him that he is promoting the belief that the music of these composers is fundamentally German, and part of Germany's rightful heritage. The very purpose of the collection (initiated by Goebbels's propaganda ministry) was, according to Potter, 'to demonstrate Germany's long history of musical hegemony in territories recently occupied by German troops'.[62]

Why did a disproportionately high percentage of academics and intellectuals collaborate with the Nazis and, after them, the Stasi? As Jonathan Petropoulos writes of academics in the art world, 'They collaborated with the Nazi leaders, whom they often recognized as brutal and vainglorious, because they perceived opportunities in terms of their own work'.[63] And also, I would add, because they were accustomed to putting their research aims ('the search for historical truth') above all other considerations. Working for dictators and thugs can be justified, for academics, if they provide the resources to support research, as the Nazis certainly did, both actually – directing funds and practical assistance to scholars working to extend the appropriation of foreign cultures into the

German cultural Reich – and through making unattractive the alternative to collaboration which, provided that the scholar kept his views to himself, meant unemployment but not necessarily persecution. It was not essential to collaborate, it simply aided one's research.

Some may feel that these things are better left alone now, and if one thinks mainly of the reputation of the individuals involved it is easy to agree. But although that is a consideration sometimes underrated in musicological writing, in this case there are far more significant issues at stake. The lessons of intellectual collaboration with the Nazis are too important to go unlearned. We have seen how the authoritarianism that Schering was able to indulge, culminating in his running the Deutsche Gesellschaft für Musikwissenschaft on the *Führenprinzip*, damaged Wolf and evicted Einstein.[64] Ficker's nationalistic views of music history were seen by him as contributing to the Nazi project, but anyway clearly play right into the ideology of German superiority, particularly through arguments that composers and developments in other parts of Europe were 'Nordic' and thus belonged within the intellectual heritage of Germans. This cannot be written off as idiosyncratic or a purely personal matter, for it was exactly this attitude that underlay the entire National Socialist agenda. As Petropoulos has written,

> Most Nazi territorial claims were based upon the notion that meritorious culture found abroad . . . had been created by Germanic peoples. The art historians were expected to use their scholarship to justify Nazi irredentism. During the war, cultural historian Hermann Aubin declared that 'the work of our ancestors . . . represents the great legal brief for territory'. . . . Cultural cleansing was accompanied by ethnic cleansing. Objects deemed to be Germanic in origin were preserved, while those of Slavic, Jewish, Sinti, and Roma cultures, among others, were destroyed. The art historians, like those in other professions . . ., played a role in the Holocaust that went far beyond that of bystander. They first provided intellectual justifications for the aggressive and genocidal program, then they served the Nazi leaders and [as did Herbert Gerigk, Wolfgang Boetticher and Guillaume de Van for music] helped denude the victims of their property. And . . . the expropriation of property was part of a continuum that culminated in murder.[65]

Seen from this perspective Ficker's culpability, or de Van's, was far from negligible. Ficker appropriated French music, presenting it as Germanic and so playing his part in the growth of a cultural justification for territorial claims. de Van assisted in identifying 'German' artifacts to be stolen from France and 'repatriated' to Germany. Besseler worked within Nazi organisations to further his career. And there were many others, some far more deeply implicated that these, including Friedrich Blume, Karl Gustav Fellerer, Rudolf Gerber, Hans Joachim Moser, Helmuth Osthoff, and above all Gerigk and his assistant Boetticher. All survived denazification relatively unscathed and all, save Besseler, found employment in West Germany after the war. None of the medievalists was as culpable as Boetticher who, under Gerigk, played a major role in the looting of Jewish property in occupied France and yet who flourished as a Privatdozent and then (from 1956) as Ordinarius at Göttingen, publishing on lute music, Lassus and the Schumanns, and producing the Urtext edition of Robert Schumann's piano works for Henle (volumes which many readers of this book may have on their shelves).

It is important to remember that musicologists used their skills and their knowledge in these ways, allowing – at the very least – their work to play into the hands of an amoral and murderous regime, and it is important also to recognise that the work itself was not blameless. Ficker's Nordic reading of so much medieval music, like Lederer's Celtic reading, or – a more extreme but still analogous case – the widely accepted doctrine of the so-called German Christians that Jesus was an Aryan, not a Jew,[66] was itself warped, regardless of how it may later have been used. It reminds us how much it matters not to fall into discriminatory thinking, whatever the evidence, and it reminds us too that we have moral obligations beyond those of our research: recovering and retelling the past is not to be pursued regardless of the cost. If, whatever the original motivation, we find our research being misused we have at least an obligation not to cooperate. Collaboration, whether intellectual or practical, may have been hard for German and Austrian scholars to avoid between 1933 and 1945, but it was not impossible. For all these reasons, those scholars are not guiltless, nor are their actions during those years best forgotten.

Among its many lessons, therefore, the story of research in medieval music teaches us how the unavoidable ideological element that is always at work in the formation of hypotheses can, under unfavourable circumstances, induce scholars to behave and to think immorally. This example may seem an extreme one, but there would be others if the origins and performance of medieval music had been an issue in other parts of Europe, or indeed in other parts of the world, during the past half-century. It would be optimistic to suppose that circumstances so conducive to perverted research will not arise again. Even leaving aside this example as untypical – which thank heavens it is – it is not hard to see how pressures from society and from government can turn research in one direction or another whenever scholars find it convenient, when it increases their power or protects their work from attack. The case of academics' response to the UK government's Research Assessment Exercise, cited at the beginning of this section, is just one recent example. The danger is there, too, whenever a powerful group comes to dominate the subject or a field within it. Given the weakness of the evidence, widespread agreement should be worrying. A healthy musicology should therefore embrace a very wide range of views, should celebrate diversity, and – for just the same reasons – should as a matter of principle resist conformity, questioning the status quo wherever it becomes visible.

AUTHORITARIANISM

Nevertheless, historical musicology has, as we have seen, a dangerous tendency towards absolutism, grounding it in the truth of securely established facts about the past and therefore in the special value given to the search for such facts. At its most extreme, the historicist project views facts as recoverable and, once recovered, as having absolute authority over us. Facts *can* be established (meaning rediscovered, although the terms are revealingly different in implication) and once established *must* be accepted. Anything else we claim *must*, as a necessary precondition of its acceptance, be reconcilable with them. From this follows inevitably the insistence that there are valid and invalid ways of handling the surviving material, appropriate and inappropriate, historical and anachronistic, historicist and modernist, and that these equate to right and wrong in absolute moral terms. I stress that such a view is extreme, but it is only an extreme realisation of a tendency that we have been able to see at work in much of the musicology we have examined.[67]

Objections to this kind of authoritarianism come in essentially two forms, one that facts cannot actually be established so securely as to warrant this kind of intellectual totalitarianism, the other that what happened 'then' does not have to restrict what we do now if we don't want it to. The first is a kind of ultra-positivism, not accepting even those securely established facts as secure enough; the second is a form of liberalism, advocating freedom of thought and expression (within socially acceptable constraints). Both are comfortably embraced by postmodernism, like so much else. Gary Tomlinson has argued persuasively that our interaction with the past takes place within a dialogical space between us and them, where we converse as far as we can, and whose boundaries are set by the limits of our non-coercive understanding. To measure their views against ours, however, is to step beyond those boundaries and to misappropriate 'them' for our own purposes.[68] Clearly this is a somewhat more sympathetic and generous, and indeed a more subtle view of the proper relation between us and them than I am proposing here. So is Bruce Holsinger's musicology of empathy, characterised by our striving to understand their beliefs, and our willingness to allow ourselves to be changed by them.[69] I find both these – very similar – views, and the tenor of postmodernism that underlies them, immensely attractive. But I have to confess, also, that I find them unrealistic, because they require us to imagine the past as present not just as images conjured up by us but as people needing our understanding and sympathy. Yet these people are dead. They no longer exist. They need nothing from us. Their surviving remains – those documents and artefacts that have not been destroyed over time – are all that there is. Heartless as it may sound, those remains are ours now and for us to use as we think best. But what Tomlinson's, Holsinger's, and the work of so many others in later fields shows – and for me this is what makes it so important – is that there are more subtle ways of thinking about our relationship to the past than were available before. We therefore have alternatives nowadays; it is no longer essential for musicologists in search of a successful career to be historians, at least not if they are happy to work with more recent music. But this is not yet true for the majority of medievalists. It is medieval studies, where there is least evidence and most likelihood of being wrong, that tries to apply the narrowest restrictions on how one studies and on the range of permissible interpretations of any body of evidence. Seen at its most positive this is precisely because everything is so uncertain; strict standards of interpretation are essential if one is to avoid unhistorical conclusions. But of course that argument only makes sense within the historicist paradigm. Seen from outside, one will say rather that insecurely founded ideologies and systems have no choice but to apply the tightest restrictions on individual freedom, because otherwise they collapse. From this perspective the special moral value attributed to the faithful 'historical' recovery of the past seems hard to justify.

The ideological walls surrounding the study of medieval music, protecting it from non-historicist work, are buttressed above all by this belief that there is a special value in seeing the past as the past saw itself when it was the present. And that belief, because it is by its nature exclusive, rejecting alternatives as necessarily wrong, is fundamentally authoritarian. We need to ask, therefore, by what principle or moral absolute the study of medieval music has to be historical. And since moral absolutes can really only be invoked in relation to harm caused to individuals, in other words in relation to human rights, we need to enquire into the extent to which individuals are damaged by work that is not grounded in securely established facts about the past. For example, who is hurt or disadvantaged by Salzer's hearing a V–I cadence in a Machaut song? Or by Riemann's moving text around to make room for instrumental interludes? Some might wish to argue that uninformed listeners were being disadvantaged by not being allowed to hear trecento song with its text where the composer put it, following the assumption that the experience would be richer. But not only might that be thought unduly paternalistic, but as we have already seen it is impossible to determine. We cannot know that Riemann's experience of medieval music as he understood it was any less rich than is our experience of the music as we understand it. It is possible to imagine justifiable cases where interpretations can be harmful. The examples of German scholarship cited above are clear examples. So is Fétis' view that Adam's harmony is crippled like him; that might very well be considered unacceptable now, liable to cause unnecessary hurt. But in general what is offered as professional ethics – being true to the past – is in fact no more than ideology. The composers and musicians of the Middle Ages are all dead; their descendants are, by and large, unidentifiable; there is no one left to be hurt by the way we write about them. We, on the other hand, are here and our rights do have to be considered. We must therefore be free to choose to be historical, if we can bear the anxiety of permanently falling short of an ideal. We must be free, too, not to be historical, but to consider medieval music as material to use and reinterpret today. In the larger picture, of course, that is what historians are doing anyway, but my point is that we should be free to do it openly and to have it regarded as legitimate musicology. Scholarship cannot be defined by what it does for the past, only by what it does for us. Work that challenges but rewards the intellect, for no other reason than the delight it brings, should, so long as it does not cause significant pain or incite others to cause pain, be accepted as scholarship regardless of its attitude to the distant past.

It is hard to see, then, that the authoritarianism that gives historical work special privileges has any moral justification. As Lydia Goehr has said of the similarly privileged notion of *Werktreue*, 'no one has answered satisfactorily the basic question as to what value fidelity [to the past] or interpretation should have and to whom it should be of value'. She goes on to show the impossibility of justifying fidelity to the past with the belief that it is possible to arrive at a way of thinking about something that is absolutely the right way. 'Claims that point to someone's having got something absolutely right, and claims that reveal a belief in the absolute rightness of an ideal' are dangerous. 'What absolutists do not generally see is that nothing important is lost by dispensing with absolutist claims except the general feeling of security that certain particular actions are "really" worth undertaking.'[70]

The ability to accept uncertainty without resorting to authoritarianism or religion is perhaps one of the most significant achievements of Western society. We no longer need to invent certainties in order to block out the fear of the unknown. Partly this greater confidence comes from a belief (not unjustified) that 'science' will come up with the answers, but partly too from an understanding that more valuable than certainties about the world around us is a sense of the worth of ourselves as individuals and as members of a compassionate society. Our view of what happens is more interesting than what 'actually' happens, and, in fact, more real. Similarly with medieval music, what we would like to have happened is actually more interesting and more important than what did happen, just as 600 years from now what we are actually thinking and doing will be of far less use than what people living then wish to think of us. We shouldn't be outraged at this thought, but it is a very difficult concept to come to terms with for anyone trained in the modern historical disciplines. From that point of view, giving greater value to our view than to what 'actually happened' is nothing more than self-indulgence. The danger with the traditional view is that it places too little value on human needs and too great a value on historical truth. It was, after all, the insistence that the search for historical truth was a greater good that allowed German academics between 1933 and 1945 to pander to National Socialism in order to secure continuing funding. Establishing what happened to people long since gone is not more important than providing something useful for those alive now, not morally, ethically nor practically.

It is not necessary to use this argument to justify intentional fictions about the past, though one could, and provided that they are clearly identified as intentional I see no problem with that. Its value for the historically minded lies rather in that it allows an honest admission of what cannot now be known, of the limits of our certain knowledge of the past. It justifies us in using what evidence we have to propose what 'may' have happened, allowing us to conclude with statements of possibility rather than exaggerated claims of probability; but, further than that, it gives us the right to expect that interpretations (recognised as such) that go beyond the evidence may be accepted as worthwhile applications of our research provided only that they offer something of interest. Put more simply, it's all right not to know what happened, it's all right to guess, and it's all right to reinterpret for today; and while it might be helpful to follow conventions of pointing out when we are guessing and interpreting, there's no good reason to forbid all these uses of evidence from intermingling in a single study. We owe no duty to the past to tell it like it was, our only duties are to be useful to the present and leave a thriving environment to the future.

Conclusion

The invention of medieval music (the reinvention if you prefer) has been an extraordinary achievement (the more so if we feel that that 're' is superfluous). From the most unpromising beginnings – Fétis' 'cacophony', Kiesewetter's 'O tempora! O mores!' – we have reached a point where performances of striking beauty are appreciated by millions of radio listeners, tens of thousands of record buyers. And they are enjoyed because the music and the manner of its performance make sense to us. The quantity of known medieval data in those performances is tiny; most of our pleasure comes from ideas that people – scholars to an extent, crucially the performers, inevitably, perhaps mostly, the listeners – have brought to the music. Those performances are medieval music in the fullest possible sense. They are the discipline's finest achievement by far.

What else has the investigation of medieval music achieved? There are, of course, the documentary remains from the Middle Ages, the manuscripts, the pictures, the textbooks, the administrative records, the liturgies and so on. Their value is inestimable. Finding and publicising such remains is the one task in musicology that seems likely to remain for the foreseeable future unquestionably worthwhile. Then there is the story of its development that has been broadly agreed since Besseler and that, as a result, we can find set out in any history of music. Some of what has been said here may have raised doubts about the extent to which that story can be trusted, not because there is anything wrong, methodologically speaking, with the research that supports it but simply because there is no way of knowing how much of it is anything like a true account of what happened and why it happened: there is too little certain evidence and there are too few possibilities for cross-checking suggestions as to what that evidence might mean. But there is not a lot we can do about that. Short of finding new documents we have to make do with best guesses. What is a best guess changes, naturally; and if that means that one's own best efforts are going to be superseded, there's not a lot to be done about that either. That interpretations change as we change indicates, I'd argue, a healthy field of research. So in assessing what the study of medieval music has achieved we can count the historical stories that have been told about it as a contribution, but one whose value must remain unclear. There are other achievements of work on medieval music that are far more certain, yet far less respectable. Here are some of them.

(1) It's provided intellectual research satisfaction. There are fascinating problems raised by the things we don't know but might be able to find out something about, not just facts about the past but, because there is so much room for interpretation, things about us too. It allows work in a wide range of sub-disciplines and encourages us to mix them in interesting ways. Musicologists of early music are particularly multi-skilled, often able to make observations in several very different specialisations and allow them to interact in their arguments, for example manuscript study, style analysis, notation and archival work all feeding into conclusions about chronology. One could go on. But basically it's fun to do.

(2) It's bolstered the concept of the Other, sensitising us to an extent unusual among lovers of Western music to the presence in our past of cultures very different from our own. In turn this fosters wider interests in and sympathy for other cultures today (as has been very evident in the close links forged in modern times between medieval and non-Western musics), and offers a broader context in which to view ourselves.

(3) It's helped to build up a sense of musical roots, supporting many different narratives that connect it to the present, offering starring roles to several different nations (France, Italy, Germany, England) and offering ways of understanding the origin and gradual development of a host of musical devices and procedures that we otherwise take for granted.

(4) It's offered a wide range of popular visions of the Middle Ages: colourful, mystical, mellifluous, raucous, fearful, lascivious, crude, intellectual, esoteric. Not everyone holds them all at once (though some try), but they all serve to enrich our imagined past.

(5) It's provided employment for scholars, performers, instrument builders, record producers, technicians, editors, publishers, printers, copyists, even, through some of the earlier Early Music groups, employment for the otherwise unemployable. And, funding all that, it's produced sales, especially of recordings, but also of instruments, music, journals, costumes, cook-books and (I'm thinking especially of the Hildegard industry) ephemera of all sorts.

(6) In sum, it's managed to accommodate a very wide range of needs and preferences. It's been a rich area for social activity, engagement and fulfilment.

Every one of these things, it seems to me, is achieved more successfully than is the verifiable reconstruction of the past. That reconstruction, ostensibly the purpose of the enterprise, is in fact the least of its achievements, barely (if one insists upon the 'verifiable') an achievement at all. Yet it has been highly productive as an aim, for it made the rest possible. Just as with the authenticity movement, to which historical musicology is so closely related, the (re-)creation of a lost tradition in modern times, however chimerical, has nevertheless produced readings that shed new and often thrilling light on old materials. Musicology of this sort may deal in illusions, but they are useful. I am going to argue, therefore, that rather than give up on 'historically informed interpretation' of medieval music – which might be tempting at this stage in the book – it makes better sense to continue with it as enthusiastically as ever, not because we are establishing 'what happened' but because the readings we produce help us to make sense – our sense – of what survives. Just as with 'historically informed performance', the views of the past we (re-)create in attempting to recover it are no less fascinating for being largely modern.[1] I want only to propose, therefore, that nothing would be lost, and quite a lot gained, by our being more open about the inevitable modernity of our stories about medieval music. It is very much in our interests to recognise and remain continually aware in all historical work that our findings cannot, on the whole, be established as facts, and it's important therefore not to pretend, even for the sake of economy of expression, that they can; because making it more difficult for possibilities to become dogmas, for claims to become required beliefs, making it more difficult for any finding to be seen as the essential starting-point for all future work, opens up and then keeps open many more possibilities for productive interaction between scholars and the material they choose to study.

Trying to work out what happened in the past is going to fascinate us for as long as our culture cares to look back: the problem is challenging, the process is hugely enjoyable. But we need to be realistic about what we achieve when we do it. After more than 200 years' research and speculation we still don't know how medieval music was typically performed, we don't even agree, except within small disciplinary communities, about the broadest outlines (instrumental accompaniment or *a cappella*). We don't know how it was composed – even fewer agree about that – nor how carefully it was listened to, nor how it was understood as musical process. But we have views on all these things, and those views offer those of us who wish to hold them ways of hearing the music ourselves.

Equally, it is perfectly possible to hear the music as coherent and interesting without having views on any of those things or knowing anything about what such views might be. To believe, as some performers in their more cynical moments do, that the scholar's job ends with the provision of some legible notes on staves, is a perfectly reasonable view for exactly this reason: people can appreciate what they hear without knowing anything about it. Nevertheless, to the extent that making the notes available involves interpretation, which for medieval music it does to a substantial degree, the scholar is already there, shaping the perceptions of anyone interested enough in music to listen. In such cases the scholarly contribution will go entirely unrecognised, and none of the higher interpretative work that scholars do with the music will be known or heeded, but the music will still be appreciated; the experience will be different, but not necessarily less intensely positive. This shouldn't worry us, because, to be realistic, we work partly to interest ourselves and one another, and only partly to serve the wider community. From a politico-economic viewpoint this may not be satisfactory, since it is the community, one way or another, that pays most of our salaries, but one of the privileges of living and working in affluent countries is that many such activities can be afforded. What we cannot justify, though, in such an astonishingly privileged position, is to use academic and financial power – the power to determine what is studied – to suppress or oppress by placing unnecessary restrictions on the kind of intellectual work that public money can be used to support. Since there is no special virtue in any one approach to studying the past, decisions about funding and employment cannot ethically be based on the privileging of one methodology or one disciplinary community over another. The only criterion, whether for funding, publication, employment or esteem, should be the extent to which work stimulates the interest of broad-minded, multi-skilled, expert readers and, if possible (though with technical work it cannot always be), the wider community as well. To adapt my earlier formulation, good musicology is whatever musicologists do interestingly as musicologists.

My underlying contention, then, is that musicologists should feel free (and I mean that quite literally) to study medieval music, or any other music, in any way they find rewarding. The responsibility is theirs to pass on that sense of fascination and excitement to readers, performers, listeners.

What follows from this is a case for re-evaluating the positive aspects of what we have created so far. Performance practice's claims for historical accuracy are largely groundless, though the practices arrived at are not necessarily wrong (whether or not they are remains to be seen). Yet the process has produced something positive, indeed remarkable: a modern but rich tradition of performance strategies capable of producing wonderful musical experiences. Similarly, other fields within medieval music studies work very largely with speculations, making claims for historical accuracy that cannot possibly be proved though are not necessarily wrong. And yet they too create a constantly shifting narrative about medieval music that we find useful, even exciting, providing a context for music that might otherwise be anchorless and largely incomprehensible, just as it was for our disciplinary ancestors Fétis and Kiesewetter in their more exasperated moments. Historical musicology has helped us make sense of the music. It may not be their sense or it may be, or it may be in part, but we cannot know whether it is or not. To accept this is to look at what we do in a different way. It is to break down the walls built unnecessarily around historical musicology to protect it from doubt, letting people inside emerge to find a far wider range of approaches and uses for musicology. Among other things, it involves removing the moral imperative that has propped up historical work in music. Quasi-historical approaches can be no more than one kind of modern response to medieval music. A great many others are possible (by which I mean plausible in *our* context – of course what is plausible changes all the time) and there seems no reason, let alone any moral imperative, not to explore them or create more.

It almost, but not quite, goes without saying that this is just my own view, one that I have tried to make interesting to anyone who cares to read it. It would be foolish not to be as sceptical about everything here as I have been about everything I've discussed. As an ultra-positivist with liberal leanings – and after working through the history of musicology and seeing its hilarious variety it seems impossible to be anything else – I find scepticism the only possible frame of mind in which to work. But that, of course, is a view as characteristic of its place and time as any.

Notes

1 Cook & Moore 1990, 12′ 34″–18′ 57″. The sketch was originally broadcast in *Not only . . . but also*, Series 2, Episode 7, on 26 February 1966.
2 On 'BBC 3', with Robert Robinson, BBC TV, 13 November 1965.
3 The beginnings of modern musicology can be seen either at the point where it became professionalised, say from 1897 when Gustav Jacobsthal was appointed the first German professor of musicology, followed by Guido Adler in Vienna the following year (though in fact Jacobsthal was appointed Reader in 1875), or when scholars began to write music history in the earlier eighteenth century, from publications such as Walther 1732, Martini 1757 and Marpurg 1759.
4 Kreutziger-Herr 2001.
5 Kramer 1995: 2.
6 The proceedings of the 1997 International Musicological Society congress, for a start (Greer 2000).
7 Interesting testimony to this appeared just as this book was about to go to press. Introducing a new edition of The New Oxford History of Music, volume III.1 (covering late medieval music), Reinhard Strohm makes just this point about the impossibility of writing a straight history at the moment. He goes on to explain, with engaging candour, that of the seventeen essays commissioned for the volume, not one of those dealing with traditional topics got written (Strohm 2001: xxvi).

THE INVENTION OF THE VOICES-AND-INSTRUMENTS HYPOTHESIS

1 E.g. Fallows 1983b.
2 E.g. Page 1977, 1982.
3 Igoe 1971.
4 Page 1993b; Greig 1995.
5 For a detailed study of eighteenth- and nineteenth-century work on medieval music see Kneif 1963.
6 Burney 1789: 587–8.

7 Buck 1932 (a revision of Wooldridge 1905) offers a late example, preserving Wooldridge's view unchanged: 'the dry melody, and the arbitrary discords which sometimes render whole passages unintelligible . . . ' (Buck 1932: 41; Wooldridge 1905: 172).

8 Fétis 1827: 5 (the full passage is quoted on pp. 158–9 below). Cf. Ambros on *Tant con je vivrai*: 'die Harmonie ist abermals horribel' (Ambros 1880: 341).

9 *Ibid.*: 7.

10 Fétis' later writings on medieval music seem likely to have been informed by the transcriptions of François Louis Perne; see the admirable survey by Lawrence Earp 2002.

11 Later corrected in Bellermann 1858: 34–6 (2/1930: 124–7).

12 Fétis 1827: 9.

13 Kiesewetter's achievement is examined in Kier 1968. For a convenient introduction, and a study of Kiesewetter's view of slightly later repertories, see Kirkman 2000.

14 Kiesewetter 1848: 144–5.

15 *Ibid.*: 147.

16 Kiesewetter 1841: music supplement p. 7, example 14. See the discussion of this example in chapter 3, pp. 159–60 below.

17 Coussemaker 1865: 67–8, 111.

18 An earlier proposal of instrumental participation, which might perhaps have influenced Coussemaker, was made in 1838 by A. Bottée de Toulmon in a paper surveying the instruments. Since the book is hard to find, I give the relevant passage here. 'Certes si d'autres renseignements ne nous indiquaient pas combien l'art musical était peu avancé à cette époque, nous en serions convaincus par ce qui vient d'être exposé. Les instruments étaient plus nombreux, il est vrai; on pourrait même croire que le système en était plus riche que de nos jours, puisque chacun avait sa famille complète. C'est précisément cela qui me fait tirer une conséquence contraire: en effet, les voix se divisent en dessus, haute-contre, taille et basse. C'était donc d'après ce système que tous les morceaux de musique étaient composés; et comme la musique instrumentale était en quelque sorte rivée à la musique vocale, il en résulta que les instruments furent obligés de suivre de point en point les voix avec lesquelles ils jouaient à l'unisson; encore cette combinaison n'est-elle venue que plus tard. Avant le xvie siècle un orchestre était la réunion bruyante et désordonnée de tous les instruments que l'on pouvait rencontre: nulle idée musicale ne présidait au choix que l'on aurait pu en faire. En effet, quel sens raisonnable pouvaient présenter en musique des instruments aussi imparfaits qu'un *flaios de saus*, une *muse de blé* et surtout une *flûte brehaigne*!' (196–7).

19 Ambros 1864: 339; 2/1880: 339; 3/1891: 372.

20 Wooldridge 1905: 25; although later in the book (p. 172) Wooldridge also follows Stainer's view of instrumental participation in the Canonici songs.

21 Riemann, trans. Shedlock, 1893–7: 7. Shedlock's translation is loose, and in the following extracts I have offered some more exact alternatives in square brackets. The corresponding German text is in Riemann 3/1887: 91.
22 Riemann, trans. Shedlock, 1893–7: 525. Riemann 3/1887: 331.
23 Riemann, trans. Shedlock, 1893–7: 526. Riemann 3/1887: 332.
24 Riemann, trans. Shedlock, 1893–7: 121. Riemann 3/1887: 470.
25 See, for example, the notes to *Vostre tres doulx regart* (Riemann 1892: 7). The manuscript is now Munich, Bayerische Staatsbibliothek, Galloram monacensis 902, most recently studied in Slavin 1989.
26 A still earlier book on notation, which suffered from the same handicap, was by Ludwig's teacher, Gustav Jacobsthal, *Die Mensuralnotenschrift des zwælften und dreizehnten Jahrhunderts* (Berlin, 1871), dedicated appropriately to Heinrich Bellermann.
27 See also the similar statements of Leichtentritt and Haas, each introducing their support for instrumental participation with the observation that until Riemann the music was thought to be purely vocal. Leichtentritt 1905–6: 317; Haas 1931: 93.
28 Riemann 1905–6.
29 Stainer 1895–6: 6.
30 Gevaert 1890: 27.
31 At least some of their music, being easily transcribable, had long been known – hence the discussion in Burney, for example – but it was not until Kiesewetter 1829 that it was placed in a clear historical frame.
32 F. Max Müller, Taylorian professor of modern European languages at Oxford 1854–68, professor of comparative philology 1868–1900, was at the time of Stainer's lecture the outstanding authority on the history of languages.
33 Stainer 1895–6: 18. At the end of the paper 'A vote of thanks was then unanimously accorded to the lecturer, and to the four gentlemen from the Royal College of Music who had played the illustrations' (p. 21).
34 Schering 1912: 3–12 and *passim*; Ludwig 1922–3: 436 n. 1; Dischner 1927: 2; Ellinwood 1939: xxxix.
35 See Harman 1952: 291.
36 Stainer 1898: 15–16.
37 For a more cautious reading of de la Marche see Fallows 1983b: 139.
38 Göttingen, Niedersächsische Staats- und Landesbibliothek, Handschrift-abteilung, Ludwig Nachlass boxes XXIII–XXVIII. It is impossible to know how much of this material had also been transcribed by Wolf, since his personal library was destroyed by Allied bombing on 22 November 1943 (Kinkeldey 1948: 7), though Wolf 1904 offers impressive testimony to the range of the materials he had by then assembled.
39 Göttingen, Musikwissenschaftliches Seminar library, MG I R 79, p. 307.
40 Ludwig 1902–3: 29–30.
41 *Ibid.*: 67.
42 Adler & Koller 1900: p. VII (dated September 1899); Wolf 1899–1900.

43 Riemann 1905–6: 530.
44 Riemann 1878, 1/1882, 1888 etc.
45 Ludwig 1902–3, preceded only by the selection of pieces published in Italy in Wolf 1901. The historiography of editions of trecento music is surveyed in Martinez-Göllner 1971.
46 Ludwig 1902–3: 46.
47 Riemann 1905: 295–6.
48 *Ibid.*: 296.
49 *Ibid.*: 305.
50 See also Riemann's treatment of this in his *Katechismus der Musikgeschichte*: 'In all secular music there pulsates a fresh natural musical life, which contrasts most advantageously with the still for the most part tortured polyphonic compositions of the higher art music used almost exclusively by the church' (Riemann 1888; 2/1901: 40; trans. 1892: 36).
51 Riemann 1905: 305–6.
52 Rehding 2000: 367, quoting Riemann 1898: 3; the italics are Riemann's, the translation Rehding's. For further comment see also Rehding 2000: 372–3.
53 Riemann 1905: 306.
54 *Ibid.*: 306–7.
55 Here Riemann lists examples: 'see among others the possible introductions, interludes and postludes of the chansons of Cesaris, p. 96, Charité, p. 99 and Dufay, pp. 102, 105, 108, 113, 127 etc., also the examples in Stainer's *Early Bodleian Music* and the selection from the Trent codices in D.T.O.' (Riemann 1905: 307).
56 *Ibid.*: 307–8.
57 *Ibid.*: 308.
58 *Ibid.*: 313–14.
59 Aubry 1907a: 7.
60 Christensen 1997, especially p. 36. Christensen's conclusion might well be applied here: 'he was truly one of the "leading personalities of German and European musical life" [Christian Wolff] – but where did he lead them?' (*ibid.*, p. 42). See also the pointed analysis of Riemann's reading of medieval music in an overall view of music history in Seidel 1995.
61 Leichtentritt 1905–6.
62 Buhle 1903.
63 Leichtentritt 1905–6: 317.
64 *Ibid.*: 329.
65 *Ibid.*: 331.
66 Aubry 1908: III, 148. For a slightly more liberal view see Aubry 1907c, especially p. 10: 'In conclusion, there were, in my view, some motets where instruments mixed with voices, and others restricted entirely to vocal performance'.
67 Aubry 1908: III, 148. For a wider view of Aubry, and the curious story of his death see Haines 1997. For Aubry's (also partly nationalistic) objections

to Riemann's work on monophony, see Haines 2001 b. For the role of nationalism in their and others' views of turn-of-the-century musicology see Haines 2001 c.

68 Riemann 1905–6: 535.

69 Quoted in *ibid.*: 307.

70 *Ibid.*: 535.

71 *Ibid.*: 537.

72 Barbieri 1890 (edition of Madrid MS 1335), containing 460 polyphonic pieces in three and four parts with texted cantus and untexted lower voices.

73 Riemann 1905–6: 539.

74 It is interesting to see that the copy of Riemann's 1893 *Illustrationen* now in the Music Department library at University of California, Berkeley, scored *a cappella*, was later updated with the addition of manuscript parts for viola and cello (on manuscript paper printed in Zurich, so probably before the volume was acquired by Berkeley), allowing it to be used in the same way as *Hausmusik*, another small indication of Riemann's success in changing views.

75 Riemann 1908: 67–70.

76 Riemann 1910: 39–43.

77 See especially Items 1–6 and the notes on them by Schering in the 1912 edition.

78 The series title is 'Handbücher der Musiklehre auf Anregung des Musikpädagogischen Verbandes zum Gebrauch an Musiklehrer-Seminaren und für den Privatunterricht' (Handbooks of music teaching as proposed by The Music-Pedagogical Association for use by trainee music teachers and for private instruction).

79 Riemann 1888; 2/1901: 40–1.

80 Riemann 1888; 3/1906: 41.

81 Riemann 1908: 67.

82 Riemann 1882; 3/1887: 91; 4/1894: 94.

83 Riemann 1882; 5/1900: 95–6; 6/1905: 109.

84 Riemann 1882; 7/1909: 117.

85 Riemann 1882; 3/1887: 470; 4/1894: 514.

86 Riemann 1882; 5/1900: 550; 6/1905: 641.

87 Riemann 1882; 7/1909: 684.

88 *Ibid.*: 477.

89 *Ibid.*: 350.

90 *Ibid.*: 414.

91 *Ibid.*: 644.

92 *Ibid.*: 798.

93 *Ibid.*: 856.

94 Riemann 1905–6: 531.

95 Adler 1909: 51.

96 Schering 1911–12: 173.

97 *Ibid.*: 177–8.

98 Riemann 1912. See especially item 3 (p. 3 of the edition), Giovanni da Firenze's *Nascoso el viso*, retexted by Riemann, with the commentary on p. 2 of the introduction by Schering.

99 Schering 1912: 25.

100 *Ibid.*: 3, n. 1, suggests that the book was issued around March 1912, and in his contribution to the Berlin meeting Schering refers to his book as 'recently appeared' (Springer 1912: 266).

101 Göttingen, Musikwissenschaftliches Seminar library, *Zeitschrift der internationalen Musik-Gesellschaft* 13 (1911–12), 266–8.

102 Leichtentritt 1912–13.

103 Schering 1913–14; Leichtentritt 1913–14.

104 Reaney 1966: 719–21, including an illustration in score of a section of Machaut's Credo, as performed in Liège in 1958. Reaney arranged instrumental parts that decorated Machaut's vocal lines, leaving them to function as a plain melodic core. He comments, 'If the method is reminiscent of Schering's *Dekolorierung* technique, it may be none the worse for that' (Reaney 1966: 719).

105 Wolf 1913: 439.

106 Reaney 1954, expanded in Reaney 1956; Harrison 1966. For fuller treatment see the following chapter, 'The re-invention of the *a cappella* hypothesis'.

107 The title-page of the programme booklet reads, 'Les Primitifs de la Musique Française: Sainte-Chapelle (Palais de Justice) Lundi 8 Juin 1914. Ces chants sont exécutés par la Maitrise de l'Eglise Saint-François-Xavier sous la direction de M. Drees, Maître de Chapelle, avec le Concours de Melle M. Babaian, Soprano, M. Jouanneau, Ténor, M. Tremblay, Baryton.'

108 Aubry 1908: no. 75, vol. II, pp. 168–9.

109 Footnote to the programme booklet p. [5]: 'Ces pièces ont été remises en partition sur le beau manuscrit du trésor d'Apt, gracieusement communiqué par M. le chanoine C. Robert, archiprêtre de la basilique, à l'occasion du Congres.'

110 Gastoué 1914: [3].

111 'Gregorian Chant: Early recordings', Parnassus PACD 96015/6, disc 1, tracks 35–7.

112 Gastoué 1922: 7.

113 On Ludwig's propensity for attributing pieces to Leonin and Perotin see Busse Berger (forthcoming).

114 Respectively Adler 1920: 19–20; Adler & Koller 1900: 178–83.

115 Ludwig 1922–3.

116 *Ibid.*: 442–3.

117 *Ibid.*: 443.

118 In view of the rarity of the programme booklet, it may be helpful to give some details here. I Musica ecclesiastica. II Musica composita: 'Leonin' *Haec dies* and *Alleluia pascha nostrum*, each followed by 'Perotin' motets on their clausulae, *Deo confitemini* and *Laudes referat*, and *Gaudeat devotio* and *Radix venie*; ten thirteenth-century motets (*Maniere esgarder/Manere*

(ed. Ludwig), *A la clarte/Et illuminare* (ed. Besseler), *Quant voi la rose/Go* (ed. Besseler), *Li doz termines/Balaam* (Coussemaker 1865: no. 32), *Ave regina/Alma redemptoris mater/Alma* (ed. Aubry 1908: no. 5), *O Maria maris stella/O Maria/Misit dominus* (ed. Aubry 1908: no. 75), *Entre Copin/Je me cuidoie/Bele Ysabelot* (Coussemaker 1865: no. 39, and Aubry 1908: no. 52), *Riens/Riens/Aperis* (ed. Müller-Blattau 1923: Anhang, no. III), *Au cuer/Je ne/Jolietement* (ed. Aubry 1908: no. 53), *Homo/Homo/Brumas e mors* (ed. Aubry 1908: no. 37, as emended in Ludwig 1922–3: 440, n. 1, and subsequently in Ludwig 1923: 203–4)) presented in two groups, separated by two of Adam's rondeaux (*Fi maris de vostre amour, A Dieu commant amouretes* (ed. Coussemaker 1872: pp. 215 and 217, and Gennrich 1921: nos. 71 and 70)); mass movements by Gratiosus de Padua and Dufay (ed. Ficker); and motets by Machaut (*Christe/Veni/Tribulatio/CT* ed. Gurlitt's Musikwissenschaftliche Seminar at Freiburg), Power (*Ave regina celorum* ed. Barclay Squire 1901: 378–9), Dunstable (*Quam pulcra es*) and Dufay (*Alma redemptoris mater, Vergine bella* ed. the Freiburg Seminar).

III Musica vulgaris: Bernart de Ventadorn *Lancan vei la folha* (ed. Ludwig), Guiraut de Bornelh *Reis glorios* (ed. Aubry 1909), Rambaut de Vaqueiras *Kalenda maya* (*ibid.*), Thibaut de Navarre *De bone amor* (ed. Ludwig), Gautier de Coinci *Ma viele* (ed. Aubry 1909); two anonymous rondeaux *Jolietement mi tient* and *Bele Ysabelot* (ed. Gennrich 1921); Walther von der Vogelweide 'Palästinalied' (credited to ed. Rietsch 1913), Neidhardt von Neuenthal 'Das Saill Herausgeg' (ed. von der Hagen 1838), Heinrich von Meiszen 'Frauenlob' (ed. Rietsch 1913); two Spielmannslieder, *Ich het czu hannt gelocket mir* and *Er hör libste Frau* ('dy trumpet') (ed. Mayer & Rietsch 1896 and Ursprung 1923); four fourteenth-century instrumental dances, *Lamento di Tristano* with *Rotta, Saltarello* (ed. Wolf 1918), *Danse royal* and *Estampie royal* (ed. Aubry 1907b); Piero *Con bracchi assai* (ed. Wolf 1904), Landini *Per la mie dolce piaga* (*ibid.*), Machaut *De toutes flours* and *Gais et jolis*; 'Binchois' *Lyesse m'a mandé, Plains de plours, Adieu mon joyeux souvenir, Margarite fleur de valeur, Adieu m'amour*; two middle Dutch songs *Al eerbaerheit weinsch, Ope es in minnen; Mein*; and finally three German songs *Mein traut gesell, Ein vrouleen edel, Der wallt hat sich entlawbet* (all ed. the Freiburg Seminar).

119 Besseler 1924–25: 49.
120 *Ibid.*: 54.
121 *Ibid.*: 48.
122 Wolf 1925: 65 and 67.
123 Handschin 1930: 2–3, n. 1; Handschin 1931, esp. 31–42: 'Excurs: Das "sekundär Instrumentale" in der mittelalterlichen Aufführungspraxis'. On Handschin's originality see Busse Berger (forthcoming).
124 Handschin 1931.
125 Handschin 1927–8: 12.
126 Handschin 1930.
127 Haas 1931: 94–7.
128 *Ibid.*, esp. 98–101.

129 Kroyer 1925: 192–3.
130 *Ibid.*, esp. 194 and 198.
131 Wolf 1926: V.
132 Potter 1998: 42. Wolf had long believed in the need to make musicology more accessible to practising musicians (Potter 1996: 74; Potter 1998: 36 and 276, n. 9). On the wider theoretical context see Potter 1998: 171–2.
133 Wolf's support for the ideals of National Socialism was, however, much less than wholehearted. Although bowing to pressure when necessary, for instance in sacking Einstein as editor of the *Zeitschrift für Musikwissenschaft* following which Wolf immediately resigned (Potter 1998: 66–7), he was considered sufficiently unreliable that Besseler forced him to resign from his post as vice-president of the International Musicological Society and German representative on its Board before the 1936 IMS meeting in Barcelona (Potter 1991a: 162–5, and Potter 1998: 82–5). The previous year Schering prevented Wolf's promotion to Ordinarius and forced his resignation from the Berlin faculty, while promoting younger National Socialists (Potter 1998: 106–7). On attempts to make musicology more accessible in this context see Potter 1996: 73–80.
134 Dischner 1927: 2.
135 Potter 1994, esp. 98–9; Potter 1998, esp. 41–6.
136 Droz & Thibault 1927: 115.
137 *Ibid.*: 119; cf. the note on no. 16, *Tant est mignonne.*
138 Perotin *Alleluya* from *Alleluya Posui adjutorium*, motets *Ad solitum vomitum/Regnat* and *Virga/Stirps/Flos*, organum *Descendit de coelis*; Vitry? *Garrit/In nova/T*, Machaut *Tu/Plange/Apprehende/CT*; Johannes de Florentia *Io son un pellegrin*, Machaut *De toutes flours*; Dunstable *Preco/Precursor/Inter*, Gemblaco *Ave virgo/Sancta Maria* (all ed. Ficker).
139 Einstein 1926–7: 498–9; see also Gratzer 1992: 48–9.
140 Ficker 1929a: 491–2; the bulk of this article, though not the beginning, is shared with Ficker 1930a with cosmetic changes. (Here cf. Ficker 1930a: 114.)
141 This relationship is the subject of a forthcoming study by Stefan Morent.
142 Mertin 1986: 6.
143 The Orlando Consort begin at 84, the Early Music Consort of London at 106, for example. ('Mystery of Notre Dame', Orlando Consort, DG Archiv 453 487–2, track 9; 'Music of the Gothic Era', Early Music Consort of London, DG Archiv 2723 045, disc 1, side 2, band 2 (reissued on CD as 453 185–2, disc 1, track 6).)
144 Gratzer 1992: 27–50 offers a fascinating reception history of Perotin's organa quadrupla from the eighteenth to the twentieth centuries.
145 Ficker 1930a: 113. See also Ficker 1925b, esp. 512–15.
146 Ficker 1930a: 114; cf. Ficker 1929a: 491.
147 Ficker 1929a: 494; Ficker 1930a: 114–15.
148 And the connection was well understood by Ficker, who says of Landini, 'With him this specific form of art, whose tendencies were first to be revived

in the Lied of the nineteenth century, came to an end' (Ficker 1929a: 499; Ficker 1930a: 120–1).

149 The influence of Huizinga on musicology was first examined in Page 1982 (esp. 441) and is explored more fully in Page 1993a, chapter 5; discussions with Page over many years have deeply informed my view of this issue.

150 Ficker 1925b: 529.

151 Ficker 1929a: 500; Ficker 1930a: 121.

152 The voice of Huizinga can still be heard in Ficker's chapter for the New Oxford History of Music, published in 1960.

153 Ficker 1929a: 505. I have left the wording of the Ficker 1929a translation of Ficker 1930a intact, even where it is free, since it so effectively demonstrates a contemporary understanding of what he was saying. For the German text see Ficker 1930a: 122–3.

154 As reported by Einstein 1926–7: 498.

155 It was arguably this same conviction that he was re-creating, not inventing the past that led Ficker a few years later to present the next volume of Trent compositions for DTÖ in original note-shapes (Ficker 1933). See also Bockholt 1971: 156.

156 The strength of Schering's belief in his view (and perhaps his insecurity over it) is reflected in his role (reported in Potter 1998: 66–7) in the sacking of Einstein as editor of the *Zeitschrift für Musikwissenschaft*, the journal of the Deutsche Musikgesellschaft of which Schering was president. In 1932 Einstein accepted an article from his friend and former professor Theodore Kroyer, sharply critical of Schering's theory (it eventually appeared in *Acta Musicologica*, Kroyer 1934). Schering appears to have used the ensuing conflict with Einstein and Kroyer as a lever to remove Einstein, a Jew, from the editorship of the journal. Soon after, Schering reorganised the society along National Socialist lines, adopting the *Führerprinzip* according to which he acquired unquestionable authority in all his decisions as president. The reorganisation was celebrated in a letter from Schering to Goebbels (Potter 1999: 306–7).

157 Schering 1931a: 16.

158 Schering 1931a: 18; Schering 1914a: 79–80.

159 Schering 1931a: 19; Schering 1914a: 85–6.

160 Schering 1931a: 13–14.

161 *Ibid.*: 14.

162 *Ibid.*: 15.

163 *Ibid.*: 12. Schering's support for such a view needs to be considered in the wider context of his belief that music history may be seen as an alternation of periods dominated by homogeneous timbres and periods dominated by a 'split sound complex' (see Potter 1998: 170–1). The extent to which such theories could take on nationalistic overtones is well illustrated by Potter's summary of Albert Wellek's 1936 Habilitationsschrift, which purported to show that Northerners tended to perceive music in a more linear way than

Southerners and that this was reflected in the northern taste for polyphony (Potter 1998: 214). Similarly Richard Eichenauer argued in his 1932 *Musik und Rasse* (Music and Race) that the innovations attributed since Ludwig to Leonin and Perotin were due to an inborn racial tendency towards polyphony (Potter 1998: 179). Thus this linear view of medieval music may have been considered, for a while, as a particular manifestation of Nordic genius, a view which Schering, with his strong Nazi sympathies, would have found attractive. (See also chapter 3, below, pp. 168–9.)

164 Brücker 1926 and Dick 1932, both from the Romanische Seminar of Gießen.

165 Ruth-Sommer 1916; von Schlosser 1920b.

166 Also von Schlosser 1920a and Brancour 1921.

167 Schneider 1924; Gurlitt 1929; Schrade 1931.

168 Schering 1931a: 110.

169 Boatwright 1973: 42. The Memling panels now belong to the Koninklijk Museum voor Schone Kunsten, Antwerp, inventory nos. 778–80.

170 Schering 1931a: 13.

171 Schneider 1931: 5.

172 *Ibid.*: 26. For a recent treatment of Odington's 'ornaments' see McGee 1998, esp. 50–3 and 77–9.

173 Schneider 1931: 29.

174 *Ibid.*: 30 and 37.

175 *Ibid.*: 22–30.

176 *Ibid.*: esp. 42–3, 50, 52. Schneider went on to compare polyphony from around the world in Schneider 1934.

177 See esp. Ribera 1924–5 and the extracts reprinted in Ribera 1928 (esp. pp. 49–64); also Ribera 1927. Other early contributions include Erckmann 1931, concentrating on poetic forms. For a contrary view see Jeanroy 1934. There is a detailed survey of previous literature in Ursprung 1934.

178 Ficker 1929a: 489–90; cf. Ficker 1930a: 113.

179 Besseler 1931: 133.

180 Schneider 1931: 72.

181 *Ibid.*: 70.

182 The development of an Arabic style by Binkley and the Studio is examined in detail in Haines 2001a, with further details in the correspondence between Sterling Jones and Haines in *Early Music* 30 (2002), 156–7.

183 Marius Schneider headed the taskforce dealing with comparative musicology in the reorganised Deutsche Gesellschaft für Musikwissenschaft from 1933. He contributed a paper on 'Fundamentals concerning musical race research' in the session 'Music and Race' at the 1938 Dusseldorf conference organised by Goebbels' Propaganda Ministry (Potter 1998: 133; Potter 1991a: 167–71).

184 Geiringer 1943: 87.

185 Wooldridge 1905: 24; Buck 1929: 244.

186 Ludwig 1902–3; Besseler 1926b; Wolf 1904.

187 Wooldridge 1905: 25; Buck 1929: 244.
188 Wooldridge 1905: 42–6; Buck 1929: 256.
189 Buck 1932: 305.
190 *Ibid.*: 310.
191 *Ibid.*: 319–20.
192 *Ibid.*: 320.
193 Page 1993b.
194 Ellinwood 1936: 201–3.
195 *Ibid.*: 203. For Ellinwood's later and more influential view, however, see below.
196 Geiringer 1943: 87.
197 *Ibid.*: 87–8.
198 *Ibid.*: 89–90. For a fuller picture of Geiringer, and amusing anecdotes about his teachers, who included Kretzschmar, Adler, Wolf and Sachs, see his autobiography, Geiringer 1993.
199 Besseler 1931: 139.
200 Gérold 1936: 310.
201 See Gérold 1932: 245, 249, 259, 284, 299, 315, 328, 331–2, 334, 336, 345, 347; Gérold 1936: 328, 335ff., 348–56, 362–3, 370, 371, 374–5, 380.
202 Gérold 1932: 315.
203 It gets a brief chapter of its own in Gérold 1936.
204 Gérold 1932: 345–8; Gérold 1936: 380 and 375.
205 Gérold 1932: chapter 20, 368–423; Gérold 1936: chapter 20, 398–418.
206 Pirro 1940, esp. 5–46. Ironically, a slightly earlier study by Pirro seems notable now for offering archival evidence for all-vocal performance, albeit still insisting that instrumental accompaniment was the norm (Pirro 1931, esp. 61). See also Gennrich 1926–7, where several extracts from fourteenth-century poems describe all-vocal performance followed by instrumental playing, yet are of interest to Gennrich only for their descriptions of instruments.
207 For further biographical details see Steinzor 1989.
208 He also had a lively interest in new music, commissioning new work as an editor at G. Schirmer and later at Carl Fischer. I am indebted to Martin Chusid, Theodore Karp, Joshua Rifkin and especially to Edward Roesner for sharing their recollections of Reese as a teacher.
209 Greenberg 1966: 314.
210 Reese 1940: 312, the phrase possibly a reminiscence of Ludwig 1922–3: 442–3, paraphrased above.
211 Reese 1940: 349, 351, 353–5, 359, 367.
212 From the folder 'M + R Listening Assignment # 15: Machaut'.
213 'Equivalent of ReMR, Chap. 1'. Naturally, Reese used his books as course texts.
214 Reese 1940: 325. Cf. Reaney: 'providing one adheres to the principle of contrast, almost any vocal-instrumental combination common to the fourteenth century may be utilised in performing the music of the period'

(Reaney 1956: 6). Igoe reports that in a conversation towards the end of his life Reese held to the view that cantus firmus should be heard in performance (Igoe 1971: 81, n. 20).

215 Reese 1940: 386.

216 For other references in Reese to instrumental participation (not always in favour) see *ibid.*: 203, 204, 307, 316, 324, 377, 379, 383–6.

217 *Ibid.*: 370–1. Cf. Ludwig 1922–3: 443; Haas 1931: 98–100; Buck 1932: 319–20; Gérold 1932: 345; Ellinwood 1936: 201–3; Apel 1950: 15; Abraham 1953: 21; Reaney 1956: 99 (generously expressed); Ellinwood 1960: 55; Fallows 1975: 257; Fallows 1985: 35. Alexander Rehding has summed up this phenomenon perfectly in commenting on a similar case, 'despite the numerous attestations that Lorenz is dead and buried, he never seemed so dead that he would not have to be ritually killed off again every time Wagner analysis is invoked' (Rehding 2001: 243).

218 Reese 1940: 361; cf. Riemann 1905: 305–6, quoted above.

219 Dart 1954: 147–59.

220 van den Borren 1960: 226–7.

221 Cape 1959–60.

222 14063 APM.

223 On Cape, the early years of Pro Musica Antiqua, and the role of Charles van den Borren as the group's mentor, see Gagnepain 1980–1: 204–19. Note also Reaney's praise for the Anthologie Sonore discs in a similar context (Reaney 1956: 4).

224 Reaney 1956: 6.

225 Mertin 1986: vii.

226 Mertin 1986: xiii.

227 Nagy 1994: 11; see also the essay by Pass in the same volume.

228 Nagy 1994: 7.

229 *Ibid.*: 6.

230 *Ibid.*: 52–4.

231 *Ibid.*: 54–5. E/E-flat clashes were perhaps not so inoffensive to his audiences. René Clemencic reports that when Mertin put on a performance of Machaut's Mass in the 1930s a member of the audience protested, 'We don't want to hear dodecaphonic music, we want to hear old music' (Interview with René Clemencic, 9 May 2000). Similarly, Scott Goddard, reviewing in *Music & Letters* in 1938, commented on Guillaume de Van's recording of Machaut's *Hoquetus David* that 'Of the music it is as difficult to speak as it would be were one suddenly faced with a new work by Berg' (Goddard 1938: 490; quoted in Davidson 1994: 310–11).

232 McGee 1990: 38.

233 *Ibid.*: 187–200. McGee's contribution to modern performance practice studies is extensive and rightly admired, including the single most important book for singers of medieval music, McGee 1996.

234 Duffin 2000.

235 Gastoué 1936: xvii–xix.

236 See Aubry 1908 (the Bamberg codex); Anglès 1931 (Las Huelgas); Rokseth 1935–9 (Montpellier). Other major editions from before 1945 (apart from Ludwig's Machaut) include Ramsbotham 1933 (Old Hall); and Husmann 1940 (three- and four-part organa).

237 Ludwig 1926, 1928, 1929. Gérold 1932: 318, n. 1, and Gérold 1936: 366–7, n. 5, reveal that a complete Machaut edition was planned by Henri Quittard, but was left incomplete at his early death in 1919. According to Gérold, his transcriptions are preserved in manuscript at the Bibliothèque de la Conservatoire in Paris.

238 Ursula Günther, interview, drawing on oral testimony of Besseler.

239 Rokseth 1935–9: IV, 220–1. For Rokseth's view of other repertories, which includes all-vocal performance of Machaut as a possibility, see Rokseth 1960, esp. 418–19.

240 Ellinwood 1936: 201; Ellinwood 1939: xxxix.

241 Ellinwood 1936: 202–3; Ellinwood 1939: xxxix.

242 Hibberd 1946.

243 Continuation of the Machaut edition was prevented by de Van's suicide in July 1949. For de Van's wartime activities on behalf of the Einsatzstab Reichsleiter Rosenberg see de Vries 1996: 202–10. On Besseler's Nazi affiliations see Potter 1998, *passim*. Armen Carapetyan (the AIM's founder and director) defended his association with de Van, and his inclusion in *Musica Disciplina* of an article by Moser, in an editorial in the second issue of 1949, following criticism by Paul Henry Lang made public in the *Journal of the American Musicological Society* (Carapetyan 1949; Lang 1949), announcing in the same issue that Besseler was to take over the Dufay edition following de Van's death. It seems safe to assume that he was unaware that Besseler had used the spectre of American competition, represented by the American Institute of Musicology, to support his application for work in the Soviet zone in 1948 (Potter 1998: 251). For more on de Van, his shadowy American background, his marriage to Yvonne Rokseth's eldest daughter, and his post-war mental breakdown, see Davidson 1994: 320–3 and 352.

244 de Van 1949a: III.

245 de Van 1949b: II. The attraction of the conviction that there was no uniform practice is noted in the discussion of Handschin's articles above. The idea that a singer might also be an instrumentalist, or vice versa, is examined below.

246 Apel 1950: 14. The volume is prefaced by a glowing endorsement from Paul Hindemith, whose practical interest in medieval music we have already seen. His analytical approach is examined in chapter 3.

247 Apel 1950: 14.

248 *Ibid.*: 15.

249 *Ibid.*

250 Of the other major editions from around this time neither Nino Pirrotta in *The Music of Fourteenth Century Italy* I (Pirrotta 1954) nor Leo Schrade in the first four volumes of Polyphonic Music of the Fourteenth Century (Schrade

1956) offers any advice to performers. (On the production of the Schrade volumes see Davidson 1994: 391–3.)

251 Reaney 1955: II.

252 de Van 1949b: II, quoted above.

253 Schering 1931b: item 24, pp. 16–17: Perusio, *Pour bel acueil.*

254 Columbia 5711, side 1: Dufay, *Christe redemptor omnium* and *Conditor alme siderum*; Choir of Westminster Cathedral, cond. Sir Richard Terry, rec. 1930.

255 Victor 45083-B: Machaut, *Douce dame jolie*; Lambert Murphy, rec. 17 March 1915, using the arrangement by J. B. Wekerlin (1853), vol. I, pp. 12–13, reproduced in Earp 2002. Other delightful harmonisations of Machaut's virelais (by Edmond Rickett) may be found in Guilbert 1926: 66–70. (My thanks to Annette Kreutziger-Herr for both these collections.)

256 Haskell 1988: 118–19.

257 Anthologie Sonore 1 (issued in the USA as AS 8). Reviewed in *The Gramophone*, December 1934, 250, and May 1935, 465–6.

258 Ficker 1929a: 498 (cf. Ficker 1930a: 120), 502 (cf. Ficker 1930a: 122); Ficker 1925b: 529.

259 Cf. the more extreme Riemann 1906: Heft III, p. 20.

260 Riemann 1906: I, p. 12.

261 HLP 5, side 1, band 7 [HMS 21, side 4]. There is another example on HLP 5, side 1, band 8 [HMS 22, side 5] where Landini's *Amar si li alti tuo gentil costumi* is sung by Jeanne Deroubaix supported by a recorder, with vielle tenor and lute contratenor, the instruments playing the end melismas and some beginnings where the voice enters after a bar or two on an off-beat (and see the accompanying booklet, Abraham 1953: 21–2).

262 Abraham 1953: 21.

263 E.g. Machaut's *Ma fin est mon commencement* (HMS 21, side '3' = HLP 5 side 1 band 5), sung by Clarence Roberts and Lemuel Hughes at *c.* $\downarrow$ = 60 with generous portamento.

264 See HLP 5 Band 2 [=HMS 20, side 1]: l'Escurel's *A vous douce debonaire* for three voices, Band 9 [HMS 22, side 5]: Piero's *Cavalcando* sung by two tenors. Oddly enough, the recordings made by Pro Musica Antiqua, including several of the same singers, in the same year for Deutsche Grammophon's equivalent Archiv series are somewhat more successful. (See 'Research Period III, The Early Renaissance [NB!], Series A: The Florentine Group: Madrigale e Caccie From the Codex of Antonio Squarcialupi.' Archive Production: History of Music Division of the Deutsche Grammophon Gesellschaft. APM 14019, side a (dated 24 June 1953) (no bands), item 4, Giovanni da Cascia: *Nascoso el viso*.) Others, however, are as unsteady as the English performances. (See 'II. Forschungsbereich, Das zentrale Mittelalter, Serie D: Ars Nova in Frankreich. Guillaume de Machaut La Messe de Nostre Dame, 10 Weltliche Werke.' 14063 APM (rec. 2/3 February 1956), band 7, Machaut: *De triste cuer/Certes je di/Quant vrais amis*).

265 'II. Forschungsbereich, Das zentrale Mittelalter, Serie C: Frühe Mehrstim-migkeit bis 1300: Ecole de Notre Dame: 2 Organa.' APM 14068 (rec. 1/2/7 July 1956), side b, band 2.

266 My grateful thanks to Annette Kreutziger-Herr for supplying me with a tape from Bavarian Radio.

267 The director the Archiv series, Fred Hamel, had trained as a musicolo-gist with Schering and with his (and Riemann's) student Friedrich Blume (Haskell 1988: 127).

268 'musical architecture as firm, majestic, intricate and varied as the architec-ture of the chapels and arcades of Notre Dame of Paris.... *Alleluia nativitas* was originally created for Notre Dame of Paris more than seven centuries ago; here it sounds again, solid and massive, like the walls that enclose it.'

269 'Notre Dame de Paris in the 13th Century', Vocal and Instrumental En-semble directed by Thurston Dart, Fontana SFL 14133 (issued 1967), side 1, band 7; also issued in Germany (with details of the performers) as Philips 839 306 EGY.

270 'Guillaume Dufay, Gilles Binchois: Ballades, rondeaux, lamentation', Harmonic Records H/CD 8719. Rec. 1987, track 1. Cf. Riemann 1906: Heft II, 12–13. (See also track 4: Dufay, *Par droit je puis.*)

271 Medieval Ensemble of London, 'Guillaume Dufay: Complete Secular Music'. Decca L'Oiseau Lyre D237D 6, 1981. Side 1, band 1: *Ce jour de l'an.* (See also Side 4, band 1, *Ce moys de may*; Side 4, band 4, etc.)

272 'Dufay Masses', Stradivarius STR33569, rec. 1999 (see the review Noble 2001); see also the Huelgas Ensemble's 'Perusio: virelais, ballades, caccia', Vivarte SK 62928, track 8, rec. 1996 (I owe these references to Christopher Page and Yolanda Plumley). Another group perpetuating Riemann's idea is Mala Punica; see their performance of Bartolomeo da Bologna's *Que pena maior* on 'Ars subtilis ytalica', Arcana A 21, track 1, rec. 1993. The disc is subtitled, 'Musica nell'autunno del medioevo', a Huizingan reference that speaks for itself.

273 'Guillaume Dufay, Gilles Binchois...', track 16: Dufay, *Vostre bruit.* Cf. Anthologie Sonore 59, 'Musique francaise au quatorzième siècle', Pro Musica Antiqua Brussels, dir. Safford Cape, Side 1: Pierre des Molins, *De ce que fol pense* (discs manufactured May 1937). The practice of octave doubling received support from a scholar in Reaney 1966: 719.

274 'Guillaume Dufay: Complete Secular Music', Decca L'Oiseau Lyre D237D 6, 1981. Side 1, band 3. Another case, that has been variously treated in recordings, is Senleches' *En ce gracieus tamps joli* whose cantus 'cucu's are imitated in an otherwise untexted triplum. Capella Cordina (dir. Alejandro Planchart, Expériences Anonymes EA 83: 'Music of the Middle Ages: Vol-ume IX – The Fourteenth Century'. Rec. Jan., May, June 1966 at Yale. Side 1, band 7) score the piece for tenor, cor anglais and bassoon, who are joined by a soprano for the imitations. The Medieval Ensemble of London ('Ce Diabolic Chant', DSDL 704, issued 1983. Side 1, band 5) keep the imitative part instrumental, Gothic Voices ('The Medieval Romantics',

Hyperion CDA 66463, rec. 1990 and 1991, track 12) give an all-vocal performance and therefore have no problem with the occasional words.
275 Schering 1931 b: 16–17; The Medieval Ensemble of London, 'Matteo da
Perugia, Secular Works', Decca L'Oiseau Lyre DSLO 577. Issued 1979.
Side 2, band 1. See also Side 2, band 6, *Gia da rete d'amor*.
276 On this see Haines 2001 a.
277 Fallows 1983b: 138.

THE RE-INVENTION OF THE *A CAPPELLA* HYPOTHESIS

1 See especially Reaney 1969 and Slavin 1991. Although Adler is discussing
sacred music and Reaney and Slavin secular, their findings are strikingly
consistent. It would be quite unreasonable, however, to expect modern
scholars to have known this, given that Adler's article had fallen on deaf
ears in the first place.
2 Besseler 1924–5: 49 and 54, quoted in chapter 1, p. 51 above.
3 Columbia 5711.
4 OL 61, 62 and 63 (1938), and OL 109 (1939). On OL 62, side [a],
Ockeghem's *Déploration sur la mort de Binchois* is sung with the lower voices
partially vocalised. For further details and more examples see the selection
of early recordings without instruments at the end of this chapter.
5 E.g. HMS 20, side 1 = HLP 5, side 1, band 1; HMS 22, side 5 = HLP 5,
side 1, band 9; APM 14019, side a (no bands), item 4; APM 14063, side a,
bands 2, 5 and 6, side b, band 7.
6 Anthologie Sonore 31 and 35 respectively. Thanks to Jerome Weber's
uniquely detailed knowledge of the production process it is possible to
date the recording of the Machaut disc to early February 1936. De Van
performed the Mass for the first time on 2 February. From Pathé codes
stamped on the shellac it is possible to deduce that the shells must have
arrived at the Chatou factory on 19 February. Similarly AS 35 can be dated
to December 1935 or January 1936. I am very grateful for Father Weber's
help in dating several of the recordings discussed here.
7 Besseler 1950: 186–7, quoted in chapter 3, n. 58 below. Cf. Riemann 1882;
7 / 1909: 684 (see p. 42 above).
8 Anna Maria Busse Berger, forthcoming.
9 Besseler 1953: 66–7.
10 *Ibid.*: 71–2.
11 Reaney 1956: 6.
12 When lais were accompanied heterophonically 'The result would be an instrumental tone-poem on the lines of an Arabian *maqam*. The parallel may
seem a little strained, but we have the same preludising, the same building
on a known structure with progressive growth, and folk-like virtuosity employing all the tricks of the trade.' And he refers for support to the *Roman
de Horn* as interpreted by Handschin 1929 (Reaney 1956: 100).

13 Reproduced in Besseler 1952: col. 1334.
14 Reaney 1956: 8; for Paulus' text, which is not quite so straightforward, see Reiss 1924–5: 261.
15 Reaney 1956: 6.
16 For examples from the 1930s and 1950s see the list at the end of this chapter. See also chapter 1, p. 84, and this chapter, p. 89. For a further, later example see the Capella Cordina's performance of Landini's *Sy dolce non sono* (on Expériences Anonymes EA 83: 'Music of the Middle Ages: Volume IX – The Fourteenth Century'; rec. Jan., May, June 1966, side 2, band 6) recorded in 1966, ten years after Reaney's article. This track was used by Reese in his teaching, incidentally (New York University, Department of Music, Reese papers, folder '14th-century Italian music, etc.').
17 See the discussion of Page 1993b on pp. 127–8 below.
18 Reaney 1966: 719, n. 72.
19 Reaney 1956: 8.
20 *Ibid.*: 99.
21 Bowles 1957: 52–3.
22 Donington 1958: 86–7. Donington had studied with Arnold Dolmetsch. He later moved to the USA where, according to his obituary in *The Times* (26 January 1990, p. 18), he became 'an active member of the American Musical Logical Society'.
23 Bowles 1959: 92. For a straightforward statement of a later, more nuanced view see Fallows 1985: 33: 'the unquestionable truth that instruments were not normally allowed in church, and particularly not during Mass, must be qualified by the equally unquestionable evidence that on many occasions instruments were used in church, specifically during Mass'. And he goes on to provide examples. Christopher Page has commented to me on Bowles' self-destructive use of the 'mirror of research' as a metaphor: 'what do we see in a mirror but ourselves?'
24 Reaney 1966: 704; Harrison 1966: 319.
25 Harrison 1966: 319; Reaney 1966: 704.
26 Harrison 1966: 328.
27 *Ibid.*: 335.
28 A listing in a fragment from *Radio Times* – unfortunately not including a date, but as far as I recall dating from the early 1970s – gives countertenor (Kevin Smith), two tenors (Martyn Hill and Duncan Robertson), fiddle and alto crumhorn (Mary Remnant), psaltery and recorder (Marylin Wailes), lute (Robert Spencer), tenor cornett and sackbut (Paul Nieman, with Anthony Moore playing a second sackbut), and organ (Reaney himself). The programme, of which I have a mono tape, is of Machaut songs and motets. A recording of a different programme, taken from a BBC Radio 3 broadcast of 5 May 1970 and introduced by Reaney, may be heard in the National Sound Archive (NP1581 W BD 1).
29 Reaney 1966: 714.
30 Interview with Andrea von Ramm, 19 April 1998.

31 'French Court Music of the Thirteenth Century', Musica Reservata, DS 3201, side b, band 3b (issued 1968).

32 'The Art of Courtly Love', The Early Music Consort of London, dir. David Munrow. SLS 863, record 1, side 2, band 1 (issued 1973), probably influenced by a similar performance recorded in 1967 by the New York Pro Musica that used recorder, viols, rauschpfeife, and an array of percussion – the first of many multi-coloured performances on record ('Ah Sweet Lady: the romance of medieval France', Decca DL 79431; see Earp 1995: 402–3 for commentary). Munrow's contemporaneous article in *Early Music* does suggest that at least some of these Renaissance instruments are being used 'in order to deputise for their ancestors' (Munrow 1973: 199). His knowledge of all these instruments is conveniently set out in Munrow 1976.

33 Sequentia, perhaps the most successful of the medieval groups to emerge from Binkley's pupils at the Schola Cantorum Basiliensis, was formed in 1977.

34 'Music of the Middle Ages and the Renaissance (Volume 1, 13th–15th Centuries)', Syntagma Musicum, dir. Kees Otten, HQS 1195 (issued 1968). The instruction on the cover reads 'File under CLASSICAL: Miscellaneous', which accurately sums up the place of such collections in contemporary views of music history.

35 'The Mediaeval Sound', David Munrow (with Gillian Reid and Christopher Hogwood). Oryx EXP 46 (n.d., reviewed in *Gramophone* in July 1971). Roger Fiske, the *Gramophone* reviewer, represents the popular view of the time when he writes of this record, 'The effect is wonderfully alive and good-humoured. Nothing could be less like the performances of medieval music the Third Programme offered us in its early days. This is not museum stuff' (Fiske 1971: col. 203).

36 Munrow 1976: 4.

37 *Ibid.*

38 Montagu 1975: 243.

39 Greenfield 1967: 598.

40 Trowell 1968: 499.

41 The key innovation, as Christopher Page has reminded me, came at the end of 1965 with the release of the Beatles' album 'Rubber Soul', in which – accompanying 'Norwegian Wood' – George Harrison played a sitar, not quite for the first time in pop (see Macdonald 1998: 146–7) but in an early and hugely influential track.

42 *Early Music* volume 1 (1973, 119) includes the following advertisement: 'Wigmore Hall, April 9. In concert: Huggett family of Canada. Recently featured on B.B.C. T.V. Music–Songs–Dances from the Royal Courts of Henry VIII, Eliz. R. in COSTUME, plus unique folk songs [*sic*] from the 'Huggetts' latest album produced by George Martin. Lute, Baroque oboe, flute, consorts of viols, krumhorns, recorders, racket, rauschfeiffe, spinet, cello, viola, guitars, percussion, etc, etc.' George Martin, of course, was the Beatles' producer.

43 Arnold 1969: 69.

44 'The people of the Middle Ages and the Renaissance liked gorgeous colours in their clothes, sharp contrasts in their paintings, highly flavoured dishes at their table. In music they liked sounds which were bright and uncompromising' (Sleeve-note to Oryx EXP 46, *c.* 1971).

45 Brown 1976. The article's most significant contribution is in its marshalling of evidence for voice accompanied by harp or lute as plausible combinations for chanson performance. In a brief article accompanying an edition of Busnois' *Faites de moy* for *Early Music*, derived from Brown 1976 but published first – indeed, as the very first article of *Early Music* – he allows for the possibility of texting the lower voices, though he clearly does not like the result: 'Singing all three voices unaccompanied also masks the supremacy of the top line, but nevertheless some evidence suggests that these chansons were at least occasionally performed *a cappella*... since [the contratenor] was sometimes sung, and the text can somewhat unhappily be forced onto it, I have made the attempt, if only as an experiment' (Brown 1973: 7; cf. p. 5). Brown's resistance to the *a cappella* hypothesis is discussed in more detail below.

46 It is a nice coincidence that the series, which began publication in 1955, presents some of the same pieces that caused Stainer to arrive at exactly the opposite conclusion seventy years earlier.

47 Reaney 1969: 246–7.

48 Reaney 1977 begins by taking a step further, pointing out that, 'If the truth be admitted, very few instruments actually seem to be suited to the music' (Reaney 1977: 3). But although repeating the main suggestions of Reaney 1969 as regards texting the lower voices, it is primarily a reiteration of previous proposals on workable instrumental combinations, based on his experience as a performer. (Cf. Reaney 1966.)

49 van der Werf 1972: 19.

50 van der Werf 1972: 21.

51 Igoe 1971: 91.

52 *Ibid.*: 92. Igoe also offers a useful corrective to 'the time-honoured concept of medieval sonority as one of timbre contrast', quoting Paulus Paulirinus on the tenor 'smoothly mixing itself in' [suaviter se inmiscendo] with the other voices in motets (p. 80). On the range of synonyms for singing/playing see especially Huot 1989.

53 Wright 1981 (paper delivered in 1977).

54 Wright published his study of 'Performance practices at the cathedral of Cambrai' the following year (Wright 1978; on the lack of instruments see esp. pp. 322–5).

55 Perkins 1981: 620–1.

56 McKinnon 1978: 25.

57 'In pursuing this survey of mass scenes there will be little explicit reference to the *a cappella* question; the reader will note simply that instruments do not

appear in the illustrations' (McKinnon 1978: 26). McKinnon 1986 offers a useful reminder that there was never any doctrinal obstacle to the use of instruments in church, rather it was a matter of circumstance.

58 Page 1974.

59 [Page's footnote 29:] 'There is, for example, an explicit reference to the performance of *teneur* and *contrateneur* on the *psalterium* in the *Pratique du Psalterium Mystique* of Jean de Gerson (*d* 1429), see Mgr. Glorieux, ed., *Jean de Gerson Oeuvres Complètes*, 10 vols. in 11, Tournai, 1960–73, 7(1), p. 421.'

60 Page 1977: 487. Page's footnote supporting this last point reads: 'See, for example, with regard to the music of the troubadours and trouvères, H. van der Werf, *The Chansons of the troubadours and trouvères: A study of the melodies and their relation to the poems*, Utrecht, 1972, and on the textless parts of the Old Hall manuscript, Margaret Bent's note to the music supplement of *Early Music*, January 1974; "Vocalization is a likely solution, and one to which modern singers of early music may have to grow more accustomed"'.

61 Page's footnote here (n. 30) refers especially to Reaney 1969 and Igoe 1971. The qualification, 'the English speaking world', intended to exclude Continental groups such as the Clemencic Ensemble who were still performing sacred music with large instrumental bands.

62 Page's footnote mentions particularly Fallows 1983b (then forthcoming), Wright 1981 and Page 1977.

63 Page 1982: 441.

64 Howard Brown, with the benefit of the subsequent (1984) critical edition of *Cleriadus et Meliadice*, suggests that Page's reading of the text here was flawed; but this has no bearing on Page's main conclusions (Brown 1991, esp. n. 43).

65 Page 1982: 449.

66 Interview with Christopher Page, 7 September 1999.

67 Interview with Andrew Parrott, 19 June 2000. The Purcell Consort used an organ for alternatim performance of the Kyrie and to reinforce the Deo gracias.

68 Interview with Andrew Parrott, 19 June 2000.

69 Indeed, Parrott was to have been the first tenor in Gothic Voices' first BBC broadcast, but was replaced at the last moment, due to illness, by Rogers Covey-Crump. Covey-Crump had sung with Parrott's Taverner Consort, and according to Page he brought with him many of the ideas on tuning he had learned from and had already tried out with Parrott. It is a nice coincidence that their seminal recordings, Parrott's of the Mass, Page's 'Narcissus', were made within weeks of each other in early 1983.

70 *The Radio Times*, 14–20 February 1981, p. 26. For the first broadcast see *The Radio Times*, 24–30 January 1981, p. 28.

71 Fallows 1984.

72 Leech-Wilkinson 1984b: 411.

73 Fallows 1983b: 109.

74 Fallows questions even one of the best known, the 'De ce que fol pense' tapestry, on the grounds that we cannot know that the music being performed is the song by Pierre des Molins (Fallows 1983b: 132, n. 52).

75 Fallows 1983b: 133.

76 Bowers 1983: 164. Archival studies have become very much more complex since then, and Bowers would have strong reservations about such statements today (personal correspondence).

77 A useful index to the first ten discs (excluding 'A Feather on the Breath of God') is provided in Earp 1993.

78 Fallows 1989: 208.

79 'A Feather on the Breath of God', Hyperion A66039, recorded (all of it) on 14 September 1981.

80 Interview with Christopher Page, 7 September 1999; interview with Ted Perry, 9 May 2000.

81 Hyperion A66087.

82 Interview with Christopher Page, 7 September 1999.

83 Examples are printed and discussed in the much later Slavin 1991, but had been easily available in print since Schoop 1971.

84 I recall reading it before reviewing the Consort of Musicke's recording of Cordiforme in 1981, and referred to it there (Leech-Wilkinson 1981a: 215). Among other places it is cited (as forthcoming) in Earp 1991:, 209, n. 16, and seems to be invoked in Slavin 1991: 186.

85 Fallows 1989: 210–12; Fallows 1991 reappeared in English, with some changes, in Fallows 1996.

86 Fallows 1996: essay X, p. 7.

87 *Ibid.*, p. 12, n. 15.

88 Fallows 1984.

89 'The Garden of Zephirus', Hyperion A66144 , recorded 1984; 'The Castle of Fair Welcome', A66194, recorded 1985; 'The Service of Venus and Mars', A66238, recorded 1986.

90 Arnold 1969 (see above, pp. 97–8).

91 Wright 1979: 124–34; Fallows 1981b: 551. Page arranged for harp a song by Loqueville (also known as a harpist) on 'The Service of Venus & Mars' (Hyperion CDA66238, track 15).

92 Hyperion CDA66286.

93 Interview, 7 September 1999.

94 Hyperion CDA66336.

95 Though other interpretations have on occasion been proposed: see chapter 1, p. 19 (Coussemaker 1865) and p. 59 (Schering 1931a) above.

96 Page 1989b.

97 Fallows 1989: 206.

98 Brown & Sadie 1989b: chapter 1 'Introduction', and chapter 2 'Instruments', *passim*.

99 Gothic Voices, 'The Marriage of Heaven and Hell', Hyperion CDA66423, recorded 1990.

100 Gothic Voices, 'The Medieval Romantics', Hyperion CDA66463, recorded 1991; 'Lancaster and Valois', CDA66588, recorded 1991.
101 Page 1993b; Greig 1995.
102 Hyperion CDA66619, recorded 1992.
103 Hyperion CDA67098.
104 Not surprisingly, Earp enthusiastically endorses Page's new lower-voice practice in his 1993 review of 'The Medieval Romantics', 'Lancaster and Valois' and 'The Study of Love', the first three Gothic Voices discs to use vocalisation throughout.
105 The same conclusion – that partial texting in the sources should be followed exactly – was reached by Timothy McGee in a study of fifteenth-century songs in Italian manuscripts a couple of years later (McGee 1993).
106 The fate of the Medieval Ensemble of London will be considered briefly below, but there is little doubt that their demise owed something to the success of Gothic Voices and to the reviews of MEL recordings written from an all-vocal perspective.
107 Page 1992a: 29.
108 Knighton 1992: 562.
109 Supportive reviews began with Knighton 1985: 459.
110 Page 1992b.
111 Cape 1959–60 is an important previous case of a director describing his decisions in detail, but Cape has little to say about the character of Pro Musica Antiqua's sound.
112 See, for example, Bent 1993, esp. pp. 630–1. There are pertinent comments on this difference of views in Holsinger 2001: 349–50.
113 In which respect, as we have seen, he was anticipated by Igoe 1971 and Huot 1989.
114 Notwithstanding McGee's book *The Sound of Medieval Song*, which is not about sound in this sense.
115 Gothic Voices, 'The Voice in the Garden', Hyperion CDA66653, recorded 1993.
116 Since then, and since this chapter was written, he has published Page 2000, which combines many of the points set out here with suggestive comments from medieval writers in order to assemble a historically informed approach to listening to a thirteenth-century motet, a performance of which, by Gothic Voices, can be played from the journal's website, *www.em.oupjournals.org*.
117 Page 1993b: 454.
118 Page cites two reviews in the August 1984 issue of *Early Music* (Leech-Wilkinson 1984a and 1984b). The point was made again more strongly in Leech-Wilkinson 1986.
119 Page 1993b: 466.
120 As I can testify from having attended a number of Gothic Voices recording sessions over many years.
121 Greig 1995: 125.

122 Gothic Voices, 'The Spirits of England and France': I, 'Music of the Later Middle Ages for Court and Church', Hyperion CDA66739, recorded 1994; II, 'Songs of the Trouvères', CDA66773, recorded 1994; III, 'Binchois and his Contemporaries', CDA66783, recorded 1995.

123 Gothic Voices, 'The Spirits of England and France': IV, 'The Missa Caput', CDA66857, recorded 1996; V, 'Missa Veterem Hominem', CDA66919, recorded 1996; 'Pierre de la Rue, Missa de Feria, Missa Sancta Dei Genitrix', CDA67010, recorded 1997.

124 Gothic Voices, 'Jerusalem: Vision of peace', Hyperion CDA67039, recorded 1998. Similarly, see 'The Earliest Songbook in England', CDA67177, recorded 1999.

125 Reaney 1956: 6.

126 Page 1989a.

127 Among a series of remarkable studies from these years, see especially Bowers 1980 and 1983.

128 Sandon had been recordings editor from 1979 to 1982; Milsom shared the books and music editorship with Fallows from 1982 to 1984.

129 Page 1993b's Appendix 1 (469), identifies and documents a 'forum' almost identical to this list; mine is based on my memory of these informal meetings, his on a thorough trawl through *Early Music* for all reviews that meet criteria he lists, essentially a particular set of views about 'correct' and 'incorrect' performance practices for medieval music. It is very striking that our lists are so similar, emphasising just how a generation of young scholars took hold of the journal and used it to popularise their views.

130 On the production-review cycle (scholar as editor – performer – scholar as reviewer – performer's reaction) see Leech-Wilkinson 1996: 176–7.

131 Fallows 1978: 235.

132 Fallows 1980: 1575.

133 Page 1980: 117–19. John Thomson, *Early Music*'s founding editor, used to say that René Clemencic came into the *EM* office after the review appeared and said he'd do it with fewer instruments in future, as indeed he has: his performance of the Machaut Mass at the 1999 Salzburg Festival used two tenors and two baritones unaccompanied.

134 Leech-Wilkinson 1980: 265. The discs' titles reflect early music marketing at the time: 'Instrumens Anciens', 'The Four Seasons', 'Woods, Women and Wine'.

135 The argument for the other side, reflecting popular views then current, is set out in a letter in *Early Music* for October 1980 from Michael Uridge, challenging the Leech-Wilkinson review and scholarly introspection (Uridge 1980).

136 Wright 1980: 410–11.

137 Leech-Wilkinson 1981a; 1981b: 273.

138 *Ibid.*: 273.

139 Fallows 1981a: 865. On the douçaine see pp. 144–5, below.

140 Leech-Wilkinson 1982a.

141 Everist 1982: 281.
142 Leech-Wilkinson 1982b.
143 Fenlon 1983: 958.
144 Fallows 1983a.
145 Fallows 1984: 898.
146 Fallows 1975: 258. Fallows tells me that this was common currency at the time, but I have not been able to find any other suggestions in print.
147 Leech-Wilkinson 1984b: 413.
148 Leech-Wilkinson 1986.
149 The Medieval Ensemble of London, 'Matteo da Perugia: Secular works', DSLO 577.
150 'Guillaume Dufay: Complete secular music', D237D6 (issued 1981).
151 'Johannes Ockeghem: Complete secular music', D254D3 (issued 1982).
152 DSDL 704.
153 'Guillaume de Machaut: La Lay de la Fonteinne, Un Lay de Consolation', DSDL 705.
154 DSDL 714, with sleeve notes by David Fallows.
155 'Josquin Desprez: Missa di dadi, Missa Faisant regretz', 411 937–1, recorded 1984; 'Josquin Desprez: Complete 3-part secular music', 411 938–1, recorded 1984.
156 Interview with Christopher Page, 7 September 1999. His interview with Peter and Timothy Davies was broadcast on BBC Radio 3, Spirit of the Age, 4 December 1993. A recording survives in The British Library, National Sound Archive, H2433/01. Page paid warm tribute to the influence of MEL in Page 1992a: 25.
157 Leech-Wilkinson 1994.
158 John Thomson's editorial in the third issue of *Early Music* (1973: 129) records evocatively, 'Meanwhile enterprise and experiment continues. London's first baroque orchestra has given a concert...'
159 Titles include 'An introduction to the crumhorn repertoire', 'First steps on the dulcimer', 'Introducing the hurdy-gurdy'.
160 Montagu 1974: 20.
161 Register of Early Music 1973: 45.
162 *Early Music* 1 (1973), 47.
163 *Ibid.*: 173.
164 *Ibid.*: 49.
165 *Ibid.*: 54.
166 *Ibid.*: 123.
167 *Ibid.*: 53, 121.
168 'Register of Early Music/Register of Early Instruments', supplement to *Early Music* April 1975: 14.
169 *The Early Music Yearbook* (1998).
170 This is, of course, a very approximate calculation that depends on judgement and a degree of guesswork. What does 'lute' mean in an advertisement:

Renaissance or Baroque or both? For how long are harpsichords Renaissance instruments? I have not attempted to do a social scientific survey here, and the figures should be taken as very rough.

171 For further bibliography see Fallows 1989: 218, n. 23.

172 Fallows 1981a: 862–5.

173 Fallows 1985: 32.

174 Myers 1983.

175 *The Early Music Shop . . . Catalogue,* March 2000.

176 *The Early Music Shop Newsletter,* Spring 2001, p. 8 (the section headed 'Reduced to tears').

177 Page 1993b: 458.

178 Brown's tendency to shoot first and ask questions later is well illustrated by his treatment of Roger Bowers whom he belittled in *Early Music* 1982 for a recent conference paper downplaying the value of iconographic evidence (a Brown speciality); yet some years after the same paper appeared in print, years during which Bowers had become a much higher-profile musicologist, Brown cited it as 'an excellent example' of performance practice research (Brown 1982: 289; Brown 1989b: 11, n. 1).

179 Brown's 'a cappella heresy' surfaced again in his article on the trecento fiddle in *Early Music* 1989 (Brown 1989a: 323) and, as already noted, was taken up ironically by Slavin 1991, Page 1992a and Knighton 1992.

180 It was never quite clear whom Brown had in mind. Later in the review he wrote, 'Page's groupies will surely argue that we cannot draw conclusions about this [the implications of a scene at the Feast of the Pheasant] since we do not know what kinds of music they were singing', which was one of Fallows' crucial points (Fallows 1983b). But it was a point also made (knowing Fallows' views) in a review by me, immediately following discussion of the Feast of the Pheasant (Leech-Wilkinson 1982b: 559) and, while scoring as many hits as possible was quite likely to have been his intention, Brown if pressed could hardly have dismissed Fallows so lightly.

181 Brown 1987: 278. Remains of this linger in the language and argumentation of Brown 1991.

182 Pestell 1987: 57.

183 The nearest thing to an overview is Fallows 1989, which has yet to be surpassed.

184 See Leech-Wilkinson 1981c. On instrumental participation in polyphony, read or memorised, see especially Polk 1992, chapter 7.

185 See in particular Bent & Bowers 1981, esp. pp. 16–17.

186 Polk 1992.

187 Fallows 1983b: 39.

188 Fallows 1985: 38.

189 Fallows 1989: 204.

190 *Ibid.:* 206.

191 Banks 1999: 296, echoing work by Louise Litterick in the 1980s (Litterick 1980 and 1981).

192 The amateur Zorzi Trombetta was learning to play from mensural notation in the 1440s, and – since he earned money at it – would hardly have
bothered if there had not already been a market (Leech-Wilkinson 1981c).
193 Banks 1999: 308.

HEARING MEDIEVAL HARMONIES

1 On the distinction between sonority and chord, the cause of much agon-
ising among theorists of medieval harmony, I am with Carl Dahlhaus:
'It would be futile to attempt ... to name specific criteria by which one
could determine whether a sonority is or is not a chord' (Dahlhaus
1990: 67).
2 Wangermée 1980; 2/2001: 747. See also Earp 2002.
3 Fétis 1827: 5.
4 Perne 1827: 231–2; quoted in Earp 2002.
5 For a tantalising introduction to Perne (and more quotations along these
lines from other nineteenth-century historians) see Earp 2002, whose typescript is my source for this extract from Perne's manuscript, now F-Pi 931,
p. 97.
6 Kiesewetter 1848: 45–6. Willy Pastor was presumably remembering this
passage, and that of Fétis quoted above, when he wrote of Hucbald in
similar terms in 1910 (quoted in Rehding 2000: 362).
7 Kiesewetter 1841: examples p. 7.
8 Kalkbrenner 1802: discussion on p. 106 and diplomatic facsimile in table 5,
fig. 1.
9 Kiesewetter 1843: 202.
10 Fétis 2/1862: IV, 158–9 (this passage not in the 1st edition, vol. 4, 1837,
pp. 464–5).
11 Ambros 1864: 341.
12 *Ibid.*: 341. For more on Ambros's beliefs see the bibliography in Kalisch
1999.
13 Kiesewetter 1848: 96–7; translated from Kiesewetter 1834: 38–9.
14 Interestingly, before more than a few fragments of medieval polyphony
were available in print the view could be rather different. An anonymous reviewer of Heinrich Christoph Koch's *Musikalischen Lexikon*, in the *Allgemeine
Musikalische Zeitung* for 1803, attempting to understand the need for musica
ficta, offers the first statement of a long-running view of medieval notation,
one that persists in some quarters to this day: 'Musica ficta is not treated
at all. ... This material – concerning which Herr Forkel in the second part
of his music history is also so brief – deserves a careful investigation, in
order to determine whether the hearing of our ancestors was not finer
than their music system' (Anon. 1803: col. 41). I am grateful to Annette
Kreutziger-Herr for drawing my attention to this passage.
15 Kiesewetter 1848: 107; translated from Kiesewetter 1834: 43.
16 Kiesewetter 1848: 98; translated from Kiesewetter 1834: 39.

17 Kiesewetter 1848: 101. This passage appears neither in the first, 1834, nor the second, 1846, edition of the German text. Kiesewetter and the translator, Robert Müller, corresponded about the translation project; some additions may have been made, but if so they are not acknowledged.
18 Bellermann 1867: 26.
19 *Ibid.*: 32–3.
20 Wooldridge 1902–3: 573.
21 Bellermann, for example, adhered as a composer to the mid-nineteenth-century 'a cappella ideal' with its elevation of Palestrina to the highest level of pre-modern musical accomplishment (Siebenkäs 1999). See also Busse Berger (forthcoming).
22 An interesting comparison can be made with the earliest modern reactions (from the mid-eighteenth century) to troubadour verse, for example Jean-Baptiste de La Curne de Sainte-Palaye's opinion that it would be 'an abuse of the press to make it roll over the crude morsels of our ancestors' (Kendrick 1996: 104).
23 Quoted more fully in chapter 1, p. 29 above. Rehding points to similar arguments in the work of Guido Adler (Rehding 2000: 363–4).
24 Compare Wooldridge (discussing the Stainers' Canonici pieces): 'In all these examples the dry melody, and the arbitrary discords which some-times render whole passages unintelligible, are to be found; they are indeed characteristic of the whole collection, and probably no specimen that might be shown could be said to be entirely free from them. The work of Cesaris given as our example is remarkable chiefly for its cacophony, not altogether surprising indeed in a pupil of Machault' (Wooldridge 1905: 42).
25 Ludwig 1902–3: 46; trans. Stephen Rice (unpublished seminar paper).
26 Busse Berger forthcoming; Garratt 2002.
27 Riemann 1905: 306.
28 Ludwig 1906: 17. For a study of this inaugural lecture on Ludwig's appointment to the University of Strasbourg see Haines, forthcoming.
29 Schering in Riemann 1912: 2. The modernity of Machaut is still being stressed by Ficker as late as 1951 (Ficker 1951: 104–5; trans. Moll 1997: 105–6).
30 Schering 1914b: 75.
31 *Ibid.*: 80–1.
32 *Ibid.*: 84.
33 Moll 1997: 17, citing Schering 1914a: 123.
34 I am very much indebted in the following discussion to a paper on Ficker by Gwendolyn Tietze, contributed to a seminar on the subject of this chapter taught at King's College in 1999. I am most grateful to her for allowing me to draw on her work.
35 Schering 1914b: 75.
36 Ficker 1920: 13; Tietze 2000a.
37 Ficker 1925b: 502; Tietze 2000a.
38 Ficker 1924–5: 195–6 (his emphasis); Tietze 2000a.

39 Ficker 1924–5: 198–9; Tietze 2000a.
40 Ficker 1924–5: 202–3; Tietze 2000a.
41 Ficker 1924–5: 209; Tietze 2000a.
42 Ficker 1929b. See Rehding 2000 for a fascinating wider context.
43 Chapter 1, p. 270 n. 163, above.
44 Potter 1998: 179.
45 *Ibid.*: 214.
46 Potter 1996: 102.
47 *Ibid.*: 81.
48 As Potter reports, 'Ficker himself pointed to his own interest in the contribution of the Nordic race in western music history, an interest he pursued since 1924, long before other scholars had taken notice of it'. She goes on, 'In 1938 he proposed setting up a musical instruments museum... and cited its importance... in areas of *Volk* and race studies' (Potter 1991 b: 270).
49 On the general persistence of Germanocentrism in musicology see Potter 1996: 107–8.
50 See also Schipperges 1999: col. 1518.
51 'Volk', of course, has entirely different connotations in German than in English, and these need to be borne in mind when considering Besseler's view in its historical context. The various Volk movements in the 1920s played an important part in rebuilding German national consciousness.
52 See also Wegman 1998, esp. 438–41. Wegman shows how Besseler's concept of *Kollektivdasein*, based on Heidegger, relates to his sense of traditional German values, and allows a view of listening that in some ways comes closer to medieval habits than to modern concert practice. On Besseler's approach to history see also Lütteken 2000.
53 Besseler 1924–5: 46.
54 *Ibid.*: 47.
55 *Ibid.*: 48.
56 [Besseler's note:] Bologna Lic. [Ms] 37... gives an authentic texting for the contratenor.
57 *Ibid.*: 49–50.
58 'Thus two clearly separate steps become visible in the history of fauxbourdon. In the 1430s Dufay's mixed-sonority fauxbourdon [Mischklang-Fauxbourdon] prevails on the continent, instrumental accompaniment assumed. In the background a liturgical music forms with alternating chorus, duets for soloists and changing sonority-groups. In the 1440s, however, one observes a striving for compositional unity by means of vocalisation of the instrumental lower voices. To this corresponds the new sung fauxbourdon with vocal tenor and increased chordal writing. The balance shifts unmistakeably in favour of uniformity. The aforementioned studies of Dufay show his intention to fill all voices uniformly with cantabile melody and to give them all text. This leads compositionally to the already mentioned "fusing-sonority", in which the individual voice no longer stands out. Since the

singer will always be considered first, vocality develops as the basic colour of the whole. How far instruments were still involved we do not know' (Besseler 1950: 186–7). See also chapter 2, p. 90 above.

59 Besseler 1924–5: 54.

60 Hereafter Besseler 1931 (its copyright date).

61 On the nationalistic slant in Besseler 1931 see Tietze 2000b: 20–2; on the influence on Besseler of Ficker's *Sederunt* see Tietze 2000b: 38–9.

62 Tietze 2000b: 13–15.

63 *Ibid.*: 16–21. Tietze also shows (pp. 24–5) how Ludwig picked up and repackaged Besseler's reading of this changed attitude from ars antiqua to ars nova.

64 *Ibid.*: 33–5.

65 *Ibid.*: 41–4.

66 Potter 1998, esp. 242–5 and 251. For analogous cases in the art world see Petropoulos 2000.

67 See especially Moll 1988 and 1997.

68 The concept of bass-controlled sonority has reappeared in a more subtle and theoretically grounded form in Moll 1995.

69 For another view from this period see Breidert 1935.

70 Besseler 1924–5: 49; see chapter 1 above, p. 51, and chapter 2, pp. 89–90.

71 Besseler 1953, discussed in chapter 2, pp. 90–1 above.

72 Leech-Wilkinson 2001.

73 Moll 1997, *passim*.

74 Apel 1938: 8.

75 Apel 1938: 12. His view was vigorously attacked by another émigré, Edward Lowinsky, who (in Lowinsky 1945) rehabilitated the theorists and provided the intellectual basis for much work on musica ficta later in the century.

76 Apel 1942: 403.

77 Apel 1950: 7.

78 Besseler 1924–5: 46; Dischner 1927: 2. The whole question is covered in depth in Kreutziger-Herr 2001; see especially Part III, Chapter I.1, 'Moderne und Mittelalter: Eine rezeptionsästhetische Konvergenz'.

79 Apel 1950: 11.

80 The pejorative sense of 'manneristic' is pointed out by Günther 1963: 106.

81 [Apel's note 51:] We are using here a terminology, introduced by C. Stumpf, in which 'consonance' and 'dissonance' express objective facts of acoustics, while 'concordant' and 'discordant' indicate subjective perceptions or interpretations . . .

82 Apel 1950: 11–12.

83 Reaney 1953: 138-40.

84 *Ibid.*: esp. 137–8 and 139–40.

85 Reaney 1968: 66.

86 Interview with Ursula Günther, 17 June 1998; Günther 1957: 25, where Reaney is much the most warmly thanked.

87 Apel, inevitably, was also a major influence, but because so much of Günther's work involved correcting him the debt may perhaps have felt

less evident. Professor Günther told me of encountering Apel in Blooming-ton. He invited her for coffee and she brought him an offprint. WA: 'What is this?'. UG: 'Another attack on Apel!'

88 Interview with Ursula Günther, 17 June 1998.

89 Once again, I owe much of the following discussion to a seminar paper on Ficker and his pupils by Gwendolyn Tietze, though she bears no responsi-bility for the light in which they are here viewed.

90 Georgiades 1937, esp. 67–9 and 83.

91 *Ibid.*: 69.

92 See especially Apfel 1962, 1963 and 1964.

93 See the multiple entries under Apfel in the bibliography below.

94 Apfel's work has been revived and justified, very persuasively, by Kevin Moll (1995) who has used a related approach to arrive at (I believe) far more significant conclusions about late medieval approaches to composition.

95 See also chapter 4, p. 243, below.

96 Apel 1950: 25, n. 61.

97 The original German text (Hindemith 1937), published before Hindemith moved to America, is less specific, *Unterweisung im Tonsatz* (Instruction in Composition), but the English version was prepared in the USA under Hindemith's supervision, so it is reasonable to suppose that the new title was his.

98 Hindemith 1942: 2 (translated from Hindemith 1937: 16. 'Pure whim' is a loose but stylish translation of Hindemith's more mechanically evocative 'willkürlich schaltender Geist').

99 Hindemith 1945: 206; from Hindemith 1937: 233.

100 'Such an anachronistic approach was typical of many of the first attempts at technical analysis of Machaut's music, such as Paul Hindemith's analysis of ballade 22. It is beyond the scope of this study to point out the many absurdities in Hindemith's analysis, although one should admit that his was an early and relatively rare attempt at systematic analysis of harmonic progressions and tonal organization in Machaut's music' (Hirshberg 1971: 90–1).

101 In Connor 1999.

102 Salzer 1962: 268.

103 Salzer 1952: I, 279–80. Is this impression the same one that underlies Leeman Perkins' remarks quoted in chapter 2, p. 103, above?

104 Salzer 1967, esp. 35–40.

105 It probably goes without saying that I write 'we' here because Salzer's attitude seemed so exactly right to me when I first read his work in the later 1970s, at a time when it still lay largely unacknowledged by medievalists. It seems naive now, of course, but to say that is anachronistic.

106 Salzer 1969: 38–40.

107 *Ibid.*: 96–7.

108 Schachter 1970.

109 Crocker 1962: 16.

110 Hughes 1956: iv.

111 *Ibid.*: 74–5.

112 'compositions starts with . . . a two-voice texture, superius–tenor, in which the superius receives primary attention' (Apel 1950: 11).

113 Hughes 1956: 101, 154.

114 *Ibid.*: 104–9.

115 *Ibid.*: 156.

116 *Ibid.*: 72–3.

117 Kühn 1973, completed in 1969 (p. 5).

118 Other recent German studies tending towards Kühn's approach include Eggebrecht 1968 and Dömling 1970. Contemporary with Kühn was Pelinski 1975. A key study that has been drawn on ever since to provide a conspectus of medieval counterpoint teaching – perhaps too readily, since its excellence has discouraged a careful reading of the originals – is Sachs 1974.

119 Fuller 1986: 53; ex. 7, b. 129.

120 Interestingly, only her later article for the same *Journal of Music Theory* uses most of these labels again, suggesting that while musicologists may have been impressed by them, they did not actually need them hereafter.

121 Fuller 1987: 58, n. 24.

122 Leech-Wilkinson 1984c. More recent studies by me that have used reductional analysis have been noticeably more careful. A 1990 book on Machaut's Mass used reductional graphs to make points about composition, but this time much more cautiously, observing local prolongations but not looking for any overall harmonic or melodic design. A 1996 article on Machaut's virelais pointed to harmonic implications and long-range melodic structures in monophonic songs. If both were relatively non-controversial (at least in these respects) it was to a considerable extent due to the general acceptance of Fuller's work. Also symptomatic was Leech-Wilkinson 1993 (drawing on an unpublished paper of 1985), which included an outline attempt to ground a reductional procedure in the counterpoint treatise of Petrus dictus Palma Ociosa.

123 For the series of her articles following and extending Fuller 1986 see the listing in the bibliography below. For some other examples see Plumley 1990 and 1996; Leach 1997; Connor 1999.

124 The number of authors who make this association during the 'instrumental period' is so large that they defy comprehensive listing. Arnold Salop provides a nice example in his 1971 history of musical style (citing Reaney 1956 in support): 'the performance practice of the time probably did not embrace the idea of blending of the separate voices, but rather of a distinct contrast between them. . . . Thus, the three notes sounding simultaneously probably would have been perceived more as separate entities – as parts of separate lines – than as constituents of a single impression (i.e., of harmony). In general, then, the play of consonances and dissonances would have been deemphasized, and might indeed have escaped perception' (Salop 1971: 44).

125 Cf. chapter 2, pp. 112–13 above.

126 'I share with others the opinion that sonority was a significant structural resource in the advanced polyphony of fourteenth-century France and, in particular, in the music of Guillaume de Machaut' (Fuller 1986: 38).

127 Including Salzer 1952; Hughes 1956; Salzer 1967; Salzer & Schachter 1969; Schachter 1970; Bashour 1975; Novack 1970, 1976 and 1983; among others. The thirty-year gap between Hughes and Fuller is especially sad.

128 There is a huge literature on problems of musica ficta, much of which could have been discussed under the topic of this chapter (and very nearly was). For valuable modern contributions see K. Berger 1987 and 1989; and Brothers 1997.

129 Some underlying conceptual problems with Bent's proposal, including, as he puts it, the 'anachronism' of analysing out a two-voice core, are outlined in Wegman 1998: 452–3. On anachronism, however, see also chapter 4 below.

130 Leach 1997: xi–xii, where the idea of a composer working beyond his time (by which she means, beyond the theorists of his time) is held to be anachronistic. For a strongly worded statement on the 'fallacy' of such views as promoted by Christian Berger see Fuller 1998b: 105–6.

131 Cf., for example, the Berkeley treatise on the one hand and pseudo Johannes de Muris and Petrus dictus Palma Ociosa on the other. The tendency to lump together 'the theorists' without taking any one as a guide – equivalent to a rather imprecise conflation of sources in textual criticism – avoids the problem that none answers all musical situations or comes from exactly the right place and time for more than a fraction of the repertory.

132 See especially Ellsworth 1977: 108.

133 Petrus dictus Palma Ociosa: 'It is permitted that the intervals mentioned above, decently standing and ordered in the aforementioned places *and in others of whatever kind,* may still be ordered and made *wherever you wish...*' (Insuper nota, quod, licet omnes species discantus antedictae decentius stant et ordinantur in locis praedictis quam in aliis quibuscumque, possunt tamen ordinari et fieri, ubicumque volueris) (Wolf 1913–14: 512). Prosdocimus: 'There are other extremely charming styles of singing [we would say composing] to be found; to write them down would be exceedingly difficult and perhaps impossible, since such styles are in a certain way infinite – and delightful in different and various ways, on account of which a variety of compositional practices arises.' (Reperiunter etiam et alii modi dulcissimi cantandi, quos scribere foret valde difficile et forte impossibile, cum tales modi quodammodo infiniti sunt, et diversis diversimodi delectabiles, qua propter insurgit diversitas componentium) (Herlinger 1984: 66–9 (with alternative readings) and, in relation to musica ficta, 94–5. Also quoted in Hughes 1956: 24).

134 Johannes Boen offers three classic examples. See the discussion in Fuller 1998c: 473–6. As well as these questions one also needs to consider the implications of the far more complex picture that emerges from Moll 1995.

135 See Burstyn 1997 for a selection of well-known quotes on this, including Jacques Le Goff's 'Medieval man is exotic for us'.
136 By far the most methodologically sophisticated attempt at such a reconciliation is Moll 1995, though (or perhaps because) it offers neither a method for analysing individual compositions nor even hints at a way of listening.
137 See especially Sloboda & Edworthy 1981; Huron 1989; Wessel 1979; McAdams & Bregman 1979.
138 Page 2000: 352; cf. Reimer 1972: I, 96–7. Page points out in a note (357), 'The interpolator of Garlandia's treatise adds that a four-part texture is especially perceived in this way "when filled out with instruments" (*maxime instrumentis completis*)' – interesting testimony for the medieval perception of that link between a linear view of harmony and instrumental performance that we found was crucial to so much of the work described in the preceding chapter.
139 As noted in chapter 1 (pp. 270–1, n. 163), Pamela Potter has shown how a related idea, that Northerners heard more polyphonically than Southerners, was abused by German musicologists during the Nazi period. Though we are here examining arguments about period, not racial differences, that exemplum should nevertheless make us wary. Having said that, there seems to be a surprising complacence among specialists in music perception about the extent to which cultural factors may affect perceptions of music. Compare, for example, the responses of Eleanor Selfridge-Field and Christian Kaden to the papers on perception and cognition presented at the 1997 IMS congress, printed in Greer 2000: 111–17.
140 Besseler made a very similar point about the impossibility of true horizontal hearing in Besseler 1926a: 150.
141 Reaney 1956: 6.
142 Burstyn 1997: 695.
143 See Wegman 1998.
144 Burstyn 1997: 697.
145 Burstyn's fundamentally optimistic view is clear also in Burstyn 1998.
146 The Tinctoris article (Page 1996) is only tangentially relevant here, yet Page's analysis of some descriptive phrases in the fifteenth-century theorist is perhaps the most challenging of the early articles in this field since, by showing how it might be done, it demonstrates that any hope of understanding what a medieval writer might have meant requires a wide knowledge of the texts he would have known and of the ways in which he filleted, paraphrased and adapted them. This range of knowledge, potentially covering the whole body of Classical philosophy and medieval Latin and vernacular literature, musicologists simply do not have. Consequently it shows with startling clarity how inadequate has been the attempt by previous scholars at a historical understanding of medieval music and particularly music theory. For anyone who believes in a historical approach it has to be one of the richest and most depressing articles in the literature. And it plays straight into the hands of those postmodernists and ultra-positivists who insist

(as I shall in the following chapter) that nothing can be known with the degree of certainty that historians have liked to claim about the way it was then. Standing up against those claims is going to be a lot harder if Page's article is accepted as a salutary lesson from the historicist side of the fence.

147 A later, but more specific context is described by Tess Knighton in the same issue of *Early Music* as contains Page's trouvère article, an issue devoted to 'Listening Practice' (Knighton 1997).

148 Botstein 1998.

149 Botstein's article introduced the proceedings of a conference organised by Rob Wegman on 'Music as Heard', held just before the issue of *Early Music* on 'Listening Practice', containing Page's, Burstyn's and Knighton's articles, appeared. Compare the remark about *Zeitgeist* that opens Wegman 1998: 434. Another important study is Fuller 1998c. In all these studies it is clear that opportunities to bring together knowledge acquired in other projects and place it in a new context are being seized eagerly.

EVIDENCE, INTERPRETATION, POWER AND PERSUASION

1 For numerous further discussions of current musicology, and references to many of the crucial studies of the past twenty years, see Cook & Everist 1999. Compare my definition with the aims of literary scholarship as defined by Robert D. Hume: 'the critic or scholar attempts to solve problems or answer questions, hoping thereby to add to or improve our understanding of our subject' (Hume 1999: 157). I have some trouble with Hume's 'our' because I am not entirely happy to see humanities subjects constructed as a matrix of problems with solutions or questions with answers. Both seem to me to narrow the possibilities needlessly. I prefer a much more open definition; for while it specifies almost nothing it leaves open the possibility of a great many more approaches that may be fruitful in ways not yet imagined.

2 It's worth bearing in mind the difficulty we have in being sure about things that happened recently, even events to which we were an eye-witness. Edmonds & Eidinow 2001 investigate an incident in a Cambridge philosophy seminar in 1946 when Ludwig Wittgenstein may have raised a poker to Karl Popper. Surviving witnesses include a judge, five professors and a non-university philosopher, men (they are all men) whose business is to be precise. No two of them agree either on the events or on their sequence. No doubt the same would be true of medieval witnesses.

3 Balkin 1998.

4 'Historicism' has had numerous meanings. I am using it in the same sense as Robert D. Hume's 'archeo-historicism', an approach to studying the past that takes as its primary aim the reconstruction of historical contexts and the interpretation of texts in relation to them (Hume 1999, esp. 1–11, 188).

5 Because of the nature of the evidence, and the circumstances that produced it, most of this work concerns later repertories than are considered here.

For an essential introduction to current methodology see Haggh 1996, and for an exemplary application Wegman 1994. The rate of discovery in this field is such that it would be absurd to maintain that there was not a vast improvement in knowledge and understanding over recent years. Partly this is due to the profusion of new foundations and endowments in the fifteenth century which greatly increased the documentation of musical activity. The period covered by this book seems, so far, to have been less fortunate.

6 Lest I be thought an out-and-out relativist let me emphasise that I am here talking about musicology, and in particular the musicology of medieval music. In science, to go to the case most used as a test of people's relativism, it is perfectly obvious that, in at least some areas, there is a gradual convergence towards verifiable knowledge. History is another matter, music yet another. Historical musicology attempts to mix these two in such a way as to borrow for the study of music some of the convergence believed to be possible in the study of history. I find the extent to which this works doubtful, both because I doubt what can be known of history and because I doubt still more what can be known historically of music.

7 In Leo Treitler's words, 'Differences or changes about what a text says are not necessarily to be charged against the frailties of interpreters; they can as well reflect differences or changes in the interests of interpreters. The idea that interpreters should shed their interests and read the "invariable" meanings of texts is, I think, not realistic' (Treitler 1989: 50).

8 The classic texts are collected in Taruskin 1995. See also Butt 2002.

9 A related factor is, I believe, influential. There is overwhelming anecdotal evidence to suggest that musicians feel that as they get older they become better at understanding music while listening to it, that their appreciation of music gets deeper with age. In that case it would be impossible to distinguish a sense that one appreciated music more through increased knowledge from a sense that one appreciated it more through increased maturity. The improvement in one's appreciation could not be broken down into parts having identifiably distinct causes. There will always be a tendency for musicologists, then, to credit their experience of music to their knowledge of it, regardless of the impossibility of knowing that that is the cause.

10 Cf. Kuhn 1962, 3/1996: 25–6.

11 Karl Popper saw Kuhn's 'normal science' as the product of poor teaching leading to a disinclination to ask awkward questions (Popper 1970: 52–3; quoted in Bent 1986: 85, n. 1). Nothing could be further from my view of normal musicology here. On the contrary, I believe that the fields listed above have produced, and continue to produce, some of the very best musicology, less dramatic but better grounded – that is to say, working within a well-established paradigm, producing clear results with a coherent methodology – than any of the 'revolutionary' work which necessarily lacks, at first, an established paradigm (and thus a tested methodology) within which to work. That is not to say that the methodologies of normal musicology cannot be questioned by revolutionary work, nor that they are immune to change as a

result, and their findings with them. (For a more realistic view than Popper's
of the problems that thorough training can bring consider 'Hume's Paradox:
the better trained the historian, the more difficult original thought becomes'.
Hume 1999: 49.)

12 For a useful commentary on and updating of Kuhn's differentiation of normal and revolutionary science see especially Bird 2000. For an angrily contrasting view see Steve Fuller 2000. Fuller argues, among other things, that
'paradigms should be seen, not as the ideal form of scientific inquiry, but
rather an arrested social movement in which the natural spread of knowledge is captured by a community that gains relative advantage by forcing
other communities to rely on its expertise to get what they want' (37). This
is certainly a plausible way of reading the insistence of scholars working
in either the 'instrumental' or 'vocal' camps that performers should follow
their recommendations; one could argue, for example, though it would be
uncharitable, that scholars advising performers on specific projects exchange
assistance with editions and historical information for a realisation of their
hypotheses in performance.

13 For Hume there are no sudden changes of view in the humanities, and therefore 'Applying Kuhn's theory to humanistic subjects strikes me as profoundly
misguided' (Hume 1999: 170). I offer these cases as counter-examples.

14 Cf. Kuhn 1962, 3/1996: 78: 'They will devise numerous articulations and
ad hoc modifications of their theory in order to eliminate any apparent
conflict'.

15 Cf. Kuhn 1962, 3/1996: 94: 'When paradigms enter, as they must, into a
debate about paradigm choice, their role is necessarily circular. Each group
uses its own paradigm to argue in that paradigm's defense.' And 148: 'The
proponents of competing paradigms are always at least slightly at cross-
purposes. Neither side will grant all the non-empirical assumptions that the
other needs in order to make its case.'

16 Cf. the discussion of Hughes in chapter 3 above: 'He was, by and large,
overlooked: he was jumping too far ahead of current thinking; and to reach
beyond him it would be necessary to go over the ground much more slowly.
As things stood, medieval music studies had, as yet, no use for his approach
or for the idea of analysis that went beyond description.'

17 Chapter 3, p. 201 above.

18 It is also worth noting, in the light of (Thomas) Kuhn's observation that
'Almost always the men who achieve these fundamental inventions of a
new paradigm have been either very young or very new to the field whose
paradigm they change' (Kuhn 1962, 3/1996: 90), that Sarah Fuller was a
newcomer to the field of late medieval harmony, having worked previously
on the Aquitanian repertory and early theory. (Kuhn's study, of course, was
first published at a time when the general masculine was still acceptable.)

19 Kuhn 1962, 3/1996: 71.

20 The failure of Adler's and then Kroyer's counter-proposals is explained by
Kuhn's analysis of an analogous situation in the history of science: 'one

reason why the theories ... failed to get a sufficient hearing was that they made no contact with a recognized trouble spot in normal scientific practice' (*ibid.*: 76). No one but Adler and Kroyer appeared to perceive a crisis, or if they did they were not willing to say so; the existing paradigm was working far too well.

21 Some of these, though not those that came to seem the most difficult, were outlined already by Fallows in his seminal *a cappella* article, Fallows 1983b, esp. 141–2.

22 Fallows 1991 and 1996.

23 Banks 1999.

24 Kuhn 1962, 3/1996: 95–6.

25 Cf. Kuhn 1962, 3/1996: section X.

26 Dawkins 1976: *passim*; Sperber 1996, esp. chapter 6.

27 Balkin 1998.

28 Another very interesting way of understanding the transmission of culture is through the epidemiological analogy developed in Sperber 1996, which helps to explain how culture mutates as it spreads.

29 On Besseler's debt to the teaching of Ludwig and Gurlitt see Tietze 2000b: 7–9.

30 Riemann 1892, 1893, 1906; Wolf 1901.

31 Chapter 2, p. 133 above.

32 Brown 1987: 278–9.

33 Needless to say, almost all the scholars covered by this book were men. My alternation of feminine and masculine pronouns over the next few pages, though intended only to be even-handed, makes that point uncomfortably clearly. Although the balance is gradually changing, there remains a danger that women will become equally active members of these groups without concomitant questioning of the values by which groups operate.

34 I am indebted in this section to the effective, at times devastating critique of academic power-play offered in Brian Martin, *Tied Knowledge: Power in higher education*, esp. chapter 3, 'Heirarchy' (*http://www.uow.edu.au/arts/ sts/bmartin/pubs/98tk/tk03.html*). For a view of the related issue of the self-replication of disciplinary communities see Bird 2000, esp. 80–2. A systematic treatment of (French) academic power is Bourdieu 1988.

35 Scholars who work outside institutions, needless to say, have a far harder time getting their work heard, since opportunities to speak and publish are so much more likely to be offered through institutional contacts. This alone is enough to demonstrate the added value that institutional power brings to a researcher.

36 For a wider view of this phenomenon see Steve Fuller 1993, esp. 330–1.

37 The transfer of power from the historicist to the postmodernist is another clear example of the kind of disciplinary discrimination to which I am pointing here. Richard Evans complains that 'Many aspects of postmodernism can be understood, sociologically speaking, as a way of compensating for the loss of power within the world at large, and within the university as an

institution. For it places enormous, indeed total intellectual power in the hands of the academic interpreter . . .' (Evans 1997: 199). But this is simply to acknowledge that the same power previously resided in the (traditional) historian whose authority, backed by the facts, seemed similarly unassailable.

38 Leech-Wilkinson 2001.

39 Another factor to consider, if only one could, is the extent to which individuals need to be different. As Frank Sulloway argues, 'Some people, it would appear, are *inclined* to challenge established truths', others are inclined to do all they can to uphold them (Sulloway 1996: 19).

40 Hoppin in Lowinsky 1989: vol. II, 680.

41 For a richly provocative view of the usefulness of rhetoric in mediating between apparently incompatible theories of knowledge see Steve Fuller 1993, esp. 17–24.

42 Cf. chapter 3, pp. 187–8 above.

43 For differently motivated statements of the same view compare Bent 1998: *passim*, and Holsinger 2001: 349, both arguing (though differing profoundly in every other way) that we must allow ourselves to be changed by the historical past.

44 See also Treitler 1989: 17, who touches on the relationship of such phrases to traditional oppositions between masculine (knowing) and feminine (known). A great deal more could be said along these lines.

45 For a succinct introduction to this translation problem and to the contrast between history and science see Evans 1997: 45–74.

46 This is mainly a rhetorical point. I have found in studying the structure of manuscripts that so long as the measurements are taken in one session they can be extremely useful. It is not clear, though, how much is gained by publishing them, since for the next scholar they may be all wrong. One simply feels good in being able to provide so much apparently precise information.

47 My use of this analogy is thus quite unlike Popper's (in 'Evolutionary epistemology'), to take a well-known example, since for him the evolution of scientific knowledge depends on the 'elimination of error'. Naturally, I see that (in his strict sense) as playing a relatively small role in musicology (Popper 1985).

48 I have made no attempt to adjust my rhetoric here in order to play down the issues of gender that it raises. On the contrary, my point is precisely that this is a traditionally gendered power game, and will remain so until forced to change.

49 Potter 1999: 307.

50 Potter 1991a: 160–1; Potter 1999: 306–7. The hope that conformity would bring funds was amply fulfilled – see Potter 1996, esp. 77–80.

51 Potter 1998: 67; chapter 1, p. 270 n. 156 above.

52 *Ibid.*: 106–7; chapter 1, p. 269 n. 133 above.

53 For the wider context see Potter 1996: esp. 77–87.

54 Ficker 1924–5: 207, 209; translation Tietze 2000a.

55 Potter 1991b: 270.

56 Besseler 1931: 100; translation after Tietze 2000b: 21.
57 Potter 1998: 179; chapter 3, p. 168 above.
58 Besseler 1931: 66; translation after Tietze 2000b: 22.
59 Potter 2001: 489.
60 Potter 1991b: 270.
61 As reported in Potter 1996: 102.
62 Potter 1996: 81.
63 Petropoulos 2000: 4.
64 For fuller references see chapter 1, p. 269 n. 133 above.
65 Petropoulos 2000: 168–9.
66 Kater 1997: 158.
67 The historicist who truly accepts the equality of other approaches is a rare beast. If one really believes in historicism one necessarily, just as with one's religion, believes that it is inherently superior. Robert D. Hume, for example, despite numerous tributes to the relativity of knowledge and the inevitability of subjectivity, lets slip in a less guarded moment that 'If . . . the commitment of the scholar is not to the discovery of what is both *true* and *documentable*, then there is no point at all to the enterprise' (Hume 1999: 29; his italics).
68 Tomlinson 1993: chapters 1 and 8, esp. 250–1.
69 Holsinger 2001, esp. 347–51.
70 Goehr 1992: 277–8. Cf. Treitler 1989: 14: 'In the politics of explanation those who stake their claims by right of objectivity wrap themselves in a mantle of absolute authority'.

CONCLUSION

1 On the notion of historically informed performance see Butt 2002.

Bibliography

Abraham, Gerald 1953, *History of Music in Sound*. Vol. III: *Ars Nova and the Renaissance, c. 1300–1540*, Oxford.

Adler, Guido & Koller, Oswald (eds.), 1900, 1904, 1912, 1920, *Sechs Trienter Codices I*, Denkmäler der Tonkunst Österreich, VII. Jahrgang, Bande 14–15 (Vienna, 1900); *II*, Jahrg. XI, Band 22 (1904); *III*, Jahrg. XIX, Band 38 (1912); *IV*, Jahrg. XXVII, Band 53 (Vienna, 1920); etc. up to *VII*, Jahrg. XL, Band 76 (Vienna, 1933).

Adler, Guido 1909, 'Über Textlegung in den "Trienter Codices"', no ed., *Riemann-Festschrift: Gesammelte Studien. Hugo Riemann zum sechzigsten Geburtstage*, Leipzig: 51–4.

(ed.) 1924, *Handbuch der Musikgeschichte*, Frankfurt.

Allaire, Gaston 1972, *The Theory of Hexachords, Solmization and the Modal System: A Practical Application*, Musicological Studies and Documents 24, n.p., American Institute of Musicology.

Ambros, August Wilhelm 1864, *Geschichte der Musik*, vol. II, Breslau.

Anglès, Higini 1931, *El Còdex musical de las Huelgas*, 3 vols., Barcelona.

Anon. 1803, review of Heinrich Christoph Koch's *Musikalischen Lexikon*, *Allgemeine Musikalische Zeitung* 6 (issue 3, 19 October): cols. 33–45.

Apel, Willi 1938, 'The partial signatures in the sources up to 1450', *Acta Musicologica* 10: 1–13.

1942, *The Notation of Polyphonic Music 900–1600*, Cambridge, Mass.

1950, *French Secular Music of the Late Fourteenth Century*, Cambridge, Mass.

Apfel, Ernst 1955, 'Der klangliche Satz und der freie Diskantsatz im 15. Jahrhundert', *Archiv für Musikwissenschaft* 12: 297–313; trans. Kevin Moll as 'The "tonal discant" and "free discant" techniques of composition in the fifteenth century' in Moll 1997: 171–92.

1959, *Studien zur Satztechnik der mittelalterlichen englischen Musik*, 2 vols., Heidelberg.

1962, 'Die klangliche Struktur der spätmittelalterlichen Musik als Grundlage der Dur-moll-Tonalität', *Die Musikforschung* 15: 212–17; trans. Kevin Moll as 'The harmonic structure of late medieval music as a foundation of major-minor tonality' in Moll 1997: 269–92.

1963, 'Spätmittelalterlichen Klangstruktur und Dur-moll-Tonalität', *Die Musikforschung* 16: 153–6; trans. Kevin Moll as 'Late medieval harmonic structure and major-minor tonality' in Moll 1997: 293–300.

1964, *Beiträge zu einer Geschichte einer Satztechnik von der frühen Motette bis Bach*, 2 vols., Munich.

1970, *Anlage und Struktur der Motetten im Codex Montpellier*, Heidelberg.

1974, *Grundlagen einer Geschichte der Satztechnik vom 13. bis zum 16. Jahrhundert*, Saarbrücken.

1981, *Geschichte der Kompositionslehre von den Anfängen bis gegen 1700*, 3 vols., Wilhelmshaven.

1982, *Diskant und Kontrapunkt in der Musiktheorie des 12. bis 15. Jahrhunderts*, Wilhelmshaven.

1987, *Die Lehre vom Organum, Diskant, Kontrapunkt und von der Komposition bis um 1400*, Saarbrücken; revised and expanded as:

1989, *Sämtliche herausgegebenen musikalischen Satzlehren vom 12. Jahrhundert bis gegen Ende des 15. Jarhunderts in deutschen Übersetzungen*, revised 2nd edn, Saarbrücken.

Arnold, Denis 1969, review of Purcell Choir disc ('Guillaume de Machaut: Messe de Nostre Dame', L'Oiseau Lyre SOL310), *Gramophone* 47 (June): 69.

Atlas, Allan W. 1975, *The Cappella Giulia chansonnier: Rome, Biblioteca apostolica Vaticana, C.G.XIII.27*, 2 vols., Brooklyn.

Aubry, (Louis François) Pierre 1907a, *La Rhythmique Musicale des Troubadours et des Trouvères: Examen critique du système de M. Hugo Riemann*, Paris.

1907b, *Estampies et danses royales*, Paris.

1907c, *Recherches sur les 'Tenors' Français dans les Motets du Trezième Siècle*, Paris.

(ed.) 1908, *Cent Motets du XIIIe Siècle publiés d'après le Manuscrit Ed. IV. 6 de Bamberg*, 3 vols., Paris.

1909, *Trouvères et Troubadours*, Paris.

Balkin, J. M. 1998, *Cultural Software: A Theory of Ideology*, New Haven.

Banks, Jon 1999, 'Performing the instrumental music in the Segovia codex', *Early Music* 27: 295–309.

Barbieri, Francisco Asenjo 1890, *Cancionero Musical de los Siglos XV y XVI: Transcrito y Comentado*, Madrid.

Barclay Squire, William 1900–01, 'Notes on an undescribed Collection of English 15th Century Music', *Sammelbände der internationalen Musikgesellschaft* 2: 342–92.

Bashour, Frederick J. 1975, 'A Model for the Analysis of Structural Levels and Tonal Movement in Compositions of the Fifteenth Century', Ph.D. dissertation, Yale University, UMI 75–24,499.

Bellermann, Heinrich 1858, *Die Mensuralnoten und Taktzeichen des XV. und XVI. Jahrhunderts*, Berlin, 2nd edn. by Ludwig Bellermann, Berlin 1930.

1867, 'Über die Entwicklung der mehrstimmige Musik', Vortrag gehalten im Saale der Singakademie zu Berlin im wissenschaftlichen Verein am XIX. Januar MDCCCLXVII. Berlin.

Bent, Margaret 1972, 'Music recta and musica ficta', *Musica Disciplina* 26: 73–100.

1986, 'Fact and value in contemporary scholarship', *The Musical Times* 127: 85–9.

1993, review of Page 1993, *Early Music* 21: 625–33.

1998, 'The grammar of early music: preconditions for analysis', in Cristle Collins Judd (ed.), *Tonal Structures in Early Music*, New York: 15–59.

Bent, Margaret & Bowers, Roger 1981, 'The Saxilby fragment', *Early Music History* 1: 1–27.

Berger, Christian 1992, *Hexachord, Mensur und Textstruktur: Studien zum Französischen Lied des 14. Jahrhunderts*, Beihefte zum Archiv für Musikwissenschaft 35, Stuttgart.

Berger, Karol 1987, *Musica ficta: Theories of Accidental Inflections in Vocal Polyphony from Marchetto da Padova to Gioseffo Zarlino*, Cambridge.

1989, 'Musica ficta', in Brown & Sadie 1989: 107–25.

Besseler, Heinrich 1925, 'Studien zur Musik des Mittelalters I: Neue Quellen des 14. und beginnenden 15. Jahrhunderts', *Archiv für Musikwissenschaft* 7: 167–252.

1924–5, 'Musik des Mittelalters in der Hamburger Musikhalle 1.-8. April 1924', *Zeitschrift für Musikwissenschaft* 7: 42–54.

1926a, 'Erläuterungen zu einer Vorführung ausgewählter Denkmäler der Musik des späten Mittelalters', in Wilibald Gurlitt (ed.), *Bericht über die Freiburger Tagung für deutsche Orgelkunst vom 27.-30. Juli 1926*, Augsburg: 141–54.

1926b, 'Studien zur Musik des Mittelalters II: Die Motette von Franko von Köln bis Philipp von Vitry', *Archiv für Musikwissenschaft* 8: 137–258.

1931, *Die Musik des Mittelalters und der Renaissance*, Handbuch der Musikwissenschaft, Potsdam. Published in instalments: pp. 1–32, 1930; 33–96, 1931; 97–128, 1932; 129–60, 1933; 161–338, 1934. Copyright date 1931.

1950, *Bourdon und Fauxbourdon: Studien zum Ursprung der niederländischen Musik*, Leipzig.

1952, article 'Chorbuch (I)', in *Die Musik in Geschichte und Gegenwart*, vol. II, Kassel: cols. 1332–49.

1953, 'Die Besetzung der Chansons im 15. Jahrhundert', in no ed. *Société International de Musicologie: Cinquième Congrès, Utrecht 3–7 Juiliet 1952*, Amsterdam: 65–72 & the ten plates following.

Bird, Alexander 2000, *Thomas Kuhn*, Chesham.

Bloch, R. Howard & Nichols, Stephen G. (eds.), 1996, *Medievalism and the Modernist Temper*, Baltimore.

Boatwright, Howard 1973, 'Hindemith's performances of old music', *Hindemith-Jahrbuch* 3: 39–62.

Bockholt, Rudolf 1971, 'Französische und niederländische Musik des 14. und 15. Jahrhunderts', in Thrasybulos G. Georgiades (ed.), *Musikalische Edition im Wandel des historischen Bewußtseins*, Musikwissenschaftliche Arbeiten 23, Kassel: 149–73.

Botstein, Leon 1998, 'Toward a history of listening', *The Musical Quarterly* 82: 427–31.

Bottée de Toulmon, A. 1838, 'Instruments de musique en usage dans le moyen âge', *Annuaire historique pour l'année 1839, publié par la société de l'histoire de France. A Paris, 1838*.

Bourdieu, Pierre, trans. Peter Collier 1988, *Homo Academicus*, Cambridge.

Bowers, Roger 1975, 'Choral Institutions within the English Church: Their Constitution and Development, c.1340–1500', unpublished Ph.D. thesis, University of East Anglia.

　1980, 'The performing pitch of English 15th-century church polyphony', *Early Music* 8: 21–8.

　1983, 'The performing ensemble for English church polyphony, *c*. 1320–*c*. 1390', in Stanley Boorman (ed.), *Studies in the Performance of Late Mediaeval Music*, Cambridge: 161–92.

Bowles, Edmund 1957, 'Were musical instruments used in the liturgical service during the Middle Ages?' *Galpin Society Journal* 10: 40–56.

　1959, reply to Robert Donington in *Galpin Society Journal* 12: 89–92.

Brancour, René 1921, *Histoire des Instruments de Musique*, Paris.

Breidert, Fritz 1935, *Stimmigkeit und Gliederung in der Polyphonie des Mittelalters*, Wunzburg.

Brothers, Thomas 1997, *Chromatic Beauty in the Late Medieval Chanson: An Interpretation of Manuscript Accidentals*, Cambridge.

Brown, Howard Mayer 1973, 'On the performance of fifteenth-century chansons', *Early Music* 1: 3–10.

　1976, 'Instruments and voices in the fifteenth-century chanson', in John W. Grubbs (ed.), *Current Thought in Musicology*, Austin: 89–137.

　1982, report on 'Expanding the horizons for research into performance practice', a conference held in New York in October 1981, in *Early Music* 10: 289–90.

　1987, review of Gothic Voices 'The Castle of Fair Welcome', *Early Music* 15: 277–9.

　1989a, 'The trecento fiddle and its bridges', *Early Music* 17: 309–29.

　1989b, 'Introduction', in Brown & Sadie 1989: 3–14.

　1991, 'Songs after Supper: how the aristocracy entertained themselves in the fifteenth century', in Monika Fink *et al.* (eds.), *Musica Privata: Die Rolle der Musik im privaten Leben. Festschrift zum 65. Geburtstag von Walter Salmen*, Innsbruck: 37–52.

Brown, Howard Mayer & Sadie, Stanley 1989, *Performance Practice: Music before 1600*, London.

Brücker, Fritz 1926, *Die Blasinstrumente in der altfranzösischen Literatur*, Giessener Beiträge zur romanischen Philologie 19, Gießen.

Buck, Percy (ed.) 1929, *The Oxford History of Music I*, Oxford.

Buck, Percy (ed.) 1932, *The Oxford History of Music II*, Oxford.

Buhle, Edward 1903, *Die musikalischen Instrumente in den Miniaturen des frühen Mittelalters. Ein Beitrag zur Geschichte der Musikinstrumente I: Die Blasinstrumente*, Leipzig.

Burney, Charles 1789, *A General History of Music*, London.

Burstyn, Shai 1997, 'In quest of the period ear', *Early Music* 25: 693–701.

1998, 'Pre-1600 music listening: a methodological approach', *The Musical Quarterly* 82: 455–65.

Busse Berger, Anna Maria (forthcoming), 'Friedrich Ludwig and the invention of the Middle Ages', in *Perspektiven auf die Musik vor 1600: Beiträge vom Symposium Neustift/Novacella 1998*.

Butt, John 2002, *Playing with History: The Culture of Historically Informed Musical Performance*, Cambridge.

Cape, Safford 1959–60, 'The Machaut Mass and its performance', *The Score* 25: 38–57 & 26 (1960): 20–9.

Carapetyan, Armen 1949, 'Editorial in reply to an incorrect statement', *Musica Disciplina* 3: 45–54.

Christensen, Dieter 1997, 'Hugo Riemann and the shaping of musicology: an ethnomusicological perspective', in Christoph-Hellmut Mahling & Ruth Sieberts (eds.), *Festschrift Walter Wiora zum 90. Geburtstag*, Tutzing: 34–43.

Connor, Kimberly 1999, 'Machaut's *Formes Fixes*: Towards a Nidus for Structure', Ph.D. thesis, University of Southampton.

Cook, Nicholas & Everist, Mark (eds.) 1999, *Rethinking Music*, Oxford.

Cook, Peter & Moore, Dudley 1990, *The Best of ... What's Left of ... Not Only ... But Also* (videotape) BBCV 4430, London.

Coussemaker, Edmond de 1852, *Histoire de l'Harmonie au Moyen Age*, Paris.

1865, *L'Art Harmonique aux XIIe et XIIIe siècles*, Paris.

1864–76, *Scriptorum de musica medii aevi*, 4 vols., Paris.

1872, *Œuvres Complètes du Trouvère Adam de la Halle*, Paris.

Crocker, Richard 1962, 'Discant, counterpoint, and harmony', *Journal of the American Musicological Society* 15: 1–21.

Dahlhaus, Carl 1990, *Studies on the Origin of Harmonic Tonality*, trans. Robert O. Gjerdingen, Princeton; originally published as *Untersuchungen über die Entstehung der harmonischen Tonalität* (Kassel, 1968).

Dart, Thurston 1954, *Interpretation of Music*, London; German translation by Andres Briner as *Practica Musica* (Bern, 1959).

Davidson, Jim 1994, *Lyrebird Rising: Louise Hanson-Dyer of Oiseau-Lyre 1884–1962*, Portland, Oregon.

Dawkins, Richard 1976, *The Selfish Gene*, Oxford.

de Van, Guillaume [William Devan] 1949a, *Guglielmi Dufay Opera Omnia 3: Missa sine nomine*, Corpus Mensurabilis Musicae 1/3, Rome.

1949b, *Guglielmi De Mascandio Opera I: La Messe de Nostre Dame*, Corpus Mensurabilis Musicae 2, Rome.

de Vries, Willem 1996, *Sonderstab Musik: Music confiscations by the Einsatzstab Reichsleiter Rosenberg under the Nazi Occupation of Western Europe*, Amsterdam.

Dick, Friedrich 1932, *Bezeichnungen für Saiten- und Schlaginstrumente in der altfranzösischen Literatur*, Giessener Beiträge zur romanischen Philologie 25, Gießen.

Dischner, Oskar [1927], *Kammermusik des Mittelalters: Chansons der 1. und 2. niederländischen Schule für drei bis vier Streichinstrumente herausgeben von Oskar Dischner*, Augsburg.

Dömling, Wolfgang 1970, *Die mehrstimmigen Balladen, Rondeaux und Virelais von Guillaume de Machaut*, Münchner Veröffentlichungen zur Musikwissenschaft 16, Tutzing.

Donington, Robert 1958, letter in *Galpin Society Journal* 11: 85–7.

Droz, Eugénie, Thibault, Geneviève, Rokseth, Yvonne & Pirro, André (eds.) 1927, *Trois Chansonniers Français du XVe Siècle*, Paris (repr. New York, 1978).

Duffin, Ross W. (ed.) 2000, *A Performer's Guide to Medieval Music*, Bloomington.

The Early Music Yearbook 1998 (no ed.), Caythorpe.

Earp, Lawrence 1991, 'Texting in 15th-century French chansons: a look ahead from the 14th century', *Early Music* 19: 195–210.

    1993, review of three Gothic Voices discs ('The Medieval Romantics', Hyperion CDA 66463; 'Lancaster and Valois', CDA 66588; 'The Study of Love', CDA 66619), *Early Music* 21: 289–95.

    1995, *Guillaume de Machaut: A Guide to Research*, New York.

    2002, 'Machaut's music in the early nineteenth century: the work of Perne, Bottée de Toulmon, and Fétis', in Jacqueline Cerguiglini-Toulet and Nigel Wilkins (eds.), *Guillaume de Machaut 1300–2000: Actes du colloque de la Sorbonne 28–29 septembre 2000*, Paris: 9–40.

Edmonds, David & Eidinow, John 2001, *Wittgenstein's Poker: The Story of a Ten-minute Argument Between Two Great Philosophers*, London.

Eggebrecht, Hans Heinrich 1962–3, 'Machauts Motette Nr. 9', *Archiv für Musikwissenschaft* 19/20: 281–93, and 25 (1968): 173–95.

Einstein, Alfred 1926–7, 'Der musikhistorische Kongreß in Wien (26.-31. März 1927)', *Zeitschrift für Musikwissenschaft* 9: 494–500.

Ellinwood, Leonard 1936, 'Francesco Landini and his music', *The Musical Quarterly* 22: 190–216.

    1939, *The Works of Francesco Landini*, The Mediaeval Academy of America, Publication No. 36 (Studies and Documents, No. 3), Cambridge, Mass.; 2/1945.

    1960, 'The fourteenth century in Italy', in Dom Anselm Hughes & Gerald Abraham (eds.), *The New Oxford History of Music III: Ars Nova and the Renaissance 1300–1540*, Oxford: 31–81.

Ellsworth, Oliver B. 1977, 'Contrapunctus and discantus in late medieval terminology', in Margot H. King & Wesley M. Stevens (eds.), *Saints, Scholars, and Heroes: Studies in Medieval Culture in Honor of Charles W. Jones*, Collegeville, Minnesota, vol. II: 105–12.

Erckmann, Rudolf 1931, 'Der Einfluß der arabisch-spanischen Kultur auf die Entwicklung des Minnesangs', *Deutsche Vierteljahrsschrift für Literaturwissenschaft und Geistesgeschichte* 9: 240–84.

Evans, Richard J. 1997, *In Defence of History*, London.

Everist, Mark 1982, review of partial reissue of Early Music Consort of London discs ('Music of the Gothic Era', DG Archiv 2547 051), *Early Music* 10: 281.

Fallows, David 1975, 'Performing early music on record–1: A retrospective and prospective survey of the music of the Italian trecento', *Early Music* 3: 252–60.

1978, review of Clemencic Consort disc ('Guillaume Dufay: Missa Ecce ancilla domini', HM 997), *Gramophone* 56: 235.

1980, review of Pomerium Musices disc ('Guillaume Dufay: Missa Ecce ancilla domini, Motets and Chansons', Nonesuch H-71367), *Gramophone* 57: 1575.

1981a, 'Medieval instruments', *Gramophone* 59: 862–5.

1981b, review of Craig Wright, *Music at the Court of Burgundy 1364–1419* (Henryville, 1979), *Journal of the American Musicological Society* 34: 545–52.

1983a, review of the Medieval Ensemble of London ('Ce diabolic chant', Decca Florilegium DSDL 704), *Early Music* 11: 557–8.

1983b, 'Specific information on the ensembles for composed polyphony, 1400–1474', in Stanley Boorman (ed.), *Studies in the Performance of Late Mediaeval Music*, Cambridge: 109–59.

1984, review of Gothic Voices ('The Mirror of Narcissus', Hyperion A66087), *Gramophone* 61: 898.

1985, 'The performing ensembles in Josquin's sacred music', *Tijdschrift van de Vereniging voor Nederlandse Muziekgeschiedenis* 35: 32–66.

1989, 'Secular polyphony in the 15th century', in Brown & Sadie 1989: 201–21.

1996, 'Texting in the chansonnier of Jean de Montchenu', in David Fallows, *Songs and Musicians in the Fifteenth Century*, Aldershot, essay X.; a slightly revised version of the original English text of section IV, 'Placement des Paroles', of the introduction to Geneviève Thibault & David Fallows (eds.), *Chansonnier de Jean de Montchenu* (Paris, 1991) pp. xxxv–xlvi.

Fenlon, Iain 1983, review of the Medieval Ensemble of London ('Ce diabolic chant', Decca Florilegium DSDL 704), *Gramophone* 60: 958.

Fétis, François-Joseph 1827, 'Découverte de plusieurs Manuscrits intéressans pour l'histoire de la musique', *Revue Musicale* 1: 3–11.

1835–44, *Biographie universelle des Musiciens*, Paris; 2/1862.

1876, *Histoire generale* vol. V, Paris.

Ficker, Rudolf 1920, 'Die Kolorierungstechnik der Trienter Messen', *Studien zur Musikwissenschaft* 7: 5–47.

1924–5, 'Formprobleme der mittelalterlichen Musik', *Zeitschrift für Musikwissenschaft* 7: 195–212.

1925b, 'Die Musik des Mittelalters und ihre Beziehungen zum Geistesleben', *Deutsche Vierteljahrsschrift für Literaturwissenschaft und Geistesgeschichte* 3: 501–35.

1927, programme booklet for concert *Musik der Gotik/Wien, Burgkapelle, 30 March 1927*.

1929a, 'Polyphonic music of the Gothic period', *Musical Quarterly* 15: 483–505.

1929b, 'Primäre Klangformen', *Jahrbuch der Bibliothek Peters* 36: 21–34.

1930a, 'Die Musik des Mittelalters', in O. Brunner *et al.*, *Das Mittelalters in Einzeldarstellungen*, Wissenschaft und Kultur III: Das Mittelalter, Leipzig: 106–23.

1930b, *Perotinus: Organum Quadruplum 'Sederunt Principes'*, Vienna.

(ed.) 1933, *Sieben Trienter Codices VII*, Denkmäler der Tonkunst Österreich Jahrg. XL, Band 76, Vienna.

1951, 'Zur Schöpfungsgeschichte des Fauxbourdon', *Acta Musicologica* 23: 92–123; trans. Kevin Moll as 'Towards a history of the genesis of fauxbourdon', in Moll 1997: 91–128.

1960, 'The transition on the Continent', chapter V of Dom Anselm Hughes & Gerald Abraham (eds.), *The New Oxford History of Music III: Ars Nova and the Renaissance 1300–1540*, Oxford: 134–64.

Fiske, Roger 1971, review of David Munrow *et al.* ('The Mediaeval Sound', Oryx EXP 46), *Gramophone* 49: cols. 202–3.

Forkel, Johann Nicolaus 1788–1801, *Allgemeine Geschichte der Musik*, Leipzig.

Fuller, Sarah 1986, 'On sonority in fourteenth-century polyphony: some preliminary reflections', *Journal of Music Theory* 30: 35–70.

1987, 'Line, *contrapunctus* and structure in a Machaut song', *Music Analysis* 6: 37–58.

1990, 'Modal tenors and tonal orientation in motets of Guillaume de Machaut', *Studies in Music: Festschrift for Ernest H. Sanders*, New York: 199–245.

1991, 'Machaut and the definition of musical space', *Sonus* 12: 1–15.

1992, 'Tendencies and resolutions: the directed progression in *ars nova* music', *Journal of Music Theory* 36: 229–58.

1992, 'Guillaume de Machaut: *De toutes flours*', in Mark Everist (ed.), *Models of Music Analysis: Music before 1600*, Oxford: 41–65.

1998a, 'Exploring tonal structure in French polyphonic song of the fourteenth century', in Cristle Collins Judd (ed.), *Tonal Structures in Early Music*, New York: 61–86.

1998b, 'Modal discourse and fourteenth-century French song: a "medieval" perspective recovered?' *Early Music History* 17: 61–108.

1998c, '"Delectabatur in hoc auris": Some fourteenth-century perspectives on aural perception', *Musical Quarterly* 82: 466–81.

Fuller, Steve 1993, *Philosophy, Rhetoric, and the End of Knowledge: The Coming of Science and Technology Studies*, Madison.

2000, *Thomas Kuhn: A Philosophical History for Our Times*, Chicago.

Gadamer, Hans-Georg 1989, *Truth and Method*, trans. Joel Weinsheimer & Donald G. Marshall, London; from *Wahrheit und Methode. Grundzüge einer philosophischen Hermeneutik* (2nd edn, Tübingen, 1965).

Gagnepain, Bernard 1980–1, 'Safford Cape et le "Miracle" Pro Musica Antiqua', *Revue belge de musicologie* 34–5: 204–19.

Garratt, James 2002, 'Performing renaissance church music in nineteenth-century Germany: issues and challenges in the study of performative reception', *Music & Letters* 83: 187–236.

Gastoué, Amédée 1914, programme booklet for concert *Les Primitifs de la Musique Française: Sainte-Chapelle (Palais de Justice) Lundi 8 Juin 1914*.

1922, *Les Primitifs de la Musique Française*, Paris.

1936, *Le Manuscrit de Musique du Trésor d'Apt*, Paris.

Geiringer, Karl 1943, *Musical Instruments*, London (New York, 1945).

1993, *This I Remember: Memoirs of a Life in Music*, Santa Barbara.

Gennrich, Friedrich 1921, *Rondeaux, Virelais und Balladen aus dem Ende des XII., dem XIII. und dem ersten Drittel des XIV. Jahrhunderts, mit dem überlieferten Melodien*, Gesellschaft für romanische Literatur 43, Dresden.

1926–7, 'Zur Musikinstrumentenkunde der Machaut-Zeit', *Zeitschrift für Musikwissenschaft* 9: 513–17.

Georgiades, Thrasybulos 1937, *Englische Diskanttraktate aus der ersten Hälfte des 15. Jahrhunderts*, Munich.

Gerbert, Martin 1784, *Scriptores ecclesiastici de musica*, St Blasien.

Gerhard, Anselm (ed.) 2000, *Musikwissenschaft – eine verspätete Disziplin?* Stuttgart.

Gérold, Théodore 1928, 'Les instruments de musique au moyen âge', *Revue des Cours et Conférences* 29 (1st series)/3, 15 January 1928: 234–9; 29/3, 15 February 1928: 459–73; 29/7, 15 March 1928: 607–19; 29 (2nd series)/12, 30 May 1928: 357–72; 29 (2nd series)/16, 30 July 1928: 740–54.

1932, *La Musique au Moyen Age*, Paris.

1936, *Histoire de la Musique des origines à la fin du XIVe siècle*, Paris.

Gevaert, François-Auguste 1890, *Les Origines du chant liturgique de l'eglise latine*, Ghent.

Goddard, Joseph [n.d.], *The Rise of Music: being a careful enquiry into the development of the art form from its primitive puttings forth in Egypt and Assyria to its triumphant consummation in modern effect*, London, no date but 1907 or 1908.

Goddard, Scott 1938, review of 'Guillaume de Machaut: Hoquetus David', OL 3, *Music and Letters* 19: 490–1.

Goehr, Lydia 1992, *The Imaginary Museum of Musical Works*, Oxford.

Grafton, Anthony 1997, *The Footnote: A Curious History*, London.

Gratzer, Wolfgang 1992, 'Bearbeitung der Bearbeitung der Bearbei…Zu Rudolf Ficker's editorischen Bemühungen um einen "Epochtermin der Musikgeschichte"', *De Editione Musices–Festschrift Gerhard Croll*, Laaber: 27–50.

Greenberg, Noah 1966, 'Early music performance today', in Jan LaRue (ed.), *Aspects of Medieval and Renaissance Music: A Birthday Offering to Gustave Reese*, New York: 314–18; R/New York, 1978.

Greenfield, Edward 1967, review of Studio der frühen Musik disc ('Carmina Burana', AWT9455 (mono) SAWT9455 (stereo)), *Gramophone* 44: 598.

Greer, David (ed.) 2000, with Ian Rumbold & Jonathan King, *Musicology and Sister Disciplines: Past, Present and Future: Proceedings of the 16th International Congress of the International Musicological Society, London, 1997*, Oxford.

Greig, Donald 1995, 'Sight-readings: notes on *a cappella* performance practice', *Early Music* 23: 125–48.

Guilbert, Yvette 1926, *Chanteries du Moyen Age*, 2 vols., Paris.

Günther, Ursula 1957, 'Der musikalische Stilwandel der französischen Liedkunst in der zweiten Hälfte des 14. Jahrhunderts', Ph.D. dissertation, University of Hamburg.

1963, 'Das Ende der ars nova', *Die Musikforschung* 16: 105–20.

Gurlitt, Wilibald 1922, concert programme booklet *Musik des Mittelalters/ Badische Kunsthalle Karlsruhe/24–26 September 1922*.

1924, concert programme booklet *Musik des Mittelalters in der Hamburger Musikhalle vom 1. bis 8. April 1924*.

(ed.) 1929, *Michael Praetorius: De organographia*, Kassel.

Haas, Robert 1931, *Aufführungspraxis der Musik*, Handbuch der Musikwissenschaft, Potsdam.

Haggh, Barbara 1996, 'Foundations or institutions? On bringing the Middle Ages into the history of medieval music', *Acta Musicologica* 68: 87–128.

Haines, John 1997, 'The "modal" theory, fencing, and the death of Aubry', *Plainsong and Medieval Music* 6: 143–50.

2001a, 'The Arabic style of performing medieval music', *Early Music* 29: 369–78.

2001b, 'The footnote quarrels of the modal theory: a remarkable episode in the reception of medieval music', *Early Music History* 20: 1–34.

2001c, 'Généalogies musicologiques: aux origines d'une science de la musique vers 1900', *Acta Musicologica* 73: 21–44.

(forthcoming), 'Friedrich Ludwig's "Musicology of the Future": a commentary and translation'.

Hamm, Charles 1968, 'Musiche del quattrocento in S. Petronio', *Rivista italiana di Musicologia* 3: 215–32.

Handschin, Jacques 1927–8, 'Die mittelalterlichen Aufführungen in Zurich, Bern und Basel', *Zeitschrift für Musikwissenschaft* 10: 8–22.

1929–30, 'Über Estampie und Sequenz I', *Zeitschrift für Musikwissenschaft* 12: 1–20.

1931, 'Die Rolle der Nationen in der mittelalterlichen Musikgeschichte', *Schweizerische Jahrbuch für Musikwissenschaft* 5: 1–42.

Harman, R. Alec (ed.) 1952, Thomas Morley, *A Plain and Easy Introduction to Practical Music*, London.

Harrison, Frank 1966, 'Tradition and innovation in instrumental usage 1100–1450', in Jan LaRue (ed.), *Aspects of Medieval and Renaissance Music: A Birthday Offering to Gustave Reese*, New York: 319–35; R/New York, 1978.

Haskell, Harry 1988, *The Early Music Revival: A History*, London.

Hawkins, Sir John 1776, *A General History of the Science and Practice of Music*, London.

Herlinger, Jan (ed.) 1984, *Prosdocimo de' Beldomandi, Contrapunctus: A New Critical Text and Translation*, Lincoln, Nbr.

Hibberd, Lloyd 1946, 'On "instrumental style" in early melody', *The Musical Quarterly* 32: 107–30.

Hindemith, Paul 1937, *Unterweisung im Tonsatz*, Mainz; trans. Arthur Mendel as *The Craft of Musical Composition*, London, 1942; rev. edn. 1945.

Hirshberg, Jehoash 1971, 'The Music of the Late Fourteenth Century: A Study in Musical Style', Ph.D. dissertation, University of Pennsylvania, UMI 71-26,031.

1980, 'Hexachordal and modal structure in Machaut's polyphonic chansons', in John Walter Hill (ed.), *Studies in Musicology in Honor of Otto E. Albrecht*, Kassel: 19–42.

Holsinger, Bruce 2001, *Music, Body, and Desire in Medieval Culture*, Stanford.

Hope, Robert 1899, *Medieval Music: An Historical Sketch*, 2nd edn, London.

Hoppin, Richard H. 1966, 'Tonal organization in music before the Renaissance', in John Glowacki (ed.), *Paul A. Pisk: Essays in his Honor*, Austin: 25–37.

Hughes, Andrew 1972, *Manuscript Accidentals: Ficta in Focus 1350–1450*, Musicological Studies and Documents 27, Rome.

Hughes, Andrew & Bent, Margaret (eds.) 1973, *The Old Hall Manuscript*, Corpus Mensurabilis Musicae 46, n.p.

Hughes, Dom Anselm & Abraham, Gerald (eds.) 1960, *The New Oxford History of Music III: Ars Nova and the Renaissance 1300–1540*, Oxford.

Hughes, David G. 1956, 'A View of the Passing of Gothic Music: Line and Counterpoint 1380–1430', Ph.D. dissertation, Harvard University.

Hume, Robert D. 1999, *Reconstructing Contexts: The Aims and Principles of Archaeo-historicism*, Oxford.

Huot, Sylvia, 1989, 'Voices and instruments in medieval French secular music: on the use of literary texts as evidence for performance practice', *Musica Disciplina* 43: 63–113.

Huron, David 1989, 'Voice denumerability in polyphonic music of homogeneous timbres', *Music Perception* 6: 361–82.

Husmann, Heinrich 1940, *Die Drei- und Vierstimmigen Notre-Dame-Organa*, Publikationen älterer Musik XI, Leipzig.

Igoe, James Thomas 1971, 'Performance Practices in the Polyphonic Mass of the Early Fifteenth Century', Ph.D. dissertation, University of North Carolina at Chapel Hill, UMI 72 10733.

Jacobsthal, Gustav 1871, *Die Mensuralnotenschrift des zwælften und dreizehnten Jahrhunderts*, Berlin.

Jeanroy, Alfred 1934, *La Poésie lyrique des Troubadours*, Paris.

Kalisch, Volker 1999, 'Ambros, August Wilhelm' in Ludwig Finscher (ed.), *Die Musik in Geschichte und Gegenwart... Zweite... Ausgabe*, Personenteil 1, Kassel: cols. 583–6.

Kalkbrenner, C. 1802, *Histoire de la Musique*, Paris.

Kater, Michael 1997, *The Twisted Music: Musicians and their Music in the Third Reich*, Oxford.

Kemp, Walter H. 1990, *Burgundian Court Song in the Time of Binchois*, Oxford.

Kendrick, Laura 1996, 'The science of imposture and the professionalization of medieval Occitan literary studies', in Bloch & Nichols 1996: 95–126.

Kier, Herfrid 1968, *Raphael Georg Kiesewetter (1773–1850): Wegbereiter des musikalischen Historismus*, Regensburg.

Kiesewetter, Raphael Georg 1829, *Die Verdienste der Niederländer um die Tonkunst*, Amsterdam.

  1831, 'Fünfter Artikel. Die Noten-Tabulatur oder Partitur der alten Contrapunctisten', *Allgemeine Musikalische Zeitung* 33 (no. 23, 8 June): 366–76 & music supplement.

  1834, *Geschichte der Europäisch-abendländische Musik*, Leipzig; English translation issued as Kiesewetter 1848.

1838, 'Ueber den weltlichen und volksmässigen Gesang im Mittelalter', *Allgemeine Musikalische Zeitung* 40, no. 15, 11 April: 234–48 & music supplement.

1841, *Schicksale und Beschaffenheit des weltlichen Gesanges vom frühen Mittelalter bis zu der Erfindung des dramatischen Styles und den Anfängen der Oper*, Leipzig.

1843, 'Ueber die musikalischen Instrumente und die Instrumental-Musik im Mittelalter und bis zu der Gestaltung unserer dermaligen Kammer- und Orchester-Musik', *Cäcilia* XXII, Heft 88: 187–238 and tables.

1848, *History of the Modern Music of Western Europe* (translation by Robert Müller of Kiesewetter 1834), London.

Kinkeldey, Otto 1948, 'Johannes Wolf (1869–1947)', *Journal of the American Musicological Society* 1: 5–12.

Kinsky, Georg 1929 (with Robert Haas & Hans Schnoor), *Geschichte der Musik in Bildern*, Leipzig.

Kirkman, Andrew 2000, '"Under such heavy chains": the discovery and evaluation of late medieval music before Ambros', *19th-Century Music* 24: 89–112.

Kneif, Tibor 1963, 'Zur Entstehung der musikalischen Mediavistik', Ph.D. dissertation, Göttingen.

Knighton, Tess 1985, review of The New London Consort ('Music at the Court of Spain', Meridian E45 77065) and other discs, *Early Music* 13: 455–9.

1992, 'The *a cappella* heresy in Spain: an inquisition into the performance of the *cancionero* repertory', *Early Music* 20: 549–81.

1997, 'Spaces and contexts for listening in 15th-century Castile: the case of the Constable's palace in Jaén', *Early Music* 25: 661–77.

Kramer, Lawrence 1995, *Classical Music and Postmodern Knowledge*, Berkeley.

Kreutziger-Herr, Annette 2001, *Mittelalterliche Musik als Imagination: Zur Rezeptionsästhetik der Musik des Mittelalters in der Neuzeit*, Habilitationsschrift, University of Hamburg (publication forthcoming).

Kroyer, Theodor 1925, 'Zur Aufführungspraxis', in Guido Adler *et al.* (eds.), *Gedenkboek aangeboden aan Dr. D. F. Scheurleer op zijn 70sten Verjaardag bijdragen van Vrienden en Vereerders op het Gebied der Muziek*, 's-Gravenhage: 191–200.

1934, 'Das A-cappella-Ideal', *Acta Musicologica* 6: 152–69.

Kuhn, Thomas S. 1996, *The Structure of Scientific Revolutions*, Chicago, 1962; 3/1996.

Kühn, Hellmut 1973, *Die Harmonik der Ars Nova: Zur Theorie der isorhythmischen Motette*, Berliner Musikwissenschaftliche Arbeiten 5, Munich.

Lang, Paul Henry 1949, report on the 1949 meeting of the International Musicological Society in Basel, *Journal of the American Musicological Society* 2: 202–4.

Leach, Elizabeth 1997, 'Counterpoint in Guillaume de Machaut's Musical Ballades', D.Phil. thesis, University of Oxford.

Leech-Wilkinson, Daniel 1980, review of discs by Les Musiciens de Provence ('Instrumens anciens', ARN 34217, 34260, 34301, 34370, 36451, 36516; 'Noel Provençal', ARN 34348) and Joculatores Upsaliensis ('Early Music at Wik', BIS LP-3; 'The Four Seasons', BIS LP-75; 'Woods, Women and Wine', BIS LP-120), *Early Music* 8: 262–5.

1981a, 'Le Chansonnier Cordiforme', *Early Music* 9: 213–16.

1981b, review of the Medieval Ensemble of London ('Matteo da Perugia: Secular works', Decca Florilegium DSLO 577), *Early Music* 9: 271–3.

1981c, 'Il libro di appunti di un suonatore di tromba del quindicesimo secolo', *Rivista italiana di Musicologia* 16: 16–39.

1982a, review of the Schola Cantorum Basiliensis ('Cantigas de Santa Maria', Harmonia Mundi 1 C 065–99 898), *Early Music* 10: 121.

1982b, review of discs by The Medieval Ensemble of London ('Guillaume Dufay: complete secular music', Decca Florilegium D237D6), *Early Music* 10: 557–9.

1984a, review of a Hilliard Ensemble disc ('Medieval English Music', Harmonia Mundi HM 1106), *Early Music* 12: 409–11.

1984b, review of discs by the Taverner Consort ('Guillaume de Machaut: Messe de Nostre Dame', EMI Reflexe 1 C 067 1435761) and Gothic Voices ('The Mirror of Narcissus', Hyperion A66087), *Early Music* 12: 411–13.

1984c, 'Machaut's *Rose, lis* and the problem of early music analysis', *Music Analysis* 3: 9–28.

1986, review of recent discs by Gothic Voices ('The Garden of Zephirus', Hyperion A66144), the Hilliard Ensemble ('Johannes Ockeghem: Requiem, Missa Mi-mi', EMI Reflexe 1 C 067 0098 1), the Medieval Ensemble of London ('Heinrich Isaac: Chansons, Frottole and Lieder', Decca Florilegium 410 107–1; 'Josquin Desprez: Missa di Dadi, Missa Faisant Regretz', 411 937–1), Ensemble Chanticleer de San Francisco and the Clemencic Consort ('Heinrich Isaac: Grand Motets Solennels', Harmonia Mundi HMC 1160), *Early Music* 14: 125–6.

1990, *Machaut's Mass: An Introduction*, Oxford; R/1992.

1993, 'Improvised and written polyphony', in Christian Meyer (ed.), *Les Polyphonies orales dans l'Histoire et dans les Traditions européennes encore vivantes*, Royaumont: 170–82.

1994, review of three Ensemble Project Ars Nova discs ('Ars magis subtiliter', New Albion NA 021 CD; 'The Island of St Hylarion', NA 038 CD; 'Homage to Johannes Ciconia', NA 048 CD), *Early Music* 22: 337–8.

1996, review of discs by Micrologus ('Landini e la musica florentina', Opus 111 OPS 30–112), Ensemble Gilles Binchois ('Fontaine de Grace', Virgin Veritas 7243 5 45066 2 8), Anonymous 4 ('Love's Illusion', Harmonia Mundi HMU 907109) and Gothic Voices ('The Spirits of England and France I', Hyperion CDA 66739), *Early Music* 24: 176–8.

2001, 'Wie überträgt man die Musik des Mittelatters?', in Wolfgang Gratzer and Hartmut Möller (eds.), *Übersetzte Zeit: Das Mittelatter und die Musik der Gegenwart*, Hofheim: 325–39.

Lefferts, Peter 1995, 'Signature-systems and tonal types in the fourteenth-century French chanson', *Plainsong and Medieval Music* 4: 117–47.

Leichtentritt, Hugo 1905–6, 'Was lehren uns die Bildwerke des 14.–17. Jahrhunderts über die Instrumentalmusik ihrer Zeit?' *Sammelbände der internationalen Musikgesellschaft* 7: 315–64.

1912–13, 'Einige Bemerkungen über Verwendung der Instrumente im Zeitalter Josquin's', *Zeitschrift der internationalen Musikgesellschaft* 14: 359–65, replies from Schering and Leichtentritt in 15 (1913–14): 11–17.

1958, *Music, History, and Ideas*, Cambridge, Mass. (Lecture series given at Harvard, 1934–5.)

Litterick, Louise 1980, 'Performing Franco-Netherlandish secular music of the late 15th century: Texted and untexted parts in the sources', *Early Music* 8: 474–85.

1981, 'On Italian instrumental ensemble music in the late fifteenth century', in Iain Fenlon (ed.), *Music in Medieval and Early Modern Europe: Patronage, Sources and Texts*, Cambridge: 117–30.

Lowinsky, Edward 1945, 'The function of conflicting signatures in early polyphonic music', *The Musical Quarterly* 31: 227–60; reprinted in Lowinsky 1989: II, 647–64.

1989, *Music in the Culture of the Renaissance and Other Essays*, Chicago.

Ludwig, Friedrich 1902–3, 'Die mehrstimmige Musik des 14. Jahrhunderts', *Sammelbände der internationalen Musikgesellschaft* 4 (1902–3): 16–69, 5 (1903–4): 179–224, 7 (1905–6): 514–28.

1906, 'Die Aufgaben der Forschung auf dem Gebiete der mittelalterlichen Musikgeschichte'; inaugural lecture, 4 Nov 1905, *Beilage zur Allgemeinen Zeitung*, 17/18 January 1906, offprint: Munich.

1909, 'Die mehrstimmige Musik des 11. und 12. Jahrhunderts' in Guido Adler (ed.), *III. Kongreß der internationalen Musikgesellschaft Wien, 25. bis 29. Mai 1909. Bericht* Vienna: 101–8.

1910, *Repertorium Organorum Recentioris et Motetorum Vetustissimi Stili* I/1 Halle.

1922–3, 'Musik des Mittelalters in der Badischen Kunsthalle Karlsruhe 24.–26. September 1922', *Zeitschrift für Musikwissenschaft* 5: 434–60.

1923, 'Die Quellen der Motette ältesten Stils', *Archiv für Musikwissenschaft* 5: 185–222, 273–315.

1924, 'Musik des Mittelalters bis zum Anfang des 15. Jahrhunderts', in Adler 1924: 157–295.

1925, 'Die mehrstimmige Messe des 14. Jahrhunderts', *Archiv für Musikwissenschaft* 7: 417–35, 8 (1926): 130.

1926, *Guillaume de Machaut: Musikalische Werke*, Publikationen älterer Musik I/1, III/1, IV/2, Leipzig 1926, 1928, 1929.

Lütteken, Laurenz 2000, 'Das Musikwerk im Spannungsfeld von "Ausdruck" und "Erleben": Heinrich Besselers musikhistoriographischer Ansatz', in Gerhard 2000: 213–32.

Macdonald, Ian 1998, *Revolution in the Head: The Beatles' Records and the Sixties*, 2nd edn, London, 1997; reissued 1998.

Machabey, Armand 1955, *Guillaume de Machault 130?–1377: La vie et l'œuvre musicale*, 2 vols., Paris.

Marpurg, Friedrich Wilhelm 1759, *Kritische Einleitung in die Geschichte und Lehrsätze der alten und neuen Musik*, Berlin.

Martinez-Göllner, Marie Louise 1971, 'Musik des Trecento', in Thrasybulos G. Georgiades (ed.), *Musikalische Edition im Wandel des historischen Bewußtseins*, Musikwissenschaftliche Arbeiten 23, Kassel: 134–48.

Martini, Giovanni Battista 1757, *Storia della Musica*, Bologna 1757, 1770, 1781.

Mayer, Friedrich Arnold & Rietsch, Heinrich 1896, *Die Mondsee-Wiener Liederhandschrift und der Mönch von Salzburg*. 2. Teil, Berlin.

McAdams, Stephen & Bregman, Albert 1979, 'Hearing musical streams', *Computer Music Journal* 3/4: 26–43, 60.

McGee, Timothy 1990, *Medieval and Renaissance Music: A Performer's Guide*, Toronto, 1985, London, 1990.

  1993, 'Singing without text', *Performance Practice Review* 6: 1–32.

  (ed.) 1996, *Singing Early Music: The Pronunciation of European Languages in the Late Middle Ages and Renaissance*, Bloomington.

  1998, *The Sound of Medieval Song*, Oxford.

McKinnon, James W. 1978, 'Representations of the mass in medieval and Renaissance art', *Journal of the American Musicological Society* 31: 21–52.

  1986, 'A cappella doctrine versus a cappella practice: a necessary distinction', in Marc Honegger & Christian Meyer (eds.), *La Musique et le Rite Sacré et Profane: Actes du XIIIe Congrès de la Société Internationale de Musicologie, Strasbourg, . . . 1982*, Strasbourg: 238–42.

Mertin, Josef 1986, *Early Music: Approaches to Performance Practice*, New York; translation by Siegmund Levarie of *Alte Musik: Wege zur Aufführungspraxis* 2nd edn, Vienna, 1978.

Moll, Kevin 1988, 'Analyzing Four-Voice Vertical Sonorities in Fifteenth-Century Sacred Polyphony', Masters thesis, New England Conservatory of Music.

  1995, 'Structural Determinants in Polyphony for the Mass Ordinary from French and Related Sources (ca. 1320–1410)', Ph.D. dissertation, Stanford University.

  (ed.) 1997, *Counterpoint and Compositional Process in the Time of Dufay: Perspectives from German Musicology*, New York.

Montagu, Jeremy 1974, 'Early percussion techniques', *Early Music* 2: 20–4.

  1975, 'The "Authentic" sound of early music', *Early Music* 3: 242–3.

Müller-Blattau, Joseph 1923, *Grundzüge einer Geschichte der Fuge*, Königsberg.

Munrow, David 1973, 'The art of courtly love', *Early Music* 1: 195–9.

  1976, *Instruments of the Middle Ages and Renaissance*, Oxford.

Myers, Herbert W. 1983, 'The *Mary Rose* "shawm"', *Early Music* 11: 358–60.

Nagy, Michael (ed.) 1994, *'Musik muss man machen': Eine Festgabe für Josef Mertin zum neunzigsten Geburtstag am 21. Marz 1994*, Vienna.

Noble, Jeremy 2001, review of Cantica Symphonia ('Dufay Masses', Stradivarius STR33569), *International Record Review* 2/3: 66–7.

Novack, Saul 1970, 'Fusion of design and tonal order in mass and motet: Josquin Desprez and Heinrich Isaac', *The Music Forum* 2: 187–263.

1976, 'Tonal tendencies in Josquin's use of harmony', in Edward Lowinsky & Bonnie Blackburn (eds.), *Josquin des Prez: Proceedings of the International Josquin Festival-Conference . . . 1971*, Oxford: 317–33.

1983, 'The analysis of pre-Baroque music', in David Beach (ed.), *Aspects of Schenkerian Theory*, New Haven: 113–33.

Page, Christopher 1974, 'Medieval fiddle construction', *Early Music* 2: 166–7.

1977, 'Machaut's "pupil" Deschamps on the performance of music', *Early Music* 5: 484–91.

1980, review of the Clemencic Consort ('Les Cantigas de Santa Maria', Harmonia Mundi MH 977–979), *Early Music* 8: 117–19.

1982, 'The performance of songs in late medieval France: a new source', *Early Music* 10: 441–50.

1987, *Voices and Instruments of the Middle Ages*, London.

1988, 'The performance of ars antiqua motets', *Early Music* 16: 147–64.

1989a, *The Owl and the Nightingale: Musical Life and Ideas in France 1100–1300*, London.

1989b, 'Polyphony before 1400', in Howard Mayer Brown & Stanley Sadie, 1989: 79–104.

1992a, 'The English *a cappella* heresy', in Tess Knighton & David Fallows (eds.), *Companion to Medieval and Renaissance Music*, London: 23–9.

1992b, 'Going beyond the limits: experiments with vocalization in the French chanson, 1340–1440', *Early Music* 20: 447–59.

1993a, *Discarding Images: Reflections on Music and Culture in Medieval France*, Oxford.

1993b, 'The English *a cappella* Renaissance', *Early Music* 21: 452–71.

1996, 'Reading and reminiscence: Tinctoris on the beauty of music', *Journal of the American Musicological Society* 49: 1–31.

1997, 'Listening to the trouvères', *Early Music* 25: 639–59.

2000, 'Around the performance of a 13th-century motet', *Early Music* 28: 343–57.

Panum, Hortense 1915, *Middelalderens Strengeinstrumenter og deres Forløbere i Oldtiden*, Copenhagen.

Pass, Walter 1994, '"Das Kunstwerk nicht nur der Form nach untersuchen, sondern daruber hinaus es auch Musik werden zu lassen": Rudolf von Ficker als Vorbild und Lehrer Josef Mertins', in Nagy 1994: 113–26.

Pelinski, Ramón 1975, 'Zusammenklang und Aufbau in den Motetten Machauts', *Die Musikforschung* 28: 62–71.

Perkins, Leeman 1981, 'Euphony – a working definition', in Daniel Heartz & Bonnie Wade (eds.), *International Musicological Society: Report of the Twelfth Congress Berkeley 1977*, Kassel: 620–1.

Perne, François-Louis 1827, 'Notice sur les manuscrits relatifs à la musique, qui existent dans les principales bibliothèques de l'Europe,' *Revue musicale* 1: 231–7.

Pestell, Richard 1987, 'Medieval art and the performance of medieval music', *Early Music* 15: 56–68.

Petropoulos, Jonathan 2000, *The Faustian Bargain: The Art World in Nazi Germany*, London.

Pirro, André 1931, 'Remarques sur l'exécution musicale, de la fin du 14e au milieu du 15e siècle', *Société internationale de Musicologie, Premier Congres Liège (1930): compte rendu*, Burnham: 55–65.

1940, *Histoire de la Musique de la fin du XIVe siècle à la fin du XVIe*, Manuels d'Histoire de l'Art, Paris.

Pirrotta, Nino 1954, *The Music of Fourteenth Century Italy* I, Corpus Mensurabilis Musicae 8, n.p., American Institute of Musicology.

Plumley, Yolanda 1990, 'Style and Structure in the Late Fourteenth-Century Chanson', Ph.D. thesis, University of Exeter.

1996, *The Grammar of 14th Century Melody: Tonal Organization and Compositional Process in the Chansons of Guillaume de Machaut and the Ars Subtilior*, New York.

Polk, Keith 1992, *German Instrumental Music of the Middle Ages*, Cambridge.

Popper, Karl 1970, 'Normal science and its dangers', in Imre Lakatos and Alan Musgrave (eds.), *Criticism and the Growth of Knowledge*, Cambridge: 51–8.

1985, 'Evolutionary epistemology', 1973 lecture first published 1975, in David Miller (ed.), *Popper Selections*, Princeton: 78–86.

Potter, Pamela 1991a: 'The Deutsche Musikgesellschaft, 1918–1938', *Journal of Musicological Research* 11: 151–76.

1991b: 'Trends in German Musicology, 1918–1945: The Effects of Method-ological, Ideological, and Institutional Change on the Writing of Music History', Ph.D. Yale, UMI 9136183.

1994, 'German musicology and early music performance, 1918–1933', in Bryan Gilliam (ed.), *Musicology and Performance during the Weimar Republic*, Cambridge: 94–106 & 195–9.

1996, 'Musicology under Hitler: new sources in context', *Journal of the American Musicological Society* 49: 70–113.

1998, *Most German of the Arts: Musicology and society from the Weimar republic to the end of Hitler's Reich*, New Haven and London.

1999, 'From Jewish exile in Germany to German scholar in America: Alfred Einstein's emigration', in Reinhold Brinkmann & Christoph Wolff (eds.), *Driven into Paradise: The Musical Migration from Nazi Germany to the United States*, Berkeley: 298–321.

2001, 'Besseler, Heinrich', in *The New Grove Dictionary of Music and Musicians, Second Edition*, London: vol. III, 489–90.

Pratt, Waldo Selden 1907, *The History of Music*, New York.

Ramsbotham, A. 1933, *The Old Hall Manuscript*, Burnham.

Reaney, Gilbert 1953, 'Fourteenth-century harmony and the ballades, rondeaux and virelais of Guillaume de Machaut', *Musica Disciplina* 7: 129–46.

1954, 'Voices and instruments in the music of Guillaume de Machaut', in Wilfried Brennecke *et al.* (eds.), *Bericht über den internationalen Musikwissen-schaftlichen Kongress Bamberg 1953*, Kassel: 245–8. Expanded as Reaney 1956.

(ed.) 1955, *Early Fifteenth Century Music I*, Corpus Mensurabilis Musicae 11, n.p., American Institute of Musicology.

1956, 'Voices and instruments in the music of Guillaume de Machaut', *Revue belge de Musicologie* 10: 3–10, 93–104.

1966, 'The performance of medieval music', in Jan La Rue (ed.), *Aspects of Medieval and Renaissance Music: A Birthday Offering to Gustave Reese*, New York: 704–22; reissued New York, 1978.

1968, 'Notes on the harmonic technique of Guillaume de Machaut', in Hans Tischler (ed.), *Essays in Musicology: A Birthday Offering for Willi Apel*, Bloomington: 63–8.

1969, 'Text underlay in early fifteenth-century musical manuscripts', in Gustave Reese & Robert J. Snow (eds.), *Essays in Musicology in Honor of Dragan Plamenac*, Pittsburgh: 245–51.

1977, 'The part played by instruments in the music of Guillaume de Machaut', *Studi musicali* 1: 3–11.

Reese, Gustave 1940, *Music in the Middle Ages*, New York.

'The Register of Early Instruments', *Early Music* 1 (1973): 179–90; 2 (1974): 61–73; cumulative list issued as supplements to issues of April & July 1975 and April & October 1976.

'The Register of Early Music', *Early Music* 1 (1973): 45–58, 120–4, 173–7, 255–9; 2 (1974): 211–13; cumulative lists for 1974, 75 and 76 issued annually as a supplement to the January issue. From 1977 published on separate subscription.

Rehding, Alexander 2000, 'The quest for the origins of music in Germany circa 1900', *Journal of the American Musicological Society* 53: 345–85.

2001, 'Trial scenes at Nuremberg', *Music Analysis* 20: 239–67.

Reimer, Erich 1972, *Johannes Garlandia: de mensurabili musica*, Beihefte zum Archiv für Musikwissenschaft 10, Wiesbaden.

Reiss, Josef 1924–5, 'Pauli Paulirini de Praga Tractatus de musica (etwa 1460)', *Zeitschrift für Musikwissenschaft* 7: 259–64.

Ribera y Tarragó, Julián 1924–5, *La Música andaluza medieval en Europa*, Madrid.

1927, *Historia de la Música árabe medieval y su influencia en la Española*, Madrid.

1928, *Disertaciones y Opúsculos* II, Madrid.

Riemann, (Carl) Hugo 1878, *Studien zur Geschichte der Notenschrift*, Leipzig; repr. Hildesheim, 1970.

1882, *Musik-Lexikon*, Leipzig; 2/1884, 3/1887, 4/1894 (Eng. trans. Shedlock, *Dictionary of Music* (London, 1893–7)), 5/1900, 6/1905, 7/1909.

1888, *Katechismus der Musikgeschichte*, Leipzig (Eng. trans. as *Catechism of Musical History*, London 1892); 2/1901, 3/1906, 4/1910.

1892, *Sechs bisher nicht gedruckte dreistimmige Chansons (für Tenor, Diskant und Kontratenor) von Gilles Binchois (c. 1425) aus dem Codex Mus. Ms. 3192 der Münchener Hof- und Staatsbibliothek in moderne Notierung übertragen mit neuem (deutschem) Text herausgegeben von Dr. Hugo Riemann. Also Manuscript gedruckt*, Wiesbaden.

1893, *Illustrationen zur Musikgeschichte. I: Weltlicher mehrstimmiger Gesang im 13.–16. Jahrhundert*, Wiesbaden.

1898, *Geschichte der Musiktheorie im IX-XIX Jahrhundert*, Leipzig; trans. Raymond Haggh, *History of Music Theory... by Hugo Riemann*, Lincoln, 1962.

1904–5, 'Zwei falsch gelöste Kanons in Stainer's "Dufay"', *Zeitschrift der internationalen Musikgesellschaft* 6: 466–9.

1905, *Handbuch der Musikgeschichte* I/2, Leipzig.

1905–6, 'Das Kunstlied im 14.-15. Jahrhundert', *Sammelbände der internationalen Musikgesellschaft* 7: 529–50.

1906, *Hausmusik aus alter Zeit: Intime Gesänge mit Instrumental-Begleitung aus dem 14. bis 15. Jahrh. in ihrer Originalgestalt in die heutige Notenschrift übertragen und mit Vortragsbezeichnung versehen von Prof. Dr. Hugo Riemann mit Originaltext und deutscher übersetzung*, 3 vols., score and parts, Leipzig.

1908, *Kleines Handbuch der Musikgeschichte*, Leipzig.

1912, *Musikgeschichte in Beispielen . . . mit Erläuterungen von Dr Arnold Schering*, Leipzig, following a 1911 edition by Riemann with the examples alone.

Rietsch, Heinrich 1913, *Gesänge von Frauenlob, Reinmar v. Zweiter und Alexander*, Denkmäler der Tonkunst Österreich, XX. Jahrgang, Zweiter Teil, 41. Band, Vienna.

Rockstro, W. S. 1886, *A General History of Music*, London.

Rokseth, Yvonne 1935–9, *Polyphonies du XIIIe Siècle: Le manuscrit H 196 de la Faculté de Médecine de Montpellier*, Paris.

1960, 'The instrumental music of the middle ages and early sixteenth century', in Dom Anselm Hughes & Gerald Abraham (eds.), *The New Oxford History of Music III: Ars Nova and the Renaissance 1300–1540*, Oxford: 406–65.

Ruth-Sommer, Hermann 1916, *Alte Musikinstrumente: Ein Leitfaden für Sammler*, Berlin.

Sachs, Curt 1920, *Handbuch der Musikinstrumentenkunde*, Leipzig.

1923, *Die Musikinstrumente*, Breslau.

Sachs, Klaus-Jürgen 1974, *Der Contrapunctus im 14. und 15. Jahrhundert*, Beihefte zum Archiv für Musikwissenschaft 13, Wiesbaden.

Salop, Arnold 1971, 'The secular polyphony of Guillaume de Machaut', chapter 2 of *Studies in the History of Musical Style*, Detroit: 39–80 and 323–6.

Salzer, Felix 1952, *Structural Hearing*, New York; R/1962.

1967, 'Tonality in early medieval polyphony: towards a history of tonality', *The Music Forum* 1: 35–98.

Salzer, Felix & Schachter, Carl 1969, *Counterpoint in Composition: The Study of Voice Leading*, New York.

Schachter, Carl 1970, 'Landini's treatment of consonance and dissonance: a study in fourteenth-century counterpoint', *The Music Forum* 2: 130–86.

Schering, Arnold 1911–12, 'Das kolorierte Orgelmadrigal des Trecento', *Sammelbände der internationalen Musik-Gesellschaft* 13: 172–204.

1912, *Die niederländische Orgelmesse im Zeitalter des Josquin: Eine stilkritische Untersuchung*, Leipzig; repr. Amsterdam, 1971.

1913–14, reply to Leichtentritt, *Zeitschrift der internationalen Musikgesellschaft* 15: 11–16.

1914a, *Studien zur Musikgeschichte der Frührenaissance*, Leipzig.

(ed.) 1914b, Arrey von Dommer *Handbuch der Musikgeschichte*, Leipzig, 3/1914.

1931 a, *Aufführungspraxis alter Musik*, Leipzig; reissued Wiesbaden 1969 and Wilhelmshaven 1975.

1931 b, *Geschichte der Musik in Beispielen*, Leipzig.

Schipperges, Thomas 1999, 'Besseler, Heinrich', in Ludwig Finscher (ed.), *Die Musik in Geschichte und Gegenwart . . . Zweite . . . Ausgabe*, Personenteil 2, Kassel: cols. 1514–20.

Schletterer, Hans Michael 1884, *Studien zur Geschichte der französischn Musik* I, Berlin.

Schluter, Joseph 1863, *Allgemeine Geschichte der Musik in übersichtliches Darstellung*, Leipzig.

Schmidt-Görg, Joseph 1946, *Musik der Gotik*, Bonn.

Schneider, Marius 1931, *Die Ars nova des XIV. Jahrhunderts in Frankreich und Italien*, Potsdam.

  1934, *Geschichte der Mehrstimmigkeit: Historische und phänomenologische Studien*, n.p.; 2nd edn Tutzing, 1969.

Schneider, Max (ed.) 1924, *Sylvestro Ganassi, Regola Rubertina*, Leipzig.

Schoop, Hans 1971, *Entstehung und Verwendung der Handschrift Oxford, Bodleian, Canonici misc. 213*, Bern.

Schrade, Leo 1931, *Die handschriftliche Ueberlieferung der ältesten Instrumentalmusik*, Lahr.

  (ed.) 1931, *Sebastian Virdung: Musica getuscht*, Kassel.

  (ed.) 1956, Polyphonic Music of the Fourteenth Century I: *The Roman de Fauvel, The Works of Philippe de Vitry, French Cycles of the Ordinarium Missae*; II-III: *The Works of Guillaume de Machaut*; IV: *The Works of Francesco Landini*, Monaco.

Seidel, Wilhelm 1995, 'Ältere und neuere Musik. Über Hugo Riemanns Bild der Musikgeschichte', in Giselher Schubert (ed.), *Alte Musik im 20. Jahrhundert: Wandlungen und Formen ihrer Rezeption*, Mainz: 30–8.

Siebenkäs, Dieter 1999, 'Bellermann: 2. Heinrich', in Ludwig Finscher (ed.), *Die Musik in Geschichte und Gegenwart . . . Zweite . . . Ausgabe*, Personenteil 2, Kassel: col. 999.

Slavin, Denis 1989, 'Genre, final and range: unique sorting procedures in a fifteenth-century chansonnier', *Musica Disciplina* 43: 115–39.

  1991, 'In support of 'heresy': manuscript evidence for the *a cappella* performance of early 15th-century songs', *Early Music* 19: 179–90.

Sloboda, John & Edworthy, Judy 1981, 'Attending to two melodies at once: the effect of key relatedness', *Psychology of Music* 9: 39–43.

Sperber, Dan 1996, *Explaining Culture: A Naturalistic Approach*, Oxford.

Springer, Hermann 1911–12, 'Der Anteil der Instrumentalmusik an der Literatur des 14.–16. Jahrhunderts', *Zeitschrift der internationalen Musik-Gesellschaft* 13: 265–9.

Stainer, Sir John 1895–6, 'A fifteenth-century MS. book of vocal music in the Bodleian Library, Oxford', *Proccedings of the Musical Association* 22: 1–22.

Stainer, J. F. R. & Stainer, C. (eds.) 1898, *Dufay and his Contemporaries: Fifty Compositions . . . transcribed from MS. Canonici misc. 213*, London.

Steinzor, Curt Efram 1989, *American Musicologists, c. 1890–1945: A Bio-bibliographical Sourcebook to the Formative Period*, New York.

Strohm, Reinhard & Blackburn, Bonnie J. 2001, *Music as Concept and Practice in the Late Middle Ages*, The New Oxford History of Music, vol. III.1, New Edition, Oxford.

Sulloway, Frank J. 1996, *Born to Rebel: Birth Order, Family Dynamics, and Creative Lives*, New York.

Taruskin, Richard 1995, *Text and Act: Essays on Music and Performance*, Oxford.

Tietze, Gwendolyn 2000a, 'Rudolf Ficker, Thrasybulos Georgiades, and Ernst Apfel', unpublished seminar paper, King's College, London.

2000b, '"Nicht nur zu historischem Verständnis, sondern zu lebendiger Wirkung wiederstehen": Heinrich Besseler's *Musik des Mittelalters und der Renaissance*, 1931', unpublished M.Mus. thesis, King's College, London.

Tomlinson, Gary 1993, *Music in Renaissance Magic: Towards a Historiography of Others*, Chicago.

Traub, Andreas 1994, 'Eine Perotin-Bearbeitung Hindemiths', *Hindemith Jahrbuch* 23: 30–60.

Treitler, Leo 1989, *Music and the Historical Imagination*, Cambridge, Mass.

Trowell, Brian 1968, review of Studio der frühen Musik disc ('Lyric Songs and Poems, 1200–1320', AWT9487, SAWT9487), *Gramophone* 45: 499.

Uridge, Michael 1980, 'Popular early music', letter in *Early Music* 8: 575–6.

Ursprung, Otto 1923, 'Vier Studien zur Geschichte des deutschen Liedes', *Archiv für Musikwissenschaft* 5: 11–30.

1934, 'Um die Frage nach dem arabischen bzw. maurischen Einfluß auf die abendländische Musik des Mittelalters', *Zeitschrift für Musikwissenschaft* 16: 129–41 & 355–7.

van den Borren, Charles 1938, 'La pureté du style et i'interpretation dc la musique du moyen-age', *La Revue Internationale de Musique* 1: 96–102, 273–9.

1960, 'Dufay and his School', chapter VII of Dom Anselm Hughes & Gerald Abraham (eds.), *The New Oxford History of Music III: Ars Nova and the Renaissance 1300–1540*, Oxford.

van der Werf, Hendrik 1972, *The Chansons of the Troubadours and Trouvères: A Study of the Melodies and Their Relation to the Poems*, Utrecht.

von der Hagen, Friedrich Heinrich 1838, *Minnesinger, Deutsche Liederdichter des zwölften, dreizehnten und vierzehnten Jahrhunderts*, Leipzig.

von Schlosser, Julius 1920a, *Alte Musikinstrumente*, Vienna.

1920b, *Die Sammlung alter Musikinstrumente*, Vienna.

Walther, Johann Gottfried 1732, *Musikalisches Lexikon*, Leipzig.

Wangermée, Robert 1980, 'Fétis, (1) François-Joseph', *The New Grove Dictionary of Music and Musicians*, London: vol. VI, 512; 2/2001: vol. VIII, 746–9 (revised by Katharine Ellis).

Wegman, Rob 1994, *Born for the Muses: The Life and Masses of Jacob Obrecht*, Oxford.

1998, ' "Das musikalischen Hören" in the Middle Ages and Renaissance: Perspectives from Pre-War Germany', *The Musical Quarterly* 82: 434–54.

Wekerlin, Jean-Baptiste 1853–7, *Echos du Temps Passé*, 3 vols., Paris.

Wessel, David 1979, 'Timbre space as a musical control structure', *Computer Music Journal* 3/2: 45–52.

Wolf, Johannes 1899–1900, review of Stainer 1898, *Sammelbände der internationalen Musikgesellschaft* 1: 150–63, 330.

1901, *Musica Fiorentina nel Secolo XIV. (Aus den Handschriften in moderne Notation übertragen von Dr. Johannes Wolf)*, La Nuova Musica Vol. II, Serie 4a. disp. 46, Florence.

1901–02, 'Florenz in der Musikgeschichte des 14. Jahrhunderts', *Sammelbände der internationalen Musikgesellschaft* 3: 599–646.

1904, *Geschichte der Mensuralnotation*, Leipzig.

1913, *Handbuch der Notationskunde* I, Leipzig.

1913–14, 'Ein Beitrag zur Diskantlehre des 14. Jahrhunderts', *Sammelbände der internationalen Musikgesellschaft* 15: 504–34.

1918, 'Die Tänze des Mittelalters: Eine Untersuchung des Wesens der ältesten Instrumentalmusik', *Archiv für Musikwissenschaft* 1: 10–42.

1925, *Geschichte der Musik in allgemeinverständlicher Form, Erster Teil: 'Die Entwicklung der Musik bis etwa 1600'*, Wissenschaft und Bildung: Einzeldarstellungen aus allen Gebieten des Wissens 203, Leipzig.

1926, *Sing- und Spielmusik aus älterer Zeit herausgegeben als Beispielband zur Allgemeinen Musikgeschichte*, Wissenschaft und Bildung: Einzeldarstellungen aus allen Gebieten des Wissens 218, Leipzig.

1926–7, *Chor- und Hausmusik aus alter Zeit* Heft I: Gesänge für gemischen Chor, Berlin, 1926; Heft II: Gesänge für gemischen Chor, Berlin, 1927; Heft III: Instrumentalmusik, Berlin, 1927; Heft IV: Instrumentalmusik, Berlin, 1927.

Wooldridge, H. E. 1902–03, 'The latest collection of early English music' (review of Early Bodleian Music 2), *Sammelbände der internationalen Musikgesellschaft* 4: 570–6.

1905, *The Polyphonic Period, Part II: Method of Musical Art, 1300–1600*, The Oxford History of Music, vol. II, Oxford.

Wright, Craig 1978, 'Performance practices at the cathedral of Cambrai 1475–1550', *The Musical Quarterly* 64: 295–328.

1979, *Music at the Court of Burgundy 1364–1419: A Documentary History*, Musicological Studies 28, Henryville.

1981, 'Voices and instruments in the art music of Northern France during the 15th century: a conspectus', in Daniel Heartz & Bonnie Wade (eds.), *International Musicological Society: Report of the Twelfth Congress Berkeley 1977*, Kassel: 643–9.

Wright, Lawrence 1980, review of René Jacobs disc ('Guillaume de Machaut: Le Livre du Voir Dit, La Messe de Nostre Dame', Mirror Music 0006-9), *Early Music* 8: 408–11.

Zipay, Terry Lee 1983, 'Closure in the Motets of Machaut', Ph.D. dissertation, State University of New York at Buffalo, UMI 8312465.

Index

Abraham, Gerald, 84
a cappella enthusiasts, 101, 107–8, 112, 116–17,
    122–3, 138, 147, 235
    membership, 132, 133–4, 150, 284 n.129
a cappella ideal, 90, 163, 288 n.21
a cappella performance
    discussed before *c*.1910, 20, 21–3, 35, 42, 44
    discussed *c*.1920–75, 53, 78, 80, 88–104, 272
        n.206, 274 n.239, 280 n.45
    discussed from *c*.1980, 13–14, 86, 104–50
    as a paradigm, 225, 227–8, 230–1
    performances before *c*.1980, 51
    on record before *c*.1980, 82, 84, 85, 89,
        154–6, 275 n.264, 276–7 n.274
    and musical analysis, 164–5, 172–3, 205,
        289–90 n.58
    see also medieval music: vocalisation
Acourt, *Je demande ma bienvenue*, 25
Adam de la Halle, 17, 18, 40, 67, 160, 165,
    167, 254
    A Dieu commant amouretes, 268 n.118
    Au cuer/Je ne/Jolietement, 50, 96, 268 n.118
    Fi maris de vostre amour, 268 n.118
    Le Jeu de Robin et Marion, 17
    Tant con je vivrai, 17, 263 n.8
Adler, Guido, 16, 51, 70, 75, 234, 262 n.3, 272
    n.198
    contra Riemann, 43–4, 46, 53, 69, 86, 88,
        103, 192, 277 n.1, 297–8 n.20
    Trent codices edition, 21, 27
Ad regnum/Noster, 154
Ad solitum vomitum/Regnat, 269 n.138
A la clarte/Et illuminare, 268 n.118
Al eerbaerheit weinsch, 268 n.118
Allaire, Gaston, 206
Alleluia pascha nostrum, 49, 267 n.118
Ambros, August Wilhelm, 16, 19, 20, 160, 166
American Institute of Musicology, 78, 79–80,
    187, 274 n.243
American Musicological Society, 150,
    278 n.22

anachronism in musicology, *see* musicology:
    anachronism
Anima mea/Descendi/Alma, 154
Anonymous 4 (group), 138
Anonymous IV (theorist), 157–8
anonymous refereeing, 237–8
Anthologie Sonore, 82, 83, 84, 85, 89, 121, 154,
    273 n.223, 276 n.273, 277 n.6
Anthonello da Caserta, *Amours m'a le cuer mis*,
    114
Apel, Willi, 72, 198, 290–1 n.87
    on performance, 80–1, 82, 85, 188
    and analysis, 179–82, 183, 187, 199, 207
Apfel, Ernst, 186–7, 188, 192, 197, 201, 207,
    234, 240
Aquitanian polyphony, 48, 57, 195
Arabic influence, *see* 'oriental' styles
Armstrong, Flt. Lt. R. N., 142
Arnold, Denis, 97–8, 117
ars antiqua, 3, 48, 118, 290 n.63
ars nova, 28–9, 166, 201, 228
    French, 48, 52, 67, 171, 172, 174, 198, 200,
        290 n.63
    Italian, 29, 32, 40, 42–3, 51–2, 67, 163, 168
ars subtilior, 28, 113–15, 117, 137, 179–82, 198–9
Atlas, Allan, 226
Aubin, Hermann, 250
Aubry, Pierre, 34, 35–6, 48, 50, 265 n.66,
    265–6 n.67
Austria, concerts of medieval music, 55–7
    emigration from, 66, 69, 179
authenticity, 5, 109, 140, 149, 153, 170, 184,
    223, 259
Ave regina/Alma redemptoris mater/Alma, 268 n.118

Bach, Johann Sebastian, 141
Baines, Anthony, 142
Balkin, J. M., 218, 233, 235
Banks, Jon, 153, 230
Barbieri, F. A., 37, 266 n.72
bards, 41

Bartolomeo da Bologna, *Que pena maior*, 276 n.272

Bashour, Frederick, 196–8, 201, 205, 227

Baude Cordier
Amans ames secretement, 114
Se cuer d'amant, 114
as harpist, 117

Bayerische Rundfunk (Bavarian Radio), 57, 84

BBC, 1, 2, 113, 118, 133, 278 n.28, 279 n.35, n.42, 281 n.69, 285 n.156

Beatles, The, 97–8, 279 n.41, n.42

Beck, Jean, 48

Beckett, John, 114

Beethoven centenary festival, 55–6, 58, 140

Bele Ysabelot, 268 n.118; *see also Entre Copin*

Bellermann, Heinrich, 161, 263 n.11, 264 n.26, 288 n.21

Benet, John, 29

Bent, Margaret, 192, 208–9, 226, 228, 281 n.60, 283 n.112, 299 n.43

Berg, Alban, 273 n.231

Berger, Christian, 207, 228, 293 n.130

Berger, Karol, 228, 276 n.270

Berkeley treatise, 293 n.131

Berlin, 59, 248, 269 n.133

Bernart de Ventadorn, *Lancan vei la folha*, 268 n.118

Berry, Mary, 97

Besseler, Heinrich, 47, 72, 139, 227, 274 n.238
attitudes and beliefs, 169–79, 289 nn.51–2
on *a cappella* performance, 48, 88–92, 99, 172–3, 289–90 n.58
Die Musik des Mittelalters, 65, 70–1, 173–4, 175, 248
contrasted with Ficker, 169–70, 174–8, 197, 227, 234, 240
hearing of music, 223, 243, 294 n.140
influence, 67, 100, 178–9, 184, 186, 257
'Musik…in der Hamburger Musikhalle', 51–2, 88–9, 171–3, 175, 223–4
and National Socialism, 174, 248–51, 269 n.133, 274 n.243
reaction to, 187, 188, 203

Binchois, Gilles, 19, 21, 50, 51, 54, 131
Adieu m'amour, 268 n.118
Adieu mon amoureuse joye, 131
Adieu adieu mon joyeulx souvenir, 268 n.118
A solus ortu cardine, 154
De plus en plus, 83
Lyesse m'a mandé, 268 n.118
Margarite fleur de valeur, 268 n.118
Plains de plours, 268 n.118
Sanctus, 154
Vostre tres doulx regart, 264 n.25

Binkley, Thomas, 66, 77, 97–8, 107, 136, 144, 279 n.32

Bird, Alexander, 297 n.12, 298 n.34

Blachly, Alexander, 134

Blume, Friedrich, 59, 72, 250, 276 n.267

Boccaccio, Giovanni, 40
Decameron, 87

Boeke, Kees, 85

Boen, Johannes, 293 n.134

Boetticher, Wolfgang, 250–1

Botstein, Leon, 213, 295 n.149

Bottée de Toulmon, A., 18, 263 n.18

Bourdieu, Pierre, 298 n.34

Bowers, Roger, 110, 133, 226, 284 n.127, 286 n.178

Bowles, Edmund, 93–4, 96, 278 n.23

Boydell, Barra, 145

Breidert, Fritz, 290 n.69

Breitkopf & Härtel, 35, 36, 37

Britain (England)
early music boom, 141–3
musicology, 107, 122–3, 132, 147–8, 184
polyphony, 41, 120, 177, 186; compared to France and Italy, 28–30, 71, 119–20, 131
research assessment, 246–7, 252
singing tradition, 25, 68, 89, 114–15, 127–30, 147
treatises, 16
see also a cappella enthusiasts
see also nationalism

Brollo, Bartolomeo, *O celestial lume*, 83

Brothers, Thomas, 228, 293 n.128

Brown, Howard Mayer, 99, 110, 133, 147–50, 235, 280 n.45, 286 n.178
'heresy', 121, 122, 148–9, 150
New Grove Handbook, 118, 119–20, 152

Brücker, Fritz, 63

Brumans est mors, see Homo/Homo

Buck, Percy, 67, 263 n.7

Buhle, Edward, 35

Bukofzer, Manfred, 72

Burckhardt, Jacob, 29, 31, 45, 162

Burgundy, court of, 58, 109, 154

Burney, Charles, 16, 17, 18, 264 n.31

Burstyn, Shai, 212, 294 n.135, 295 n.149

Busnois, Antoine, 19
Corps digne/Dieu quel mariage, 19
Faites de moy, 280 n.45
In hydraulis, 44

Busse Berger, Anna Maria, 277 n.8, 288 n.21

Butt, John, 296 n.8

Caldwell, John, 106, 138

Cambrai cathedral, 102, 109, 110, 134

Canonici manuscript, *see* manuscripts: Oxford

Cantica Symphonica, 85
Cantigas de Santa Maria, 65, 134, 136
Cape, Safford, 75, 77, 83–4, 89, 95, 140, 273 n.223, 283 n.111
Capella Antiqua München, 95
Capella Cordina, 156, 276 n.274, 278 n.16
Cara, Marchetto, 19
Carapetyan, Armen, 274 n.243
Carmina burana, 97, 138; *see also* Orff
Carpenter, R. H. S., 142
Castil-Blaze, 161
Cesaris, Johannes, 54, 265 n.55, 288 n.24
    A l'aventure, 81
Charité, 265 n.55
Chorale Yvonne Gouverné, 89, 154–5
Christensen, Dieter, 34, 265 n.60
Chusid, Martin, 272 n.208
Ciconia, Johannes, 174
Clemencic Ensemble, 120, 281 n.60
Clemencic, René, 76, 85, 134–5, 138, 273 n.231, 284 n.133
Cleriadus et Meliadice, 106, 117, 133, 281 n.64
conductus, 19, 29, 59, 94, 111, 117–18, 119, 131, 167, 172
Confort d'amours, 117
Congaudeant catholici, 155
Congaudeant turbe, 154
Connor, Kimberly, 192, *204*, 205–6, 291 n.101
Consort of Musick, 135, 282 n.84
Cook, Peter, 1–3
Cooke, J., 131
Cordiforme chansonnier, *see* manuscripts: Paris
Coucy, Chatelain de, 16
Coussemaker, Edmond de, 16, 19, 165
    motet publications, 17, 24, 48, 234
    on performance, 19–20, 21, 35, 36, 59, 263 n.18
Covey-Crump, Rogers, 113–14, 115, 281 n.69
Crocker, Richard, 197, 200–1, 223, 227
Curtis, Gareth, 109, 133

Dahlhaus, Carl, 287 n.1
Danse royal, 268 n.118
Dart, Thurston, 74–5, 77, 84–5
Dauby, Lina, 83
Davidson, Jim, 274 n.243, 275 n.250
Davies, Peter, 138–9
Davies, Timothy, 138
Dawkins, Richard, 232
de la Marche, Olivier, 26, 264 n.37
Deo confitemini, 267 n.118
Deroubaix, Jeanne, 84, 275 n.261
Der wallt hat sich entlawbet, 51, 88, 268 n.118
Descendit de coelis, 269 n.138

Deschamps, Eustache, 113, 132
    Art de dictier, 105
Deutsche Gesellschaft für Musikwissenschaft, 247–8, 250, 271 n.183
Deutsche Musikgesellschaft, 247–8, 270 n.156
de Van, Guillaume (William Devan), 79–80, 81, 274 n.243
    and National Socialism, 250, 274 n.243
    recordings by, 89, 273 n.231, 277 n.6
de Vries, Willem, 274 n.243
Dick, Friedrich, 63
Dischner, Oskar, 54, 57
Dobson, Eric, 106
Dolmetsch, Arnold, 278 n.22
Dömling, Wolfgang, 292 n.118
Dommer, Arrey von, 165
Donington, Robert, 93–4, 148, 149, 278 n.22
Droz, Eugénie, 55
du Fay, Guillaume, 54, 90, 103, 132, 172, 174–7, 196, 265 n.55, 289–90 n.58
    editions of, 42, 50, 54, 79–80, 274 n.243
    performance of, 25–6, 70, 90, 109, 172
    performances of, 24–5, 50, 51, 172, 268 n.118, 276 n.270
    recordings of, 85, 89, 136, 138–9
    Alma redemptoris mater, 50, 83, 172, 268 n.118
    Ave regina celorum, 109
    Ce jour de l'an, 25, 85
    Ce moys de may, 19, 276 n.271
    Christe redemptor omnium, 154, 275 n.254
    Conditor alme siderum, 154, 275 n.254
    Et in terra [Gloria] ad modum tubae, 44
    Estrines moy, 25–6
    Je prens congié, 19
    Mass *Ecce ancilla domini*, 134
    Mass for St Anthony of Padua, 109
    Mass *Se la face ay pale*, 83, 89
    Par droit je puis, 276 n.270
    Resveilles vous, 81, 85
    Salve regina, 50
    Vergine bella, 268 n.118
    Vostre bruit, 276 n.273
Dunstable [Dunstaple], John, 21, 25, 29, 70, 90, 131
    O rosa bella, 22
    Preco / Precursor, 269 n.138
    Quam pulcra es, 51, 88, 172, 268 n.118
Dyer, Louise, 89

Early Bodleian Music, 28, 162, 265 n.55
Early Music, influence of, 107, 113, 123, 133, 141–7, 235, 238, 284 n.129, n.133
early music business, 141–6
Early Music Consort of London, 86, 96, 269 n.143, 279 n.32

Early Music Group of Oxford, 105
Early Music Group of York, 105, 107
Early Music Shop, 146
Earp, Lawrence, 122, 149–50, 279 n.32, 282
    n.77, n.84, 283 n.104, 287 n.5
Eggebrecht, Hans Heinrich, 292 n.118
Eichenauer, Richard, 168, 248, 271 n.163
Einstein, Alfred, 38, 53, 56, 72
    and National Socialism, 247, 248, 250, 269
        n.133, 270 n.156
Ein vrouleen edel, 268 n.118
Ellinwood, Leonard, 68, 77–8, 79, 80
England, *see* Britain
En mal la rousée, 154
Ensemble Gilles Binchois, 85, 138
Ensemble Organum, 120, 138, 206, 209
Ensemble Project Ars Nova, 138, 139–40
Ensemble Ricercare de Zurich, 135–6
Entre Copin/Je me cuidoie/Bele Ysabelot, 51, 268
    n.118
Er hör libste Frau, 268 n.118
Erkmann, Rudolf, 271 n.177
Estampie royal, 268 n.118
Evans, Richard, 298–9 n.37, 299
    n.45
Everist, Mark, 133, 136

Fallows, David, 86, 107, 108, 112, 119, 122,
    132–8 *passim*, 148, 149, 151–2, 230, 278
        n.23, 284 n.128, 286 n.180, 298 n.21
    on the douçaine, 136, 144–6
    'Specific information', 87, 108–11, 150
Feast of the Pheasant, 87, 149, 286 n.180
Fellerer, Karl Gustav, 251
Fenlon, Iain, 137
Fétis, François-Joseph, 16, 17, 19, 158–9, 160,
    170, 203, 254, 257, 261, 263 n.10
Ficker, Rudolf (von), 82, 288 n.29
    attitudes and beliefs, 57–8, 130, 167–71, 180,
        182, 270 n.155
    and orchestration, 38, 52, 56–8, 85, 228
    Beethoven centenary concert, 55–6
    and Besseler, 169–71, 174–8, 197, 227, 234,
        240
    influence, 75–6, 84, 87, 122, 173, 178–9, 186,
        290 n.61
    and the Nordic/Gothic, 65, 71, 76, 167–9,
        175, 248, 251, 289 n.48
    reactions to, 187–8
    relation to National Socialism, 168, 174,
        248, 250–1
fifers, 18
Fiske, Roger, 279 n.35
Florentine ars nova, *see* ars nova: Italian
Forkel, Johann Nicolaus, 17, 287 n.14

France,
    concerts of medieval music, 48–9
    French music compared to Italian, *see* Italy:
        polyphony
    see also ars antiqua; ars nova; ars subtilior;
        nationalism
Franco of Cologne, 17, 161
Fuller, Sarah, 173, 190, 199, 201–3, 205, 206,
    213, 293 n.130, n.134, 295 n.149, 297 n.18
Fuller, Steve, 297 n.12, 298 n.36, 299 n.41
Fux, Johann Joseph, 161

Gadamer, Hans-Georg, 6
Gagnepain, Bernard, 273 n.223
Ganassi, Sylvestro, 63
Garlandia, *see* Johannes de Garlandia
Gastoué, Amédée, 48–9, 77–8
Gaudeat devotio, 267 n.118
Gautier de Coinci, *Ma viele*, 268 n.118
Gebrauchsmusik, 170
Geiringer, Karl, 66, 69–70, 85, 272 n.198
Gemblaco, Johannes, *Ave virgo/Sancta Maria*,
    56, 269 n.138
Gennrich, Friedrich, 272 n.206
Georgiades, Thrasybulos, 186, 197, 234
Gerber, Rudolf, 251
Gerigk, Herbert, 250–1
Gérold, Théodore, 63, 71–2
Gerbert, Martin, 16, 17, 19, 21
Germany
    concerts of medieval music, 49–53 (*see also*
        Hamburg, *see also* Karlsruhe)
    emigration and exile from, 66, 72, 179, 189,
        192, 290 n.75
    musicology in, 30, 54, 168–70, 185, 247–52,
        254, 255
    special role in music history, 30, 71, 168
    Volk and music, 170, 174, 247, 249, 289 n.48,
        n.51
    see also nationalism; National Socialism
Gerson, Jean de, 281 n.60
Gevaert, François-August, 24
Giotto, *Coronation of the Virgin*, 75
Giovanni da Cascia (da Firenze), 82
    Io son un pellegrin, 56, 269 n.138; *see also*
        Vincenzo
    Nascoso el viso, 155–6, 267 n.98, 275 n.264
    Nel mezzo a sei, 32, 33, 83
Gloria in cielo, 83
Goebbels, Joseph, 169, 247, 249, 270 n.156,
    271 n.183
Goehr, Lydia, 254–5
Goethe, Johann Wolfgang von, 31
Goddard, Scott, 273 n.231
Gombosi, Otto, 72

Gothic; *see* Racial theories, Nordic/Gothic
Gothic Voices, 107–8, 111–32 *passim*, 147, 149,
    205, 206, 210, 235, 276 n.274, 281 n.69
  'A Feather on the Breath of God', 115, 282
    n.77
  'A Song for Francesca', 117, 119, 122
  'Jerusalem', 131
  'Lancaster and Valois', 120, 124, 283 n.104
  'Music for the Lion-Hearted King', 117–18,
    119, 122, 131
  'The Castle of Fair Welcome', 121, 148–9,
    282 n.89
  'The Garden of Zephirus', 117, 282 n.89
  'The Marriage of Heaven and Hell', 118, 120
  'The Masters of the Rolls', 121
  'The Medieval Romantics', 120, 122, 124,
    283 n.104
  'The Mirror of Narcissus', 108, 111, 113,
    115–16, 126, 137, 205, 281 n.69
  'The Service of Venus and Mars', 120, 138,
    282 n.89, n.91
  'The Spirits of England and France', 126,
    130–1
  'The Study of Love', 121, 283 n.104
  'The Voice in the Garden', 126–7
Gouverné, Yvonne, *see* Chorale Yvonne
    Gouverné
Gramophone, influence of, 97–9, 199, 196, 197
Gratiosus de Padua, 268 n.118
Greenberg, Noah, 73, 77, 95, 140
Greenfield, Edward, 97–8
Greig, Donald, 14, 120–1, 129–31
Gratzer, Wolfgang, 269 n.139, n.144
Grenon, Nicholas, 54
Grocheio, Johannes de, 171
Guermant, H., 83
Guido of Arezzo, 17
Guilbert, Yvette, 275 n.254
Guiraut de Bornelh, *Reis glorios*, 268 n.118
Günther, Ursula, 184–6, 187, 188, 198, 274
    n.238, 290 n.80, 290–1 n.87
Gurlitt, Wilibald, 49, 51, 59, 63, 171, 234

Haas, Robert, 47, 53, 264 n.27
Haec dies, 267 n.118
Haggh, Barbara, 295–6 n.5
Haines, John, 265–6 n.67, 271 n.182, 288 n.28
Halbig, H., 155
Halle, Adam de, *see* Adam de la Halle
Hamburg, concerts in, 49, 51–3, 55, 57, 60, 66,
    234
  see also Besseler
Hamel, Fred, 276 n.267
Handschin, Jacques, 52, 72, 152–3, 234, 268
    n.123, 277 n.12

Harnoncourt, Nikolaus, 141
Harrison, Frank, 48, 94–7, 106, 134
Harrison, George, 279 n.41; *see also* Beatles
Hausmusik, 37–8, 44–5, 54
Haussmann, Valentin, 54
Hawkins, Sir John, 16, 17
Hayne van Ghizeghem, *De tous biens plaine*, 55
Hebrews, music of the, 41
Heidegger, Martin, 170, 289 n.52
Heine, Heinrich, 31
Heinrich von Meiszen, 'Frauenlob', 268 n.118
Herlinger, Jan, 293 n.133
Hibberd, Lloyd, 79, 103, 105
Hildegard of Bingen, 108, 115, 258
Hill, Martyn, 278 n.28
Hilliard Ensemble, 114, 137, 138
Hindemith, Paul, 64, 72, 140, 188–9, 190–2,
    198, 274 n.246
Hirshberg, Jehoash, 206
historicism, 7, 211–12, 294–5 n.146, 295 n.4,
    298–9 n.37
  ethical status of, 7, 215, 243–4, 252–6, 261,
    300 n.67
'History of Music by Ear and Eye', 82, 89, 154
'History of Music in Sound', 83–4, 89, 155
Hogwood, Christopher, 279 n.35
Holsinger, Bruce, 253, 283 n.112, 299 n.43
Homo/Homo/Brumans est mors, 50, 268 n.118
Hope, Robert, 66
Hoppin, Richard, 240–1
Hucbald, 158–9, 287 n.6
Huelgas Ensemble, 276 n.272
Huggett family, 279 n.42
Hughes, Andrew, 206, 226
Hughes, Dom Anselm, 155
Hughes, David, 198–200, 207, 227, 293 n.127,
    293 n.133, 297 n.16
Hughes, Lemuel, 275 n.263
Huizinga, Johan, 58, 72, 93, 106, 122, 148, 270
    n.149, n.152, 276 n.272, 280 n.44
Hume, Robert D., 295 n.1, n.4, 296–7 n.11,
    297 n.13, 300 n.67
Huot, Sylvia, 152–3, 280 n.52, 283 n.113
Husmann, Heinrich, 59, 185
Hyperion, 115, 120

Ich het czu hannt gelocket mir, 268 n.118
Igoe, James, 14, 101, 105, 273 n.214, 281 n.61,
    283 n. 113
instrumental music, 42–3, 45–6, 52, 106, 151,
    153, 268 n.118
instrumental performance, 13–156 *passim*
instruments
  aulos, 41
  bassoon, 56, 58, 136, 276 n.274

instruments (*cont.*)
  bells, 56, 74, 95
  celesta, 56–8
  chrotta (rote), 41, 143
  cithara, 41
  citole, 96
  cittern, 143
  clarinet, 97
  clavichord, 55
  cor anglain, 56, 276 n.274
  cornemuse, 136, 142, 143, 145, 146
  cornett, 18, 63, 92, 96, 97, 131, 141, 142, 278
    n.28
  crumhorn, 81, 96, 97, 105, 140–6 *passim*, 278
    n.28, 279 n.42, 285 n.159
  cymbals, 58
  douçaine (dulcina, dulzaina), 136, 143, 144–5
  drums, 141
  dulcimer, 141, 143, 285 n.159
  dulzian, 142
  fiddle, *see* vielle
  fife-and-tabor, 135
  flageolet, 135
  flute, 50, 51, 58, 64, 76, 142, 279 n.42
  fortepiano, 140
  gemshorn, 97
  gittern, 143
  glockenspiel, 56, 58, 60
  guitar, 97, 142, 279 n.42
  harmonium, 135
  harp, 55, 60, 63, 74, 106, 114, 117, 119, 122,
    137, 142, 152, 154, 280 n.45, 282 n.91
  harpsichord, 140, 286 n.170
  horn, 56, 58, 75
  hurdy-gurdy, 141, 143, 285 n.159
  kortholt (kurtal), 135, 142
  lute, 36, 55, 60, 63, 69, 75, 76, 97, 105, 119,
    122, 143, 153, 275 n.261, 279 n.42, 280
    n.45, 285–6 n.170
  lyre, 24, 41
  Mary Rose pipe, 143
  nakers, 96
  oboe, 56, 97, 136, 279 n.42
  organ, 18, 26, 42, 45, 46, 48, 55, 58, 59–60,
    63, 65, 68–9, 74, 77, 85, 93, 101, 102, 106,
    128, 152, 178, 278 n.28
  orpharion, 143
  psaltery, 41, 60, 63, 143, 160, 281 n.60
  rabab, 98
  racket, 140, 142, 279 n.42
  rauschpfeife, 97, 142, 279 n.32, n.42
  rebec, 96, 142–3
  recorder, 50, 64, 84, 85, 91, 96, 97, 131, 135,
    140, 141, 142, 146, 148, 275 n.261, 279
    n.32, n.42

  regal, 155
  sackbut, 97, 105, 134, 278 n.28
  shawm, 75, 134, 142, 143, 146
  sitar, 279 n.41
  sordun, 142
  spinet, 160, 279 n.42
  tabor, 96
  triangle, 58
  tromba marina, 60, 63, 135, 143
  trombone, 18, 55, 56, 60, 63; *see also* sackbut
  trumpet, 18, 56, 63, 73, 93, 268 n.118
  vielle (fiddle), 20, 41, 48, 59, 83, 84, 105, 141,
    143, 149, 152, 275 n.261, 278 n.28, 286
    n.179
  vihuela, 122
  viol, 20, 24–5, 41, 44, 55, 58, 64, 69, 75, 76,
    78, 87, 91, 97, 105, 131, 136, 142–3, 155,
    165, 279 n.32, n.42
  viola, 24, 50, 56, 60, 143, 279 n.42
  viola da gamba, 50, 56
  violin, 97, 142, 143
  violoncello, 143, 279 n.42
instruments
  iconography of, *see* medieval music:
    iconography
  organology, 63, 69–70, 72, 144–5, 228
  popular uses of, 95–9, 229
International Musicological Society, 46, 150
  Barcelona congress (1936), 269 n.133
  Berkeley congress (1977), 101–4, 132, 232
  London congress (1997), 262 n.6, 294
    n.139
  Paris congress (1914), 48
  Utrecht congress (1952), 90
Isaac, Heinrich, 54
Italy
  importance of trecento, 20, 29, 34, 40, 47–8,
    67, 72, 265 n.45
  Italian music compared to French, 26–31,
    41, 42, 51–2, 67, 71, 74, 162–5, 168, 172,
    186, 199–200, 248
  text setting, 32–4, 45, 59, 82
  see also ars nova

Jacobs, René, 135
Jacobsthal, Gustav, 234, 262 n.3, 264 n.26
Jacopo da Bologna, *Un bel sparver*, 68
J'ay prins amours, 55
Jeanroy, Alfred, 271 n.177
Jerome of Moray, 119
Je voy / Fauvel, 154
Jochum, Eugen, 57, 84
Johannes de Garlandia, 166–7, 210, 294 n.138
Jolietement mi tient, 268 n.118
Jones, Sterling, 271 n.182

jongleurs, 16, 40, 42, 67, 76, 100–1
Josquin des Pres, 19, 54, 139, 151, 172

Kaden, Christian, 294 n.139
Kalkbrenner, C., 160
Karlsruhe, concerts in, 49–53, 55, 57, 60, 66, 89, 177, 234
Karp, Theodore, 272 n.208
Kenyon, Nicholas, 113
Kier, Herfrid, 263 n.13
Kiesewetter, Raphael Georg, 16, 17–19, 32, 159–62, 166, 170, 203, 257, 261, 263 n.13, 264 n.31
King, Catherine, 121
Kinkeldey, Otto, 46, 72, 264 n.38
Kinsky, Georg, 63
Kirkman, Andrew, 263 n.13
Klemperer, Otto, 188
Knighton, Tess, 122–3, 133, 150, 295 n.147, n.149
Koch, Heinrich Christoph, 287 n.14
Koller, Oswald, 21
Körber, Günther, 144
Kneif, Tibor, 262 second n.5
Kramer, Lawrence, 9
Kretzschmar, Hermann, 16, 72, 234, 272 n.198
Kreutziger–Herr, Annette, 6, 275 n.254, 276 n.266, 287 n.14
Kroyer, Theodore, 48, 53, 88, 89, 90, 234, 238, 248, 270 n.156, 297–8 n.20
Kuhn, Thomas, 225–31, 297 n.18, n.20
Kühn, Hellmut, 201, 227–8, 292 n.118

La Borde, Jean-Benjamin de, 18
La Curne de Sainte-Pelaye, Jean-Baptiste, 288 n.22
Lamento di Tristan, 268 n.118
Landini Consort, 114
Landini, Francesco, 18, 43, 45, 54, 68, 70, 77, 79, 196, 269 n.148
  Amar si li alti tuo gentil costumi, 275 n.261
  Gran piant'agl'occhi, 50, 51
  Per la mie dolce piaga, 268 n.118
  Sy dolce non sono, 156, 278 n.16
Lang, Paul Henry, 274 n.243
Lantins, Arnold de, *Puisque je voy*, 83
Lassus, Orlando de, 152
Laudes referrat, 267 n.118
Leach, Elizabeth Eva, 192, 208–9, 228, 293 n.130
Leech-Wilkinson, Daniel, 108, 127–8, 133, 135, 136–7, 137–8, 203, 205, 284 n.135, 286 n.180, 292 n.122
Lederer, Victor, 251

Lefferts, Peter, 207
Le Goff, Jacques, 294 n.135
Leichtentritt, Hugo, 35, 47, 74, 264 n.27
Leipzig, 30, 35, 36, 37, 59, 234
Lennon, John, *see* Beatles
Leonin, 49, 57, 65, 168–9, 195, 248, 249, 267 n.118
l'Escurel, Jehannot de, 67
  A vous douce debonaire, 155, 275 n.264
Les Arts Florissants, 115
Les Musiciens de Provence, 135
Letroye, René, 156
Lewis, Ann, 133
Li doz termines / Balaam, 268 n.118
Liebert, Reginaldus, 167
listening practice, 211–14, 259, 260
Litterick, Louise, 102, 286 n.191
Lochamer Liederbuch, *see* manuscripts, Berlin
London Medieval Group, 47, 95
Loqueville, Richard, 282 n.91
Lorenz, Alfred, 273 n.217
Lowinsky, Edward, 241, 290 n.75
Ludwig, Friedrich, 16, 17, 29, 44, 48, 52, 77, 78, 90, 166, 169, 170, 186, 222, 240, 267 n.113, 290 n.63
  comments on others, 40, 42, 43, 47
  'Die mehrstimmige Musik', 23, 28, 32, 67
  'Musik des Mittelalters', 70–1, 162–3, 164–5, 179
  'Musik des Mittelalters in . . . Karlsruhe', 50, 51, 234
  unpublished transcriptions, 26, 78, 185, 187, 228, 234
Lütteken, Laurenz, 289 n.52

Machabey, Armand, 184
Machaut, Guillaume de,
  before *c*.1977, 18, 43, 54, 56, 67, 71, 76, 81, 90, 92, 159–61, 166, 175, 182–4, 185, 190–3, 288 n.24, n.29
  after *c*.1977, 105, 128, 140, 196, 206, 254, 292 n.122, 293 n.126
  editions of, 78, 80, 274 n.237, n.243
  recordings of, 114, 131, 137–8, 139, 156, 275 n.255, 278 n.28
  Christe / Veni, 51, 172, 268 n.118
  De toutes flours, 114, 268 n.118, 269 n.138
  De triste cuer / Certes / Quant, 156, 275 n.264
  Douce dame jolie, 82, 96
  Dous viaire gracieus, 18, 159–60
  Gais et jolis, 268 n.118
  Hoquetus David, 273 n.231
  Il m'est avis, 190–2
  Livre dou Voir Dit, 135
  Ma fin est mon commencement, 275 n.263

Machaut, Guillaume de (*cont.*)
Mass, 47, 50, 73, 75, 76, 80, 81, 89, 98, 106,
108, 137, 156, 159, 160, 165, 267 n.104,
273 n.231, 281 n.69, 284 n.133, 292
n.122
Ploures, dames, 165
Rose, lis, printemps, verdure, 114, 203, 205
S'amours ne fait, 59
Se pour ce muir, 59
Tu/Plange, 56, 58, 269 n.138
Maier, J. J., 21
Mala Punica, 121, 206, 276 n.272
Maniere esgarder/Manere, 267 n.118
manuscripts
Apt, Basilique Sainte-Anne, Trésor 16bis,
48, 77, 267 n.109
Bamberg, Staatsbibliothek, Lit. 115, 35, 50,
274 n.236
Berlin, Staatsbibliothek, Preußischer
Kulturbesitz 40613 (Lochamer
Liederbuch), 40, 50
Bologna, Civico Museo Bibliografico
Musicale Q15, 51, 289 n.56
Burgos, Monasterio de Las Huelgas, 274
n.236
Chantilly, Musée Condé 564, 90–1, 163
Engleberg, Stiftsbibliothek 314, 154
Florence, Biblioteca Medicea Laurenziana,
Med. Pal. 87 (Squarcialupi Codex), 46,
72, 155, 275 n.264
Göttingen, Niedersächsische Staats- und
Landesbibliothek, Handschriftabteilung,
Ludwig Nachlass, 264 n.38
London, British Library, Add. 28550
(Robertsbridge Codex), 45
London, British Library, Add. 57950 (Old
Hall), 120, 226, 274 n.236, 281 n.60
Madrid, Biblioteca de Palacio Real II-1335,
266 n.72
Modena, Biblioteca Estense e Universitaria
α.X.1.11, 172
Montpellier, Bibliothèque
Inter-Universitaire, Séction Médecine
H196, 24, 78, 154–5, 171, 274
n.236
Munich, Bayerische Staatsbibliothek,
Galloram monacensis 902, 21
Oxford, Bodleian Library, Canonici misc.
213, 23–6, 27, 54, 64, 86, 125, 263 n.20,
288 n.24
Paris, Bibliothèque de la Conservatoire, 274
n.236
Paris, Bibliothèque Nationale de France,
Rothschild 2973 (Chansonnier
Cordiforme), 116, 135, 138

Santiago de Compostella, Biblioteca de la
Catedral Metropolitana (Codex
Calixtinus), 155
Segovia, Achivo Capitular, 153
Trent codices, 21, 37, 43, 54, 172, 265 n.55
Marpurg, 262 n.3
Martin, Brian, 298 n.34
Martin, George, 279 n.42
Martinez-Göllner, Marie Louise, 265 n.45
Martini, 262 n.3
'Mary Rose', 146
Mason, Colin Scott, 113–14, 117
Matteo da Perugia, 82, 135, 138, 276 n.272,
277 n.275
Gia da rete d'amor, 277 n.275
Pour bel acueil, 85
McCartney, Paul, *see* Beatles
McCrae, Peter, 117
McGee, Timothy, 76–7, 124, 271 n.172, 273
n.233, 283 n.114
McKinnon, James, 104–5
Mediaeval Academy of America, 79
Medieval Consort (Milwaukee), 142
Medieval Ensemble of London, 81–2, 114, 115,
122, 138–9, 283 n.106, 285 n.156
'Ce diabolic chant', 137, 139
'Dufay: Secular music', 85, 136, 138–9, 276
n.274
'Matteo da Perugia', 135, 138, 139, 277
n.275
medieval music
analysis of, 32–4, 45, 157–214 *passim esp.*
189–209, 222, 226, 227, 238, 243;
reductional analysis, 196, 197–8, 200–5,
207, 292 n.122, n.123
certain knowledge of, 218–24
compositional procedure, 30–1, 74, 106, 117,
119, 160–1, 164–7, 169, 175–7, 181–2,
182–3, 186–7, 196, 199, 200, 259, 292
n.112
counterpoint, 17, 18, 28–31, 70, 114, 118,
126, 157–214 *passim*, 223
editorial practice, 32–4, 37–8, 43–4, 77–82,
84, 99–100, 167, 187–8, 208, 240, 267
n.98, 270 n.155
harmony, 5, 11–12, 17, 18, 19, 30, 52, 54, 67,
70, 76, 89–90, 92, 113, 114, 132, 138,
157–214 *passim*, 227–8
histories of, 16–43, 52, 53, 57, 66–8, 70–4,
257
iconographic evidence, 35, 60–4, 65, 70, 75,
90–1, 93, 102, 104, 108, 110, 116, 148, 229,
286 n.178
lower-voice performance, 101, 106, 109–10,
123

ornamentation, 65, 68, 74, 148
performance as scholarship, 44–5, 111–12,
116–17, 120, 123–4, 130, 132, 189, 206,
280 n.48
pronunciation, 98–9, 106–7, 117–20
in relation to modern, 24, 28, 31, 32, 34,
54–5, 58, 78, 97–8, 121, 140, 165, 171, 173,
180, 182, 190–2, 239, 288 n.29, 290
n.78
scoring, 18, 20, 24–6, 35–42, 49, 50–8,
60–4, 67, 72–7, 82–6, 95, 96, 106–7,
109–10, 114, 119, 134, 139, 265 n.66, 266
n.74, 270 n.163, 272 n.214, 276 n.273
text expression, 38, 82–3, 92, 121, 131, 154–5
texting, 19, 20, 21, 23–6, 31, 34, 37–8, 44–5,
46–7, 48, 53, 59, 68–9, 76, 79, 83, 99–100,
102, 116–17, 118, 121–2, 149–50, 153
theory, 16, 17, 157–8, 161–2, 166, 183, 186–7,
193, 194, 197, 201, 206–7, 208–9, 223,
227–8, 292 n.122
tonality, 28, 31, 32–3, 174–6, 186, 193–5, 243
tuning, 92, 106–7, 116–20, 126–7, 131, 137,
281 n.69
vocalisation, 19, 20, 67, 91, 94, 101, 102, 105,
109–10, 115–20, 122–5, 131, 135, 137, 139,
151, 281 n.60
Meier, Bernhard, 207
Meili, Max, 83
Mein, 268 n.118
Mein traut gesell, 268 n.118
Memling, Hans, 60–4
Mengelberg, Willem, 187
Mertens, Franz, 156
Mertin, Josef, 57, 75–7, 85, 273 n.231
Milsom, John, 133, 284 n.128
Minnesang, 71
minstrels, 20, 40, 93, 152, 225
Moeck, Herman, 145
Molins, Pierre des, *De ce que fol pense*, 276 n.273,
282 n.74
Moll, Kevin, 166, 174–5, 178, 201, 291 n.94,
293 n.134, 294 n.136
Montagu, Jeremy, 97, 141
Montpellier, *see* manuscripts
Moore, Anthony, 278 n.28
Moore, Dudley, 1, 3
Morent, Stefan, 269 n.141
Morley, Thomas, 25
Morphy, Don G., 36
Morrow, Michael, 77, 106, 114
Moser, Hans Joachim, 169, 251, 274 n.243
Mountney, Rev. F. H., 142
Müller, Max, 24, 264 n.32
Müller, Robert, 288 n.17
Münchinger, Karl, 187

Munrow, David, 77, 96–7, 99, 134, 136, 279
n.32
Muris, Johannes de (Jean de Murs), 161, 165,
167, 293 n.131
Murphy, Lambert, 82
musica ficta, 172, 179, 206, 208, 228, 287 n.14,
290 n.75, 293 n.128
Musical Association (later Royal Musical
Association), 23
Musica Reservata, 86, 95–9, 105–6, 114, 209
musicology, 2–11, 257–61, 262 n.3, 289 n.49,
294 n.146, 295 n.1
achievements of, 257–9, 261
anachronism in, 105, 183, 187–8, 192, 198,
201, 220, 243–4, 252, 291 n.100, n.105,
293 n.129, n.130
authoritarian, 252–5
competitive, 150, 231, 237, 244–5
as discipline, 217, 257
email in, 232–3
gender issues in, 244–5, 298 n.33, 299 n. 44,
n.48
hypothesising in, 7, 219–20, 222, 224–31,
237–9, 242–3, 245–6, 251
groups in, 231–6, 245
paradigms in, 221, 225–31, 235, 236, 242–6
patronage in, 238, 246, 260
and performers, 13–16, 95, 145–6, 198, 206
personality in, 239–42, 245–6
politics and, 246–52, 260, 299 n.50
power relations in, 236–8, 243–6, 252, 260
rhetoric in, 29, 148–9, 202, 217–18, 219,
225, 236, 239, 242–6, 278 n.23, 299 n.46
women in, 298 n.33
see also historicism: ethical status
Myers, Herbert W., 146

Najera, Santa Maria de Real, 60
Napoleon Bonaparte, 30
National Early Music Association, 142
nationalism, 14
English, 68
French, 71–2, 265–6 n.67
German, 30–1, 34, 40, 53–4, 71, 168–70,
174, 248, 249, 250, 289 n.51, 290 n.61
see also Racial theories
National Socialism, 7, 54, 66, 168–9, 189,
247–51, 255, 269 n.133, 271 n.163, 271
n.183, 294 n.139; *see also* Racial theories
Navarre, Thibaut de, *see* Thibaut de Navarre
Neihardt von Neuenthal, 'Das Saill
Herausge', 268 n.118
New Oxford History of Music, 262 n.7, 270
n.152; *see also* Oxford History of Music
New York, Metropolitan Museum, 64, 188

New York Pro Musica, 73, 86, 279 n.32
Nieman, Paul, 278 n.28
Noble, Jeremy, 276 n.272
Noorman, Jantina, 98
Nordic, *see* Racial theories
Norwegian Wood, 279 n.41
Not only ... but also, 1
Notre Dame (Paris), 76, 85, 276 n.268
    see also conductus; Leonin; organum; Perotin

Obrecht, Jacob, 47
Ockeghem, Johannes, 42, 64, 139, 172
    Déploration sur la mort de Binchois, 154–5, 277
        n.4
    L'autre d'antan, 55
    Ma bouche rit, 55
    Missa L'Homme armé, 60–4
Odington, Walter, 65, 271 n.172
Odo of Cluny, 158
Old Hall manuscript, *see* manuscripts, London
O Maria maris stella / O Maria / Misit Dominus, 48,
    51, 171, 268 n.118
Orff, Carl, *Carmina Burana*, 57
organum, 17, 20, 28, 29, 42, 58, 59, 158–9,
    167–8, 170, 193
    see also Leonin; Perotin
'oriental' styles, 64–6, 69–70, 71, 74, 85–6, 91,
    97–8, 228; *see also* Racial theories
Orlando Consort, 107, 138, 269 n.143
Osthoff, Helmut, 59, 251
Otten, Kees, 279 n.34
Oxford History of Music, 20, 66–7

Page, Christopher, 86, 92, 152, 205, 229, 238,
    270 n.149, 278 n.23, 279 n.41, 281 n.69
    reactions to, 120–1, 147–50, 280 n.45
    'Around the performance', 210, 283 n.116
    'English *a cappella* Renaissance', 68, 127, 147,
        235, 284 n.129
    'English *a cappella* heresy', 122, 150, 285
        n.156
    'Going beyond', 123–4
    'Listening to the trouvères', 212
    'Machaut's "pupil"', 104–5, 106, 111, 123,
        135, 143, 281 n.62
    'Performance of ars antiqua motets', 118, 143
    'Performance of songs', 105–6, 108, 110, 117,
        136
    'Polyphony before 1400', 118–19, 126
    see also Gothic Voices
Palestrina, Giovanni Pierluigi da, 90, 163, 170,
    186, 288 n.21
Panum, Hortense, 63
Parrott, Andrew, 106–7, 108, 114, 137
Pastor, Willy, 287 n.6

Paulus Paulirinus, 91, 280 n.52
Paumann, Conrad, 18
Pelinski, Ramón, 292 n.118
Pérès, Marcel, 77
Perkins, Leeman, 103, 132, 291 n.103
Perle, George, 188
Perne, François Louis, 159, 263 n.10
Perotin, 51, 56, 57, 157, 168–9, 248–9, 269
    n.144
    Alleluia Nativitas, 84–5
    Alleluia Posui adjutorium, 48, 56, 195, 269
        n.138
    Sederunt principes, 56–7, 84, 157, 186, 290
        n.61
Perry, Edward (Ted), 115
Perusio, Matheus de, *see* Matteo da Perugia
Pestell, Richard, 148
Petrarca, Francesco, 40, 45
Petropoulos, Jonathan, 249, 250
Petrucci, Ottaviano, 19
Petrus de Cruce, 174
Petrus dictus Palma Ociosa, 292 n.122, 293
    n.131, n.133
Philipoctus da Caserta, *En remirant*, 113–14
Philpot, Margaret, 113–14, 115
Pickett, Philip, 138
Piero
    Cavalcando, 275 n.264
    Con bracchi assai, 268 n.118
Pirro, André, 55, 72, 272 n.206
Pirrotta, Nino, 84, 274 n.250
Plamenac, Dragan, 72
Planchart, Alejandro, 109, 156, 276 n.274
Plumley, Yolanda, 207
Polk, Keith, 286 n.184
Popper, Karl, 295 n.2, 296–7 n.11, 299 n.47
Potter, Pamela, 55, 168, 247, 248, 249, 269
    n.132, n.133, 270 n.163, 274 n.243, 299
    n.50
Pourtois, Willy, 156
Power, Leonel, 29, 54, 175
    Ave regina celorum, 172, 268 n.118
Praetorius, Michael, 63, 96, 140
Pro Musica Antiqua Bruxelles, 75, 83–4, 273
    n.223, 275 n.264, 283 n.111
Prosdocimus de Beldemandis, 293 n.133
Purcell Consort, 98, 106
Pycard, 120, 124

Quant voi la rose / Go, 268 n.118
Quittard, Henri, 274 n.237

Racial theories
    Northerners and Southerners, 71, 168, 248,
        270–1 n.163, 294 n.139

Nordic/Gothic traits, 71, 168–9, 175, 186, 248, 250, 251, 271 n.163, 289 n.48
'the Oriental', 65–6
see also Germany: *Volk*; nationalism; National Socialism
Radix venie, 267 n.118
Rambaut de Vaqueiras, *Kalenda maya*, 268 n.118
Rameau, Jean-Philippe, 163
Reaney, Gilbert,
  as performer, 47, 278 n.28
  on performance, 48, 75, 81, 85, 91–2, 94, 96, 99–101, 105, 131, 272 n.214, 273 n.223, 276 n.273, 277 n.1, 280 n.48, 281 n.61
  on harmony, 182–4, 185, 198, 207, 211, 292 n.124
Reed, Gillian, 279 n.35
Reese, Gustave, 72–4, 95, 220–1, 272 n.208, n.213, 273 n.214, 278 n.16
Regis, Johannes, 19
Register of Early Instruments, 143
Register of Early Music, 141–3, 146
Rehding, Alexander, 30, 273 n.217, 289 n.42
Remnant, Mary, 278 n.28
Ribera y Tarragó, Julián, 65, 98
Rickett, Edmond, 275 n.254
Riemann, Hugo, 16, 19, 49, 59, 88, 90, 101, 107, 112, 125, 162, 164–5, 171, 174–5, 178, 201, 202, 228, 254, 264 n.27, 265 n.60
  attitudes and beliefs, 20–3, 27–34, 37–8, 41, 58, 239, 240
  influence, 35–6, 38–40, 43, 47, 66–9, 71, 72, 74, 76–7, 79, 82–5, 87, 168, 200, 229, 233–4, 238, 276 n.267, 276 n.272
  reactions to, 43–6, 50, 51–3, 68, 74, 81, 84, 172, 186, 187, 228–9, 273 n.217
  as self-publicist, 37–40
  'Das Kunstlied', 23, 27, 36–7, 43
  Geschichte der Musiktheorie, 30, 197
  Handbuch der Musikgeschichte, 23, 26–34, 35–6, 38, 40, 83, 87, 164
  Hausmusik aus alter Zeit, 37–8, 39, 42, 44–5, 83, 266 n.74
  Illustrationen zur Musikgeschichte, 21, 266 n.74
  Katechismus der Musikgeschichte, 38, 40, 265 n.50
  Kleines Handbuch der Musikgeschichte, 40–1
  Musik-Lexikon, 20, 38, 41–3
  Sechs bisher nicht gedruckt dreistimmige Chansons, 21
Riens/Riens/Aperis, 268 n.118
Rifkin, Joshua, 272 n.208
Roberts, Clarence, 275 n.263
Robertson, Duncan, 278 n.28
Robertson, Robert, 262 n.2

Robson, C. A., 106
Rockstro, W. S., 19
Roesner, Edward, 272 n.208
Rokseth, Yvonne, 55, 78, 274 n.239, n.243
Roman d'Alexandre, 16
Roman de Fauvel, 91, 154
Roman de Horn, 277 n.12
Ross, Annie, 95
Rotta, 268 n.118
Royal Musical Association, *see* Musical Association
Ruhland, Konrad, 76
Ruth-Sommer, Hermann, 63

Sacchetti, Franco, 36
Sachs, Curt, 63, 69, 72, 82, 154, 272 n.198
Sachs, Klaus-Jürgen, 292 n.118
Sadie, Stanley, 136
St Martial, Limoges, *see* Aquitanian polyphony
Salop, Arnold, 292 n.124
Saltarello, 268 n.118
Salzer, Felix, 188, 192–6, 197, 199, 202, 203, 205, 227, 243, 254
Sandberger, Adolf, 234
Sanders, Ernest, 117–18
Sandon, Nick, 133, 284 n.128
Schachter, Carl, 188, 196, 197
Schenker, Heinrich, 192, 194, 197–8, 202–3, 213
Schering, Arnold, 36–7, 44–7, 49, 53, 59–65, 85, 88, 90, 98, 100, 101, 165, 166–7, 175, 178, 223, 228, 234, 238, 239, 266 n.77, 267 n.100, 270 n.163
  and National Socialism, 247–8, 250, 269 n.133, 270 n.156, 271 n.163
  influence, 47, 52–3, 66, 68, 70, 72, 73, 74, 76, 79, 82–3, 87, 122, 181, 188, 267 n.104, 276 n.267
  reactions to, 46–7, 50, 53, 68, 79, 81, 84, 104, 187
Schletterer, Hans Michael, 19
Schluter, Joseph, 19
Schneider, Marius, 65, 70, 74, 85, 98, 271 n.176, n.183
Schneider, Max, 63
Schola Cantorum Basiliensis, 140, 279 n.32
Schola Cantorum (Paris), 49
Schoop, Hans, 282 n.83
Schrade, Leo, 63, 72, 274 n.250
Schumann, Clara and Robert, 251
Seidel, Wilhelm, 265 n.60
Se je chant, 154
Selfridge-Field, Eleanor, 294 n.139
Senfl, Ludwig, 54

Senleches, Jacob
  En ce gracieus tamps, 276 n.274
  La harpe de melodie, 139
Sequentia, 121, 138, 279 n.33
Shedlock, John, 264 n.21
Singbewegung, 170
Slavin, Denis, 121–2, 149–50, 264 n.25, 277
  n.1, 282 n.83, n.84
Smith, Kevin, 278 n.28
Solage, *Le basile*, 117
Solazzo, Il, 87
Spain, 36, 40, 41, 122, 150
Sperber, Dan, 232, 298 n.28
Springer, Hermann, 47
Squarcialupi, Antonio, 46, 275 n.264
Squarcialupi codex, *see* manuscripts, Florence
Stainer, Sir John, and family, 19, 23–6, 27, 31,
  32, 34, 37, 41, 64, 76, 86, 88, 125, 126,
  228, 263 n.20, 265 n.55, 280 n.46, 288
  n.24
Steinzor, Curt, 72
Stockhausen, Karlheinz, *Stimmung*, 98
Stoltzer, Thomas, 54
Strohm, Reinhard, 262 n.7
Strunk, Oliver, 72
Studio der frühen Musik, 66, 95–6, 119–21,
  137, 140, 144, 210
Stumpf, Carl, 290 n.81
Sulloway, Frank, 299 n.39
Super/Presidentes, 91
Susato Consort, 142
Swingle Singers, 95
Syntagma Musicum, 96

Tant est mignonne, 269 n.137
Taruskin, Richard, 109, 296 n.8
Taverner Consort, 138, 281 n.69
Terry, Sir Richard, 88, 154, 275 n.254
Thatcher, Margaret, 143
Thibault, Geneviève, 55
Thibaut de Navarre, 16
  De bone amour, 268 n.118
Thomson, John, 284 n.133, 285 n.158
Tietze, Gwendolyn, 288 n.34, 298 n.29, 299
  n.54, 300 n.56, n.58
Tinctoris, Johannes, 96, 212
Tomlinson, Gary, 252–3
trecento polyphony, *see* Italy; *see* ars nova
Treitler, Leo, 296 n.7, 299 n.44, 300 n.70
Trombetta, Zorzi, 287 n.192
troubadours, 16, 20, 29, 30, 40, 41, 42, 48, 59,
  100, 288 n.22
trouvères, 16, 48, 100, 135, 212–3, 284
  n.122
Trowell, Brian, 97–8

trumpetum, 91
Tusa, Andrew, 121
Tyas, Shaun M., 135–6
Tynan, Kenneth, 2

Uridge, Michael, 284 n.135
Ursprung, Otto, 271 n.177

van Ackere, Albert, 84
van den Borren, Charles, 74–5, 83, 95, 156,
  273 n.223
van der Werf, Hendrik, 100, 281 n.60
Va t'ent souspir, 83
Vellard, Dominique, 77
Veni sancte spiritus, 154
Vienna Concentus Musicus, 141
Vincenzo da Rimini
  Io son un pellegrin, 82 (*see also* Giovanni da
    Cascia)
  Ita se nera, 82–3
Virdung, Sebastian, 63
Virga/Stirps/Flos, 269 n.138
Vitry, Philippe de, 28, 30, 43, 166, 169,
  249
  Garrit/In nova , 56, 269 n.138
  Impudenter/Virtutibus, 48
  Tuba/In arboris, 72
vocalisation, *see* medieval music: vocalisation
vocal performance, see *a cappella* performance
voices and instruments, 13–87 *passim*, 150–3,
  163–4, 188–9, 222, 225, 228–9
Volk and music, *see* Germany
von Fischer, Kurt, 75
von Ramm, Andrea, 278 n.30
von Schlosser, Julius, 63

Wagner, Richard, 163, 190
  Das Rheingold, 57
Walcha, Helmut, 187
Walter von der Vogelweide, 'Palästinalied', 50,
  268 n.118
Walther, 262 n.3
Wathey, Andrew, 133
Waverly Consort, 73, 86, 95
Weakland, Rembert, 95
Weber, Father Jerome, 154–5, 277 n.6
Wegman, Rob, 293 n.129, 295 n.149, 295–6
  n.5
Wekerlin, Jean-Baptiste, 275 n.255
Wellek, Albert, 168, 270 n.163, 294 n.139
Westrup, Jack, 67–8, 69
Wilkins, Nigel, 142
Winternitz, Emmanuel, 64
Wiora, Walter, 59
Wittgenstein, Ludwig, 295 n.2

Wolf, Johannes, 16, 17, 27, 32, 44, 50, 67, 72,
    84, 222, 228, 264 n.38, 265 n.45, 272
    n.198
  and National Socialism, 247–8, 250, 269
    n.133
  and Riemann, 107, 233–4
  contra Schering, 46–7
  and the public, 53–4, 269 n.132
  Geschichte der Mensuralnotation, 23, 26, 27,
    28–9, 37, 45, 67, 77, 86, 162, 165, 179,
    234, 264 n.38
Wolff, Christian, 265 n.60
Woodley, Ronald, 133

Woods, Dr B., 142
Wooldridge, H. E., 20, 66–7, 162, 263 n.7,
    n.20, 288 n.24
Wright, Craig, 101–4, 109, 110, 117, 132, 134,
    229, 281 n.62
Wright, Lawrence, 133, 135

Yale, 64, 72, 156, 188, 192
York Early Music Festival (1977), 106–7, 111

Zimmermann, Reinhold, 168–9,
    249
Zipay, Terry Lee, 196